# AMERICAN ENVIRONMENTAL HISTORY AND POLICY

## A Troubled Journey to Reform

Frank T. Manheim

BRISTOL
UNIVERSITY
PRESS

First published in Great Britain in 2026 by

Bristol University Press
University of Bristol
1–9 Old Park Hill
Bristol
BS2 8BB
UK
t: +44 (0)117 374 6645
e: bup-info@bristol.ac.uk

Details of international sales and distribution partners are available at bristoluniversitypress.co.uk



DOI: 10.51952/9781529250732

British Library Cataloguing in Publication Data
A catalogue record for this book is available from the British Library

ISBN 978-1-5292-5070-1 hardcover
ISBN 978-1-5292-5072-5 ePub
ISBN 978-1-5292-5073-2 ePdf



Cover design: Andrew Corbett
Front cover image: pidba.org/All Fluted Points
AI disclaimer: The author utilised ChatGPT as an expanded search engine beyond Google for initial research. The analysis and conclusions in this book are the author's own.
Bristol University Press uses environmentally responsible print partners.
Printed and bound in Great Britain by CPI Group (UK) Ltd, Croydon, CR0 4YY

FSC
www.fsc.org
MIX
Paper | Supporting responsible forestry
FSC® C013604

Bristol University Press' authorised representative in the European Union is:
Easy Access System Europe, Mustamäe tee 50, 10621 Tallinn, Estonia,
Email: gpsr.requests@easproject.com

To Lucy

# Contents

# List of Figures and Tables

## Figures

## Tables

# About the Author

Frank T. Manheim joined the Schar School of Policy and Government, George Mason University, as an Affiliate Professor and Distinguished Research Fellow in 2003 after a career as a federal ocean scientist. His main field is environmental policy, with a special interest in political history and the origin of the US's political polarization. He received the Swedish Academy of Science Pettersson Medal for Excellence in Ocean Chemistry in his former field and has authored more than 60 publications in the policy area. He is a long-time reviewer of books in environmental science and policy for *Choice Magazine*. In 2021 he began contributing articles on policy issues to leading US political media.

# Acknowledgments

My move from ocean and Earth science to policy research began in 2003 at the School of Public Policy at George Mason University. I'm indebted to my colleague, Professor Don E. Kash, for discussions and insights into energy policy. Kash shared background from service as chief of the US Geological Survey's Conservation Division, responsible for oversight over offshore oil and gas and minerals exploration and leasing. Kingsley Haynes, founder and dean of the School of Public Policy (now the Schar School of Policy and Government), gave me valuable guidance, and I deeply appreciate the support of his successor, Dean Mark Rozell.

Despite the massive literature on environmental policy,[1] publications on major environmental developments showed surprising gaps. To fill these, I interviewed key officials involved in environmental affairs from the 1960s to the 1990s and later (see Table 0.1). They provided insights unavailable in literature sources.

Queried about President John F. Kennedy's 1963 response to *Silent Spring*, Rachel Carson's influential 1962 book on the pesticide problem, Kennedy's speechwriter and advisor Theodore Sorensen referred me to Secretary of the Interior Stewart Udall. In a telephone interview, Udall informed me that he gave Kennedy, who was concerned about environmental pollution, a copy of Carson's book before its formal publication. Udall had maintained contact with Carson after she retired as chief editor of Fish and Wildlife Service Publications.

During a European tour in 2007, I interviewed the director of the Swedish Environmental Protection Agency, officials at the Finnish Environmental Protection Agency and Geological Survey, senior Hungarian and Austrian counselors for environmental policy, officials at the Ukrainian Forestry University, Lviv, and the head of the energy division of German Greenpeace in Hamburg, Germany. Simone Koritnig, a counselor with the German Consulate in New York City, provided detailed background on German environmental policy. Staff of the Norwegian Embassy, Washington, D.C. kindly undertook search for Norwegian regulations for offshore oil and gas leasing during this period.

As tabulated below, Russell Train and John Whitaker provided personal insights into activities of the Council for Environmental Quality and events in the Nixon administration. Richard Ayres, a founder of the Natural Resources Defense fund, stated that the Natural Resources Defense Council had no input to the framing of the *Clean Air Act Amendments of 1970*, but was active in hearings prior to final passage. Becky Norton Dunlop, Vice-President at the Heritage Foundation, shared difficult interactions with Environmental Protection Agency (EPA) officials in the Clinton administration and gave me a full list of her conservative books. Daniel Sarewitz, professor and co-founder of the Consortium for Science, Policy & Outcomes at Arizona State University, provided a jacket endorsement for my first book. Istvan Kesmarky, formerly with the Eotvos University in Budapest, provided a review of my 2009 book from European and Hungarian perspectives. The Lyndon B. Johnson Library delivered a critical collection of documents on the Johnson administration's environmental policy actions.

Over the years, I received responses to queries from David Doniger, senior policy advisor at the National Resources Defense Council, and had a telephone interview in 2024. Interviews with Professor Lee Talbot, former chief scientist for the Council on Environmental Quality, revealed that he had toughened the final version of the *Endangered Species Act of 1973*.

Peter Kolb, forestry professor at the University of Montana, provided key insights into US and German forest management policy. Daniel Fiorino, an EPA administrator and author of a leading book on environmental policy reform, provided a tour of the EPA's Performance Track program. Marcia McNutt revealed that the low remuneration of experts appointed as science agency heads in the first Obama administration was a major factor in their inability to continue their service. They earned a small fraction of the pay of executives with comparable responsibilities in the private sector. Detailed comments were received on a lengthy paper relevant to this book by Adam White (convenor) and other participants at a C. Boyden Gray Center Roundtable at the Scalia Law School, George Mason University. David Schoenbrod served as a critic of the paper on a podcast by the C. Boyden Gray Center. Economist Peter Dorman kindly offered a critique of Chapter 6. David Lampo provided an excellent proofreading of the final manuscript, partly supported by Dean Mark Rozell.

I am grateful for two important contributions to the book. Dr. David Anderson, a director of the Paleoindian Database of the Americas, provided the Paleoindian Database of the Americas (PIDBA) book cover illustration that depicts North America at the time of first human entry. He graciously reviewed the chapter on Indian arrivals to North America. Dr. James Hansen, a noted climate scientist (Columbia University Program on Climate Science, Awareness and Solutions), generously provided the updated global temperature plot that opens Chapter 8. Jason Force, Jacqueline Albergotti, and Marcel Schwab assisted with manuscript preparation. Special thanks to Jason Force for technical assistance with final manuscript submission. My wife, Lucy McCartan Manheim (a PhD geologist), provided indispensable editing and other assistance and sacrificed to let me give full attention to the writing. Finally, I deeply appreciate the thorough review of the final text, and the recreation of deficient figures by Bristol University Press when I became hospitalized with a leg infection.

**Table 0.1:** Communications: interviewees and their positions

| | |
|---|---|
| Stewart Udall, 2006 | Secretary of the Interior (Kennedy and Johnson administrations) |
| Russell E. Train, 2007 | Chairman, Council on Environmental Quality (Nixon administration) |
| John C. Whitaker, 2007 | White House Staff and Undersecretary of the Interior (Nixon administration) |
| Richard E. Ayres, 2007 | Co-founder, Natural Resources Defense Council (NRDC), 1970s |
| Leon Billings, 2007, 2008 | Legislative Director, Senate Subcommittee on Air & Water Pollution (Nixon administration); Assistant to Senator Edmund Muskie; later President of the Muskie Foundation, Lewiston, ME |
| William van Ness, 2007 | Chief Consel, Senate Committee on Energy and Natural Resources (Nixon administration) |
| William Bettenberg, 2007 | Budget Director, Department of Interior; Acting Director, Minerals Management Service (Reagan administration) |
| William K. Reilly, 2007 | EPA Administrator (George H. W. Bush administration) |
| Becky Norton Dunlop, 2007, 2008 | Secretary of Natural Resources, Commonwealth of Virginia (George Allen administration); subsequently Vice-President of the Heritage Foundation |
| Marcia McNutt, 2013 | Director of the US Geological Survey, now President of the US Academy of Science |
| Lee Talbot, 2018, 2019 | Chief Scientist for the Council on Environmental Quality (Nixon administration) and a co-author of the Endangered Species Act (final draft); interviewed while Professor of Environmental Science, Policy, and International Law at George Mason University |
| David Schoenbrod, 2020, 2021 | Early activist with the NRDC; Professor of Law at New York University and subsequently law reform advocate |
| Peter Dorman, 2023 | Emeritus Professor of Economics, Evergreen Stage College |
| David Doniger, 2024 | Senior attorney, NRDC |

# Preface

This book is the product of more than 20 years of research that began with the goal of tracing the origin of the US's conflict over environmental policy. The research was conducted while I was (and am) Affiliate Professor and Distinguished Research Fellow at the Schar School of Policy and Government, George Mason University. I came to political science and policy research with a background and goals that were different from those of most political scientists. However, in my first career as a federal ocean scientist, I already had an interest in societal issues owing to the influence of my father, an internationally known sociologist and anthropologist.[1]

From the late 1970s, national conflict over environmental issues grew. It affected my work and that of my agency, the US Geological Survey (USGS). Federal employees were limited by the Hatch Act from engaging in political activities outside their official duties, so I limited my interest in policy to attending lectures at the Marine Policy program of the Woods Hole Oceanographic Institution and collecting federal government reports and academic publications. Direct engagement in policy issues came first during a leave of absence to serve as chairman of the University of South Florida's Department of Marine Science.[2] Our department, together with the Florida State Ocean Institute (SUSIO), led a consortium of academic institutions in the first US Bureau of Land Management-sponsored survey of offshore environmental conditions before petroleum leasing in the MAFLA[3] area in the eastern Gulf of Mexico. I also initiated a Master's track in marine policy for our department.

Returning to the USGS, I was a leader in research on ocean mineral deposits. However, national controversies during the first Reagan administration (1981–1989) terminated USGS field investigations. I moved to environmental research, including contaminated sediments in US coastal estuaries and water bodies. My interest in environmental policy led to my participation in panels sponsored by the National Academy of Science and the National Oceanic and Atmospheric Administration, as well as assessments by the US Environmental Protection Agency (EPA).

During my USGS career, I found no explanation for the increasing national conflict over environmental policy. After 1990, gridlock in Congress blocked legislation on environmental, energy, and natural resource policy as well as other critical national issues. On retiring from the federal government in 2002, I committed myself to tracking the origin of the contretemps. I was fortunate to join the School of Public Policy (now Schar School of Policy and Government) at George Mason University), Arlington, Virginia in 2003. At this time, Don E. Kash served as a professor of public policy. A national expert on energy policy, Dr. Kash had been appointed chief of the Geological Survey's Conservation Division by President Jimmy Carter. Among its responsibilities, this agency monitored offshore oil and gas exploration and drilling operations.

Serving as my mentor and colleague, Kash noted that policy think tanks, university institutions, and government efforts to bridge differences over environmental and energy policy had been unsuccessful. He suggested that a critical development in the post-Second World War period had been the collision between two major movements: the environmental movement and the powerful US offshore oil industry. I confirmed his concept, identifying the Santa Barbara offshore oil spill of January 1969 as a watershed event, which can be graphically confirmed by querying on "environmental conflict" using Google's Ngram Viewer.[4]

Several years of intensive research on academic literature failed to yield answers to key policy questions like details on the framing of the groundbreaking environmental laws of the 1970s. This led me to interview principals and knowledgeable officials involved with the environmental legislation and politics of the 1970s and later developments (see Acknowledgments). Leaders who would have been unapproachable during their active careers readily shared their experiences, which included startling revelations.

With student assistance, I began compiling a comprehensive database of US environmental and land-use laws dating back to the founding of Congress (Manheim and Fuhs, 2007; Manheim, 2014). The results of the earlier studies were published in a book in 2009,[5] which offered much new information, including confirmation of the absence of partisan conflict over environmental policy in the 1970s. *The Clean Air Act Amendments of 1970* were approved *unanimously* in the Senate en route to overwhelming passage by Congress and signature by President Nixon.

Work for the 2009 book convinced me that more research on environmental and policy history was needed to understand the origin of major policy problems, and that earlier US history and politics should be included. Subsequent research and publications led to the present book's dual goals. The first is to provide a coherent review of the environmental and policy history of the US from early arrivals to North America to the present. It includes underemphasized but important political developments like Andrew Jackson's spoils system. The second goal is to offer new research detail on the origin and evolution of turbulent policy developments beginning with the environmental revolution of the 1970s. The final three chapters offer a comparison between US and European environmental history and progress, a synthesis of earlier chapters, review of policy issues, and attempts at a realistic exploration of policy pathways for the future.

Wikipedia has not been accepted as a reference in most past academic literature. However, with over 7 million articles in the English edition, its coverage has expanded to the point that it has been critical for this book, often providing the only substantive data sources, especially for more recent political developments. Articles are frequently documented by hundreds of references and are continuously updated. They are distinguished rom normal references in this book by being cited in the text.

The final manuscript for the book was delivered on January 5, 2025, after Donald Trump's election on November 7, 2024. US policy status at that time is reflected in the body of the book. Dramatic changes that took place during the first three months of the new administration are reviewed in the Afterword.

1

# An Introduction

This book has two goals. The first is to present a brief but coherent review of American environmental and policy history, focusing on important developments. The story begins with the first humans to arrive in North America (illustrated by Figure 2.1) and ends at the present. In subsequent chapters, relevant political developments are included. The second goal, with a greater level of detail, is to trace the history of issues that have roiled the American political scene since the environmental revolution of the 1970s. In recent decades political polarization has critically affected environmental policy and progress—dramatically in the case of elections of Donald Trump in 2016 and 2024. Current problems have roots in the past. The book argues that without balanced knowledge of history, we are hindered in understanding problems and identifying solutions.

This book traces national characteristics that have affected US society throughout its history. The perceptive French student of American democracy, Alexis de Tocqueville, noted 180 years ago that Americans tended to have unwarranted confidence in the validity of their opinions. On the positive side, confidence in visions led to bold achievements like electrical illumination, skyscrapers, landing a man on the Moon, and the internet. Taken to extremes on the negative side, distorted beliefs led to the assassination of four presidents and 19 assassination attempts—most recently, two attempts on presidential candidate Donald Trump. This is a record more extreme than for any other advanced nation. The book traces how well-intended political zeal and overreaction since the Second World War contributed to political polarization, dysfunction in governance, and, arguably, the election of President Trump.

In spite of a large literature on environmental policy, I found little information on the origins and development of the transformative environmental laws of the 1970s when I began policy research 20 years ago. It could be a reflection of an old saying attributed to Mark Twain: "People who love sausage and respect the law should never watch either one being made." New information on the origin of US conflict over environmental policy emerged in the course of exploration of the framing of key environmental laws and subsequent events. This book offers new data on the history of the groundbreaking *National Environmental Policy Act of 1969* (NEPA), the *Clean Air Act Amendments of 1970* (CAA), and the *Endangered Species Act of 1973* (ESA).

Chapter 2 begins with pre-European Indian cultures and land-use practices. Research since the 1960s transformed assumptions about pre-European North America, but left significant controversy. In contrast to earlier assumptions of the Indian population in North America before European colonization as low as one million, recent estimates extend to 18 times higher. The short but spectacular migration period was noted for the hunting of large, now-extinct mammalian species with devastatingly effective stone spear points (Clovis and Folsom). Unlike Mesoamerican and Andean Indigenous empires based on intensive agriculture, North American Indian cultures became highly diverse after dispersing throughout the subcontinent, adapting lifestyles to local conditions. Subsequent periods remain under active research. In the precolonial and colonial times, the Haudenoaussee (Iroquois confederacy) had sophisticated political systems that included political autonomy and personal liberty. A Congressional resolution in 1988 acknowledged that insights from the political organization of Indian society influenced the framing of the US Constitution.

Discussion of Indian land use in North America is followed by colonial impacts and land use (Chapter 3). European principles of land ownership with commercial value differed from Indian concepts of ownership based on use. Historian Alan Taylor noted that while "Europeans were not innately cruel and violent, they exercised superior power in inflicting misery on native American cultures." Settlers in the 13 British colonies initially employed agricultural practices from the European societies from which they came, but soon developed more exploitative practices owing to ready availability of land. Boston is of special interest as having the oldest continuous American records relating to environmental and health measures, dating from the 17th century.

The American colonies were outposts of the Enlightenment, a time that valued insights from science and rational inquiry, and sought a more humane society. Free from the corruption of European aristocracy and with weak oversight by British governors, the colonies developed advanced governance systems, even as the "New World" was marred by the ugly legacy of slavery.

Three founders stand out as active students of natural science as well as politics: Benjamin Franklin, James Madison, and Thomas Jefferson. Among his many innovations, Franklin traced the path of the Gulf Stream by compiling data from the logs of merchant vessels. Madison has been called the first American environmentalist, and Thomas Jefferson had wide-ranging interests in natural history and social science that include what we now call archeology and anthropology. Jefferson collected relics of extinct animals and compiled dictionaries of Indian languages as a means of tracing the migration of the Indigenous peoples of North America. He also chaired a panel that created the first law governing land management.

Scholars of administrative practice have noted the advanced management systems for government administration adopted by the first six presidents, but this period came to an end in 1829 with President Andrew Jackson's spoils system for appointment of government officials and workers. The subsequent turnover of government after presidential elections prevented the establishment of stable and effective administrative systems. The patronage system in presidential administrations contributed to the despoliation of land and contamination of water resources as a result of mineral exploitation in Western federal territories. In a book first published in 1835, Alexis de Tocqueville expressed surprise at the lack of vision in American politicians, in contrast to the gifted political leaders active during the Revolutionary War period.

The 19th century (Chapter 4) was a time of expansion, rapid growth and technological development—often at the expense of native Indian populations. It was also the time of naturalists who collected and recorded Indigenous plants and wildlife, and expressed concern for the preservation and prudent management of environmental resources. Henry David Thoreau and John Muir's activities are best known, but the most influential individual in his time was George Perkins Marsh, a diplomat and polymath who served US embassies in Europe. Marsh's phenomenal linguistic skills allowed him to compile data from European archives into accounts of practices that caused the decline of earlier European and Near Eastern civilizations. His groundbreaking book in 1864 (*Man and Nature*) warned Americans against repeating this experience in the new nation.

The post-Civil War period was characterized by economic booms and busts (panics), with pervasive corruption and veniality in federal and state governments; it was also a time of private-sector monopolies under the "robber barons" of industry. Reform of the Jacksonian patronage system began in the administration of Rutherford B. Hayes and his crusading Interior secretary, Carl Schurz. A milestone was the passage of the *Pendleton Act of 1883*, which created the merit system for the appointment of government employees and remained in force until 1978.

The role of engineers during this period deserves special attention. Beginning as an elite corps in the US Army in the early 19th century, American engineers took pride in maintaining professional standards. They played critical roles in waterway management and public health systems, as well as in infrastructural development and manufacturing.

By 1900, the Progressive reform movement led both parties to accept the principle (though not always the practice) that federal agencies should be led by independent leaders chosen for professional competence. Growth of public trust in federal agencies enabled Congress to pass short laws that gave agencies missions and goals, and allocated funding while delegating operating policies to the agencies. Congress drew on the expertise of these agencies in making and amending law (Chapter 5).

The early decades of the 20th century saw the expansion of protected national forests by President Theodore Roosevelt. The Public Health Service used advances in biomedical science to counter epidemics and disease; the United States became the first nation to provide nationwide access to safe drinking water such that customers at any restaurant would automatically get a glass of water. Besides infrastructure that included a comprehensive national rail network, skyscrapers, and New York City's subway system, advanced municipal sewage systems were built for major urban communities. However, health problems such as infectious diseases associated with crowded industrial conditions, poor hygiene, and poor sanitation remained severe. Coal miners were affected by dangerous working conditions.

New ecological and environmental movements emerged toward the middle of the 20th century. Leaders included Aldo Leopold, who began work with the US Forest Service, Robert Marshall (Chief of Recreation and Lands for the Forest Service), and Jay Norwood "Ding" Darling, who became a leader in national park and wildlife preservation movements.

The Great Depression, which began with the stock market crash of 1929, descended like a gray blanket on the Roaring Twenties. Limitation on domestic activity during the Second World War continued to keep pollution low, but the postwar economic boom and replacement of rail transport by automobiles and trucks dramatically increased air and water pollution; deaths due to air pollution occurred in populated areas during inversions. The threat of extinction of the bald eagle, America's revered national bird, set in motion a new national awareness about pesticides and environmental pollution. National concern was heightened by a 1969 offshore blowout that fouled the white beaches of Santa Barbara, California with crude oil.

Chapter 6 begins with that event, which occurred shortly after the inauguration of President Richard Nixon. A sense of national environmental crisis spurred passage of two groundbreaking laws, the *National Environmental Policy Act of 1969* (signed into law by President Nixon on January 1, 1970) and the *Clean Air Act Amendments of 1970* (CAA). The latter was spearheaded by five senators on the Senate Subcommittee for Air and Water Pollution. In contrast to current partisan divisions over environmental policy, three of the five were Republicans, and the law was approved overwhelmingly by Congress.

The CAA transferred authority for controlling air pollution from the states to the federal government. It prescribed unprecedentedly rigorous provisions enforced throughout the nation by the new US Environmental Protection

Agency. The CAA set the pattern for other laws to control environmental concerns like water pollution, endangered species, waste disposal, and effects on the marine environment. The CAA made rapid progress in reducing air pollution, winning grateful approval from environmentalists. However, it had a negative impact on the economy and fostered litigiousness. The rigorous provisions and costs of the CAA and subsequent laws contributed to an unexpected economic recession in the 1970s. There was an exodus of business entrepreneurs from manufacturing and related industries to less affected economic sectors like banking, finance, real estate, and law. Production began moving abroad.

The decline in the economy and simultaneous inflation (stagflation), along with the Iranian hostage crisis in 1979, led to a landslide victory by Ronald Reagan over President Jimmy Carter in 1980 (Chapter 7). Committed to re-establishing the legitimacy of business and profit, the Reagan administration won sharp reductions in personal tax rates from earlier levels of 70 percent for the top tax brackets. As heads of key federal agencies, Reagan appointed zealous advocates for reducing regulatory burdens on business and industry and leasing of federal lands. The actions of Environmental Protection Agency (EPA) administrator Ann Gorsuch and Secretary of the Interior James Watt in rolling back the enforcement of environmental laws resulted in a backlash from Congress. Among other actions, Congress imposed moratoria on all offshore oil and gas leasing except for grandfathered areas in the Gulf of Mexico and the Pacific coast. Gorsuch and Watt were forced to resign by 1983. Gorsuch was replaced by William Ruckelshaus, the respected first administrator for the EPA, who returned enforcement to previous levels. However, it was too late; conflict over environmental policy widened to partisan and political polarization.

Chapter 8 begins with climate change. It highlights James Hansen, director of the National Aeronautics and Space Administration's (NASA) Goddard Center for Space Studies, and his dramatic Senate testimony in 1988 regarding global warming. Scientists normally qualified their statements, but Hansen stated that there was a 99 percent certainty that the Earth was warming. His testimony galvanized the environmental community and marked a critical change for environmental and energy policy in the United States. Outlays for climate research rose steeply under Bill Clinton and Al Gore, though with relatively little decrease in greenhouse gases. However, concern over global climate change also sharpened domestic conflict.

In the presidential election of 1988, George H. W. Bush defeated Massachusetts governor Michael Dukakis after a campaign in which Bush claimed he would be "the environmental president." Bush, a scion of a family committed to public service, had been defeated in the Republican primary of 1980 by Ronald Reagan, but became vice-president in the Reagan administration. He led a task force on deregulation and oversaw the administration's lasting administrative reforms. Gaining the presidency in

1988, Bush issued an executive order for a federal moratorium on offshore oil and gas leasing beyond the grandfathered areas. He gave strong support to the *Clean Air Act Amendments of 1990*, which became one of the last updates of the major environmental laws of the 1970s.

In 1992, Bush was defeated for re-election by the Democratic ticket led by former governor of Arkansas, William Clinton, a centrist Democrat, and Senator Al Gore, in a close election. The Clinton-Gore administration was noteworthy for its "Reinventing Government" initiative, headed by Gore. It also achieved the last federal balanced budget. No new laws emerged from the Reinventing Government initiative, but regulatory procedures of federal agencies were simplified, and the Environmental Protection Agency sought better communication with industry.

Chapter 9 begins with the administration of George W. Bush, son of George H. W. Bush. The younger Bush defeated Al Gore and Joe Lieberman in the controversial election of 2000 (Chapter 9). Led by campaign manager Karl Rove, Bush's campaign claimed that he would reduce greenhouse gas emissions, but this commitment was abandoned once Vice President Richard Cheney gained influence over administration policy. Bush refused to join the Kyoto Protocol and the United States lagged behind European nations in moving toward renewable energy use. Environmental organizations accused it of undermining climate science and cutting environmental safeguards to support mining and oil interests. However, buoyed by public approval of his response to the Al-Qaeda attack of September 11, 2001, Bush defeated Democratic challengers John Kerry and John Edwards in the election of 2004.

The election of Barack Obama, an African American, as President in 2008 was a milestone event. Obama pursued the issue of global climate change with urgency. The Obama-Biden administration won re-election over Republican challengers Mitt Romney and Paul Ryan in 2012, but polarization increased. Obama's Clean Power Plan was reversed after the surprise election in 2016 of real estate mogul Donald Trump, who tapped into a vein of disillusion in the US public (Chapter 9). Trump's public support increased as the nation achieved energy independence thanks to the growth of hydraulically fractured oil and gas, but it was diminished by his handling of a COVID-19 epidemic and actions that led to two impeachment motions by the Democratically controlled House of Representatives. President Trump was acquitted by the Republican-controlled Senate both times.

President Trump and his vice presidential candidate Mike Pence lost the 2020 election to the Democratic ticket of Joe Biden and Kamala Harris, although the former president continued to make claims for election fraud that were overwhelmingly rejected by the courts. The incoming Biden administration ran on a green energy platform. Assuming the presidency, Biden canceled Trump's executive orders regarding environmental and energy issues and soon announced a comprehensive plan to combat climate change.

Laws passed in 2022, particularly the *Inflation Reduction Act*, committed unprecedented resources to infrastructure and renewable energy development. However, extreme policy differences between Republican and Democratic administrations and gridlock in Congress posed obstacles to progress against climate change. The delayed commitment of President Biden to withdraw from his re-election campaign and support his vice president, Kamala Harris, was a factor in the surprising election of Donald Trump to a nonsequential second term. Support of Trump by working-class Americans in contrast to support of Harris by college-educated voters marked a reversal of previous demographic alignments. Among Trump's radical government reform agenda, his proposed policies rejected US commitments against climate change.

Comparisons of American and European policies (Chapter 11) reveal that European climate policies minimized environmental contention and allowed Europe to become the world leader in renewable energy development, surpassing US progress. Ironically, federal agencies under the civil service system before 1969 had some comparable features, but were transformed in the 1970s.

Chapter 12 reviews environmental policy issues, including the history and origin of conflict, American characteristics that affected the nation through its history, relevant literature, law, and constitutional debates. The concluding Chapter 13 explores current political polarization that has inhibited environmental policy and progress against climate change and has culminated in a popular revolt against the status quo. It recognizes that bipartisan reform legislation has little promise in the foreseeable future—the parties hold widely divergent views. The incoming Trump administration proposes dismantling previous climate change programs. Recognition that past attempts by each party to dominate politics have failed and polarization has corrupted basic political relationships could allow more constructive approaches to resolving the governance problems of the US in future administrations. One such approach would be through administrative reforms. These, combined with nonpartisan, professional development of legislative reform measures, offer pathways to gain broad public support for more effective policies. Given the reversion by President Trump to extreme patronage policies, the suggested policies would apply to future recognition of the futility of polarized politics and the importance of a return to an apolitical, professional civil service.

Throughout the body of the book, I have attempted to address issues straightforwardly, seeking to maintain balance and support unfamiliar or controversial points with documentation. The body of the book presents status as of Donald Trump's election, but before his inauguration and the unexpected subsequent developments. The Afterword summarizes developments in the first 120 days of Trump's second administration and presents concluding perspectives.

2

# North American Indians and Land Use before European Colonization

## The arrival of Indigenous populations to the American continent

Thomas Jefferson was the first in US history to take a keen interest in fields that we would now call archaeology and anthropology. He collected skeletal remains of extinct animals and had a special interest in American Indians and their origin. Recognizing that Native Americans had Asian affinities and putting this together with James Cook's 1778 maps of the coasts of Siberia and Alaska, Jefferson concluded that the human population of North America migrated to North America from Siberia across the Bering Strait (Jefferson, 1785). However, the timing and circumstances of the origin of Native Americans long continued to be poorly known and remain in contention. Active interest and debates intensified in the early 20th century. An example is provided by a noted anthropologist and curator of the American Museum of Natural History (now the Smithsonian National Museum of Natural History), Aleš Hrdlička. Hrdlička conducted detailed studies of skeletal remains from Tibet, Siberia, Alaska, and the Aleutian Islands (from 1927), and was the first to publish documentation regarding the colonization of the American continent from East Asia. He claimed that this took place less than 3,000 years ago (Wikipedia—Hrdlička), but that claim has since been superseded by later research. An excellent review of the history of discoveries and controversies relating to early arrivals to North America is provided by anthropologist David J. Meltzer (Meltzer, 2021).

The first multifaceted scientific breakthrough regarding the time and origin of Indigenous peoples' arrival in North America came in 1964 when C. Vance Haynes, a professor of anthropology at the University of Arizona (Haynes, 1964), reported on his studies that utilized the new technique of Carbon 14 ($^{14}C$) dating on Clovis spear point discovery sites (see Figures 2.1 and 2.2), indicating they were at least 11,500 years old.[1] Clovis points were

**Figure 2.1:** Distribution of Clovis and related points in North America and the ice-free corridor c. 13,000 years ago

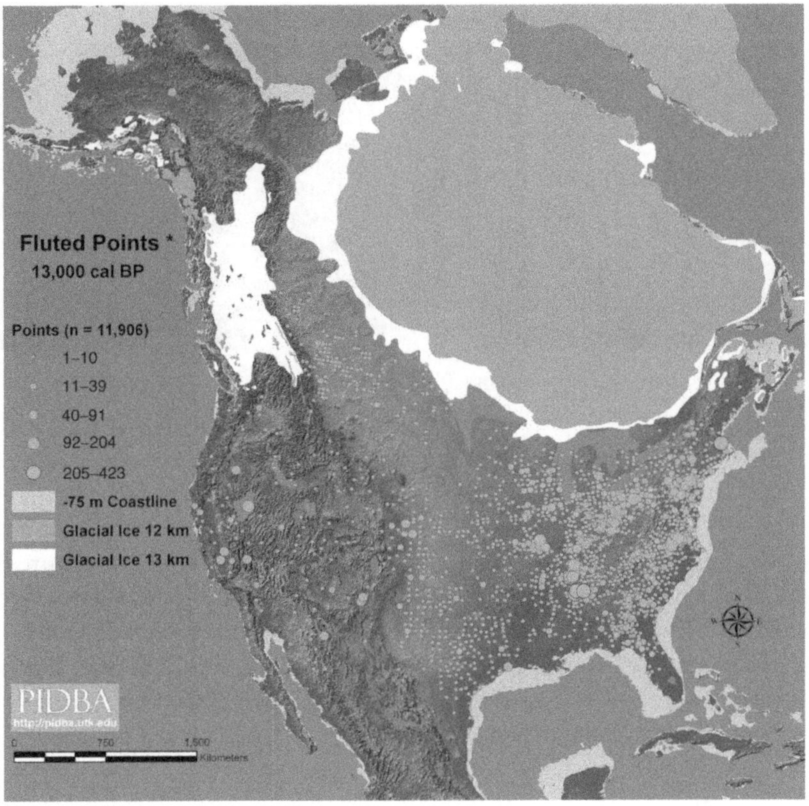


Note: * The light dots in the map encompass all Clovis and Clovis Variants, plus all untyped fluted forms that have not yet been unequivocally assigned to a later type like Folsom, Barnes, Cumberland, and so on in the database.

Source: PIDBA (2019). The PIDBA database is described by Anderson et al (2010), reproduced with permission. The color map can be accessed at https://pidba.org/content/fluted.JPG

artfully produced stone spear points that permitted hunters to kill large animals, and their age roughly corresponds with the opening c. 12,000–14,000 years ago of an ice-free corridor between the Cordilleran ice sheet covering the Northwestern United States and Canada, and the Laurentian ice sheet centered on Hudson Bay. As the vast, mile-thick glaciers melted, a narrow time window allowed travel across the land bridge between Siberia and Alaska before it was inundated by rising seas. Incoming migrants had a ready pathway through Alaska and Canada into the interior of the continent (Figure 2.1). Beautifully worked Clovis spear points, first found in the 1930s near Clovis, New Mexico (Figure 2.2), would be found dispersed in some 1,500 sites along this pathway and throughout North America before traces of the Clovis people disappeared (PIDBA, 2019). Corroborated by tooth

**Figure 2.2:** Clovis points from the Rummells-Maske site, 13CD15, Cedar County, Iowa

Note: Office of the State Archaeologist Collection

Source: Wikipedia—File: Clovis Rummells Maske.jpg

studies (Turner and Scott, 2014), the data provided the basis for the widely adopted "Clovis-first" school of early human dispersal in North America. Native Americans of the Paleo-Eskimo and modern Inuit cultures are documented to have migrated across the Bering Strait at dates after 6,000 BP. The primacy of the Clovis-Beringia concept was dramatically challenged by the discovery of an earlier complex human habitation site at Monte Verde, southern Chile, by Thomas Dillehay in 1977. Questions about its dates were countered by exhaustively detailed documentation (Pino and Dillehay, 2023) that dated the site to ca. 14,400–14,600 BP.

The Monte Verde discovery set off a flood of reports of older site claims in North America, as well as Central and South America. In the new research environment opened by the Monte Verde site, some authors even claimed migration of early arrivals from Japan (Fiedel et al, 2020) and from the Solutrean culture of Europe across the Atlantic Ocean (Bradley and Stanford, 2004). For migration from the Bering Strait area, dates for earlier human occupancy posed the following riddle: how could pre-Clovis migrants have arrived south along the American continent before a corridor opened through ice masses that were obstructing travel from Beringia?

Boats have long been known to transport early humans across long water distances, and experts have proposed that pre-Clovis groups reached Pacific coast areas by this means. However, Meltzer (2021) offered a critical review of alternative migration routes by boat or land migration along the Pacific shore, noting that these would have been obstructed by the Aleutian ice mass and periglacial coastal obstacles. He suggested that the navigation dilemmas have not yet been resolved. He also questioned a number of the proposed pre-Clovis site claims as having potential sources of contamination from older nonhuman deposits, or for other reasons (Meltzer, 2021).

Nevertheless, a book by Dillehay (2000) offers multiple arguments, including linguistic evidence, that American Indian cultures in South America were diverse, unlike the coherent and widespread Clovis culture in North America. The sites feature stone tools that are different from the Clovis types. The Dillehay book illustrates the fact that almost every aspect of early American human history remains controversial. A problem is that virtually all examples older than the Clovis period are isolated and lack unequivocal diagnostic artifacts like the Clovis point itself. Should there not have been further traces of early arrivals? A recent article posing further questions about older sites was published by Surovell et al (2022), which, using stratigraphic analysis on North American sites, reaffirmed late (Clovis-age) arrivals.

An impressive genetic study reported by a large group of researchers in the premier science journal *Nature* (Moreno-Mayar et al, 2018) concluded that all North American Indians stemmed from a single Eurasian culture that diverged from later occupants of Siberia around 36,000 years ago. This culture is suggested to have lived in the Land Bridge area for thousands of years until the melting of the ice masses opened the corridor to North America and allowed migration to the American continent (Tamm et al, 2007; Elias, 2014).

A succinct and insightful synthesis of the early settlement on the North American continent was provided by Alan Taylor (2002):

> Early migrants in Siberia lived in small bands on land inhospitable to farming. They existed largely by pursuing large roaming and grazing animals. It was a hard, cold, and usually short life, in which hunger alternated with big kills. Once they arrived in North America, however, they found a vast grassland that sustained large herds of slow-moving herbivores initially inexperienced in defending themselves against a predator as cunning, numerous, and cooperative as humans. The beasts included immense mammoths, mastodons, bison, horses, and camels, as well as caribou and deer. The Paleoindians found beavers as big as bears … after centuries of subarctic hardship, the first Americans found a hunter's Eden.

Anthropologist J. M. Adovasio (Adovasio and Page, 2002) offered an elaborated scenario about North American migration, which can be paraphrased as follows. In the Tanana Valley that led into the upper Yukon River basin, a people Adovasio referred to as Nenana moved south on the Yukon plateau in the warmer summers, eating plants, fish, waterfowl, and game that they could kill with their wooden spears. The retreat of the mile-high glaciers let them venture successively further south. Eventually, a vast Canadian plain opened. Reaching Boone Lake near Grand Prairie in Alberta, they spotted a herd of mammoths in a poplar grove. These were giant beasts unlike anything they had ever seen before. They attacked and wounded a young mammoth, only to have its mother charge them. Their wooden spears merely bounced off her tough hide. They ran for their lives. These hunters realized that only longer spears with more penetrating tips could bring down animals of this size. After much trial and error, a toolmaker devised stone spear points with a groove that helped fasten the points to a wooden lance. Voila—Clovis Man.

As first modeled by Mosimann and Martin (1975) and described by Taylor (2001), the abundant new protein diet led to explosive population growth, which quickly depleted local food resources, leading bands to subdivide and move in search of more distant animal herds. "Through some combination of climatic change and the spread of highly skilled hunters, almost all the largest animals died out," helping account for the disappearance of the Clovis spear points, and perhaps many of the people who produced them.

Adovasio again elaborates, partly based on documentation including an infant found buried at the Anzick site near Wilsall, Montana, 3,500 miles from the upper Tanana Valley: "The world became drier with year after year of drought. Water tables dropped and big game gathered around remaining water holes, making them easy prey to skilled hunters." In the last stages of the Pleistocene epoch, the Younger Dryas (which began ca. 12,850 years ago and ended ca. 11,700 years BP), the big game, what have been called Pleistocene megafauna, disappeared, leaving only bison, musk ox, moose, deer, and a few other large game animal species.

As the large animals became extinct, the environment became more diverse. Global warming shrank grasslands and expanded forests, also "expanding the range of plants and small animals that could be gathered for food. Nomadic bands had to learn to exploit local environments to harvest shellfish, fish, birds, nuts, seeds, berries and tubers" (Taylor, 2001). In the ensuing Archaic period (see Table 2.1), the Paleolithic populations increased

**Table 2.1:** Precolonial American Indian periods, cultures, and sites

| Date | Period/event | Reference/notes |
|---|---|---|
| 14,400–14,600 BP | Monte Verde site, Chile | Pino and Dillehay, 2023 |
| 13,050–12,750 BP | Clovis period | Waters et al, 2020 |
| 13,000–8,000 BP | Paleoindian period | NPS, 2025 |
| 9,600 (8,000) BCE–1000 BCE | Archaic period | NPS, 2023 |
| 1000 BCE–1000 CE | Woodland Period | NPS, 2016 |
| 200–1300 CE | Anasazi Culture | Hurst, 1994 |
| 800–1600 CE | Mississippian culture | King, 2020 |
| 1492 CE | Columbus voyage | |

Notes: Dates can vary depending on location of cultures and author interpretations; controversial dates prior to the Monte Verde site are not included.

in terms of both size and skill at living in diverse new environments. As Indian groups proliferated, so did their languages, cultures, and kinship systems.

The classification of American Indian history in North America remains most controversial for the earliest arrivals, and dates of periods vary in synthesis reports by different authors. Popular encyclopedias and websites such as the *History of Pre-Colonial America* frequently cite unsubstantiated earlier dates for initial arrivals to North America that are not included in the classification in Table 2.1.

## The transformation of concepts of American Indian populations and impacts on the land

Popular perceptions of North America before European arrivals were long influenced by images of virgin wilderness and romantic novels like those of James Fenimore Cooper's *The Last of the Mohicans*, "which portrayed the Indian man as an admirable brave or a fiendish warrior" (Dippie, 2023). Discoveries in the 20th century transformed earlier concepts of "museum landscapes," revealing that North America "had been shaped by thousands of years of indigenous burning, pruning, sowing, selective harvesting, and tilling" (Anderson and Moratto, 1997).

Based on early encounters, it was assumed that pre-European North America was sparsely populated. From detailed tribal estimates, Smithsonian anthropologist J. L. Mooney (Mooney, 1928) calculated the population of preconquest Indian populations north of Mexico at 1,153,000. The pioneering American anthropologist Alfred Kroeber (Kroeber, 1939) reduced estimates of aboriginal populations to around 900,000.

Despite the early assumptions, numbers for Central American Indian populations had already been questioned by archeologist and anthropologist H. J. Spinden (Spinden, 1928), who noted the appalling number of Mayan Indian deaths reported by the Franciscan priest Toribio de Benaventa de Motolinia in 1536. The first comprehensively documented challenge to low Indigenous population estimates was published by Henry F. Dobyns (Dobyns, 1966), whose intensive analyses of early reports on the effect of disease on Central American populations concluded that low population estimates were subject to major bias. His work indicated that estimates of Indian populations by European observers were based on contact with native populations that had already been reduced by exposure to European diseases.

Dobyns reported that a single sick Spanish sailor introduced the smallpox that "hopscotched" through Central America, ravaging vast native populations. Europeans living with domestic animals for thousands of years had acquired substantial immunity to diseases like smallpox and measles, but American Indians had no such immunity. Their communities suffered losses of up to 90 percent through spread of disease even without direct contact with Europeans. Compounding loss from disease in Central America was famine, the demoralization of society, and deaths during forced labor by Spanish conquistadores. Dobyns concluded his seminal report with an estimate of 90 million persons for the entire hemisphere, a number that has been modified to varying degrees by later writers. Mortalities were greatest in densely populated areas of Central America and were lowest in sparsely populated areas in North America (Dobyns, 1983).

The effects of decline in Indian populations in New England were summarized by environmental historian William Cronon (Cronon, 1983), who observed that "It is tempting to believe that when the Europeans arrived in the New World, they confronted Virgin Land, the Forest Primeval, a wilderness which had existed for eons uninfluenced by human hands." Cronon cited descriptions by an early English traveler, the philosopher and natural scientist Henry David Thoreau, about his regret over loss of the former forests, lush vegetation, and wildlife: "bear, moose, deer, porcupines, the grim-fac'd Ounce, and rav'nous howling Wolf, and beaver." He continued: "Not only the mammals of the land were gone; the sea and air also seemed more empty. Bass had once been caught two or three thousand at a time." However, Cronon noted that: "Nothing could be further from the truth [that this was the environment before European settlement] … Indians had lived on the continent for thousands of years, and had to a significant extent modified its environment to their purposes." It was the decimation of Indian populations that created the verdant earlier landscape envisaged by Thoreau.

Another pioneer in environmental history, William Denevan, who began research on South American cultures in the 1960s (Denevan, 1992), provided similar observations: "Forest composition had been modified, grasslands had been created, wildlife disrupted … Earthworks, roads, fields, and settlements were ubiquitous. With Indian depopulation in the wake of Old World disease, the environment recovered in many areas. A good argument can be made that the human presence was less visible in 1750 than it was in 1492." In short, new discoveries in the post-World War II period provided major new insights on early colonial history of North America. A summary of some 50 years of research became widely known through a bestselling popular review by Charles Mann (2006).

## Fire and evolving agriculture: mound builders and town dwellers

In contrast to popular conceptions, mature forests offer little food for humans or game animals; Native Americans made them more productive for human needs using fire. In addition to clearing large tracts of wooded land for farming, "the burning of large areas was useful to divert big game (deer, elk, bison) into small unburned areas for easier hunting" (Williams, 2003, p 3), and was used to reduce fuel accumulation that could lead to unwanted fires (Anderson and Moratto, 1997).

Over many generations, Indians learned to cultivate and crossbreed wild plants. "By 1,500 BCE Indians in central Mexico learned to cultivate maize from inch-long ears … to hybrids with multiple ears, protective husks, and cobs with multiple rows of kernels" (Dennis et al, 2016). The authors noted that "Indians practiced calculated and extensive resource management in central areas of North America." By 1000–1600 CE in the Mississippian Era, complex agricultural societies were present across much of the Southeast and Midwest and into the Great Lakes region, including the dense population centers in the American Bottom at and around Cahokia, near the confluence of the Mississippi and Missouri Rivers. "Nor were the people of the Midwest simple nomads," the authors continued, "but urbanized engineers, long-distance traders, and large-scale farmers."

According to historian Joshua J. Mark (2021): "The largest urban center (c. 650–c. 1,350 CE) was Cahokia, now southern Illinois, a grand city with a wide central plaza, shops, ball fields, a solar calendar, residences for the lower class and for the elite, and fields of corn and other crops." Cahokia's most prominent feature was a huge earthen pyramid, covering ca. 14 acres and with a height of 100 feet, originally topped by a wooden temple (Taylor, 2001; Pauketat, 2004). Agriculture, which furnished the main food supply in Cahokia, was highly labor-intensive without animal support, using only bone or stone hoes. Overreliance on one plant, maize (corn), was not as healthy as the diverse diet of hunter gatherers; skeletal evidence of early farmers reveals childhood malnutrition and loss of stature from overconsumption of corn. An increase in the population of the Cahokia community is interpreted as having led to depleted woodlands, associated game, and loss of soil fertility, and this and other factors, such as changes in rainfall regimes and the rise of possible political rivals, ultimately led to the decline of the Cahokia community beginning around 1200 CE (Pauketat, 2004; Benson et al, 2009). Dates for Cahokhia's early history vary among authors.

Other complex cultures, called Hohokam and Anasazi (Pueblo group) by scholars, developed in the American Southwest about the same time, over the last two millennia. Both cultures incorporated different linguistic groups, but built substantial towns or villages headed by male political or religious hierarchies. Exchange took place with populations of Mesoamerica, from whom the Southwestern groups learned how to grow cotton and weave cloth. In their arid areas, the cultures built elaborate systems of dams, reservoirs, and ditches to irrigate plants (Lekson, 2018). During the 12th and 13th centuries, the groups experienced crises due to overpopulation and excessive reliance on maize. Drought further aggravated conditions, forcing the population to disperse to new environments and lifestyles.

## The Pacific coast and eastern North America

Varied environments in western areas of North America required relevant adaptation by Indian tribes (see, for example, Raab and Jones, 2004; Anderson and Moratto, 1997). In the high-rainfall Pacific Northwest, "the hunting, gathering, and fishing complex was so productive that native peoples did not feel the pressures that elsewhere led to horticulture ... With a bountiful diet and leisure, Indians of the Northwestern raincoast developed elaborate rituals, art, and status hierarchies" (Taylor, 2001; see also Ames and Maschner, 1999; Moss, 2011).

In Eastern coastal areas, fish and shellfish supplied a significant part of Indian food supplies, but unlike in the Pacific coast, agriculture was a part of mixed diets, except in Florida (Hutchison et al, 2016), Historian Alan Taylor (2001) reported that maize plants supported bean vines; squash and pumpkins spread along the ground, discouraging weeds. Fires were set twice a year to reduce brush and undergrowth, favoring hardwoods that bore edible nuts. This practice opened up patches of sunlight that "promoted ground-hugging plants like grasses and berries, which sustained deer herds, to the benefit of human hunters." Because they did not store large quantities of food, tribes that were more distant from coastal waters periodically suffered from hunger.

Knowledge of North American land-use patterns before European influence remains in the early stages of development. Some authors regarded Indian influence on vegetation as ubiquitous in the Eastern areas, while others proposed that prehistoric Native-American land use involved a "shifting mosaic" of managed areas (Munoz et al, 2014). It is assumed that, except along the coast, where populations were more concentrated and had incentives to maintain stable dwelling areas, a dominant practice was "slash and burn" agriculture, which refers to growing crops until the soil becomes depleted and then moving on to new areas.

## Land use, social organization, and warfare

While cultural patterns were highly diverse, the concept of land ownership common to all Indian tribes was based on use, with ownership belonging to the community. This principle differed from the colonial interpretation of land ownership in terms of tangible value that could be assigned, bought, and sold. A corollary was a community-oriented society, in contrast to the intensely individual-centered societal pattern that later become dominant in American society.

Regarding gender roles in society, men "were generally responsible for hunting, warfare, and interacting with outsiders," as well as formal leadership. Women engaged in agriculture and food gathering, owned family housing and goods, and reared children. "Because of their central role in community welfare," women had a higher status than was the case in most European societies. Clan membership, as in the Iroquois Six Nations, often descended matrilineally (Anonymous, 2018).

Indian culture was no exception to the universal predisposition to warfare by males, which has been traced to the earliest human records (Wrangham and Peterson, 1996). But with the exception of more complex chiefdom and state-level societies, violence rarely involved the massive killing and complete domination seen during the Spanish conquests in Central and South America (Dye, 2009). Some Eastern populations actively participated in the slave trade following conquest (Ethridge and Shuck-Hall, 2009). A frequent motivation for raids included the capture of enemy villages to incorporate parts of their populations, a practice accentuated in Eastern areas after losses from European-initiated disease (Taylor, 2001). However, after 1570, a Huron leader named Dekanawida ("The Peacemaker") initiated a famous Iroquois (Haudenosaunee) confederation of five Eastern Indian tribes: the Mohawk, Oneida, Onondaga, Cayuga, and Seneca. They were later joined by a sixth tribe, the Tuscarora, in 1722. The objective of the compact was to "advance peace, civil authority, righteousness, and the Great Law" (Brittanica, 2023).

The confederation succeeded in maintaining peace between its members and developed a sophisticated political organizational structure that involved representative governance as well as personal autonomy for tribal members. Instead of control by a powerful leader, ritualized formal procedures governed decision making, both within tribes and by representatives from each tribe. The confederation was devastatingly successful in warfare against other tribes, coming to control vast areas from New York State and Pennsylvania to the Mississippi River. Remarkably, it "maintained autonomy vis-à-vis both the French and English." Its Grand Council still exists.

## Indian influence on colonial government and the constitution

Americans in the Revolutionary War era had differing attitudes toward Indians. Founders like John Adams, George Washington, Benjamin Franklin, and Thomas Jefferson respected Indian culture and ideas regarding governance and human freedom (Miller, 1993). Jefferson believed that Indians had the same abilities as Europeans and regarded them as having a superior moral culture. His view of Indians' abilities contrasted with his negative opinion of the abilities of African Americans (Jefferson, 1785). On the negative side was the inexorable push of colonists for new land, and "the threat posed by Indian tribes toward the new United States government" (Miller, 1993).

As will be reviewed in Chapter 4, wholesale violation of treaties and forced Indian removals first took place during the presidency of Andrew Jackson.

The Albany Congress of 1754, designed to develop a plan for union of British colonies in America and stabilize relationships with the Iroquois Six Nations, included 150 Indian representatives. Benjamin Franklin, who was a delegate from Pennsylvania, was especially impressed by Indian governance and was said to have been influenced by it in his plan presented to the Congress in 1754 (Wikipedia—Albany Plan). More recently, a Congressional resolution recognized Indian contributions to the framing of the US Constitution (Udall, 1988).

# 3

# Colonial History up to 1829

## Colonization

Five European nations colonized North America. The first permanent colonists in North America were the Spanish, who founded settlements in St. Augustine, Florida, in 1565, and in New Mexico in 1598.[1] These were followed by British settlers in Virginia, Massachusetts, and the Carolinas. The Dutch established a thriving colony, the New Netherlands, in parts of New York, Connecticut, and New Jersey. Its capital at New Amsterdam (subsequently New York) was on the southern tip of Manhattan Island.

New Sweden grew along the Delaware River, including current parts of New Jersey, Pennsylvania, Delaware, and Maryland. These latter colonies were included in New Netherlands ceded to Great Britain as part of the Treaty of Westminster (1674) that ended the third Dutch–British war. Henceforth, the British Crown controlled 13 American colonies that extended from Spanish Florida to the Canadian border. Canada was settled by the French and belonged to France until 1763, but it was ceded to Britain after the French–British War (1754–1763). Alan Taylor (2001, p 25), the previously cited award-winning historian writing on the colonial history of North America, pointed out that "European colonists were no crueler or harsher than other people of their time, but they were capable of inflicting unprecedented misery on the native population".

Most of the 13 colonies underwent major boundary changes during the colonial era. New Hampshire and New York covered an area that would become Vermont; the area that later became Maine was a separate part of Massachusetts. Carolina was one colony before North and South Carolina were separated, and Georgia's boundaries also changed 1732 to 1763. Before 1763, maps of the 13 colonies extended to the Mississippi River. Following its victory in the French–British war, the British government established the Proclamation Line of 1763 along the Appalachian Mountains as a Western boundary for the American colonies. Beyond this point, settlement was prohibited (see Figure 3.1). With the peace treaty of 1783 that ended the

**Figure 3.1:** Map of North America, translated from the French of d'Anville

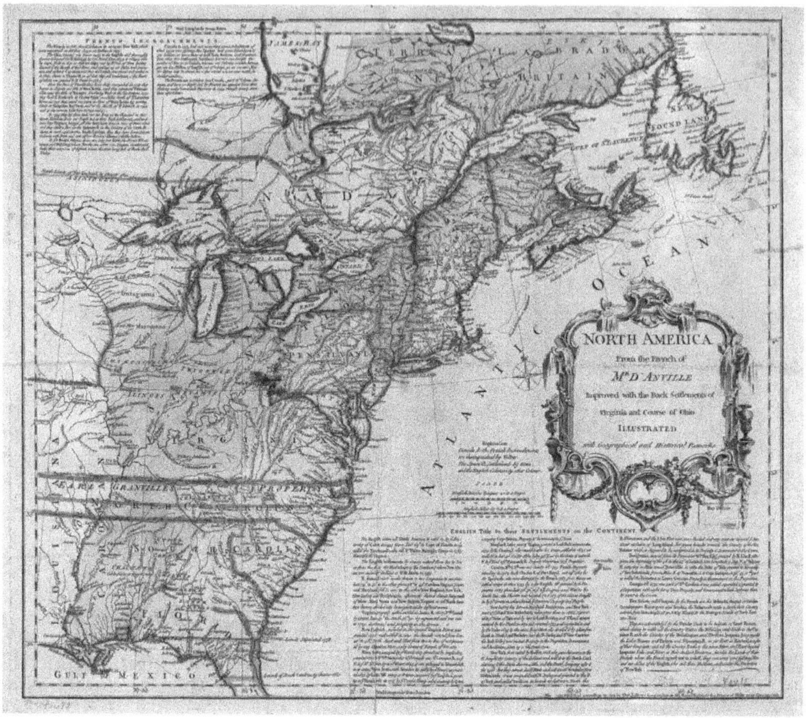


Source: Jefferys, T. and d'Anville, J. B. B. (1758) *North America* (Map). Library of Congress, available from: https://www.loc.gov/item/73696679/

Revolutionary War, maps again extended to the Mississippi River, with variable state boundaries. The map in Figure 3.1, by Jean Baptiste d'Anville,[2] the most famous cartographer of the 18th century, shows Virginia with a huge area that was later reduced by the Land Law of 1785 and other changes. For a time, the boundaries of North and South Carolina and Georgia were also expanded.

The 13 colonies were incorporated by subcontracts from the king of England or Parliament. The earliest colonists in Virginia's Jamestown settlement were poorly prepared for their new life and had unrealistic attitudes, not least of which was their brutal behavior toward Indian tribes. The unhealthy, mosquito-infested climate of the colony, combined with poor relations with Indians, led to the Jamestown settlement's collapse. The Chesapeake settlements did better in the fertile lands adjoining the bay. They came to specialize in production of tobacco, which was valuable as an export to the European continent. The Chesapeake colonists in this area also displayed hostile behavior toward the Algonquin Indians, who launched retaliatory attacks, but were ultimately defeated by disease and the superior numbers of the intruders. One of the most nuanced sources for American colonial history is again the work by Alan Taylor (2001), whom I cite extensively in this and the previous chapter.

Intensely religious and diligent, the Puritans who survived the devastating early winter in Massachusetts (1624) had good initial relationships with the Indians, which was of major benefit to them, though ultimately not to the Indians. The Wampanoags and other local tribes maintained productive agriculture and effective use of land, as noted in the previous chapter, but the settlers changed land-use practice to English methods, clearing and fencing land, building structures, cutting forests, and exterminating predatory animals like bears and wolves. Relations with Indians deteriorated when the colonists expanded southward into Connecticut and the Mystic River Valley, leading to the Pequot War. Provoked by colonists, King Philip's war in 1675 was a bloody confrontation with Wampanoag Indians of Massachusetts.

The Carolinas north of Spanish Florida were colonized by English West Indian planters, who brought slaves with them. They soon attracted English settlers from Barbados, the Chesapeake area, and England, including indentured servants who were put to work building farms—activities that Indians resisted. Livestock thrived in the mild climate, and the Carolinas became the main producer of cattle in the British Empire. The Carolinas also became a major producer of lumber and tar, obtained by tapping and boiling pitch from pine trees. Georgia, colonized in 1733 and named after King George II, was the only North American colony in which slavery was initially banned, along with rum, lawyers, and Catholics. According to the *New Georgia Encyclopedia*, General James Oglethorpe and other trustees of the Georgia grant were not opposed to slavery on principle:

> They banned slavery in Georgia because it was inconsistent with their social and economic intentions. Given the Spanish presence in Florida, slavery also seemed certain to threaten the military security of the colony. Spain offered freedom in exchange for military service, so any African captive brought to Georgia could be expected to help the Spanish in their efforts to destroy the still-fragile English colony.

The Cherokees were one of the most populous Indian tribes in the southeastern US and were close allies of the British until the Seven Years' War of 1756–1763. They became subject to territorial encroachment by both the British and the Americans after the Revolutionary War. As described in the *New Georgia Encyclopedia*, the tribe showed resilience in the face of territorial loss and made significant progress in nation building, but most were ultimately removed to Oklahoma as a result of the *Indian Removal Act of 1830*, instigated by Andrew Jackson and labeled by historians as the Trail of Tears. A moving memorial center about that sad chapter in American history is now located in Pulaski, Tennessee.

As noted by Taylor, planters learned the skills of rice cultivation from West African slaves and adapted it to the lowlands and tidal areas of the Carolinas. As a result, the Carolinas became the British Empire's great rice colony, with production increasing from 400,000 pounds in 1700 to 43 million pounds in 1740. Rice production required importation of African slaves, who came to outnumber free colonists by two to one by 1730. However, brutal working conditions ("the disease-ridden lowland environment produced a slave mortality in excess of the birthrate") required continual importation of slaves. Lowland rice production by slaves was mentioned in a dispute over slavery importation during the Constitutional Convention, which we will discuss later.

## Governance and land use

In theory, governors of colonies appointed by the king had nearly total authority, but colonial legislatures elected by property-holding males soon gained effective control. Paying the salaries of governors and providing other emoluments gave them further influence, so governors had little incentive or effective means to interfere with the legislatures' activities. As Lord Kenneth Clark observed in the noted BBC TV series *Civilisation* (Clark, 1969), the American colonies were outposts of the Enlightenment. Their distance and freedom from the corruption associated with aristocracies in England and France allowed them to develop advanced forms of self-governance (Friedman, 2005). Eleven of the colonies had written constitutions at the time they became states, and these constitutions and experience in writing laws contributed to the quality of the later US Constitution. While James Madison and other leaders dominated the final writing, other delegates had sufficient background to provide meaningful input as well.

Land in England was expensive while labor was cheap, a relationship that was reversed in the New World. Land use was initially influenced by practices in the nations from which the immigrants came, but except for stable populations in coastal areas, the easy availability of land soon led to wasteful and exploitive agriculture and wanton cutting of forests (Kawashima and Tone, 1983). In contrast with the labor-intensive land-use practices of the Indians, which were not highly disruptive geomorphologically, European settlers' "advanced technologies and economic incentives led them to rapidly clear land, plow deeply, mine and exploit resources," leading to erosion and sedimentation (James, 2011).

A universal feature of land and water use in the colonies was the European "nuisance" principle. No one had the right to use property in such a way as to injure a neighbor, and upstream users of waterways were not to pollute or affect downstream users. The nations from which immigrants came maintained oversight over land use, especially England and the Netherlands, which were more densely populated.

Progress and interest in national science grew rapidly in the 18th century. King George III appointed John Bartram, an American-born Quaker, as Botanist for the North American colonies. Advanced forest management practices in nations like Sweden (Sweden's first forestry law was passed in 1600), Germany, and Austria were not adopted, but an extensive review of colonial statutes countered earlier claims that legislatures minimally regulated land use (Kawashima and Tone, 1983).

Town boards determined access of land to settlers and owners and established land-use boundaries and properties such as fencing, grazing, mining, and water use. Statutes often required consistency or diligence in land use; that is, farmlands would be required to be cleared and actively worked or they could be allocated to other users. Wetlands might be required to be drained where they were deemed suitable for converting to grazing or farming. Thanks to the influence of William Penn, early ordinances in Pennsylvania required property owners in Philadelphia to plant trees.

## Boston: disease and early environmental regulations

The most virulent early disease, smallpox, arrived with a sick sailor on a ship from England in 1721. Initial mortality for Europeans was about 30 percent, but it reached 90 percent for Indians (O'Fallon, 2011). Learning of the practice of inoculation from his African slave, Onesimus, the noted Puritan minister Cotton Mather advocated the procedure in the face of initial opposition (Blakemore, 2021). It was successfully applied to soldiers in the Continental Army by George Washington.

Bylaws of the city of Boston, Massachusetts, provide the most complete historical data on health policy available from the colonies. An earlier review (Manheim, 2009) showed that Boston was remarkably effective in managing public health, land use, and labor law, given the knowledge of the times. Though the germ theory was unknown, communicable diseases were associated with "filth." Accordingly, sewage discharge into Boston's harbor was forbidden beginning in the 17th century up until the early 1830s. This and other measures explain the fact that Boston was spared from the worldwide cholera epidemic of 1832, which claimed thousands of lives in other American cities, especially New York and New Orleans, where controls were less stringent. Boston relaxed controls in the early 1830s and was impacted by subsequent cholera epidemics introduced by Italian immigrants arriving in New York in 1848 (Martinez, 2013).

## The Constitution and the slavery issue

On the 200th anniversary of the Constitutional Convention in 1787, Thurgood Marshall, the first Black Supreme Court justice, refused an invitation to attend a celebration. Instead, he released a shocking indictment of the founders: "The government they devised was defective from the start, requiring several amendments, a civil war, and momentous social transformation to attain the system of constitutional government, and its respect for the individual freedoms and human rights, we hold as fundamental today" (Mintz, no date). One-hundred-and thirty-three years earlier, on July 4, 1854, abolitionist William Lloyd Garrison issued a similar challenge at a meeting outside Boston: he lit a copy of the Constitution on fire, calling it "a covenant with death and an agreement with hell" (Williford, 2013). These statements referred to passages in the Constitution that allowed slavery. Garrison's reference to "death" would be vindicated by the horrific toll of the Civil War that began six years later. Because slavery continues to be a subject of contention (Hannah-Jones and *New York Times Magazine*, 2021), this chapter includes historical detail from the Constitutional Convention debates in order to better appreciate the issues and challenges facing the framers at this critical point in American history.

King Louis X of France prohibited slavery in France as early as 1315, followed by Sweden in 1335. Slavery in Britain ended in 1772, but the British Crown continued to support the slave trade until 1807, and slavery in British colonies was not finally abolished until 1833. After re-establishing the slave trade in sugar-producing colonies in 1802, Napoleon finally ended the French slave trade in 1815 (Wikipedia—Timeline of Abolition of Slavery and Serfdom In America); however, slavery in Georgia and the Carolinas was entrenched. Virginia and Maryland were also slave states, but in the 18th century, anti-slavery sentiment grew, supported by Presbyterian and Methodist clergy and a majority of Baptists. Under British rule, individuals could own slaves in the northern states.

Thanks to James Madison's comprehensive, 660-page record of the Constitutional Convention of 1787, combined with his active participation in the debates, which "nearly killed him," historians have a nearly stenographic account of the debate over slavery (Madison, 1987, republished from the 1840 edition). Paradoxically, Madison's records reveal that it was leaders of the slave state of Virginia who most actively opposed slave importation. George Washington, Thomas Jefferson, James Madison, Edmund Randolph, Henry Lee, and Patrick Henry recognized the inhuman nature of the institution. Soon after the beginning of the Revolutionary War (1778), Virginia banned slave importation. Delegate George Mason, a large slaveowner, was the most vehement voice against slavery at the convention. He later refused to ratify the Constitution because of the slavery provision:

> This infernal traffic originated in the avarice of British merchants. The British government constantly checked the attempts of Virginia to put a stop to it ... The Western people are already calling for slaves for their new lands and will fill their country if they can be got thro' S. Carolina and Georgia. Every master of slaves is a born tyrant. They bring the judgment of Heaven on a country. (Madison, 1987, pp 503–504)

Discussing problems associated with manumission, the voluntary freeing of slaves by their owners, Mason felt that slaves needed to be educated before being freed. Gouverneur Morris of Pennsylvania and John Dickenson of Delaware were also outspoken opponents of the slavery provision, as was Luther Martin of the slave state of Maryland. He proposed a variation of Section 4, Article VII to prohibit or tax slave imports, saying that the importation of slaves "was inconsistent with the principles of the revolution and dishonorable for the American character" (Madison, 1987, p 502).

However, Georgia and the two Carolinas adamantly opposed the prohibition of the slave trade. Two Pinckney relatives, Charles Pinckney and General Charles Cotesworth Pinckney, served in the South Carolina delegation. Charles Pinckney stated: "South Carolina can never receive the plan if it prohibits the slave trade," adding "If the states be all at liberty in this subject, S. Carolina may by degrees do of itself what is wished, as Virginia and Maryland have already done" (Madison, 1987, p 503). General Pinckney argued that "if himself & all his colleagues were to sign the Constitution ... it would be of no avail to obtain the consent of their constituents. S. Carolina and Georgia cannot do without slaves" (Madison, 1987, p 505). Convention delegates Hugh Williamson of North Carolina and Abraham Baldwin of Georgia also insisted on the continuation of the importation of slaves.

A paradoxical feature of slavery debate was that representatives of states with slaves or close to the slave states were the strongest advocates of banning slave imports. In contrast, Roger Sherman of Connecticut argued: "It was better to let the S. States import slaves than part with them, if that was their sine qua non." Oliver Ellsworth of Connecticut suggested that Virginia wanted to prohibit slave importation so it could breed slaves and supply the "sickly rice swamps" of the Carolinas and Georgia, which needed to replenish slaves. Representatives from Northern states like New Jersey and New Hampshire were not heard from in Madison's records.

In hindsight, a better solution to the constitutional dilemma over slavery might have been to let the Carolinas and Georgia remain outside the new US. Virginia would have remained in the union, and the slave states' influence in elections of the president and other high offices would have been avoided. This could have avoided the accession of new slave states to the union, preventing the devastating Civil War. As delegate Pinckney suggested, slave states might have ultimately moved in the direction of Virginia and Maryland. Unfortunately, in order to achieve compromise over this issue, the southern states were not only allowed to import slaves until 1808, but also gained representatives corresponding to three-fifths of the slave population, through which they dominated key government offices, including the Supreme Court. In the unified US, the opposite of Pinckney's suggestion took place. Virginia moved into the pro-slavery state camp and South Carolina's pro-slavery stance hardened. New slave states were admitted, pro-slavery presidents were elected after 1829, and Virginia ultimately became a leader in the Confederacy.

Other than the fateful slavery provision, the remainder of the Constitution has long been regarded as one of the most significant political achievements in world history (de Tocqueville, 1835). Created in less than four months in 1787, the US Constitution marked the first representative political system since the fall of the Roman republic in 27 BCE, which had a constitution, laws, elected officials, and a senior governing body of senators. The remainder of the new Constitution showed exceptional vision into human and political behavior. Amendments to the Constitution were wisely made difficult in order to avoid arbitrary changes sought for immediate concerns, but they were attainable when sufficient support for constitutional modification emerged.

An example of the ability of the founders to look beyond their times and devise sophisticated governmental mechanisms was the provision for impeachment. At the time of the Constitutional Convention, George Washington was sure to become the first president. He was a man of unquestioned character who had resigned his commission at the height of his power and popularity, but the founders recognized the likelihood of abuses by future presidents and high officers in government. They invested the initiation of impeachment in the most democratic branch of government, the House of Representatives, but required approval by the Senate, whose longer terms meant that incumbents would represent larger proportions of constituents, have longer experience, and presumably more balanced judgment.

The vision displayed in the Constitution was also displayed in early law making. Administrative history scholar Paul Light has suggested that the first ten years of Congress might be considered as an evolution of administrative practice from the Constitution (Light, 2009). Groundbreaking laws passed by the early Congress included the *Bill of Rights*, the *Federal Judiciary Act*, the Department of Treasury, the Postal Service, and the Decadal Census. The first national land management act, the *Confederation Congress's Lands*

*Act of 1785*, banned slavery and laid out principles for the subdivision and surveying of land in territories that would become Illinois, Ohio, Indiana, Michigan, Wisconsin, and part of Minnesota. Surveying was to include environmental features like water bodies, forests, and salt licks on maps submitted to the Surveyor General and made accessible to the public. The quality of law making regrettably did not continue in later Congresses.

## Natural science and land use: James Madison and Thomas Jefferson

Interest in natural science in the 18th century was demonstrated by the appointment of John Bartram as royal botanist for the North American colonies by King George III. In 1780, John Adams, John Hancock, Bowdoin, and 60 others founded the American Academy of Arts and Sciences in Boston during the Revolutionary War in 1780. The most prominent of the founders in terms of scientific interests were Benjamin Franklin, James Madison, and Thomas Jefferson. Franklin became world famous for his studies on electricity and his charting of the path of the Gulf Stream, while Jefferson had a famous dispute with the leading French encyclopedist of natural history, Georges-Louis Leclerc, Comte de Buffon. As President, Jefferson was visited by the famed German explorer and scientist Alexander von Humboldt (Anonymous, 2018).

James Madison has been called the first American environmentalist (Wulf, 2012). In a remarkable speech to the Albemarle Agricultural Society, Madison reviewed what we would now call animal and plant ecology and chemistry in terms of the scientific knowledge of the time (Madison, 1818). He detailed farming practices in quantitative terms, such as the area of fodder crops needed to support animals and acres of forest required to maintain sustainable farmstead use. He reviewed soil manuring in depth and emphasized the need to maintain nutrient balance in farming. Madison also pointed out that China and Japan had maintained sustainable agriculture for thousands of years. In contrast, poor agricultural practices in Virginia stripped soil of essential nutrients and eroded the land because land was cheap and labor was scarce.

Thomas Jefferson is a singular figure in American history. Because of current sensitivity to the US's historical treatment of African Americans (Hannah-Jones and New York Times Magazine, 2021), Jefferson's candid opinion about their inferior endowments, and his alleged poor treatment of slaves on his plantation (Wiencek, 2012) have made him the most criticized of the founders. However, he had an astonishing variety of scientific and societal interests, and made many contributions to the fledgling nation.

Jefferson was a founder of the University of Virginia, the author of the Declaration of Independence, served as US representative in France, Secretary of State in Washington's administration, and was elected President of the United States for two terms. He chaired the panel that wrote the first law governing land management, the Confederation Congress Land Law of 1785. He "gathered scientific data on the size and variety of American plants, animals" (Anonymous, 2015) and has been called the first American paleontologist. Initiating the Lewis and Clark Expedition, he directed explorers to prepare for description and documentation of the findings of the expedition by training in botany, astronomy, and land surveying. An example of the remarkable records of the Lewis and Clark Expedition is presented in the next chapter.

Jefferson compiled a large collection of vocabularies of Indian languages, in part by requesting that military officers serving in the territories record them from Indians with whom they came in contact. As noted in Chapter 2, he deduced that Indians had a common ancestry from Siberia. Linguistic similarities and differences would provide information on affinities and the timing of separation of tribes during the settlement and migration in North America. Unfortunately, a thief rifled the contents of a trunk being shipped to Monticello, and the contents were thrown into the James River. Only remnants in muddy condition were recovered (APS, no date). Subsequently, the pioneering French linguistic scholar, Peter Stephen Duponceau, vastly expanded collection and study of Indian languages and concluded that all Indian languages, from the Arctic to Tierra del Fuego, had a unique way of compounding words from a variety of roots that he called polysynthesis. This differed fundamentally from other languages and gave Indians the ability to express complex ideas in single words (Smith, 1983).

In his *Notes on the State of Virginia* (Jefferson, 1785), Jefferson showed pride in what we would now call community-based services in Virginia. For example, Jefferson referred to community subsidies for the placement of sick, disabled, or indigent persons with farm families, where they would get "far better care than would be the case in institutions in European countries."

The era that included Jefferson and Madison closed with the sixth President, John Quincy Adams (1825–1829), son of John Adams and a precocious intellect. As a boy of 14, he accompanied Francis Dana, the US envoy to Russia, as his private secretary and French translator. Initially avoiding politics, he was appointed ambassador to the Netherlands by George Washington in 1794 at the age of 27. He became a one-term senator from Massachusetts in 1802 and was appointed ambassador to imperial Russia by President Madison. He then became Secretary of State in the James Monroe administration and was later termed the greatest diplomat among presidents, formulating the Monroe Doctrine. He was also an ardent abolitionist who successfully defended African mutineers of the slave ship *Amistad*, saving them from certain death. As a Federalist, Adams proposed an ambitious agenda that included federal infrastructure projects like canals and bridges, the establishment of a national university, and greater involvement with the countries of Latin America, but Congress failed to approve many of his initiatives. He was out of touch with the growing populist sentiment of the day and was attacked by Andrew Jackson and his partisans as a symbol of the elites. He was soundly defeated in a bid for a second term by Jackson.[3] After that defeat, Adams narrowly lost a bid for governor of Massachusetts, but was elected to the House of Representatives, where he served from 1831 to his death in 1848. Adams was also a supporter of women's and Indian rights.

# 4

# The 19th Century

## Land distribution

The 19th century saw a vast expansion of the territory of the US (see Table 4.1). Earlier methods of distributing land, with conflicting borders and ownership rights, were replaced by the Congress of the *Confederation Land Act of 1785*, which was drawn up by a panel chaired by Thomas Jefferson. The law, whose provisions were incorporated in the first US environmental/ land law, the Northwest Ordinance of 1787, applied to areas north of the Ohio River and west of the Mississippi River, including ten future states. It called for a Public Land Survey System that divided land into townships that were then further subdivided. The law banned slavery in the area, called for surveying natural resource features, allocated land for schools, and provided for the submission of maps to the Survey General of the US. The maps were to be accessible to the public. The system's advanced features governed federal land law until the *Homestead Act of 1862*, which offered minimal federal oversight and covered three quarters of the US land area.

According to historian Richard Andrews: "Over 78% of total of 2.3 billion acres of the US was once owned by the federal government, and more than a third was federal land as recently as 1970, including 45 percent of California, 52% of Oregon, 86% of Nevada, and 97% of Alaska" (Andrews, 1999). Land was distributed to veterans of both the Revolutionary War and later wars, to private companies to raise money, to land grant universities and other civic developments, and states, including canal, river, and reclamation areas. Huge allocations of land were distributed through the railroad acts of 1862 and 1864 to allow completion of transcontinental railroads and the *Homestead Act of 1862*, signed by President Abraham Lincoln. The latter Act provided 160 acres for settlers who would gain deeds once they improved land and lived on it for five years. This was supplemented by the *Southern Homestead Act of 1866*, which included land for African Americans, and the *Timber Culture Act of 1873*. One hundred and sixty acres might be sufficient east of the Mississippi River, but it was inadequate in the more arid lands of the

**Table 4.1:** Main land additions to the 13 original colonies

| Name of new area | Land acquisition | Date | Country acquired from |
|---|---|---|---|
| Northwest Territories (10 states) | Northwest Ordinance | 1787 | US and states |
| Tennessee | North Carolina session | 1790 | North Carolina |
| Alabama-Mississippi | Georgia session | 1802 | Georgia |
| Land west of the Mississippi River | Louisiana Purchase | 1803 | France |
| Florida, part of Louisiana | Treaty with Spain | 1819 | Spain |
| Texas | Annexation of Texas | 1845 | Viceroyalty of New Spain and Texas |
| Part of Arizona | Gadsden Purchase | 1854 | Mexico |
| Oregon and Idaho | Oregon Treaty | 1846 | Agreement with British North America |
| Alaska | Purchase from Russia | 1867 | Russia |
| Hawaii | Annexation | 1897 | Hawaii |

West, where farmers could also suffer catastrophic losses due to drought and storms. The *Kincaid Amendment of 1904* granted a full section, 640 acres, to settlers in western Nebraska, and the *Enlarged Homestead Act of 1909* doubled the acreage to 320 acres and eliminated residence requirements. The *Stock-Raising Homestead Act of 1916* granted 640 acres for ranching purposes.

The distribution of land was a massive contributor to American wealth creation in the 19th century. A shadow side of American economic development was slavery in the South, which accounted for the bulk of the region's wealth. Slavery was declining in the late eighteenth century, and leaders of the state of Virginia opposed the slave trade in the Constitutional Convention, as previously noted, but the invention of the cotton gin in 1793 gave slavery a new impetus.[1] By 1850, the American South was producing three quarters of the world's cotton with slave labor. Virginia had moved from opposing the importation of slaves to joining the pro-slavery states that formed the Confederacy.

## Andrew Jackson and the spoils system

As was noted in the previous chapter, the first six presidents generally followed the apolitical, competence-based system for appointing officials and employees initiated by George Washington. Profound change in governance took place with the landslide victory of Andrew Jackson over John Quincy Adams in the election of 1828. Jackson claimed that the victory of Adams in the election of 1824 was stolen and attacked elites. He was the first president born in poverty. Rough-hewn, violent,[2] and charismatic, he rose to be a Tennessee representative, senator, and a general in the Tennessee militia. He became a hero as the victor in the Battle of New Orleans in the War of 1815, which raised him to national prominence. Jackson was long held in high regard as a strong leader, symbol of a new democratic order, and founder of the Democratic Party. In the first poll of historians organized by historian Arthur Schlesinger Jr., his best-known and hagiographic biographer,[3] Jackson was rated as the sixth greatest president, ahead of Theodore Roosevelt (Schlesinger, 1948).

Since the Civil Rights movement of the 1960s and the recent movement for the rights of Indigenous people, Jackson's reputation has become shadowed. He was a slaveowner and a vigorous advocate of slavery, including its expansion in the West. He abhorred abolitionists and defied a Supreme Court decision against a proposal to violate a treaty and deprive Creek Indians of their lands (Remini, 1999). His forcible removal of 50,000 Cherokee Indians from their ancestral lands in Florida, Alabama, and Tennessee through the *Indian Removal Act of 1830*, during which up to 50 percent of the Indians died (Perdue and Green, 2008), has been called the greatest act of ethnic cleansing in American history. In his speech to Congress on Indian removal, Jackson wrote: "What good man would prefer a country covered with forests and ranged by a few thousand savages to our extensive Republic, studded with cities, towns, and prosperous farms" (Jackson, 1830). Because of Jackson's changed reputation, his portrait on the $20 bill is scheduled to be replaced by Harriet Tubman in 2030.

Jackson's flawed policies included undermining the Second National Bank, which triggered the Panic of 1837. However, his most lasting adverse action was replacing qualified, permanent government positions by appointees who supported him and his policies. "Jackson claimed to be purging the corruption, laxity, and arrogance that came with long tenure, and restoring the opportunity for government service to the citizenry at large through 'rotation in office'" (Feller, 2007–2009). Alexis de Tocqueville, the noted French student of American democracy, observed that while it might be thought that this would strengthen the presidency, turnover of government at presidential elections weakened government by preventing the establishment of stable administrative structures (de Tocqueville, 1835, p 151).

Unlike land and water laws in the states, there were essentially no controls on land use in the vast federal territories in the West. After the California gold strike in 1849, the exploitation of rich mineral deposits in the West led to widespread contamination of soil and water with mining and processing wastes. Some remain in Superfund sites today. After the Civil War, the effects of the spoils system continued in the form of federal corruption and inability to implement controls on monopolistic policies of financial barons and exploitation of labor. Jackson's legacy continues to impede efforts to transition to renewable energy.

## Milestones of environmental history

The extraordinary achievements of Thomas Jefferson's Lewis and Clark Expedition (1804–1806) is epitomized in Figure 4.1, providing the first detailed tracing of the river systems of the Northwest. No further federal government surveys of major scope were undertaken until the late 1860s, in part due to limitations imposed by the spoils system on development of federal government institutions. The Coast Survey of 1807 was the first federal land survey given explicit responsibility for scientific investigation. Other milestones are summarized in Table 4.2.

Additional dates for formation of relevant agencies include: the Department of the Interior (1849), the Bureau of Chemistry (1862), the Fish Commission (1871), the Bureau of Biological Service (1885), and the Department of Agriculture (1889). A full listing of federal scientific and technical agencies and their dates of origin is provided in Manheim (2014c).

Henry David Thoreau's *Walden* and John Muir's writings on the High Sierra are well known, as is Muir's battle with Gifford Pinchot over the Hetch Hetchy dam that would inundate the beautiful Yosemite Valley in California. Thoreau's writings anticipated 20th-century ecological movements, but the pioneering environmental historian William Cronon indicated that the most influential 19th-century book on the interaction between humans and the natural environment was *Man and Nature* by George Perkins Marsh (Marsh, 1864). David Loewenthal, Marsh's biographer, stated that its influence was second only to Charles Darwin's *Origin of the Species* in its time (Loewenthal, 2003).

There are few parallels to describe Marsh's multiple activities. A leading philologist, he knew 20 languages and advocated for sign language for the deaf. He published the first English-language Icelandic grammar guide in 1838 and translated classic works from Old Norse, Danish, and Swedish into English. Marsh first trained in law, worked in farming and manufacturing, was a commissioner in charge of restoring fish populations in Vermont, served four terms as a Vermont representative, and helped found the Smithsonian Institution (Manheim, 2009). His book *Man and Nature* (Marsh, 1864) drew on his experience of more than two decades as a US diplomat in Turkey and Italy. During this time he combined observations from Europe and the Middle East with information from books and maps in the great libraries of Europe.

Marsh documented in detail that ancient civilizations helped bring about their collapse by abuse of the environment. He also observed the contemporary destruction of birds (passenger pigeons), buffalo, walrus, and

**Figure 4.1:** Map from the Lewis and Clark Expedition showing the sources and tributaries of the Missouri and Columbia river systems

Source: Lewis et al (1804)

**Table 4.2:** Milestones and important figures in US environmental history

| | | |
|---|---|---|
| Coast Survey | 1807 | Designed and first led by Austrian immigrant Ferdinand Hassler (1777–1843), who "invented the modern science agency." It used scientific measurements, formal publications, and emphasized merit appointments and integrity. |
| John J. Audubon | 1785–1851 | Ornithologist, naturalist, hunter, renowned painter of birds. |
| George Perkins Marsh | 1801–1882 | Called an originator of the US environmental movement and influential in Europe; fish commissioner for Vermont and congressman; envoy to Turkey and Italy. His influential book *Man and Nature* (Marsh, 1864) warned of the effect of man on nature. |
| Henry D. Thoreau | 1817–1862 | Abolitionist, irrepressible individualist, naturalist, and writer. |
| Asa Gray | 1810–1888 | Leading 19th-century American botanist; author of definitive manuals on flora of North America; professor of natural science at Harvard; provided information for Darwin's *Origin of the Species*. |
| Spencer F. Baird | 1823–1887 | Professor of natural history, ornithologist, natural history author and compiler, assistant secretary of the Smithsonian, US Commissioner of Fish and Fisheries. |
| Frederick Law Olmsted | 1822–1903 | Most prominent landscape architect and park designer. |
| Yellowstone Park | 1872 | First National Park, set aside by President Ulysses S. Grant. |
| US Geological Survey (USGS) | 1879 | Under the first three directors (Clarence King, John Wesley Powell, and Charles Walcott), the USGS became the world's foremost Earth science organization and conducted the first forest and soil surveys. Powell created the first ethnological maps of North American Indian cultures. |
| John Muir | 1838–1914 | Scottish-born champion of Western environment and wilderness; campaigned for Yosemite Valley; wrote influential articles and influenced presidents Benjamin Harrison, Grover Cleveland, and Theodore Roosevelt; founded the Sierra Club in 1892. |
| *Forest Reserve Act* | 1891 | Act to temporarily protect forest areas of high value. |
| Theodore Roosevelt | 1858–1919 | As president, he established forest and wildlife conservation as a key principle for US government; he also added many parks, established the US Forest Service, and increased national forest area from 46 to 148 million acres. |
| Gifford Pinchot | 1865–1946 | Leading forest expert; head of the Division of Forestry and first chief of the US Forest Service. |

Source: Manheim (2009, modified)

narwhals, and the massive cutting of forests in America. His impact came from his warning that what was done to Europe could happen to North America if Americans did hot behave in more responsible ways. The breadth of his scientific insights is indicated by his comment that if the Gulf Stream were diverted into the Pacific Ocean through the isthmus of Panama, it would bring on an ice age in Northern Europe.

After the Civil War, and with the recent availability of photography, "writers associated with a national park movement, like Clarence Dutton, Ferdinand V. Hayden, Clarence King, Nathaniel P. Langford, John Muir, and John Wesley Powell, described the spectacular scenery of the Western United States" (Parks, no date). In 1867, Congress authorized four explorations of the West headed by Clarence King, Ferdinand V. Hayden, John Wesley Powell, and Lt. George Wheeler of the US Army Corps of Engineers. Primarily focused on geology, the expeditions were merged into the US Geological Survey (USGS) (Harbaugh, 1975) in 1879. Clarence King, the first director of the USGS, wrote: "Eighteen sixty-seven marks ... a turning point, when the science ceased to be dragged in the dust of rapid exploration and took a commanding position in the professional work of the country" (USGS, 2019).

In the eastern US, the Appalachian Mountain Club, one of the first private conservation organizations, was founded in 1876 with the goal of protecting and preserving the Eastern wilderness. Focused on the West, John Muir founded the Sierra Club in 1892, and the organization exists to this day. Both organizations had a powerful influence on the growth of the conservation movement.

Influenced by Marsh and Muir, Theodore Roosevelt's administration is considered to be the culmination of the Progressive movement, embedding a conservation ethic into national policy. President Roosevelt was instrumental in creating 150 national forests, 51 bird reservations, four game preserves, five national parks, and 23 reclamation projects (NPS, 2017), leaving a lasting legacy of environment progress.

## The critical role of American engineers

Great buildings and other construction in Europe date back to Greek and Roman times, when such structures were initiated by major institutions like governments or the church. The history of American infrastructure development in the 19th century took a more pragmatic turn. Its success can be attributed to two factors: (1) the willingness of political leaders and populations to accept bold initiatives; and (2) competent executors of those visions. The enabling factor was the rise and role of engineers in American society.

Engineers began as elite units in the US Army. The Corps of Engineers was separately established in 1802, and formal engineer training, based on the model of the French Polytechnic University, carried high responsibilities and prestige. Only top cadets were admitted into Corps of Engineers training, and there was intense competition for engineers who left the military. American engineers would become indispensable in developing public water supplies and sanitation, as well as transportation, infrastructure projects, and manufacturing.

The first and most spectacular political and engineering initiative in US history was the 363-mile Erie Canal to connect agricultural products of the Midwest with the East Coast. Given the obstacles to overland transport, to get to the East Coast or Europe, products had to be transported down the Mississippi River and through the Gulf of Mexico by barges and sailing vessels. As described by Kevin Baker (Baker, 2016), the canal was initially rejected by Presidents Jefferson and James Madison on the grounds of practicality—its costs were estimated at three quarters of the US federal budget at the time.

Determined to pursue the canal, DeWitt Clinton got himself elected governor of New York in 1817, and three months later, shovels were in the ground (Wikipedia—Erie Canal). Blasting with gunpowder and with the hazardous labor of 50,000 workers, the canal opened in 1825, two years ahead of schedule. Shipping costs dropped from $100/ton to $9, and backward villages and towns overnight became industrial cities. This construction was led by three engineers: Benjamin Wright, later named The Father of US Civil Engineering; Charles Brodhead; and Canvass White, who traveled some 2,000 miles in Europe inspecting constructions and, on his return, patented a cheaper hydraulic cement that was critical for canal construction.

The Rensselaer Polytechnic Institute celebrates the founding of the first civil engineering program in America in conjunction with the Erie Canal construction. Rensselaer's engineering program was followed after 1840 by other academic institutions such as Michigan, Harvard, Yale, Union, and Dartmouth. The Massachusetts Institute of Technology's engineering program was initiated in 1864. The American Society of Civil Engineering (ASCE) was founded in 1852.

In 1861, Andrew Atkinson Humphrey, a West Point graduate, completed a monumental, 11-year Congressionally authorized hydrologic study of the Mississippi River. The report was hailed throughout Europe as a major breakthrough in hydrologic science (Barry, 1997) and led to Humphrey's election to membership in leading scientific societies in America and Europe, earning him the post of Chief Engineer of the Corps of Engineers. The reputation of engineers was heightened by achievements like the completion of the Brooklyn Bridge in 1857 and the first all-steel bridge over the Mississippi River, designed by James Buchanan Eads in 1861.

Cholera epidemics in major cities in Europe and America spurred the construction of sewer systems in the 1850s. Major cholera outbreaks in the growing Chicago metropolis led to development of innovative sewage collection and transport systems from 1863 to 1889. Engineers reversed the Chicago River and ultimately directed the flow from Chicago sewers through an enlarged canal system into the Mississippi River. The system gained international attention and awards, but a lawsuit from the downstream city of St. Louis succeeded in the courts, and the novel system had to be replaced by water treatment.

As is summarized in a more detailed review in Manheim (2009), from which much of this engineering discussion is taken, civil engineers did not consider major construction projects in isolation. In addition to science and mathematics, engineer training included administration and finance so that they were prepared to estimate the costs and requirements of construction, subsequent operation, and maintenance. Officials' and the public's confidence in the professional competence and integrity of engineers was a key factor in willingness to entrust them with costly and potentially dangerous infrastructure. The engineering profession prided itself on its high standing in society.

A famous example of an engineer who maintained integrity in the face of corruption in the Gilded Age was Peter Anthony Dey, Chief Engineer of the Union Pacific Railroad. Dey resigned "the best position in my profession this country has ever offered to any man" when he became aware that the railroad's leaders had inflated his cost estimates for westward expansion of the railroad line. His resignation was part of the *Chicago Sun*'s 1872 revelations of the Crédit Mobilier scandal that would implicate 16 politicians: senators, representatives, and even the Vice President of the US, Schuyler Colfax (Wikipedia—Peter A. Dey).

### *Boston's sanitation and water supply history*

The breakdown of early Boston's prohibitions against discharge of sewage into Boston Harbor led to cholera outbreaks from 1849 to 1853, and again from 1868 to 1873. A doctor-led public protest movement ended with the city commissioning an innovative and comprehensive wastewater management system. Basic designs drawn in 1875 were built in stages and completed shortly after 1900. These consisted of collectors, interceptors, and tunnels under Boston Harbor that led to the mouth of the main channel connecting the harbor with Cape Cod Bay. The ingenious system discharged sewage in the deep channel on outgoing tides. Plans called for periodic engineering reviews that would propose expanded capacities to keep pace with population growth. Even after 100 years, this construction still provided two thirds of the under-harbor sewage system.[4] Design drawings of the subharbor structures are so striking that many are displayed on the walls of the Massachusetts Water Resources Authority in Boston.

Because of their broad training, engineers filled high-level administrative positions in cities and states. In 1895, the Chief Engineer of Massachusetts State Board of Public Health, Frederick P. Stearns, responded to expanded requests for water supplies to Boston and its growing suburban areas. He recommended an extraordinarily ambitious plan involving the construction of the Wachusett Reservoir in a watershed 45 miles west of the center of Boston. The plans involved great expense, but the plan was accepted against competing proposals involving water filtration because of Stearns's achievements and the care with which the plan was developed. His project, which included the creation of the largest reservoir in the world, gained a gold medal at the Paris Exposition in 1900 and was completed in 1906. Stearns was elected President of the ASCE and a fellow of the American Academy of Arts and Science as a result of his success.

An even more ambitious water supply system for the Boston area was initiated by Stearns's former protégé, Walter Goodenough, who was named chief engineer of the Massachusetts State Board of Public Health after Stearns. This controversial project, which required moving four villages, involved the Quabbin watershed, nearly 70 miles from Boston. It was completed in 1930, 20 percent under budget, and continues to supply the greater Boston area with high-quality water. The Quabbin Reservoir also preserved a large area for wildlife and recreation.

Fern Nesson's detailed history of Boston water system described earlier points out the "uncharacteristic willingness" of the Massachusetts legislature to "choose long-range, grand-scale, expensive plans in 1895 and 1926 over cheaper short-term alternatives." The reasons cited were provision for pure, unfiltered water from an uncontaminated watershed, respect for Stearns's objectivity, and skill and thorough presentations by polite, literate engineers with long terms of service (Nesson, 1983).

### *Engineering effectiveness and reliability*

The preceding examples might appear to idealize engineers, but in fact, construction failures in the 19th century were extremely rare. One noted failure was the South Fork Dam near Johnstown, Pennsylvania, in 1889, which collapsed and led to a flood that killed 2,200 people (NPS, 2023). Engineers were aware that even low rates of mistakes could lead to spectacular failures in high-risk structures like underwater tunnels, bridges, and overhead railway systems, Likewise, poor financial planning or management could undermine the trust-based system that gained public acceptance of bold engineering innovations, including later skyscrapers. As a result, where risk was high, only exceptionally high levels of motivation and no-compromise performance and planning were accepted.

Through the Second World War, engineering attracted the nation's top scientific talent[5] and the kinds of individuals who welcomed the challenges and risks; the profession maintained unusually high-quality performance standards. This system, under which completion of projects to schedule and within budget was the norm, broke down after the Second World War as a result of new societal priorities described in Chapter 6.

## The Gilded Age

Despite the patronage system, major federal financial corruption before the Civil War was avoided because the government was on a lean diet, its main income coming from import duties, land distribution, and stamp sales. However, during the Civil War, federal revenues grew from a small stream to a mighty river. They were fed by income and other taxes levied to pay for the war.[6] President Lincoln and leaders in Congress anticipated the postwar need to expand railroads to the Western territories. The task of extending the railroad from Missouri to the West Coast was a daunting logistical challenge, given the problem of construction across deserts and mountains, in territories often occupied by hostile Indian tribes. The federal government chartered the Union Pacific Railroad to extend subsidized railway track from Missouri to the West Coast from 1864 to 1868.[7] Wartime taxes continued to help reduce the debt and provide funds for railroad subsidies that were not discontinued until 1872.

The availability of tax revenues offered inducements to collusion between private operators and the government, whose officials served at the pleasure of the president. During the administration of Ulysses S. Grant, a huge scandal discovered by the *Chicago Sun* in 1872 revealed that the leaders of Union Pacific had secretly captured the bonding company and bank Crédit Mobilier (CM), through which the government subsidized construction. An elaborate fraud involving inflated invoices had been aided by a Massachusetts congressman and investor in the venture, Oakes Ames. He had distributed cash bribes and discounted stock in CM to 16 other congressmen to ensure the approval of the Congressional subsidies; even the Speaker of the House and later Vice President, Schuyler Colfax, was implicated (Wikipedia—Crédit Mobilier Scandal).

President Ulysses S. Grant was a war hero and was not personally corrupt. Biographers have emphasized his critical role in the Civil War, his early support for Reconstruction, and for successfully attacking the Ku Klux Klan (KKK) (Brands, 2013). However, prize-winning Grant biographer William McFeely (2002) summarized the changes in Grant during his administration:

> Grant, though never a crusader for good causes, once had a fellow feeling for the ordinary citizen but gradually lost it as fame led him to

> depend upon the applause of the people en masse ... He abandoned a potentially generous policy toward the Indians as well as any commitment to the aims of Reconstruction.

The Grant administration marked a high point in terms of government veniality. Grant's first administration included a few able men like Hamilton Fish, Secretary of State in both administrations, George W. Bristow, Secretary of the Treasury, and Alphonse Taft, the Secretary of War, but corruption emerged in seven cabinet departments, including the Navy, Justice, War, Interior, the Post Office, and the Customs House. Bristow's investigations of the notorious Whiskey Ring that defrauded the Treasury of huge tax revenues uncovered the involvement of Grant's personal secretary, Orville Babcock, effectively his chief of staff.

The absence of effective national administrative systems allowed gifted men with ambition to achieve enormous wealth in the rapidly expanding nation. Some did so through bribery and subornation of influential government officials, Congressional members, and even the majority of state legislatures (Lawson, 1906). Corrupt political machines ruled in major cities. Scandals involving federal land in the West were associated with railroad interests. Financial machinations contributed to the economic panics of 1873 and 1893. A list of the so-called robber barons of the era is provided in Table 4.3. Animus against the "robber barons," a term popularized by the title of a 1934 book by Matthew Josephson, arose from the contrast between their enormous riches and the poverty and squalor of the lowest-paid workers employed in manufacturing.

A revisionist school of history that sought to modify the image of the robber barons was initiated by Robert Higgs (1971). Conservative historian Burton Folsom (1991) distinguished between magnates whose wealth involved innovation and superior management, such as Marshall Field, J. P. Morgan, Andrew Carnegie, and John Rockefeller, and those who accumulated wealth through financial or stock manipulations, fraud, and corruption of government, such as Jim Fisk and Jay Gould. An extreme representative of the revisionist school (Klein, 1997), extolled Gould, Harriman, and the Union Pacific railroad for their praiseworthy entrepreneurship.

The existence of "malefactors of great wealth," famously cited by Theodore Roosevelt,[8] should not denigrate the contributions of gifted entrepreneurs like Fred Weyerhauser (lumber and paper), John J. Hill (the only railroad developer who did not use federal funds and who promoted development of advanced farming methods), Henry Flagler, who was responsible for many technical innovations developed by Standard Oil, and a host of inventors like Robert Fulton, Elias Howe, Charles Goodyear, Alexander Graham Bell, and Thomas A. Edison, who contributed to national development without riches as their primary goal.

**Table 4.3:** Nineteenth-century individuals of great wealth, who have been listed among "robber barons"

| Name | Dates | Source of wealth |
|---|---|---|
| Cornelius Vanderbilt | 1794–1877 | Shipping; railroads. |
| David Drew | 1797–1879 | Railway management and speculation. |
| Russell Sage | 1813–1878 | Whig politician; railroad executive and associate of Jay Gould. |
| Collis Huntington | 1821–1900 | Railroad developer, bituminous coal; Northwestern rail developer; Newport News Shipbuilding. |
| Jay Cooke | 1821–1905 | First major investment banker; marketed federal bonds during the Civil War (reaping substantial profits); Northern Pacific Railroad. |
| Marshall Field | 1834–1906 | Department store pioneer in service and quality. |
| Jim Fisk | 1835–1872 | Commodity and stock manipulator; partner with Jay Gould and Daniel Drew; famously murdered. |
| Andrew Carnegie | 1835–1919 | US Steel technical and operational integrator (vertically integrated corporation and market consolidation); philanthropist. |
| Jay Gould | 1836–1892 | Land, stock, and commodity investor and manipulator; expert in securing favorable government policies and suborning officials. |
| J. P. Morgan | 1837–1913 | Investment banker; initiator of trusts and industrial pools; supported government in fiscal crises. |
| John D. Rockefeller | 1839–1937 | Pioneer in integrating petroleum production and distribution; created the first vertically integrated corporation; initiated commodity futures. |
| Edward H. Harriman | 1848–1909 | Land, railroad owner and financier; attacked by Theodore Roosevelt. |
| Henry Frick | 1849–1919 | "Baron of coke," joined with Andrew Carnegie; steel union strikebreaker. |

The peak in veniality and corruption took place when Congress passed the *Legislative, Executive, and Judicial Expenses Appropriation Act of 1873,* popularly called the "Salary Grab" Act. The legislation, signed by President Grant, doubled the salary of the president to $50,000 a year and the salary of Congressmen from $5,000 to $7,500. Its most brazen provision, passed on the last day of the Congressional term, was a retroactive payment of about $4,000 to each Congressman. In 2023 dollars, the act awarded the president a salary of over $1,100,000 and the one-time Congressional bonus was equivalent to $97,000 in 2023 dollars (CPI Index). Public outrage was so great that the Act was rescinded in January 1873. Ironically, it coincided with the publication of Mark Twain and Charles Warner's satirical novel *The Gilded Age*, which pilloried the graft and materialism of the times (Twain and Warner, 1873).

## The reform movement

An exception to the employment of the patronage system for cabinet appointments among presidents after Andrew Jackson was Abraham Lincoln, who chose most of his cabinet members for their qualifications rather than for their personal or party loyalty. For example, he appointed his bitter rival for the Republican nomination, William Seward, as Secretary of State. All cabinet appointees except his first Secretary of War, Simon Cameron, served effectively in critical posts during the Civil War, described in riveting detail in the award-winning book by Doris Kearns Goodwin, *A Team of Rivals* (Goodwin, 2006). However, Lincoln was plagued by the usual parade of office seekers for other government positions.

President Grant initially favored civil service reform and appointed George William Curtis, a strong reform advocate, to chair a Civil Service Commission in 1871. But once exposed to the realities of reform, Grant's distrust of reformers and the impact of their policies on his sources of support soured him on reform. Seeing his own reform proposals routinely rejected, Curtis resigned, and the Commission became defunct when Congress refused to reauthorize it in 1875 (Rausch, 2006).

Public corruption in the Grant administration was symbolized by the title of a book, *The Era of Good Stealings*, a play on "The Era of Good Feelings," a term applied to the earlier presidency of James Monroe (Summers, 1993). The bankruptcy of the investment house of Jay Cooke triggered widespread bank failures, labeled the Panic of 1873, with repercussions throughout American society. A wave of public revulsion led both political parties to nominate reformers for the election of 1876. Eager to regain their political viability after the Civil War, the Democrats nominated Samuel F. Tilden, the Governor of New York, who had participated in the movement that broke the power of the Tammany Hall machine (Boss Tweed). The Republicans nominated Rutherford B. Hayes, a graduate of Harvard Law School, who was breveted as a Major General after being wounded in the Civil War and was elected representative and then Governor of Ohio after the war. Hayes and his wife were abolitionists; he defended Black escapees crossing the Ohio River in court during his law career in Cincinnati.

The election of 1876 was the most controversial in US history. Tilden gained a plurality of votes, but a controversy over 20 electoral votes moved the decision to Congress. After four months of deadlock, an 8–7 partisan vote in an electoral commission appointed by Congress gave Hayes the election in exchange for agreement to withdraw federal troops from the South (Hoogenboom, 1988a). Angry Democrats famously called Hayes "Rutherfraud" and "His Fraudulency." However, the Miller Center review of Hayes' presidency (Millercenter, 2014) notes that: "By the time Hayes took office, Reconstruction had already ended in the entire South except in Louisiana and South Carolina … and Republican control was limited to small areas surrounding state houses in the capitals of New Orleans and Columbia, protected by small detachments of federal troops."

Hayes's reputation has been adversely affected by the 1876 election, his formal ending of Reconstruction, and the steel strike of 1877. However, Hayes's presidency has been underrated. He was moral and courageous, committing himself to only one term in order to reform the federal government, including "radical and complete civil service reform." He antagonized powerful Republican senators with independent cabinet appointments, including Carl Schurz, the nation's most influential advocate for reform, as Secretary of the Interior (Figure 4.2). Schurz withstood pressure to transfer the Indian Bureau to the War Department, which favored pacification programs, and introduced the federal government's first examination-based appointment system in the scandal-ridden Department of the Interior.

Hayes's most important contribution was the overhaul of federal government employment through a merit-based system. To this end, he commissioned Dorman Bridgman Eaton to undertake a review of international civil service systems. Eaton completed his survey and published a detailed account of the British civil service system in 1880, with recommendations for reform of the US government (Eaton 1880). But the changes were too radical for Congress or Hayes's successor as president, James A. Garfield, who allowed politics to guide his appointments. However, when Garfield was assassinated by a disgruntled office-seeker, public anger against the existing system of appointments led to the passage of the *Pendleton Act of 1883*, based on Eaton's plan. Vice President Chester A. Arthur, who assumed the presidency after Garfield's death, had earlier been part of the venial New York Customs House, but as president, he surprised many by his commitment to government reform and active support for the Pendleton Act.

The Act, only eight pages long, set up a three-person Civil Service Commission appointed by the president with the consent of the Senate, with no more than two being from the same party. It called for rules to be created for competitive examinations for all classified positions and grading to fill offices by rank in examinations. It also provided for systematic review to increase classified positions and safeguards against abuses. The first Chairman was Dorman Eaton.

The leading scholar of the civil service system, Paul P. van Riper, reported that the Act initially covered only 10 percent of government employees, but the number of classified employees steadily increased because of the bipartisan makeup of the commission and effective leadership by Commissioner Eaton (Van Riper, 1958). President Grover Cleveland sometimes deviated from his commitment to civil service reform, but in his second term, he appointed two highly qualified Republican commissioners. He also instituted the practice of allowing the party-out-of-power commissioner to serve as chairman of the commission, a convention that remained in place until the Truman administration. The Pendleton Act remained in force until President Jimmy Carter's *Civil Service Reform Act of 1978.*

Nineteenth-century reform was aided by other movements, an important one being the crusading press. The *Chicago Sun*'s breaking of the Union Pacific scandal was noted earlier. One of the most popular reform-oriented papers was *Harper's Weekly*, founded by James Gordon Bennet. One of the paper's famous cartoonists, Thomas Nast, has been called the father of the political cartoon. Figure 4.2 shows Rutherford B. Hayes's Secretary of the Interior, Carl Schurz, cleaning up corruption in the Indian Bureau.

Schurz was a symbol for reformist immigrant movements. As a revolutionary student in Germany in the 1848 revolution in Europe, he escaped a death sentence and emigrated to the US. In America he became involved in the abolitionist movement and the Republican Party, boosting Lincoln's popularity with German-speaking immigrants. He also served with distinction as a general in the Civil War, after which he was elected a senator from Missouri. Losing re-election to a former Confederate politician, he served as a crusading editor for several newspapers before joining the Rutherford B. Hayes administration as Secretary of the Interior Department.

Another reform movement in the 19th century was women's suffrage (voting rights), led by Elizabeth Cady Stanton (1815–1902), who was known for her oratory and leadership of women's organizations, and Susan B. Anthony (1820–1906) (Wikipedia—Womens' Suffrage in the United States). Anthony contributed organizational and tactical skills to a 50-year partnership with Stanton. A convention called for in Seneca Falls, NY, by Stanton and Lucretia Mott in 1848 has been regarded as launching the American women's rights movement. The reformers were also staunch abolitionists. 1878 Stanton drafted a federal suffrage amendment. It was introduced in every US Congress until the 19th Amendment granted women the right in 1920.

The political reform movement begun under Presidents Hayes and Arthur reached a peak in the Progressive Era, whose beginning is placed in 1900 by the Library of Congress. Historian Paul van Riper (Van Riper, 1983) regarded Theodore Roosevelt as the ultimate reformer, who aggressively attacked abuses of public trust and promoted progressive causes in many areas. Roosevelt began his political career with his election to the New York General Assembly in 1882, where he soon established a name for himself by exposing corruption (Brands, 1998). By 1883, he had become minority

**Figure 4.2:** Thomas Nast cartoon: Carl Schurz Cleaning out Corruption in the Indian Bureau

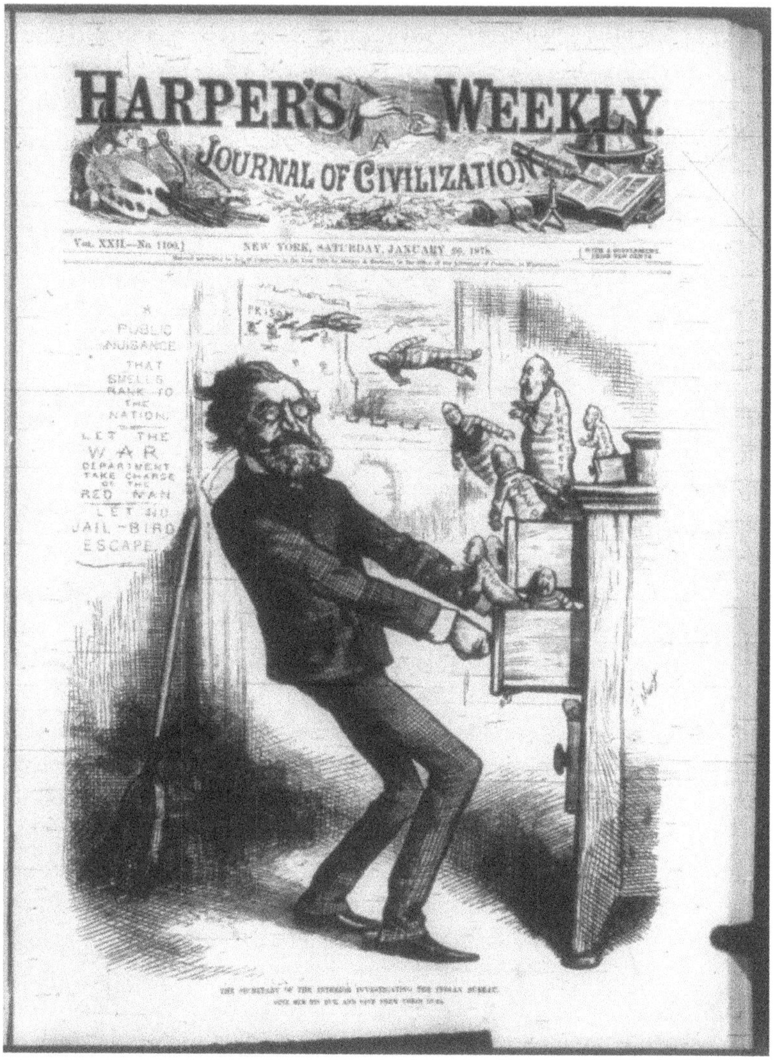


Source: Nast, T. (1878) *The Secretary ... investigating the Indian Bureau/Th. Nast.*, 1878 (Photograph), Library of Congress, available from: https://www.loc.gov/item/2004676470/

leader in the State Assembly. After losing the election for mayor of New York City, Roosevelt moved west, immersing himself in life as a cowboy, hunter, and deputy sheriff. He returned to public life in 1889 when he was appointed by President Benjamin Harrison as a commissioner for the Civil Service Commission, and he was re-appointed by President Grover Cleveland in 1893. After serving as Police Commissioner in New York City, Secretary of the Navy, and head of the Rough Riders in the Spanish American War, Roosevelt was nominated as Vice President under President William McKinley. When McKinley was shot by an anarchist in 1901, Theodore Roosevelt, at age 42, became the youngest president in US history.

Teddy Roosevelt had no peer for the ferocious energy he focused on legislative and government reform and achieving a fairer society. In addition to his environmental accomplishments, he promoted and signed the *Pure Food and Drug Act of 1906* and recognized that the "the problems of modern industrialization had to be faced squarely" (Morrisey, 2009). Referred to as the "Trust Buster," Roosevelt attacked the excesses of industrial magnates, engineering the first breakup of a major trust, the Northern Security Company, and subsequently the American Tobacco Company. Continuing his initiatives, a decision of the Supreme Court broke up the industrial colossus of John D. Rockefeller's Standard Oil Co. in 1911. Balance was critical for Roosevelt's public approval and effectiveness. In his autobiography he wrote: "Corporations have become indispensable in the business world. It is folly to try to prohibit them, but ... also folly to leave them without thoroughgoing control" (Fallone, 2012). In keeping with the principles of the Progressive movement, Roosevelt attached special importance on qualifications in his appointments, which included Gifford Pinchot as chief of the Forest Service. He cemented his legacy as one of the most reform-minded presidents in the United States, but has been criticized for glorifying war and, for a time, favoring the country's imperial expansion.

Unlike "born in a log cabin" presidents that began with Andrew Jackson and ended with James Garfield, Roosevelt was born into privilege and educated at Harvard. However, early on, he embraced the progressive reform movement and endeared himself to the nation through his vigorous life and personality. His culminating achievements would come as president after the assassination of McKinley in 1901 (see Chapter 5).

# 5

# The 20th Century up to 1969

Presiding over the peak in the Progressive movement, Theodore Roosevelt was the first president to successfully break up a major trust using the *Sherman Antitrust Act of 1890.* The trust, Northern Securities, was a railroad conglomerate controlled by J. P. Morgan, John J. Hill, and E. J. Harriman that dominated rail traffic in the northern US. Of a total of 43 trusts that Roosevelt attacked, the largest was John D. Rockefeller's giant Standard Oil Co., against which Theodore Roosevelt's Justice Department brought action in 1906. Standard Oil was split up into 34 separate companies after it was held to violate the Sherman Antitrust Act. It had controlled most of the oil production, refining, marketing, and transportation in the US from 1870 to 1911.

Unlike contemporary progressivism, which is associated with a specific political party, early 20th-century progressives were in both political parties and reflected a variety of interests, from industrial monopolies to unethical trade practices. Opposing Social Darwinism, they engaged with issues of public health, working conditions like child labor, social fairness, and women's suffrage and segregation. It has been claimed that until 1890, when cities began inspecting milk, the US spent more on animal than human health. Conservation was an important concern for Progressive reformers. Influenced by conservationists and preservationists like John Muir, Roosevelt protected national forests and preserved large numbers of natural scenic areas through the *American Antiquities Act of 1906.*

Roosevelt was immensely popular, but did not run for re-election in 1908 because of a commitment to not seek a third term. Instead, Republican William Howard Taft was elected as president, but contending that Taft had abandoned progressive goals, Roosevelt split with the Republican Party. In 1912, he decided to run again on the Progressive Party (Bull Moose) ticket. Although he gained more votes than Taft, he lost, and Woodrow Wilson, the Democratic candidate, was elected. Even with just a plurality of the popular vote, Wilson gained the largest electoral college victory since James Monroe's unopposed election in 1820. Progressive leader Robert LaFollette challenged Taft for the Republican nomination in that election, but did not support Roosevelt. He later made an independent presidential bid representing the Progressive Party in the 1924 election.

## New federal appointment and law-making systems

Reflecting the progressive ethic, both parties accepted the concept that human problems could be solved through education and intelligent action by the federal government. Accordingly, they advocated that federal agencies should have leaders capable of informed and independent decision making, an extension of the merit principle to federal employment in high leadership positions. As president, Taft continued Roosevelt's antitrust activities, and though he had a more conservative social policy, he emphasized that he would seek "the best men" for cabinet positions.

Woodrow Wilson also embraced the principle of selecting well-qualified cabinet and agency leaders, but his legacy has been diminished by racial bias—long-underrecognized regressive actions against African American government employees (Sosna, 1970). Soon after his victory over Taft, Roosevelt, and Socialist Eugene Debs in the election of 1912, Wilson introduced an economic reform package he labelled "the New Freedom." This agenda, which passed Congress at the end of 1913, included tariff, banking, and labor reforms, and introduced the federal income tax. Wilson also expanded the executive branch with the creation of the Federal Reserve, the Federal Trade Commission, and the Internal Revenue Service (Link, 1954).

With growing proportions of classified federal workers and presidential appointees hired through the merit system, and under the principle that presidentially appointed policy makers should be chosen on the basis of qualifications and ability to exercise independent leadership, public and Congressional trust in federal agencies grew. Congress gave agencies missions and tasks, and authorized funding, but operational policy was delegated to agency leaders. Consequently, many laws were short, contrasting with subsequent developments. An extreme example was the *Forest Transfer Act of 1905*, which moved responsibility for forest management from the Department of Interior to the Department of Agriculture: it was a mere half-page long. Another law, the *American Antiquities Act of 1906*, was four paragraphs long. Another characteristic of the era of independent federal agencies was that apolitical experts from the agencies assisted Congress in drafting or modifying legislation. A parallel system is employed today by European nations, which will be detailed in Chapter 11.

A reason why this system worked for science and technology agencies was that agencies had in-depth expertise, conducted advanced research, and provided guidance and services, but largely lacked regulatory responsibilities. Such functions affecting commerce and industry could bring political pressures from the executive branch or private interests. An exception to the lack of regulatory policies for agencies was the *Rivers and Harbors Act of 1899* (ten pages long, as of 2018, amended), which authorized the US Army Corps of Engineers to regulate construction, modification, navigation, and introduction of sewage or other pollutants into navigable bodies of water.[1]

The convention for appointing qualified agency heads continued though the Taft and Wilson administrations, but faltered during President Warren Harding's administration. Harding's flawed cabinet appointments were highlighted by Albert Fall, Secretary of the Department of the Interior. Fall was famously indicted and sent to prison for accepting bribes from oil companies in the notorious Teapot Dome Scandal of 1921–1924.

Competence and independence for agency heads were re-established in the administration of Franklin D. Roosevelt, whose dynamic leadership earned him a high rank among presidential historians. Driven by the crisis of the Depression and by the leftist orientation of key advisors, "This period of extraordinary [government and] regulatory growth changed the nature and scope of American government permanently" (Kurian, 1998). A respected assessment of Roosevelt's New Deal policies (Leuchtenburg, 1963) indicates that when appointing cabinet and agency leaders, Roosevelt prioritized competence and leadership qualities over partisan loyalty. For example, Harold Ickes, Secretary of the Department of the Interior in all four Roosevelt terms, was a moderate Republican who often disagreed with Roosevelt. His agency had responsibility for the massive public works programs in the New Deal era (Figure 5.1).

Assisted by his trusted Harry Hopkins and other advisors, Roosevelt created many new federal agencies and initiatives (for example, the Federal

**Figure 5.1:** Plaque for a typical public works construction project

Source: Public Works Administration archives, cited in Wikipedia—Public Works Administration

Deposits Insurance Corporation, the National Labor Relations Board, the Federal Waters Power Act, the Federal Register, and the Code of Federal Regulations), as well as major initiatives to cope with national unemployment. Despite huge outlays of funds, no financial scandals were reported during the four terms of the Roosevelt administration (Leuchtenburg, 1963).

Opinions on the effectiveness of Franklin D. Roosevelt in dealing with the Depression range from positive (Nester, 2024) to negative (Powell, 2004). What is not in dispute is the efficiency with which most of the New Deal agencies and programs operated. For example, between July 1933 and March 1939, the Public Works Administration (PWA) funded and administered the construction of more than 34,000 projects, including airports, large electricity-generating dams, major warships for the Navy, over 11,000 bridges and roadway projects, and 70 percent of the schools and a third of the hospitals built from 1933 to 1939. Projects were regularly completed within projected timeframes and cost estimates. The PWA electrified much of rural America, and its total activity required a two-year budget of $3.3 billion compared with a total GDP of $65 billion. Another program, the Works Projects Administration, was designed to employ unemployed breadwinners for families. Though its most famous Project No. 1 employed musicians, artists, actors in drama products, and literary projects, it also concentrated on construction, building 620,000 miles of streets and 10,000 bridges. Its first appropriation in 1935 was $4.9 billion, or 6.7 percent of 1935 GDP (Wikipedia—Works Project Administration), making it the largest employer in the nation. However, even the distinguished liberal historian John Kenneth Galbraith recognized that hostility between the Roosevelt administration and industry weakened the recovery of the private sector (Galbraith, 1955), delaying it until the nation united during the Second World War.

## Federal health developments

The medical discoveries by Louis Pasteur, Robert Koch, and Joseph Lister revolutionized our understanding of the role of bacteria and microorganisms in disease from the 1860s to 1890s. By 1900, most major American cities had established health departments, though their quality varied. Discussion of public health is largely taken from a detailed monograph on the history of American health providers by John Duffy (Duffy, 1992):

> By World War I municipal health departments began to assume their present form … the first 40 years of the 20th Century saw transformation of state boards of health from weak, ineffective agencies … to relatively strong departments staffed by permanent health professionals. By 1916 the California State Board, the nation's

> largest and best health system, was administering seven bureaus … and three laboratories.

An *Act for the Relief of Sick and Disabled Seamen of 1798* established the Marine Hospital Service (MHS) in the Treasury Department, but during the 19th century, the US was slow to develop national health services. Although the MHS expanded services to respond to yellow fever epidemics, it opposed the development of a national health service. A coalition of Christian Scientists, anti-vaccinationists, anti-vivisectionists, and the patent-medicine industry also opposed a national health service. After interim steps in the early years of the 20th century, the name of the MHS was changed to the US Public Health Service (PHS) in 1912, and its responsibilities and funding were increased. It soon engaged vigorously with water quality, treatment of disease, and other health issues. Rupert Blue, assistant surgeon general with the MHS, who had gained a national reputation overseeing rat extermination and urban sanitation to combat a bubonic plague epidemic in San Francisco, was appointed surgeon general and head of the PHS.

Stimulated by the recently created *British National Insurance Act of 1911*, a movement for national American health insurance grew. A plan created by the influential American Association for Labor Legislation gained approval in editorials in the *Journal of the American Medical Association* (*JAMA*), in health associations, and among many state politicians. In his presidential address to the American Medical Association (AMA) in 1916, Rupert Blue strongly endorsed it. He attributed the excessive morbidity of unskilled workers to the fact that they did make enough money for healthful living, saying: "To meet the situation, there are unmistakeable signs that health insurance will constitute the nest great step in social legislation" (Duffy, 1992). Blue's endorsement met with wide support, but in spite of the approval of AMA leadership, member physicians were neutral or dubious about national health insurance. Effective lobbying by medical societies and the Prudential Life Insurance Company[2] led to the failure of both a national plan and state bills in California and New York.

A temporary advance in support for healthcare was the *Sheppard-Towner Act of 1921*, enacted as a result of the influence of women's organizations after women had achieved suffrage through the 19th Amendment in 1920. The act provides annual appropriations of $1,240,000 for the "Advancement of Maternal and Infant Welfare," which corresponded to $21.1 million in today's dollars. In spite of opposition by the AMA, the act was reauthorized by a narrower margin in 1926.

Safe drinking water became an early concern of Surgeon General Rupert Blue. Contamination of drinking water by a Salmonella bacterium was a major cause of deadly typhoid fever. As he confided in a letter to the Secretary of the Treasury (Blue, 1913), the PHS only had authority to set water quality standards for interstate commerce (that is, drinking water in railroads). However, Blue predicted that standards set by the PHS would likely set precedents for state and local action, so he therefore issued detailed and rigorous standards. His prediction proved to be accurate: by the mid-1920s, the US became the first nation in the world in which customers at restaurants would be automatically provided a glass of safe drinking water.

## Other science and technology agencies

Federal science agencies in the 19th century were created because of specific needs for professional services—for example, coastal bathymetry; expertise in fish, chemistry, biology and entomology, Earth science and mapping; and engineering in its many manifestations. The chronology of former and existing agencies is shown in Figure 5.2 and the explanatory table for acronyms (Table 5.1).

Creation of the civil service system by the *Pendleton Act of 1883*, which required prospective employees to pass qualifying examinations, undergirded the professionalism of federal agencies. Some of the nation's most noted environmental leaders gained experience in or became known in the course of their employment in these agencies. Examples include Gifford Pinchot, first head of the US Forest Service (1906), Aldo Leopold, who studied forestry science at Yale and immediately joined the Forest Service, Howard Zahnhiser, with the Bureau of Biological Survey, and Rachel Carson, who rose in the Fish and Wildlife Service to become chief editor of all its publications before retiring to write books. Nine of the first 30 scientists hired by the first director of the US Geological Survey, Clarence King (1879–1981), became members of the National Academy of Sciences. Although different in kind from the service-oriented agencies, one should also mention the Smithsonian Institution—part library, part museum, part laboratory and research center, whose founding director was Joseph Henry, the country's greatest physicist in the 19th century (Dupree, 1957).

## Engineering, infrastructure, and changes after the Second World War

During the 20th century, American engineers continued to be critical in the development of the nation's infrastructure. By 1900: "The civil engineer ... was ideally well educated, cultured, and imbued with a sense of social responsibility. His jobs were large, socially significant, and often publicly financed projects" (Merritt, 1969). Their role in the achievement of efficient infrastructure construction and maintenance across the country is illustrated by the New York City subway system. Authorized by the *New York Rapid Transit Act of 1894*, which created a Rapid Transit Commission to manage

**Figure 5.2:** Chronologies of federal science agencies with links to land, the environment, and health

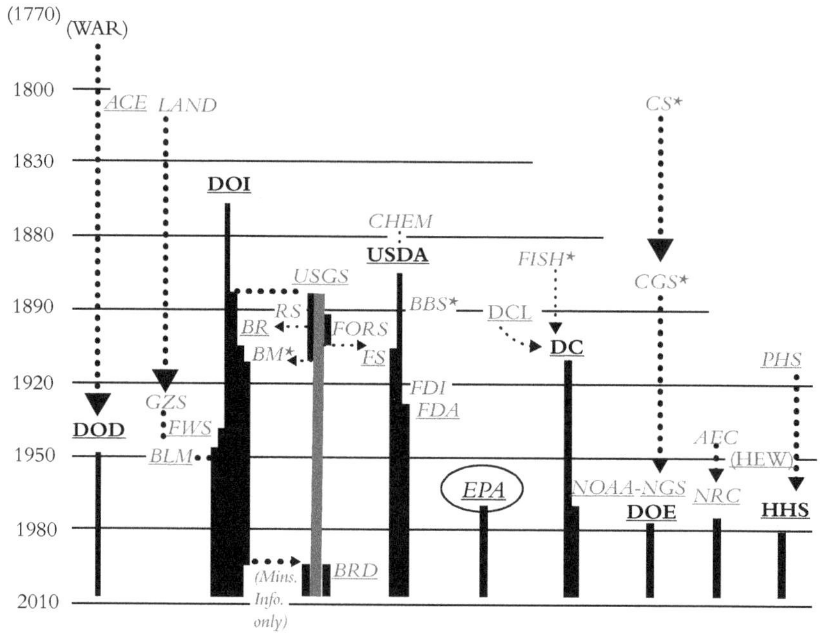


Notes: Solid vertical line segments represent the timeframes for given agencies, which are added to or removed from host agencies. Thus, for example, Reclamation Service (RS) and mining functions were moved from the USGS to become separate bureaus (Bureau of Reclamation [BR] and Bureau of Mines [BM]) in the Department of the Interior in 1905 and 1910, respectively. The BM was abolished in 1996, except for one function, which was returned to the USGS in 1996. The USGS is within the Interior Department, but is shown in a lighter shade to delineate its former agencies. Dotted lines connect independent agencies to a later organization. Some changes are too complex to be shown on the graph. For example, in 1996, much of the Department of Agriculture's Bureau of Biological Survey, along with some biologists from the Fish and Wildlife Service, were moved to the USGS and combined to form the Biological Resources Division. The EPA is circled for emphasis because of its primary importance to environmental regulation. An asterisk indicates an agency that has been part of agencies other than those listed.

Source: Manheim (2009). Abbreviations are given in Table 5.1.

development, the new system was designed by a team of engineers led by Chief Engineer William Barclay Parsons, designer of the Cape Cod Canal. Construction began in 1899 after receiving bids from construction companies. The Interborough Rapid Transit line (IRT) was completed in 1904 despite the disruptive nature of subway construction before tunnel-boring machines. Throughout major expansions of the subway system, the cost for riders remained a nickel until 1944 (Markowitz, 2003).

Another notable New York project was the Chrysler Building, completed without loss of a worker in 1930 after 20 months of construction. With 77

**Table 5.1:** List of abbreviations used in Figure 5.2

| Symbol | Organization | Symbol | Organization | Symbol | Organization |
|---|---|---|---|---|---|
| ACE | Army Corps of Engineers | DOD | Department of Defense | HEW | Health Education and Welfare |
| AEC | Atomic Energy Commission | DOE | Department of Energy | HHS | Health and Human Services |
| BBS* | Bureau of Biological Survey | DOI | Department of the Interior | LAND | Land Office |
| BLM | Bureau of Land Management | EPA | Environmental Protection Agency | NGS | National Geodetic Survey |
| BM* | Bureau of Mines | FDA | Food and Drug Administration | NOAA | National Ocean Atmosphere Administration |
| BR | Bureau of Reclamation | FDI | Food Drug Insecticide Administration | NRC | Nuclear Regulatory Commission |
| BRD | Biology Resources Division | FISH* | Fish Commission | PHS | Public Health Service |
| CHEM | Bureau of Chemistry | FS | Forest Service | USDA | Department of Agriculture |
| CGS* | Coast Geodetic Survey | FWS | Fish and Wildlife Service | USGS | Geological Survey |
| CS* | Survey of the Coast | FORS | Forestry Survey | RS | Reclamation Survey |
| DC | Department of Commerce | GZS | Grazing Service | WAR | War Department |
| DCL | Department of Commerce and Labor | | | | |

Note: Asterisks refer to agencies associated with organizations not in Figure 5.2.

floors and 1,047 feet high, it was at the time the world's tallest building. It remains a gem in the New York City skyline and is widely regarded as the best example of the Art Deco style (Figure 5.3). Requiring only one year and 45 days for construction, the Empire State Building was completed in 1931 and surpassed the Chrysler Building in height, becoming another New York City icon and engineering marvel.

Key elements for efficient construction of major infrastructure projects were quality designs and plans supplied by engineers qualified to respond

**Figure 5.3:** The Chrysler Building

Source: Chrysler Building by David Shankbone (2007), available from: https://en.m.wikipedia.org/wiki/File:Chrysler_Building_by_David_Shankbone.jpg

to questions and criticisms, and gain approval from city and state reviewing boards. The second factor was effective coordination. Consider the complexity associated with the construction of the towering Chrysler or Empire State Buildings, which required provisions for electric power, water and sewage systems, and transportation in the crowded New York City. Meteorological research involving historic wind velocities was undertaken to ensure safety in storms. Cooperation with city officials who understood the work of construction engineers and had the authority to provide necessary city support and services was an essential factor.

## Postwar changes: the decline in the prestige of engineering and construction

After the Second World War, America underwent major changes. Engineers' previously pre-eminent status was replaced by scientists, symbolized by the international nuclear physicists whose theoretical work underlay the atom bomb. President Franklin D. Roosevelt asked his science advisor, Vannevar Bush, to prepare a plan for the postwar employment of science in service of society. His famous book *Science: The Endless Frontier* extolled the potential role of science in society. Its main recommendation was the creation of a National Science Foundation, which, after initial controversy, was created in 1950 to fund the brightest scientists for basic research projects. Bush was an engineer's engineer, but his "linear" theory was that basic research by scientists would create breakthroughs that would in turn lead to practical applications (Zachary, 1997).

The National Science Foundation began with modest outlays. However, with the launch of the Soviet Sputnik in 1957, America was shocked into support for science at all levels. The *National Defense Education Act of 1958* and other federal research programs dramatically increased funding to colleges and universities, and graduate research programs and research publications boomed (see Figure 5.4). However, the new policies had unexpected outcomes. By 1975, technological advances began a steep decline, and in 1980, the US was surpassed by Germany.[3] A large fraction of the nation's technical talent moved to scientific fields, while engineers' status and their recruitment to university programs declined. The technological decline coincided with a decline in patenting and economic impacts. There was greater support for basic science than applied science.

Engineering historian Bruce Seeley observed that college and university engineering programs responded to the new societal paradigm by replacing traditional courses with engineering science (Seeley, 1999). New theoretical courses like fluid dynamics, differential equations, numerical methods, indeterminate structures, and systems design were added to the curriculum. The Academy of Engineering was added as an affiliate to the National Academy of Science in December 1964. "Only schools that embraced scientific engineering received large federal projects ... the downside was that engineering schools were basically training engineers to become professors at engineering schools—not to work in industry" (Seeley, 1999).

A factor with a paradoxically negative effect on infrastructure development was federal support for local initiatives. A dramatic example came with Boston's "Big Dig," a road project designed to move 3.5 miles of the interstate highway system adjacent to Boston Harbor underground. It was promoted by Massachusetts officials with the support of the House of Representatives speaker, Tip O'Neill, so that Massachusetts would pay only 10 percent of

**Figure 5.4:** Technical advances, federal funding, and research publications, 1950–1980

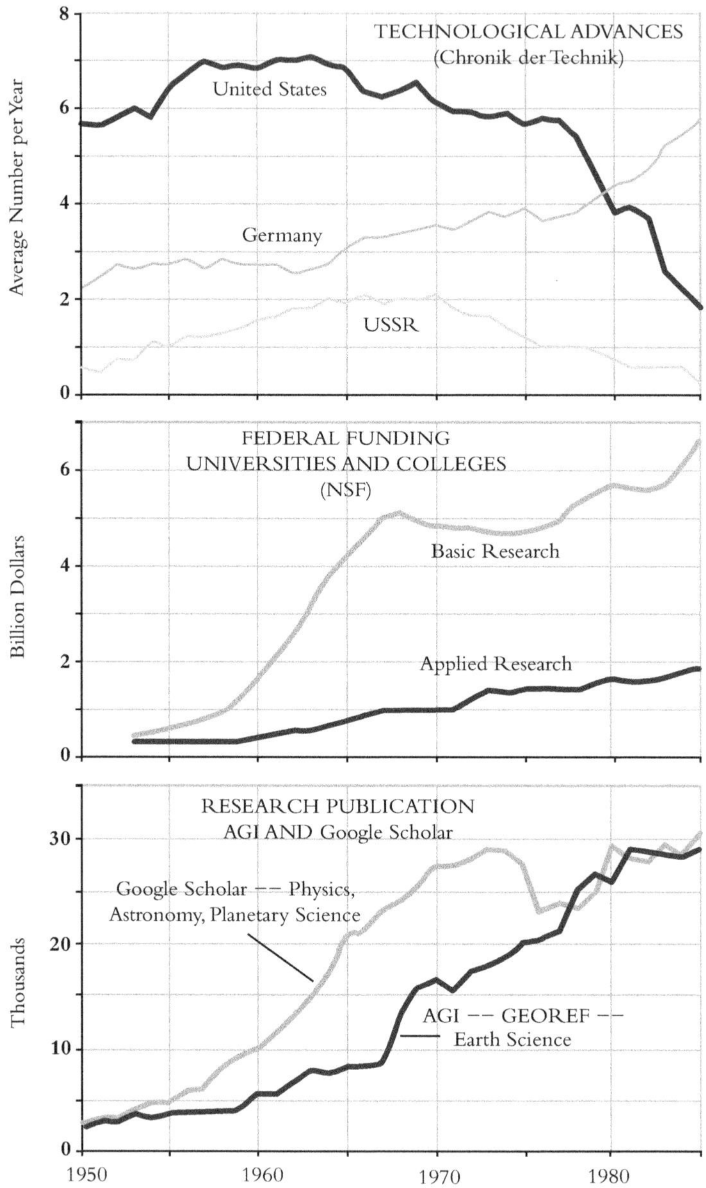


Source: Manheim (2009, p 28)

the cost. Designed in 1982, it required nine years to gain all the necessary federal permits and was completed only in 2007, with a 3.6-fold increase in cost from initial estimates (Gelinas, 2007). Many of the increases in costs occurred because the project became a milch cow for local communities.

The Big Dig pointed to a major problem with federal support for state and local infrastructure projects. Statutory requirements for federal funding include five subtitles of the federal administrative code, with a total of 270 categories, each of which can run to dozens of pages. Only experienced and well-connected contractors can navigate this complex system. Requirements for federal support generally stipulate regional stakeholder representation. This diffuses decision-making and management authority, contrary to the system that allowed efficient construction in America from the 19th century up to the Second World War. The 1970s environmental movement added multiple permitting authorities and authorized litigation against proposed projects. An overlooked human factor is that great projects have generally been led by bold and visionary leaders, but such leaders avoid projects that involve protracted bureaucratic delays.

## The environmental movement

### *Environmental organizations*

The first major American environmental organization was the Sierra Club, which was founded in 1892 by John Muir. Muir was enamored by the spectacular landscape and ancient forests of the northern Pacific area, as the name of the organization implies. Subsequent organizations are listed in Table 5.1 and vary in terms of their focus and philosophies; there are thousands of smaller organizations, including groups formed for specific local action. As a consequence of post-Second World War developments, environmental organizations (nongovernmental organizations often referred to as NGOs) experienced major growth (Table 5.2). Further growth took place in response to the countermovement against environmental regulations that will be described in Chapter 7.

The Sierra Club is unique in its diverse structure. The club provides access to nature trails and recreational opportunities; local chapters engage in regional environmental initiatives, while the national organization focuses on political lobbying and litigation. The National Resources Defense Council also prioritizes political activity and litigation, as does Friends of the Earth, whose slogan is "Because the Earth Needs a Good Lawyer."[4] The Nature Conservancy seeks to acquire and preserve private lands that have environmental value, and the World Resources Institute is primarily a research institution; neither it nor the Nature Conservancy pursues litigation.

**Table 5.2:** Major environmental organizations and their membership

| Organizations | Founding | Membership (1,000s) | | $ (millions) |
|---|---|---|---|---|
| | | 2004 | 2008 | 2023 |
| Sierra Club | 1892 | 736 | 750 | 1+ |
| National Audubon Society | 1905 | 550 | 600 | 2 |
| National Parks Conservation Association | 1919 | 375 | 1,000 | 1 |
| Wilderness Society | 1935 | 225 | 300 | 1+ |
| National Wildlife Federation | 1936 | 650 | 4,000 | 4+ |
| Defenders of Wildlife | 1947 | 463 | 130 | 2.2 |
| Nature Conservancy | 1951 | 972 | 1,000 | 1+ |
| World Wildlife Fund—United States | 1961 | 1,200 | 1,200 | 1.2 |
| Environmental Defense Fund | 1967 | 350 | 500 | 1.5 |
| Friends of the Earth | 1969 | 35 | 1,000 | >2 |
| Natural Resources Defense Council | 1970 | 450 | 1,200 | 2.4 |
| Greenpeace Global | 1975 | 250 | 250 | 3.5 |
| World Resources Institute | 1982 | - | - | - |

Source: Founding, membership, and operating budget data in 2004 are from Wikipedia—US Environmental Movement. Data for 2008 are from Manheim (2009); data for 2023 are from Wikipedia—US Environmental Movement and online data for organizations.

## *Ecology*

The term "ecology" was first used in the English title of a book (Warming and Vahl, 1909) translated from a Danish textbook by Johannes Eugenius Bülow Warming (Warming, 1895). However, the founder of ecology is considered to be Alexander von Humboldt (1769–1869), a German natural scientist and polymath for whom the concept of the unity of nature included earth and physical properties, animal and plant life, as well as humans. Among von Humboldt's works (with Aime Bonpland) is his *Essay on the Geography of Plants* (von Humboldt and Bonpland, 1807), with a 2 x 3-foot color foldout of a cross section of Chimborazo, a snow-capped mountain peak in central Ecuador (elevation 20,702 feet). The illustration details measurements of altitude, temperature, humidity, atmospheric pressure, and animals and plants (with scientific names) found at each elevation, based on his own observations and existing Spanish sources. An East-West cross-section delineates the three zones of Amazonia, from the mountains to the coast. Von Humboldt[5] also created isothermal maps of the globe, which he linked to the biogeography of plants. His monograph on Cuba is an astonishing synthesis, not only describing the geography and geology, including earthquakes, soils, climate, fauna, and flora of the island, but also human history, politics, and social institutions.

A national wilderness movement was marked by the founding of the Wilderness Society in 1935 by Robert Marshall (chief of recreation and lands for the Forest Service), Aldo Leopold, and others. However, the founding of the modern ecology movement in the US is attributed to Aldo Leopold's book, *A Sand County Almanac* (Leopold, 1949), or Eugene Odum, author of the first American textbook on ecology, *Fundamentals of Ecology*, which Odum published in 1953 with his younger brother and fellow ecologist, Howard Odum. "It was the discipline's only textbook for more than a decade" (Southwick, 1976). Southwick cites William Vogt, Fairfield Osborn, and Aldo Leopold as challenging the materialistic bases of American society and suggesting that "man was out of balance with his environment and must soon pay the consequences." Southwick cites the conclusion to the book by Osborne (1948): "Man must recognize the necessity of cooperating with nature. He must temper his demands and use and consider the natural living resources of the earth in a manner that alone can provide for the continuation of civilization."

Leopold wrote: "It is inconceivable to me that an ethical relation to land can exist without love, respect and admiration for land, and a high regard for its value."

The field of ecology encompasses *species populations* and *communities*, populations of plants and living together in given *habitats*. The 2024 *Merriam-Webster* online dictionary defines "environment" as "the complex of physical, chemical, and biotic factors (such as climate, soil, and living things) that act upon an organism or an ecological community and ultimately determine its form and survival." An *ecosystem* includes populations, communities, habitats, and environments, and refers to the dynamic interaction of all parts of the environment (Southwick, 1976). A major branch of the ecology movement emerged for forest ecology—see, for example, Spurr (1980) and Franklin (2005). It became engaged along with environmental NGOs in the "Northern Spotted Owl wars" against the lumbering industry in the 1980s (Franklin, 2008).

Radical variants of the ecology movement emerged in the 1960s and 1970s. One was the deep ecology-ecological anarchist movement represented by Murray Bookchin (Bookchin, 1964), the Norwegian ecologist Arne Naess, and the American, George Sessions (Naess and Sessions, 1984). Naess and Sessions argued that the richness and diversity of life have value in themselves and are reduced by human interference. These values require reduction of the human population. A modern review of Herbert Marcuse's eco-Marxist analyses (1960s–1990s) of the movement is provided by Reitz (2022).

An extreme radical movement, Earth First!, was founded in 1980 by Dave Foreman (Foreman, 1985). Its purpose was to engage in "civil disobedience and 'monkeywrenching' in defense of Mother Earth." In the first years after the group's formation, the use of direct actions—standing in front of bulldozers and putting spikes (for example, metal rods or nails) in trees to prevent them from being cut—attracted national news coverage.

## Postwar environmental problems

The post-Second World War economic and industrial boom, the replacement of rail by automobile and truck transportation, and other factors led to a major increase in environmental pollution. Newspaper headlines featured events like burning debris in the Cayuhoga River, toxic chemicals buried in the Love Canal, and deaths due to atmospheric pollution. African-American populations from the Southern states had migrated north to work in the war industries, and the continued movement of rural populations to the cities put pressure on water supplies and sewage treatment facilities. Boston, the site of earlier innovative sewage treatment systems described in Chapter 4, failed to maintain its previously excellent system. New waste treatment facilities established in 1968 on Deer Island, near the entrance to Boston Harbor, were already inadequate for the needs of the greater Boston area. When holding capacities were exceeded during rains, raw sewage was discharged into Boston Harbor. Willingness to make major investments was held back by anticipation that an increasingly restive Congress would provide subsidies for the modernization of municipal wastewater treatment facilities (Manheim, 2009).

Greater Metropolitan New York City also had major waste disposal problems and serious coastal pollution. The industrial steel manufacturing belt south of the Great Lakes region belched out smoke and other combustion products. When local pollution was reduced by adding higher smokestacks, smoke, soot, and sulfur dioxide were carried by higher air currents to clean areas hundreds of miles away.

Some state agencies moved to deal with environmental problems. The name of the US Environmental Protection Agency is said to have been influenced by the Illinois Environmental Protection Agency.[6] Federal agencies had qualified staff and experienced leaders, but the mobilization of the federal government to deal with the challenges, announced by President John F. Kennedy, was not pursued after Vice President Lyndon B. Johnson became president following Kennedy's assassination in 1963. As will be elaborated later on in this section, documents in the Johnson Library showed that no significant action on pollution emerged from the administration. Political pressure increased on federal agencies and science advisory bodies (Jasanoff, 1998).

A special set of problems emerged in forest management policy. The US Forest Service had long enjoyed a positive image. As described earlier, based on the recommendations of Aldo Leopold, the Forest Service created the first wildlife refuge in the Gila Forest of New Mexico in 1924. The concept of designating areas as wilderness:

> withdrawing it from timbering or other developments, was first conceived by a Forest Service landscape architect named Arthur Carhart ... The founder of the Wilderness Society, Robert Marshall, went on to become the Forest Service's Director of Recreation and convinced the agency to classify over five million acres as wilderness or primitive areas. (O'Toole, 1988)

O'Toole also noted the earlier practice of the Forest Service: "most national forest timber was managed using selection cutting: individual trees were cut when they were mature, leaving behind beautiful stands of younger trees. When done right, a selection-cut forest is hard to distinguish from wilderness."

However, the suburban housing boom, as well as the *Multiple-Use Sustained-Yield Act of 1960*, gave the agency perverse incentives to increase lumber production from national forests from 5.6 billion board feet in 1950 to 12.8 billion by 1968. Much of the new wood production was achieved by clear cutting, which created antagonism because of its visual impact.

## Rachel Carson's *Silent Spring*

A major impact on the public regarding the environment and pollution came with the blockbuster book by Rachel Carson in 1962, entitled *Silent Spring*. As described by Manheim (2009), Carson anticipated that her work would arouse antagonism. Dichlorodiphenyltrichloroethane (DDT) was a safe pesticide used to delouse populations in postwar Italy, saved millions from malaria in Africa, and enhanced farm production. It gained a Nobel Prize for Paul Muller, the Swiss chemist who discovered its useful properties. But Carson revealed for the first time that DDT threatened the extinction of the nation's revered national symbol, the bald eagle.

After the bestselling *The Sea around Us* and *The Edge of the Sea*, Carson spent five years writing *Silent Spring* (Carson, 1962). She researched her work exceptionally carefully for a book written in a popular and accessible style. It contained more than 500 references and a carefully annotated index. A flavor of her unique book can be gained from a passage whose message she repeated with variations throughout the volume:

> These sprays, dusts, and aerosols are now applied almost universally to farms, gardens, forests, and homes—nonselective chemicals that have the power to kill every insect, the good and the bad, to still the song

> of birds and the leaping of fish in the streams, to coat the leaves with a deadly film, and to linger on in soil—all this though the intended target may be only a few weeds or insects. Can anyone believe it is possible to lay down such a barrage of poisons on the surface of the earth without making it unfit for all life? They should not be called "insecticides" but "biocides."

*Saturday Review* called *Silent Spring* "a devastating attack on human carelessness, greed, and irresponsibility." Other publications described terrifying revelations. Published in September 1962, 100,000 copies were sold in bookstores by the end of the year; the book was featured by the Book of the Month Club, stayed on the bestseller list for 86 weeks, and sold two million copies (Gottlieb, 1993). There was a tidal wave of letters to Congress and government agencies about the book, and by the following year, 63 bills had been introduced in various states to deal with the problem (Graham, 1970).

DDT was highly insoluble in water, but Carson showed that minute quantities of DDT or its breakdown product, DDE, could be taken up by phytoplankton, eaten in turn by zooplankton, minnows, larger fish, and, ultimately, fish-eating birds. An osprey might have 25 ppm (parts per million) in its tissue, 600 times more than in zooplankton, which in turn are highly enriched over plankton (Heinz and Hoffman, 1998). Adult birds were not necessarily made ill by the pesticide, but they failed to reproduce. Concepts like magnification in the food chain were new even for biological scientists; they were not understandable from personal observation or common sense. But the effects of these chemicals, valued by industry and government for supporting public health and farm productivity, were demonstrated to have devastating effects on wildlife.

Not all reviews of *Silent Spring* were positive. National magazines asserted that Carson's statements were exaggerated or polemic. However, environmentally engaged persons were incensed when the chemical industry and parts of the medical industry attacked both her book and her person (Brinkley, 2022).

Interior Department Secretary Stewart Udall gave President John F. Kennedy a copy of Carson's book before its publication (Udall, 2006). Kennedy tasked his science advisor, Jerome Wiesner, to convene a panel and provide recommendations for action on pesticides. Chaired by Colin Macleod, the panel's study was released as a White House Report on May 15, 1963 (Macleod, 1963). In his preface, Kennedy indicated his plan to submit legislation to Congress to implement and fund the program. After the release of the report, Kennedy took a five-day pollution tour with Wisconsin Senator Gaylord Nelson. His plans and potential influence were cut short by his assassination on November 22, 1963.

Preoccupied by Great Society programs, civil rights issues, and the Vietnam War, President Lyndon B. Johnson deferred to his science advisor, Donald F. Hornig, for action on the Kennedy environmental report. The President's Science Advisory Council (PSAC) delivered a 38-page report with 11 scientific appendices (Hornig and Tukey, 1965). Documents provided by the LBJ Library found that the PSAC pollution panel report was sent to the ten scientific agencies, whose unedited responses constituted the full report to the president. Scientific and technical appendices were of high quality. However, a blunt statement from the Federal Water Quality Commission said that the entire report was more of a collection of ad hoc comments than a blueprint for action: "The Report, although thought-provoking, has major weaknesses and it is not a useful document from the standpoint of guiding, programming and planning for the water pollution control program" (Manheim, 2007).

It appears that the pollution panel, which consisted of Hornig, 22 professors or academic administrators, and two participants from the AT&T and IBM laboratories, was overwhelmed by the multiplicity of organizational options, and there was no effective synthesis and organization of the effort. The only environmental law that emerged from the White House during the Johnson Administration was PL 285, the *Highway Beautification Act of 1965*, a project led by the First Lady, Lady Bird Johnson. From 1965 to 1968, the Senate led the way in producing the *Endangered Species Conservation Act of 1966*, the *Air Quality Act of 1967*, and the *Wild & Scenic Rivers Act of 1968*. None of these focused on pesticide control. Two years later, a national crisis would lead to the transformation of US environmental management.

6

# The Environmental Revolution of the 1970s

## Collision: the Santa Barbara oil spill of 1969

A fateful environmental event occurred on January 28, 1969, four days after the approval of Walter Hickel, President Richard Nixon's Secretary of the Interior. Union Oil Company's Platform A blowout took place in the faulted Santa Barbara channel. Union Oil Co. was the operating company for a consortium that included Gulf Oil, Mobil Oil, and Texaco (Manheim, 2009). The well, in federal waters, had been drilled to its maximum depth of 3,479 feet. The US Geological Survey's Conservation Division was responsible for monitoring oil and gas operations, but it was later revealed that the regional oil and gas supervisor in Los Angeles agreed to a request by Union Oil Co. to place casing to only 239 feet below the sea floor.

The crew on the platform, which stood in 188 feet of water, were removing drill pipe in preparation for electrical logging when a column of mud and gas projected 20 feet upward from the rig floor. The pressure prevented the mud-drenched men from screwing a blowout preventer into the pipe. They closed the massive steel ram below the rotary table, dropping 2,759 feet of drill pipe hanging below the drill floor to the bottom of the hole. The ram closed off the blowout at the platform, but not the oil that surged through the hole below the casing. Large boils soon appeared along a geological fault near Platform A, beginning a discharge of what was later estimated at between 3.4 and 4 million gallons of crude oil—the biggest offshore spill in US history not associated with a tanker accident (Nash et al, 1972).

Had the supervisor insisted on the 1,200 feet of casing required by California State regulations, the spill would have probably not occurred. In two days, the spreading oil slick extended over 150 square miles, from Santa Barbara to Ventura. The blowout was finally brought under control on February 7, but by that time, a black tide of crude oil had fouled the beaches of Santa Barbara and drenched grebes, ducks, and other seabirds, seals, and sea lions in crude oil.

Pictures of oiled beaches and wildlife were seen by up to 20 million viewers on the nation's TV screens in nightly news broadcasts that, unlike today, were widely viewed. They were featured in newspapers and magazines, and created a sensation at a time sensitized to environmental issues. A local anti-oil movement, GOO (Get Oil Out), gained support. The crisis created doubts about the ability of the federal government to protect the environment from powerful economic forces; it created a collision between the booming offshore oil industry and the new environmental movement.[1]

### *Federal officials performed, but demand for reform grew*

Federal officials that had oversight over the Santa Barbara oil spill were Interior Secretary Walter Hickel and Director William Pecora of the US Geological Survey. Hickel was the Republican Governor of Alaska when nominated by President Nixon to be Secretary of the Interior. Hickel's nomination was controversial and Senate confirmation hearings lasted so long that Hickel was not approved until after President Nixon's inauguration.

Secretary Hickel surprised everyone with his decisive response to the Santa Barbara crisis. Before moving into his office, he flew to California to inspect the spill. According to witnesses, while there, he informed Fred Hartley, President of Union Oil, that he would shut the rigs down (which Hartley questioned) and called the Attorney General's office to "find me authority" to declare a temporary moratorium on all offshore operations. He subsequently supported strong environmental action, but rejected scapegoating of Union Oil (Marco et al, 1987). Recognizing that Hickel's bold response to the offshore environmental issues calmed some of the furor, Nixon gave him discretion to act. However, after Hickel expressed sympathy with student protesters of the Vietnam War, his subsequent meeting with Nixon led to a departure as dramatic as his entrance.

Secretary Hickel established a close relationship with USGS Director, Dr. William T. Pecora, an accomplished Earth scientist and a member of the National Academy of Sciences. Pecora had people skills and a forthright approach; he is regarded by agency historians as one of the best administrators in the USGS's history (Wallace, 1996). Pecora's performance in the crisis contributed to his appointment as Undersecretary of the Department of the Interior in 1971, although he died soon after of diverticulitis. The response of Interior officials was effective, but did not change the view of Congressional activists and a large part of the US public that new laws were needed.

## The federal government response

The crisis triggered by the Santa Barbara oil spill received an immediate response from the Nixon administration. President Nixon's interests were mainly aligned with the business community and on foreign policy, but he was aware of the importance of the environmental movement and was determined to take leadership in this area (Flippen, 2000). To this end, he brought respected environmental leaders into the White House, including Russell Train,[2] John C. Whitaker,[3] and Gordon J. F. MacDonald.[4] Senior advisor John Ehrlichman had active environmental interests and assisted in recruitment. President Nixon issued an executive order for an Environmental Quality Council (EQC) on May 19, 1969. After intensive debates on alternative agency organizations, described in the book by Whitaker (1976), Nixon proposed the Environmental Protection Agency in his Reorganization Plan, signed on July 5, 1970 (Nixon, 1970). It assumed formal operations on December 2, 1970.

As mentioned in the previous chapter, administrative law-making initiatives before the 1970s were often drawn up or advised by apolitical civil service experts in federal agencies, a system that characterizes current European practice by ministry task groups. Nixon's major message to Congress on February 10, 1970 listed 37 initiatives and 23 legislative proposals prepared by Whitaker's task group with agency staff (Whitaker, 1976). In addition to his environmental credentials, Train had leadership skills and a diplomatic style. Whitaker likewise believed in cooperative solutions, as is indicated by the title of his book, *Striking a Balance*. However, as will be noted in the next section, White House efforts were soon overtaken by Congressional initiatives. By 1974, President Nixon became disenchanted with environmental legislation, but environmental supporters in Congress and the courts nullified his actions (Lazarus, 2023).

### *The* National Environmental Policy Act

As noted in the previous section, Nixon administration environmental initiatives were supplanted by Congressional law makers; the train of environmental reform soon steamed down the tracks (Manheim, 2009). That train carried the precedent-setting *National Environmental Policy Act of 1969* (NEPA) and the *Clean Air Act Amendments of 1970* (CAA), which provided a model for later laws. NEPA was approved by Congress on December 23, 1969, and signed by President Nixon on January 1, 1970. It was sponsored by Senator Henry (Scoop) Jackson, a Democrat of Washington State and chairman of the Committee of Interior and Insular Affairs, in cooperation with Representative John Dingell (D-MI). The legislation was largely prepared by Jackson's advisor, Lynton Caldwell, a professor of political science at the University of Indiana and regarded as the nation's leading environmental policy expert. He led preparation of a massive, two-volume annotated bibliography of environmental policy (Caldwell et al, 1969). His work with Jackson's committee had been supported by Russell Train through the Conservation Foundation (Flippen, 2006). The Act was toughened in hearings by the influence of public groups like Environmental Action and by a visit by Senator Edmund Muskie (D-ME) (van Ness, 2007).[5]

Only seven pages long, NEPA proclaimed environmental quality as national policy and required that all federal agency actions must be preceded by deliberations supported by environmental impact analysis. It called for a Council on Environmental Quality[6] (CEQ) that would advise the president, prepare reports for Congress, and oversee environmental impact statements. The environmental impact statement feature was subsequently adopted by many nations. While the law was short, regulatory guidelines were expanded by the CEQ and by court decisions. It became highly controversial, as will be described later.

In his book on NEPA in 1998, Caldwell echoes a quote by Robert Nisbet that the environment was the most important movement of the 20th century, citing four basic dimensions of the act (Caldwell, 1998, p 21):

1. *Substantive*: "a declaration of goals, principles and values for Americans to which their governments are expected to adhere."
2. *Instruction*: "to the federal agencies of the principles and procedures to be followed in plans, programs and decisions having major impacts on the human environment".
3. *Evaluative*: "a means to reinforce and, where needed to reform the values, perceptions and behaviors of the American people in relation to their environment, which must henceforth be understood to encompass the planetary future".
4. *Progressive*: "its goals and principles, global and transgenerational, provide a foundation agenda for the future".

The foregoing dimensions illustrate Caldwell's Moses-like conviction about the importance of a statute intended to be nonpartisan and harmonize economic and environmental values in America. Nearly 30 years later in his 1998 book on the law, Caldwell reaffirmed its value. However, he admitted disappointment and frustration that the "the NEPA process has overshadowed NEPA's purpose" (Caldwell, 1998, p 52). He regretted that a statute designed to promote wise policy had become an administrative procedure (Lindstrom and Smith, 2002):

> Though environmental organizations tacitly supported Senator Jackson's bill at the time of its enactment, they subsequently showed

> interest in NEPA primarily as the environmental impact requirement that enabled them to stop or delay specific government programs or projects to which they objected. (Caldwell, 1998, p 35)

As noted earlier, the first two groundbreaking environmental laws passed after the Santa Barbara offshore oil spill were NEPA and the CAA. NEPA has been referred to as "our basic national charter for protection of the environment" (Lochridge, 2011), requiring all federal agencies to perform meaningful evaluation before taking actions with potential effect on the environment. Its outcomes are discussed later on in this chapter. The CAA set precedents not only for subsequent environmental laws, but also helped lead to new conventions for Congressional law making. Both laws enhanced the role of federal courts. Signed by President Nixon just before the CAA, the *Occupational Safety and Health Act of 1970* marked the culmination of efforts concerned with workplace safety dating back to the 19th century.

## *The* Clean Air Act Amendments of 1970

Concern over air pollution triggered by the New York City smog of Thanksgiving 1966 (Figure 6.1) led to the *Air Quality Act of 1967* and numerous state laws, but left demands for more stringent controls. The Nixon administration's bill, prepared by the House Commerce Committee with support from the Public Health Service and submitted to Congress in February 1970, went beyond all previous laws. For the first time, the bill set national air pollution standards for hazardous pollutants (ground ozone, nitric oxide, carbon monoxide, sulfur dioxide, and lead). It also set stringent standards for motor vehicle emissions and other sources of air pollution and designated air pollution regions.

The administration's bill, to be enforced by the Department of Health, Education, and Welfare (HEW), was well received in the House of Representatives but not in the Senate, where Senator Muskie was Chairman of the Senate Subcommittee on Air and Water Pollution. Muskie was also a potential Democratic rival to Nixon in the 1972 presidential election. Muskie favored enhancing enforcement of the 1967 Act, but retaining primary responsibility by states. However, the president's bill and proposal for national air quality standards, announced in a national speech, undermined Muskie's position.

Moreover, Muskie's 1967 bill and his new legislative proposal were attacked in a book on air pollution by a member of Ralph Nader's groups[7] (Nader and Esposito, 1970). It suggested that Muskie was in the pocket of the Maine paper industry and should be stripped of his title of "Mr. Pollution

**Figure 6.1:** Air pollution in New York City, November 1953

Note: Air pollution shown in Figure 6.1 is estimated to have caused 200 deaths.

Source: New York City/World-Telegram photo by Walter Albertin. LC-USZ62-114346. https://www.loc.gov/pictures/item/95508508/

Control." Muskie was a politician with intellect[8] and ethical principles, but these pressures led to a change in his air pollution policy.

Leon Billings, Legislative Director of the Senate Subcommittee on Air and Water Pollution, reported that Chairman Muskie brought together four additional senators to work with him on a new air quality law (Billings, 2007/2008; Manheim, 2014a). Three were Republicans: Howard Baker (TN), John Sherman Cooper (KY), and Caleb Boggs (DE). The other Democrat in the group was Thomas Eagleton (MO). The five senators came together in regular meetings to prepare the statute, an approach that differed from normal Congressional law making in committees. With a background in engineering, Baker contributed most of the scientific and technical detail in what became the CAA of 1970 (Billings, 2007).

The new statute was "dramatic, sweeping, and uncompromising" (Lazarus, 2004, p 67). It required the EPA to set rigorous national air pollution standards without regard to cost. Standards were set for automotive emission and other sources of air pollutants, and detailed procedures were prescribed for the EPA to follow. Major policies could not be changed without Congressional approval: revisions would require new laws or amendments.

The booming economy of the 1960s was fueled by America's manufacturing and industrial companies, but these were also the main sources of environmental pollution. A major concern was "regulatory capture," or fear that regulators would be influenced by powerful economic forces. To counter such concerns, Senator Eagleton advocated citizen litigation that could enforce environmental laws by suit in federal court, an approach based in part on a Michigan statute written by Joseph Sax (Sax, 1970). It had been a model for a 1970 Senate bill sponsored by Senators George McGovern (D-SD) and Philip Hart (D-MI), but not approved (Manheim, 2022a). Another provision to ensure environmental progress was "forcing technology," which was advocated by Senator Baker (Baker, 2005). It was to be implemented by mandating future dates for achieving goals that were not attainable with the current technology. The following list summarizes key features of the law, modified from Manheim (2009):

- *Pre-emptive detail.* Laws before 1970 gave discretion to agencies to make and modify operational policies to adapt to new information or problems and plan for the future. Federal agencies also guided Congress in preparing legislation. The CAA transformed this convention. Congress determined basic policies for agencies to follow.
- *Specificity.* Unlike NEPA, which emphasized many-sided evaluations of environmental issues, the CAA focused on a specific environmental problem—in this case, air pollution. Specificity lent itself to standard operational procedures. This approach was later extended to water pollution, toxic waste disposal, and other environmental issues.
- *Uniform standards.* The EPA established regulations and rules, including standards for maximum permissible pollutant levels (for example, stack emissions), that would be applicable throughout the nation.
- *Technology-forcing standards.* This meant setting standards beyond existing capabilities, requiring producers of pollutants to achieve compliance within given timeframes.

- *Priority for environmental protection.* Environmental protection took precedence over other values in enforcement, except where explicit options to seek waivers were provided.
- *Monitoring and publication of results.* Emitters of pollution were required to monitor emissions and report the results (independent checking could be employed). The enforcing agency would disseminate data to the public in accessible form.
- *Delegation to states.* States were given authority to implement the application of the laws and oversee monitoring. If they did not agree, or if their plan for compliance was found unacceptable, the federal government could take over and enforce the laws.
- *Rigorous enforcement and punitive measures for violations.* Penalties were defined for failure to meet standards and other violations. Violators could be taken to court either by agency legal staff or through attorneys for the Department of Justice. Disputes were referred to federal courts.
- *Citizen enforcement.* Citizens and citizen groups (including environmental NGOs like the Sierra Club and the Natural Resources Defense Council [NRDC]) were empowered to sue operators and regulatory agencies, including the EPA, in federal court. Citizen action was encouraged by provisions allowing reimbursement of reasonable costs (Kramer, 1982).

The law's provisions facilitated citizens' and their attorneys' monitoring of environmental performance. Extensive professional training would not be needed to identify violations and bring suit. Priority for environmental protection meant that economics could not be used as a defense against a failure to meet standards (Manheim, 2020). The intent of the framers regarding the primacy of the environment in enforcement of law was reaffirmed in the Supreme Court decision in *Whitman v. American Trucking Associations, Inc.* (2001). In that opinion, written by Justice Antonin Scalia, the Court ruled that the EPA could not consider cost in implementing national ambient air quality standards. A number of subsequent environmental laws adopted similar provisions for citizen suits.

Radical environmental ideas abounded in the early 1970s—for example, some activists advocated banning automobiles from cities. However, Leon Billings claimed that the framers of the law were not influenced by radical theories; several served on corporate boards (Billings, 2007/2008). Richard Ayres, a founder of the NRDC and a clean air activist, reported that the NRDC had no part in the initial framing of the law, but was active in hearings that led to modifications (Ayres, 2007). A factor promoting the unanimous vote in the Senate was the stature of the law's framers and their active participation in hearings. Muskie was a nationally respected leader, and Thomas Eagleton would become a vice-presidential nominee on the Democratic ticket of George McGovern for the 1972 election. Howard Baker was later minority and majority leader in the Senate and is known for his role in the Watergate hearings. Caleb Boggs had a key role in earlier pollution legislation. Unlike more recent legislation, the language of the law was clear; much of it could be understood by laypersons.

## Subsequent environmental laws

Major environmental laws followed the CAA in rapid succession. The *Federal Water Pollution Control Act Amendments of 1972* were spearheaded by the same group of senators as the CAA. It was also endorsed unanimously in the Senate en route to overwhelming passage by Congress. Like the CAA, it set ambitious requirements, calling for "fishable and swimmable waters" throughout the US by 1983 and "zero" discharge of pollutants by 1985. Complaining about its excessive costs, the president vetoed the bill, but his veto was overridden by Congress (Flippen, 2000).

The following is a list of the most important subsequent laws:

- *Federal Environmental Pesticide Control Act Amendments 1972 (FIFRA)*
- *Marine Mammal Protection Act 1972*
- *Marine Protection, Research and Sanctuaries Act 1972*
- *Coastal Zone Management Act (CZM) 1972*
- *Endangered Species Act (ESA) 1973*
- *Safe Drinking Water Act (SDWA) 1974*
- *Fishery Conservation and Management Act 1976*
- *Toxic Substances Control Act (TSCA) 1976*
- *Resources Conservation and Recovery Act (RCRA) 1976*
- *Federal Land Policy and Management Act (FLPMA) 1976*
- *Clean Air Act Amendments 1977*
- *Surface Mining and Control Act (SMCA) 1977*
- *Comprehensive Environmental Response, Compensation and Liability Act (CERCLA) 1980*

All but one of the foregoing laws, the most important of which are referred to by acronyms, deal with specific environmental issues.[9] For example, TSCA regulates the generation, transportation, treatment, storage, and disposal of hazardous wastes. Three of the laws, ESA, FLPMA, and CERCLA (Superfund), are especially significant and are briefly described in this chapter. For the remaining ones, the EPA has a well-organized and clearly written website (rare for US federal agencies) that describes all the laws under its jurisdiction (EPA, 2024a). It does not get into controversy, but its historical vignettes, including articles by key leaders like the first and fifth EPA administrator William Ruckelshaus (1932–2019), can include candid statements, which are also rare in contemporary government publications.

## *The* Endangered Species Act of 1973

One of the most powerful and controversial environmental laws is the ESA. Following earlier statutes in 1966 and 1969, the Act was inspired by domestic and international concern for the preservation of fish and wildlife facing threats of extinction. ESA in 1973 added plants to fish and wildlife species. According to a well-referenced article on ESA (Wikipedia—*Endangered Species Act of 1973*),[10] the initial law was prepared under the leadership of Russell Train, assisted by Earl Baysinger at the EPA, Dick Gutting, and Gerard A. Bertrand, who was transferred from his post as senior scientific advisor to the US Army Corps of Engineers to the White House Council on Environmental Quality. The draft included provisions requested by Representative John Dingle (D-MI), chief sponsor of the legislation. Bertrand is said to have written the "infamous 'takings' clause."

Lee Talbot was chief scientist for the Council on Environmental Quality in the Nixon administration.[11] He was not referenced in the Wikipedia article, although he is cited as a co-author (Carter, 2023) and has candidly described his personal role (Talbot, 2013). He reported that the Fish and Wildlife Service, under Nathan Reed, Assistant Secretary for Fish, Wildlife, and Parks, had overseen the preparation of the legislation, but Talbot felt it was too weak. Just before final submission, he and Frank Potter, chief counsel for the Environmental Committee for the House Committee on Merchant Marine and Fisheries, restored Talbot's earlier recommended language and removed qualifying statements like "insofar as practicable."

The final version of ESA made no attempt at balance with respect to economics or other values. It prohibited the federal government from actions that could threaten endangered species and also placed rigorous restrictions on private land that was a habitat for endangered species. Violators of the law faced severe punitive provisions. It made significant progress in saving endangered species and remains the object of deep respect and approval in many quarters. For example, a 2023 article by the US Department of the Interior (Anonymous, 2023a) states:

> The Act has saved hundreds of species from extinction and continues to protect and preserve some of our most beloved animals and plants. It has also helped to create a better understanding of how human activities can impact the environment and how we can work together to protect it.

However, the article from which this statement is taken fails to mention that the law also created antagonism and has been one of the costliest of the 1970s laws. The following assessment of the law is taken from a Department of the Interior description of ESA in the G. W. Bush administration (Jones, 2005a):

> In the past, the way the ESA was implemented placed legal and regulatory burdens on landowners and other members of the regulated community. As a result, many landowners do not want listed species on their property and have been unwilling to engage in activities that would attract species that are or could be listed in the future for fear of increased regulation and negative impacts on their property. To put it more plainly, landowners finding endangered species on their property have killed them lest use of their property be impaired.

The disparity in assessments by the same federal agency reflects the variability of policies by federal agencies concerned with environmental issues depending on the politics of the administration. The public was at first enthusiastic about ESA, seeing it as a protector of popular species, but the first indication of its broader implications came in 1978, when a Supreme Court decision confirmed that protection of the snail darter, a two-inch-long fish, required shutting down a 95 percent completed dam on the Tellicoe River.[12] A 1978 *TIME* magazine article reported that the conservation of a single wildflower, Maine's Furbish lousewort, blocked a $668 million hydroelectric project (Raymond, 2018), although a later account listed the value at $227 million (Green, 2019), indicating potential variability in media reports. The ESA differs from European laws on endangered species by uncompromising provisions that do not allow administrators to seek creative solutions to conflict.

## *The* Wilderness Act of 1964 *and the* Federal Land Policy Management Act of 1976

The Forest Service (FS) was a long-respected agency and the subject of an approving cover article in *Newsweek* magazine of June 2, 1952. It had mainly employed selective logging of mature trees (O'Toole, 1988) as well as preventative measures against disease and fire. However, in response to postwar suburbanization and expanded demand for lumber, Congressional appropriations and the *Multiple Use Sustained Yield Act of 1960* built perverse incentives into the FS's budget authorizations (Manheim, 2010); the FS quadrupled lumbering from federal land, mainly by clear-cutting methods. Opposition to the FS's new policies, as well as longstanding interest in federal wildlife preserves dating back to 1935, led to passage of the *Wilderness Act of 1964*. Except for grandfathered activities, the Act preserved some nine million acres in as natural a state as possible, excluding roads or mechanical transport means, and authorized future additions.

Subsequent controversies between environmental organizations and the lumbering industry and other user groups led to the *Federal Land Policy Management Act of 1976* (FLPMA). It imposed new requirements and restrictions on logging and federal management of land used for lumbering, grazing, mining, and other commercial activities. In 2015, Chief Forester Thomas Tidwell reported that since 1964, wilderness areas increased from 9 million to 110 million acres, an area greater than California (Tidwell, 2015).

### *The Superfund law*

CERCLA, commonly known as the Superfund law, was signed by President Jimmy Carter in 1980, but it is here grouped with the groundbreaking sequence of laws of the previous decade. It was designed to restore lands impacted by pollutants and recover costs through the implementation of the "polluter pays" concept. Unlike most regulatory laws that control current activities, Superfund looked backward to clean up past environmental harms. Authored and sponsored by Representative James Florio (D-NJ), the bipartisan-sponsored legislation was enacted during the "crisis window" after the discovery of a number of toxic waste sites. When the concept for CERCLA was developed, a relatively manageable number of major sites was envisioned, the costs for recovery of which might be offset by assigning responsibility to large existing organizations. After it came into effect, "spending on Superfund dwarfed all other programs in EPA combined" (Nakamura and Church, 2003).

## Outcomes of the environmental revolution

The environmental laws of the 1970s marked a dramatic shift in US environmental management policy, responding to urgent concerns and a sense of a national environmental crisis. Given this, an online search of post-2000 books describing the decade of the 1970s yielded surprising results. The books cited culture and fashion, race relations, feminism, the Vietnam War, Watergate, the energy crisis, hyperinflation, the Iran hostage crisis, deregulation, and more, but only one book among the first ten examined listed the word "environment" as a chapter or as a major topic. Was it avoidance of unsettled issues? Whatever the explanation for the lack of recognition of environment as a significant development in the 1970s, the following discussion summarizes positive outcomes of the new laws as well as their unintended consequences.

## *The reduction of pollutants*

The environmental laws of the 1970s made rapid though uneven progress against pollution and environmental hazards. The EPA estimated that ambient lead levels declined 64 percent from 1975 to 1982 after use of unleaded gasoline was sharply curtailed. Other industrial air pollutants, like polyaromatic hydrocarbons (PAHs) and polychlorinated biphenyls (PCBs), were reduced by more modest levels. Most PAH pollution was emitted by automobiles and trucks. Reduction in their concentration in ambient air levels required changes in manufacturing technology and therefore could not be achieved rapidly. PCBs were used in dielectric fluids to reduce the risk of explosion in capacitors and transformers; they were widely used in plasticizers and flame retardants in building materials and paint. Since 1970, airborne pollutant concentrations have declined by 77 percent (EPA, 2020). Sulfur dioxide saw major reductions mainly under later, more innovative approaches than were available in the early 1970s. Reduction in nitric oxides, which mainly came from power plants and other stationary sources, made the least progress.

Progress against water pollution was more dramatic. Environmental historian Richard N. L. Andrews (Andrews, 2008) noted that in his first week at the EPA William Ruckelshaus had issued pollution abatement orders to three major cities, Atlanta, Detroit, and Cleveland. According to John Quarles (Quarles, 1976), Chief Legal Officer at the EPA, Ruckelshaus's policy of gaining public support by taking strong action against the entrenched power of industry was successful: "editorials hailed the agency's vigorous, purposeful response" (Andrews, 2008, p 57).

The history of pollution conditions in the nation's waterways can be reconstructed because "bottom sediments in waterways have memories" (J. Schubel, cited in Manheim et al, 1999). An ingenious study sponsored by the National Oceanic and Atmospheric Administration (NOAA) (Presley et al, 1998) measured the concentration of pollutants in a 90-cm sediment core taken in the Mississippi Delta, which could be regarded as representative of average waterborne sediments in the US because the Mississippi River and its tributaries drain 41 percent of the US's area (Corps, no date). The ages of the sediments were dated by $^{14}C$ and $^{210}Pb$ radiometric methods. Figure 6.2 illustrates the age of sediments versus their pollutant concentration, offering a striking profile of waterborne pollutants in the US from 1890 to 1990.

Figure 6.2 shows that toxic PAHs rose dramatically from low levels before the 1950s (the end of the Second World War) to peaks six times higher by the late 1960s; this was followed by a remarkably sharp drop coinciding with the passage of the CAA and the *Federal Water Pollution Control Act (Clean Water Act) Amendments of 1972*.

**Figure 6.2:** Polyaromatic hydrocarbons in a dated sediment core from the Mississippi River Delta

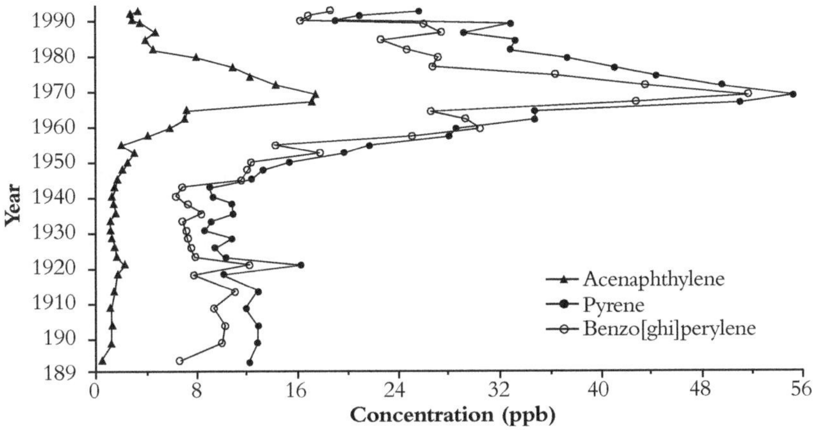


Note: The original figure includes the errors on the x-axis.

Source: Presley et al (1998). The document did not include data tables for these constituents.

## *Pesticides*

As described in the previous chapter, Rachel Carson's 1962 book revealed the threat of DDT to extinction of valued bird species, and a number of states banned its use. When the EPA was established, it took over responsibility for the regulation of pesticide use from the Department of Agriculture. Administrator William Ruckelshaus announced the final cancellation of all crop uses of DDT in June 1972. Its use for public health, quarantine use, and exports was not affected. The pesticide industry and the Environmental Defense Fund (EDF) contested the latter part of the order. Industry sought to nullify the ruling, while the EDF sought to extend it to all uses. On December 13, 1972, the US Court of Appeals supported the EPA administrator's ban. Meanwhile, the *Federal Environmental Pesticides Control Act of 1972* amended the *Federal Insecticide, Fungicide and Rodenticide Act of 1947* (FIFRA), providing the EPA with more rigorous authority to regulate pesticides.

New pesticides, for example, organophosphates and chlorinated hydrocarbons like chlordane were introduced to replace DDT; chlordane was later discontinued and more recently was replaced by chlorpyrifos. Banning pesticides registered before 1972 required approval by a special board. Reregistration of pesticides proceeded slowly and was canceled in 1976 after revelations that a testing laboratory, Industrial Bio-Test Laboratories (IBT), had been falsifying data. Reregistration was resumed in 1978.

## The *National Environmental Policy Act*

The Environmental Impact Assessment (EIA) requirement incorporated in NEPA was the most widely emulated feature of American environmental law. European nations adopted the fact-finding function envisioned by the framers whereas in the US, NEPA took more legalistic and adversarial pathways (Manheim 2009; see comments on NEPA earlier in this chapter). The law initially enjoyed wide approval and its future role was not foreseen by the framers or President Nixon.

Applications of NEPA were influenced by two landmark court cases: *Calvert Cliffs v. US Atomic Energy Agency* and *Scenic Hudson Preservation Conference v. Federal Power Commission, 1981.* In the first case, the Baltimore Gas and Electric Company began construction of a nuclear power plant at Calvert Cliffs on the Maryland coast of Chesapeake Bay in 1968 with a license from the US Atomic Energy Agency. After the passage of NEPA in 1970, the Calvert Cliffs Coordinating Committee claimed that environmental precautions were inadequate and violated NEPA. The D.C. Circuit court ruled that Section 102 of NEPA required that federal agencies must carry out NEPA's procedural requirements "to the fullest extent possible" and that these were judicially enforceable. Judge J. Skelly Wright also held that, under NEPA, federal agencies must consider alternatives that would reduce environmental damage. The plant was approved after a delay, during which Atomic Energy Commission (AEC) regulations were modified to meet the new requirements. The case moved policy from the framers' emphasis on planning and coordination to make NEPA an administrative act. Among other effects, it opened up later nuclear power plant proposals to regulatory challenge. These increased after public concern over the partial meltdown of a nuclear reactor at the Three Mile Island plant in Middletown, Pennsylvania in 1978 and the Chernobyl disaster near Pripyat, Ukraine, in 1986; these developments and the attendant increased costs of regulations essentially shut down the opening of new nuclear plants in the US.

The second case involved the power company Consolidated Edison, which proposed plans to build the US's largest pumped-storage hydroelectric plant on Storm King Mountain, adjacent to the Hudson River in New York. The plans were opposed by an environmental consortium, whose case was rejected by the federal agency, but were approved by the Second Circuit Court of Appeals, which ruled that the organization, Scenic Hudson, had legal standing because of its "special interests in aesthetic, conservational, and recreational aspects" of the mountain (Wikipedia—Scenic Hudson Preservation Conference v. Federal Power Commission). This ruling opened virtually any proposed activity to challenge by local residents on esthetic as well as a variety of other grounds. While NEPA has no provision to deny proposed activities, suits could require extensive studies, modifications, or be followed by new claims that could delay initiation or increase costs to the point that projects would be abandoned.

A classic case was the Cape Wind Project for Horseshoe Shoals in Nantucket Sound, between Martha's Vineyard and Nantucket Islands, Massachusetts. A wind turbine field capable of producing electrical power for 75 percent of the combined power requirements for Cape Cod, Martha's Vineyard, and Nantucket, was proposed in 2001. A Corps of Engineers Environmental Impact Statement (EIS) of 3000 pages involved some 20 separate laws or permits that the project had to navigate (Manheim, 2009, p 127). Battles between proponents and opponents raged until 2017, when the project was finally abandoned. Another striking example of the impact of the environmental impact statement was the report cited by Lazarus (2004) that environmental impact statements for the controversial Alaskan Pipeline weighed 50 pounds.

## Environmentalist reactions

Environmentalists were and remain euphoric about the environmental revolution. The EPA is a powerful organization with a strong science base and thousands of professional staff assigned to ten regions of the nation and units that deal with specific environmental concerns. The Office of Compliance and Enforcement has the responsibility to enforce laws over which the EPA has jurisdiction, which are as follows (EPA, 2024):

- Clean Air Act (CAA)
- Clean Water Act (CWA)
- Comprehensive Environmental Response, Compensation and Liability Act (CERCLA, or Superfund)
- Emergency Planning and Community Right-to-Know Act (EPCRA)
- Federal Insecticide, Fungicide, and Rodenticide Act (FIFRA)
- Marine Protection, Research and Sanctuaries Act
- Oil Pollution Act (OPA)
- Resource Conservation and Recovery Act (RCRA)
- Safe Drinking Water Act (SDWA)
- Toxic Substances Control Act (TSCA)

The CAA required that the EPA make pollution monitoring results promptly available to the public. It issued proposed regulations followed by opportunities for affected industries to respond before it issued final regulations. Fear of regulatory capture by powerful industry forces was dealt with by the new laws' specification of detailed operational procedures that the agency was required to follow. The CAA, as well as its water pollution equivalent, the CWA, had strong punitive measures along with authorization for private suit in federal court for a failure to meet the law's requirements. Industry's fear that the agency would become a "runaway bureaucracy of environmental zealots" was met by the specificity of provisions and supplemental imposition of hundreds of regulatory deadlines (Andrews, 1999). After decades of operation, the views of major environmental NGOs about the EPA and the basic environmental laws of the 1970s are summarized in the following list:

- The NRDC:
  "The EPA plays a vital role in safeguarding our environment, ensuring that environmental laws are enforced to protect our air, water, and land for current and future generations."
- Sierra Club:
  "Environmental laws, upheld by the EPA, stand as the guardians of our planet. They are the foundation upon which we build a sustainable future, fostering a balance between human development and the preservation of nature."
- World Wildlife Fund (WWF):
  "The EPA and environmental laws are the cornerstones of our commitment to a healthier planet. They empower us to work collaboratively, promoting responsible stewardship and conservation of biodiversity."
- Greenpeace:
  "Environmental laws, upheld by the EPA, are powerful tools in the hands of those who seek to defend our planet. They represent a collective promise to hold industries accountable and preserve the delicate balance of nature."
- Friends of the Earth:
  "In the face of environmental challenges, the EPA and robust environmental laws are our allies. They embody the principle that every individual has the right to a clean and healthy environment, inspiring action and positive change."

As will be described in later chapters, global climate change became a primary concern of these organizations. A limitation by the CAA and CWA (*Federal Water Pollution Act Amendments of 1972*) was the requirement that permit holders use "best available technology" (BAT). In practice, this meant that advanced experimental technologies could not be used and facilities could therefore undergo unreasonable degrees of treatment. Experts on environmental regulation like Richard Andrews (1999) and Daniel Fiorino (2006) pointed out that the regulatory system mandated standards, but provided no incentive to exceed them. The CAA and the CWA passed in 1977 sought to correct operational problems, but many remained.

The impact on business and industry by the CAA, the CWA and other laws led to divisions in society. Sharon Beder, an Australian environmental writer, chronicled efforts by American corporations to mobilize public opinion against regulations (Beder, 2006). A book critical of the three major auto makers listed details of their tactics to slow down regulations (Dawes and Majkut, 2023). Beyond "playing the energy/jobs card," the book cited a 1972 General Motors report, *Study on the Environment*, that "concluded that the pressure on Congress to pass the CAA was the result of twenty years of faulty print and broadcast reporting on air pollution." Later discussion will show that while industry complaints could have valid elements, its campaigns against regulations designed to control climate change became deceptive.

## Economic impacts of the environmental laws

The new environmental management system had major impacts on the US economy. Analyses by Ira Magaziner and Robert Reich (the latter a professor of management and policy at Harvard University and later Secretary of Labor in the Carter administration) reported disproportionate economic industrial declines in the 1970s, when the US fell behind nine other nations (Magasiner and Reich, 1982). Median family income had increased by more than 30 percent in the previous two decades, but declined by 6.7 percent in the 1970s. The US share of electronics production went from 50 percent in the 1960s to 8 percent. A long list of manufactured goods was now made abroad. There are contrary views on the regulatory impact of the 1970s laws,[13] but the most comprehensive study, based on "1.75 million plant observations from the Census of Manufactures" (Greenstone, 2002) reported that in the first 15 years of operation of the CAA, "nonattainment counties [alone] lost approximately 590,000 jobs, $37 billion in capital stock, and $75 billion (1987 dollars) of output in pollution-intensive industries." These included printing, organic chemicals, rubber, plastic products, fabricated metals; motor vehicles, bodies, and parts; inorganic chemicals, lumber and wood products, nonferrous metals, petroleum refining; stone, clay, glass, and concrete; pulp and paper, and iron and steel. Manheim (2009) found mining, followed by primary metals, to be the most adversely affected economic sector in the 1970s. More recently, sectors of the economy most affected by federal regulations were manufacturing and healthcare, based on RegData (Al-Ubaydli and McLaughlin, 2015).

Figures 6.3, 6.4, and 6.5 display economic indices over time. The historical plot of income quintiles in the US from the end of the Second World War up to 2022 (Figure 6.3 shows incomes on a base 2 log scale). This records relative proportional changes in different income levels Note the sudden change to

**Figure 6.3:** Semi-log plot of US family income quintiles, 1948–2020

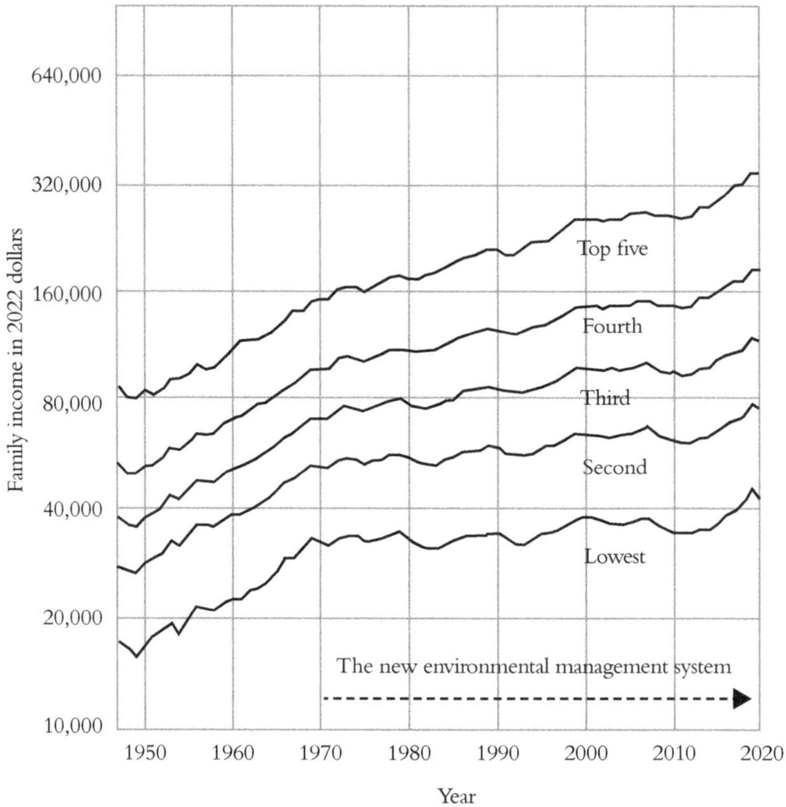


Note: The quintiles refer to the upper limit of each quintile and the lower limit of the top 5 percent of family incomes.

Source: Figure drawn from US Census Bureau, Current Population Survey data

a slower increase in income for all income levels after 1970, corresponding to the passage of the CAA. Prior to 1970, the lowest income quintile grew more rapidly than higher quintiles. After 1970, the trend reversed, with little change in inflation-adjusted income for the bottom quintile to the present. Other factors have been suggested to affect the economy during the 1970s, but none to my knowledge account for the sharp change in 1970 except the CAA.

Another economic measure with negative change from the beginning of the decade is hourly compensation, as given in Figure 6.4. This is explained by the movement of jobs from manufacturing and industry. Manufacturing jobs offer higher wages than service jobs because of their multiplier effect on productivity. There is an accompanying impact on the economy, as the loss of 100 manufacturing jobs has been claimed to lead to the loss of 744 other jobs in society, in comparison with 122 other jobs lost with the loss of 100 retail positions (Bivens, 2019). These data refer to the recent

**Figure 6.4:** Time plot of productivity and hourly wages, 1948–2025

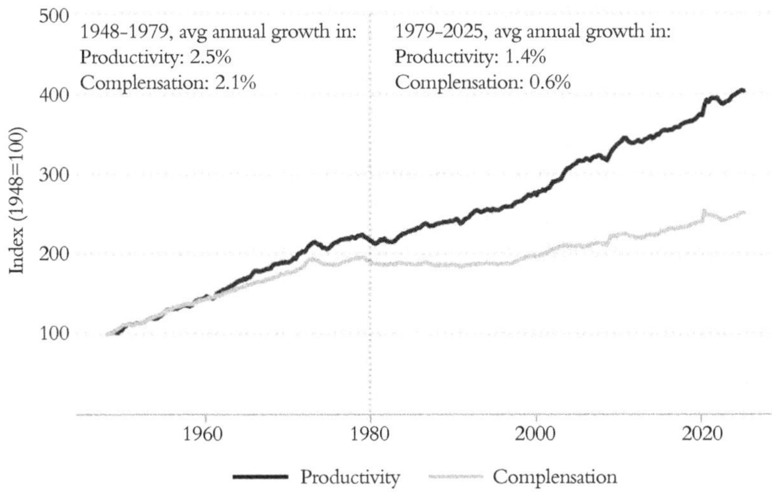


Note: The gap between productivity and a typical worker's compensation has increased dramatically since 1979.

Source: Economic Policy Institute (EPI, 2019), calculated from data of the Bureau of Labor Statistics and the Bureau of Economic Data. Reproduced with permission

conditions, but similar effects would have probably been noted during the 1970s and 1980s.

A search of reports from industrial organizations or individuals about the impact of the new laws at the time of their passage had marginal success. A rare report about the impact of the regulations on the industrial community can be found in a book on the crisis and revival of the Chrysler Motor company by Reich and Donahue (1985). In 1979, Chrysler Motor Corporation was facing bankruptcy. Its chairman, John Riccardo, spoke with Stewart Eizenstat, President Carter's chief domestic advisor, about relief from regulations: "fully half of the retooling for the next five years, he claimed, was due to government regulations" (Reich and Donahue, 1985, p 88). The adverse effect on Chrysler's competitiveness was increased because of the rapid development of German and Japanese cars during that period.

An economic measure relevant to the changes in the 1970s and subsequently is trade status. This is compared for the US and Germany in Figure 6.5. Before 1970, the US maintained trade surpluses for 100 years. Figure 6.5 shows that the US began foreign trade deficits after 1970. Claims that concerns about outsourcing and foreign exchange deficits or are based on myths (Mankiw and Swagel, 2006) defy the logic that loss of US manufacturing industries would be accompanied by increased imports and trade deficits. Germany was also subject to the pressures of Asian competition, but retained its manufacturing sector and has maintained trade surpluses.

**Figure 6.5:** Historical trade balance for the United States and Germany, 1970–2024

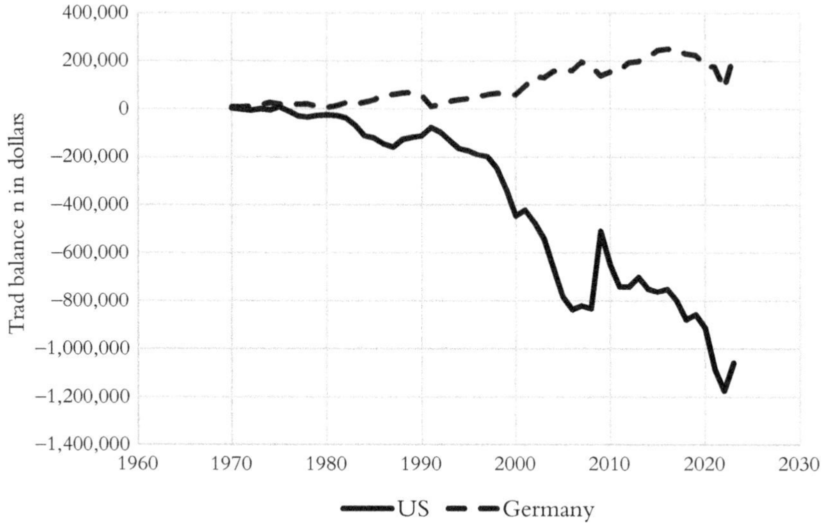


Source: US Trade data Census Bureau Historical Series: US International Trade in Goods and Service (2025); German data, Statistisches Bundesamt (Destatis, 2025) Aussenhandel; conversion of euros to dollars "Historical Currency Converter by Date."

This implies an industrial and political climate able to maintain jobs and economic development in the face of foreign competition.

The new regulatory system appears to be the primary cause of changes in the economy indicated in Figures 6.3, 6.4, and 6.5. The onset of change pre-dates the Arab oil embargo of 1973, which had a temporary effect. Transformation of the US's former strength in manufacturing and industry to a service-dominated economy was also influenced by additional factors, such as the competitive growth of manufacturing in Asian and European nations. An early econometric analysis of the unexpected economic decline and stagflation in the 1970s (Dennison, 1979) examined 17 potential causative factors, but emphasized environmental controls. To this, Ullman (1988) added military pre-emption of industrial effort and scientific and technical talent, excessive taxes on capital gains, and poor policies on the part of business.

The sudden, common change in economic trends around 1970 may have been accentuated by the psychological impact of the new CAA regulatory regime on business executive planning and decision making. Penalties of $25,000 a day for violation of pollution standards ($196,000 in 2023 dollars) and authorization of citizen suits in federal court, meant that from their earlier positive status, manufacturing and industry were now regarded by the government as dangers to health and the environment and needed stringent control. Multiple pathways for control were regarded as desirable and extended to states and local permitting authorities (for example, state versions of NEPA). Large companies could create special entities to deal with regulatory requirements, but the new regulatory regime hit smaller companies especially hard (Bardach and Kagan, 1987). Companies canceled plans for expansion and new hires, transferred capital investments to meet regulatory requirements, and moved to offshore suppliers. There was an exodus of firms from manufacturing to less affected economic sectors like banking and finance, real estate, and law. The sudden imposition of stringent controls came at an inopportune time, when, as previously noted, European and Asian manufacturing was expanding rapidly.

A factor emphasized by Bluestone and Harrison (1987), who did not mention environmental controls, was greedy and shortsighted managers who drove industry abroad. This theme was sounded by former Senator Byron Dorgan of North Dakota in a book that passionately excoriated free trade policies and the readiness of giant American corporations like Walmart and major pharmaceutical companies to lower costs and increase profits by offshoring production and services (Dorgan, 2006). Movement of industry abroad was exacerbated by the readiness of the American public to buy cheaper products regardless of their origin. This differs from populations of European nations, who express strong preference for domestic products or those from the EU. A minority of writers—for example, Ikenson (2014)—have argued that deindustrialization of the US is a myth, and a formerly widely held concept has been that moving from manufacturing to a service industry was a natural development for advanced economies (Rowthorn and Ramaswamy, 1997).

Why did the framers of the 1970s laws not consider the potential impact of the new system on the economy more seriously? There are two suggested answers to this. The first was the urgency for environmental controls triggered by the Santa Barbara offshore oil spill, whose ugly consequences were transmitted throughout the nation by nightly TV news programs. The second was a perception of the overwhelming financial power and vitality of American industry, exemplified by a box shown in a popular almanac in 1965. Its headline was "US CONTINUED TO SET RECORDS IN 1965," noting that this continued the longest boom since the Second World War. Gross national product (GNP) exceeded government estimates. With their deep concern about the potential of powerful economic forces to influence environmental regulators, the framers of the CAA assumed that the resilience of US industry would be able to accommodate the new regulatory demands. This is supported by an interview with former Senator Howard

Baker shortly before his passing. A major contributor to the provisions of the CAA and the CWA, Baker acknowledged that the framers of these laws did not sufficiently anticipate their impacts on the economy (Manheim, 2014a).

## Other developments in the 1970s

### *Litigiousness*

Before the EPA, most federal scientific and technical agencies lacked regulatory authority and could take balanced positions. The EPA was a new kind of agency; it had research functions but also far-reaching regulatory responsibilities as an enforcer with prosecutorial functions of laws on behalf of the environment. Adjudicating disputes was assigned to federal courts. Civil penalties for violation of pollution standards or other regulatory requirements could be imposed by the EPA on its own or through state agencies. Knowing or willful violation of regulations was a criminal offense and could be referred to the courts for punitive action, including imprisonment. However, such cases were rare compared with civil cases.

Figure 6.6 shows the dramatic increase in the number of environmental laws passed per year and the number of cases in federal courts in the 1970s. In 1978, legal columnist Linda Demkovich concluded that clogged federal courts might reflect "new laws guaranteeing more social and civil rights ... and the growing number of lawyers" (Demkovich, 1978; see also Halliday [1986] on the astonishing increase in the number of lawyers after 1970). Alexander Solzhenitsyn's famous critique of the West at a Harvard commencement noted that: "A society based on the letter of the law and never reaching any higher, fails to take advantage of the full range of human possibilities."

The *Civil Rights Act of 1964* was the first law to empower citizens' suits against governmental agencies. The precedent-setting CAA that initiated adjudication of disputes in federal court, soon followed by the CWA, embraced this provision. Stimulated by these and subsequent laws, litigation took on an expanded role in society. The number of environmental law cases in the 1970s was small compared to the total number of cases in federal court, but they could have a major economic impact. For example, the "Northern Spotted Owl" decision, based on the Endangered Species Act, resulted in decline in lumbering in West Coast states by up to three quarters.

The new environmental management system, especially NEPA, the CAA, and the CWA, had special impacts on infrastructure development, which will be described in greater detail in Chapter 12. The latter two laws encouraged citizen litigation in federal courts against proposed projects by allowing for the reimbursement of legal costs for successful suits, a practice not found in any other advanced nation. The addition of esthetics as justification for suit added an incentive for suits; laws designed to control pollution and harm to

**Figure 6.6:** The number of environmental laws passed per year with a superimposed plot of environmental lawsuits filed in federal court per year

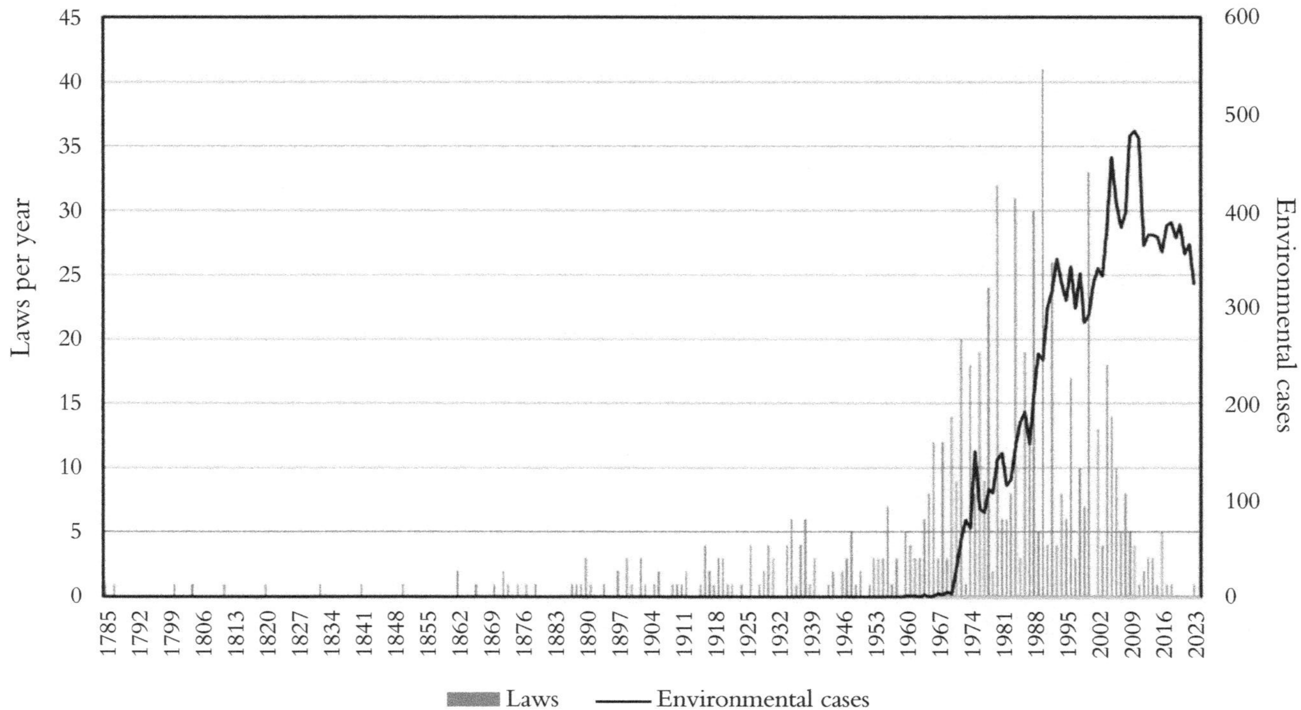


Source: Laws data are from the environmental database of Manheim and Fuhs (2007), partially updated. Environmental law cases are taken from federal court cases in the LexisNexis database.

endangered species became vehicles to stop or delay infrastructure needed to control a greater threat—global climate change.

### *A retrospective review of law making in the United States*

Earlier chapters described cycles in federal law making. After the Constitutional Convention in 1787, Congress established governance for the new nation by enacting laws providing for payment of the national debt, a national census, authentication of records in the courts, copyright provisions, patents, immigration and naturalization, and other practical measures (Wikipedia—List of United States Federal Legislation 1789–1901). The early laws enabled the new nation to grow rapidly. A monograph by administrative scholar Paul Light emphasizes the importance of Alexander Hamilton, Secretary of the Treasury, in establishing effective administrative procedures for the new nation (Light, 2009).

President Andrew Jackson's spoils system in 1829 dismantled the foregoing system, leading to turnover in government after presidential elections. This inhibited the establishment of stable administrative structures and discouraged the passage of laws that would require responsible management. The *Homestead Act of 1862* and the *Railroad Act of 1862* are among the relatively few laws dealing with land management that were subsequently passed, but there were no agencies capable of overseeing them or resolving problems. The latter Act, designed to extend the rail system to the Pacific Coast, led to one of the major scandals in American history.

By 1900, the progressive reform movement, beginning with the merit-based federal appointment system, restored trust in federal agency operations. It permitted the expansion of law making as well as the effective execution of President Franklin D. Roosevelt's many federal programs to ameliorate the effects of the Great Depression.

From 1900 to the late 1960s, the text of most laws was short, rarely exceeding 20 pages, because Congress delegated operational policy to career civil-service administrators who led agencies beneath presidentially appointed heads. This system changed with the passage of two groundbreaking laws. The first arose from major concern about coal mine health hazards and accidents. The Bureau of Mines had formal expertise regarding coal mining, but the mining industry resisted giving it adequate authority to inspect and provide mining safeguards. The *Federal Coal Mine Health and Safety Act of 1969* therefore broke with previous conventions. The new law laid out rigorous requirements at the record-breaking length of 62 pages and stipulated operational systems that enforcement bodies could not modify without Congressional approval.

The CAA followed this pattern and had a far greater impact. The initial CAA was 37 pages long, but amendments in 1977 reached 111 pages.

**Figure 6.7:** Historical plot of laws versus number of pages in laws

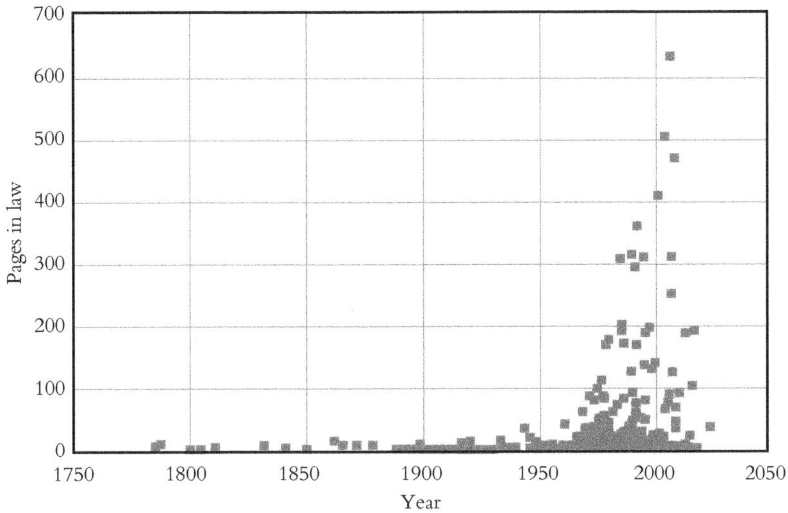


Source: Database of US environmental and land-use laws (Manheim, 2014c)

From that time, the length of laws continued to increase, as may be seen in Figure 6.7. The last CAA amendment in 1990 runs to 470 pages. After the 1970s, Congressional activism in addressing societal problems through detailed law making extended to other sectors of society. The *Affordable Care Act of 2010* reached 2,300 pages.

A more comprehensive system for controlling environmental pollution and hazards was needed. "There was no national clean air legislation, no federal clean water act program, no hazardous waste or toxic substance laws. There was not even a federal environmental protection agency prior to the 1970s" (Lazarus, 2001). The environmental regulatory system enacted in the 1970s produced rapid progress against environmental pollution and environmental hazards. The problem was that Congressional activism in the 1970s had unintended consequences. It assumed inexhaustible resilience on the part of industry and expanded regulations beyond reasonable limits. It fostered litigiousness and produced conflict in society. Given unremitting subsequent controversy over environmental regulations, it is surprising that there has been so little re-examination of the laws in recent decades. I suggest that there are reasons for this on both sides of the political aisle.

The environmental and scholarly community may be reluctant to re-examine the 1970s laws in part because of the first Reagan administration's countercampaign in the 1980s (see Chapter 7) and because this would tend to support industry's continuing battle against regulations. The campaign against climate change has called for more stringent regulations, not reform.

On the conservative and business side, companies object to regulations that impede and raise the cost of their activities. Major oil companies maintain legal staff to litigate against the EPA's proposed regulations and defend against suits by environmental NGOs. Trade organizations have more extensive research capabilities. After 2000, the US Chamber of Commerce produced detailed assessments of regulatory issues in an effort to curb the effect of regulations on commerce and industry. But these focused on restraining regulations through measures like the *REINS Act of 2023* that would restrain regulations, rather than considering reform of basic laws that were presumably set in stone, even though it is these that mandate regulations. Because of the positive image of Ronald Reagan, the excesses of the Reagan administration in 1981 are not mentioned in conservative/business publications. Minimal attention has been paid to environmental concerns and the creation of balanced policy since the reform proposals of the Natural Resources Committee under Chairman Richard Pombo in 2004–2006. A discussion of the problems associated with the existing laws is provided in Chapter 12.

In short, consideration of more cooperative and effective regulatory systems like those of the EU (Chapter 11) has been rare. The framers of the CAA and the CWA in the Subcommittee on Air and Water Pollution were a rare bipartisan group. They were committed to nonpartisan legislation (Manheim, 2014), but that perspective would be lost in the future. Congress's creation of complex regulatory systems with profound impacts on the economy inevitably politicized regulatory policy. By the 1980s, liberal environmental law experts like Thomas McGarity recognized that "the means that agencies used to implement the social reform legislation of the late 1960s and early 1970s had become too intrusive" (McGarity, 1987). However, conflict over regulatory policy had reached the point where reform was no longer possible. The result was political conflict and ultimately gridlock, described in Chapter 7.

# 7

# Other Developments in the 1970s and 1980s, and the Reagan Countermovement

## President Gerald Ford and the offshore oil and gas industry

President Richard Nixon recognized the importance of the environmental issue and brought environmental leaders into his White House. However, the administration's environmental initiatives in the early 1970s were overtaken by legislation spurred by the Santa Barbara offshore oil spill in 1969. The groundbreaking new laws enacted by Congress during the decade were largely approved by overwhelming bipartisan vote. They made rapid progress against environmental pollution. However, their impact on manufacturing and industry, the downturn in the economy created antagonism in the business community.

Nixon resigned in 1974 as a result of the Watergate scandal, famously investigated by the *Washington Post* reporters Bob Woodward and Carl Bernstein (Woodward and Bernstein, 1974). Vice President Gerald Ford became President. The Ford Library and Museum's section on environment begins by citing Ford's position: "I am committed to the Nation's effort to clean up the environment. At the same time, I am concerned about the costs and impact on the economy. We can't do it all tomorrow" (Library, 1976). According to an assessment of US environmental budgets from 1970 to 2010 (Conant and Balint, 2016), Ford's overall environmental budget proposals were moderate and differed little from final Congressional authorizations (-3.9 percent).

The US had been self-sufficient in oil and gas in the 1950s, but by 1970, it was importing 30 percent of its petroleum needs. Growth of the offshore oil industry was supported by both parties. The offshore industry had begun in the Gulf of Mexico after the Second World War, operating under the *Submerged Lands* and *Outer Continental Shelf Lands Acts of 1953* (Public laws

81–65 and 81–212) and the *Recreation and Public Purposes Act of 1954*. States could lease energy and mineral rights within three miles of their coasts (three leagues or nine miles off the Texas and Florida Gulf coasts). The Interior Department's BLM conducted competitive lease sales for tracts in federal waters beyond these limits, and companies could exploit oil and gas resources to the edge of the continental shelf or its extension. The US Geological Survey's Conservation Division was given responsibility for monitoring exploration and drilling activity and collecting revenues, though its budgets for this purpose were so meager that inspection staff had to use company boats to get to offshore rigs (Kash, 2006).

The first seafloor blowout preventer, seismic data collection system, undersea pipelines, and subsea well completions were all achieved in 1961, and the later 1960s saw advanced drill ships, microwave data transmission, computerized well-data-monitoring systems, and satellite navigation systems. By 1970, platforms were placed in water depths exceeding 1,000 feet. Experts described the offshore oil industry as comparable with the space program in terms of its technical sophistication and complexity.

The Central Gulf of Mexico became the dominant offshore oil region. Production in state waters off California was stopped after the Santa Barbara oil spill in 1969. Exploratory drilling in the Atlantic margin began in 1975, and 51 holes were drilled from 1975 to 1984, although ten lease sales brought no commercial production. Rogers C. B. Morton, Ford's Secretary of the Interior, undertook the controversial step of initiating offshore oil and gas leasing in the MAFLA (Mississippi, Alabama and Florida) area of the Eastern Gulf of Mexico. Offshore leasing and drilling were booming in the Central and Western Gulf, but the Santa Barbara oil spill raised environmental sensitivities. Florida's Democratic governor, Reuben Askew, was concerned about spills affecting his state's important tourist industry. He lacked the ability to influence leasing in federal waters until Republican Congressman Bill Young called attention to the governor's prerogative to approve pipeline permits. Subsequently, negotiations between Askew and Morton in 1974 produced the first-ever agreement that offshore leasing would be preceded or accompanied by comprehensive baseline investigations of the seafloor environment in lease areas.[1]

## The James E. (Jimmy) Carter Administration

An Arab Oil embargo of the US and other Western nations that supported Israel in the Yom Kippur War began in October 1973 and lasted until March 1974, creating a profound economic shock to the US. The US was then importing 32 percent of its oil needs, and the embargo led to long lines at gasoline stations and other shortages. The crisis led to expansion of oil and gas exploration and production.

Jimmy Carter defeated President Ford in the election of 1976. Carter was the first US President elected directly from the Deep South since Zachary Taylor in 1848. He has been described as combining a "gentle-Jesus mien" with "ambition, flinty resolve and bulletproof self-assurance" (Stephen Phillips, cited in Manheim, 2023a). As President, Carter showed deep concern for the energy problem, describing it as: "The moral equivalent of war" (Hakes, 2022). He signed the *National Energy Conservation Act of 1978*, created a new Department of Energy, and launched a bold subsidy program for solar energy and other renewable energies, However, his energy policies, as well as his plans for healthcare, government reorganization, consumer protection, and labor reform produced meager results. His prediction that by 2000, the US would be using 20 percent renewable energy was not realized.

Carter was straightforward in articulating policy positions, but tended to micromanage rather than delegate authority. He lacked the political skills of Lyndon Johnson, but also the latter's ideological bent. His achievements included deregulation of the airline, trucking, and rail industries, reducing costs for consumers and industry. Notable in foreign policy was his mediation of the Camp David Accord between Egyptian President Anwar Sadat and Israeli President Menachem Begin in 1978. He signed significant environmental legislation, for example, the *Surface Mining Control and Reclamation Act of 1977* and the *Comprehensive Environmental Response, Compensation and Liability Act of 1980*, but his presidency was troubled by stagflation and the Iran conflict. These factors helped lead to his resounding defeat by Ronald Reagan in the election of 1980.

A strong environmentalist, Carter used the four-paragraph *American Antiquities Act of 1906* to sequester 56 million acres of Alaskan land as national monuments in 1977, the largest designation up to this time. In a candid memorandum about Alaskan environmental issues, Carter acknowledged that his action angered Ronald Reagan, who regarded it as a "land grab" (Carter, 2000). His major land redesignations were included the *Alaskan National Interest Conservation Act of 1980* (ANILCA), signed by the President on December 2, 1980, in the last month of his presidency. It "designated more than 100 million acres of Alaskan land as new or expanded conservation land systems" (Wilta et al, no date).

An action that would have major consequences for environmental decision making was the revision of the merit-based federal government appointment system by the *Civil Service Reform Act of 1978* (CSRA). Carter was accustomed to the "pliant, one-party Georgia legislature" and wanted federal agencies to be more responsive to the President's policies (Manheim, 2023). He replaced the eight-page Pendleton Act and its bipartisan Civil Service Commission with an Act 173 pages in length that created three agencies: the Office of Personnel Management (OPM), the Merit Systems

Protection Board, and the Federal Labor Regulations Authority. The OPM was headed by a presidential appointee, and presidential power was enhanced by a new Senior Executive Service (SES), whose personnel could be assigned by the OPM. The President was also given authority to appoint 10 percent of temporary SES personnel as administrators who would serve under top presidential heads of agencies. Carter could not take full advantage of the new powers because he was defeated in 1980. However, it allowed the subsequent Reagan administration to control key government agencies.

## Reagan: early history and governorship

Ronald Reagan graduated in 1932 from Eureka College, a small Christian college in Illinois. His majors were economics and sociology. He was a mediocre student who participated in football and drama, and showed a gift for leadership. He became president of the student body and participated in a student strike that resulted in the college president's resignation. After a stint as a successful sports broadcaster, Reagan moved to California, where he became a nationally known film actor. He began as a Democrat, regarding Roosevelt as "a true hero." Accordingly: "He worked with the AFL–CIO to fight right-to-work laws ... and spoke out against racism in Hollywood ... Reagan supported Harry S. Truman in the 1948 presidential election, and Helen Gahagan Douglas for the US Senate in 1950" (Wikipedia—Ronald Reagan).

Concerned by communists in the film industry, Reagan moved rightward and supported the presidential campaigns of Dwight D. Eisenhower in 1952 and Nixon in 1960. He registered as a Republican in 1962 and gave an electrifying speech at the Barry Goldwater convention in 1964. The *Washington Post*'s senior commentator, David Broder, called it "the most successful national political debut since William Jennings Bryan in 1896" (Wikipedia—"A Time for Choosing"). With endorsements by Hollywood figures and financial support from the business community, Reagan soundly defeated incumbent Governor Pat Brown and was elected Governor of California in 1966 at a time of growing radical movements, notably the Free Speech Movement at the University of California, Berkeley (see Figure 7.1). He cracked down on university radicalism. He also raised taxes, erasing California's budget deficit (Wikipedia—Ronald Reagan).

Throughout his career, Reagan relied on advisors and appointees to define and execute his policies while he generally maintained cordial relations with political opponents. He appointed Norman Livermore, a former director of the Sierra Club, as Secretary of Resources, and Livermore is credited with advising Reagan on environmental policies as governor (Wikipedia—Ronald Reagan.).

Reagan signed a bill creating the Air Resources Board that consolidated air pollution control agencies in 1967, rejected a highway bill that would split

**Figure 7.1:** Mario Savio addressing a student crowd during the Free Speech Movement at the University of California, Berkeley, 1964

Source: View of students in Sproul Plaza surrounding police car, October 1, 1964. Mario Savio speaking from roof of car, photographer Wilson Lon, October 1, 1964, Free Speech Movement Photographs Collection, 1964–1984, bulk 1964 [UARC PIC 24B:1:3] University Archives, the Bancroft Library, Berkeley Library, University of California, Available from: https://digicoll.lib.berkeley.edu/record/287011?v=uv#?xywh=-378%2C-80%2C2289%2C1582]

the John Muir trail, and supported blocking further oil platform construction in the Santa Barbara Channel, buying back-channel leases. He signed a law creating a three-mile sanctuary around California Channel Islands (Easton, 1972). After his governorship, Reagan initiated an unsuccessful challenge for the Republican nomination for president in 1976 before winning election in 1980.

### *Reagan biographies*

Most biographies on Reagan have focused on his colorful life, persona, and political skills. Only three books (with different political views) have been found to offer treatment of his environmental policies. Reagan tends to be lionized by conservatives for relegitimizing business and profit, the recovery from the economic crisis of the early 1980s, and for leading a countermovement against the pervasive role of government in American society. The conservative Heritage Foundation launched a massive preparatory effort before the Reagan inauguration in 1981. It compiled a list of potential experts for staff positions in the administration and submitted policy proposals for each major agency in its 1,000-page *Mandate for Leadership* (Heatherly and Foundation, 1981). Among liberal critics, a book by Will Bunch (2010) held that Reagan's charisma and articulateness lent support to reactionary trends toward inequality in society and failed to deal with the nation's longstanding racial injustices.

The most detailed chronicler of Reagan's presidency (Cannon, 1991) provided a summary of his legacy in a Miller Center (University of Virginia) series on the US presidency (Cannon, no date):

> In domestic affairs, he set out to revitalize the economy, reduce taxes, balance the federal budget, and reduce the size and scope of the federal government. In foreign affairs, he vowed to rebuild the American military and confront the Soviet Union and its allies with new vigor and purpose. He promised to negotiate with the Soviets from a position of strength. He feared that the accepted national policy of deterring the Soviets through a balance of nuclear terror ("mutual assured destruction") would lead to a nuclear war.

However, Cannon's book contains minimal information on the campaign to roll back environmental regulations in the first Reagan administration. A terse statement about Ann Gorsuch Burford, the first EPA administrator, contrasts with events that take up much of a book authored by Jonathan Lash and co-authors (Lash et al, 1984): "The Environmental Protection Agency under Anne Gorsuch was rocked by charges of political favoritism and mismanagement." Historian and social critic Wallace Stegner described this book in the back-cover summary:

> The record of the Reagan administration on environmental matters is, in one word, appalling—and this book lays it out chapter and verse, without too much partisan rhetoric and with compelling documentation. The book becomes a partisan political document only because the record it reports is so dreadful. [It is] the best evidence of Mr. Reagan's environmental illiteracy.

In his preface to Cannon's book, historian Arthur Schlesinger Jr. notes that Reagan maintained a certain distance even from friends, as well as from his own political actions. This gained him credit for successes, but avoided full responsibility for problems. However, Reagan maintained warm personal relations with Democratic House Speaker Thomas P. ("Tip") O'Neill, despite their ideological differences. On multiple occasions, their relationship led to political compromise. Reagan is credited by both the right and the left for the combination of strength and flexibility that helped destabilize the Soviet Union and end the Cold War.

## The first Reagan administration

President Reagan was committed to deregulation, reduction in the role of government, and tax relief. Ironically, critical support for this quest was supplied by President Carter's CSRA of 1978. Previous presidents appointed agency heads and high officials listed in the Plum Book of positions to be filled by the chief executive. Presidents assigned goals and tasks and committed funding to agencies through proposed budgets, but executing laws and determining agency policies was largely in the hands of career civil service administrators. However, after President Carter's changes, the new OPM, mobile SES administrative staff, and temporary presidential SES appointees provided a layer of presidential designees to work under top officials. The administration's power under the new system was dramatically illustrated in the opening address of Secretary Watt to Interior employees, cited later. The Office of Management and Budget (OMB) was and is a critical office with major influence on all federal programs and expenditures. Lash et al (1984) observed:

> Already in the last years of his Administration, Jimmy Carter had increased OMB's power to keep watch over federal regulatory agencies requirements that made industry spend. He embarked on a campaign to give OMB the same kind of control over agency regulations that it already had over their budgets.

Accordingly, the OMB had a central role in the Reagan administration's policies. The transition team for the incoming administration chose a brilliant young Republican representative from Michigan, David Stockman, for the critical position of director. Despite his youth (34 years), Stockman was equipped with the intellect and zeal to lead the pruning federal agencies and budgets.

Reagan relied on the advice of trusted persons for appointments. One was Colorado beer magnate Joseph Coors, an active supporter of conservative causes, who had supported Reagan's campaign for Governor of California and was a member of Reagan's kitchen cabinet. Following a recommendation by Paul Laxalt, a Republican senator from Nevada, and after initial reservations about a woman serving in this position, Coors supported Ann Gorsuch for EPA administrator. Gorsuch was a former deputy district attorney, corporate counsel, and Colorado representative. She had no federal governmental or environmental experience but had a sharp intellect, brusque manner, and was strongly committed to the President's agenda.

Senator Laxalt, chairman of Reagan's presidential campaign and his closest advisor, recommended James Gaius Watt, a Wyoming native who had served as Deputy Assistant Secretary for Water at the Department of the Interior and Vice-chairman of the Federal Power Commission, as Secretary of the Interior. According to (Arnold, 1982): "Paul Laxalt asked two rewards for his faithful service: 'I want to pick the Secretary of the Interior, and I want to play tennis on the White House courts': The story goes that he got to do both."

## *Reagan's Environmental Protection Agency*

The book by Lash et al (1984) provides quoted passages and most of the other material about the EPA in the first two years of the Reagan administration in this chapter. It is an extraordinarily detailed and candid account, made possible by interviews with many EPA employees. Reagan appointed Rita Lavelle as Assistant Administrator for Solid and Hazardous Waste and Emergency Response at the EPA, a position that also directed the $1.6 billion Superfund program. Lavelle was a former assistant in the Reagan administration in California and made a national name for herself at Aerojet General as a manager responsible for manufactured chemicals, industrial and chemical intermediates, and waste treatment systems for liquid rocket engines. Appointed against Gorsuch's wishes, she would make a different kind of splash in 1982.

The Clean Air Act required the EPA to regulate emissions from 150 million cars, trucks, and buses; over 20,000 factories; and water pollution from 100,000 sources. In 1981, the EPA had 14,500 employees in 20 states and a budget of $1.35 billion. It administered $3.5 billion in construction grant programs (equivalent to $12 billion in 2024), and the Superfund Act added $1.6 billion in waste cleanup funds. Gorsuch's initial proposal in 1981 called for cuts in the EPA budget of 28 percent, 30 percent in the EPA workforce, and 40 percent in research. However, this did not satisfy Stockman's OMB, which demanded cuts of nearly 50 percent. Gorsuch battled back against Stockman in a conflict that was finally settled by President Reagan, resulting in a 29 percent cut in the agency budget, 30 percent in staff, and 42 percent in research. Gorsuch's stated goal was to reduce costs through greater efficiency and reduction of excessive and unnecessary rules:

> Under her direction, EPA had cleaned up backlogs in pesticide registration and emergency use exemptions ... but by 1982 EPA had adopted only one new air pollution standard. It had made no progress in regulating toxic air pollutants or cleaning up hundreds of waste dumps. Enforcement had virtually slowed to a standstill. Over a thousand regulatory actions had been reviewed by OMB [but] virtually all were delayed or simply disappeared. (Lash et al, 1984)

Proposals to reduce the stringency of the Clean Air Act by Michigan representative John Dingell (D) in 1981 and 1982 were "stalled by public opposition and defeated in the House by astute maneuvering by Congressmen Henry Waxman and Timothy Wirth" (Lash et al, 1984). Senator Dingell was a supporter of the Michigan auto industry and opposed excessive stringency in regulations. However, as Chairman of the House Energy and Commerce Subcommittee, with jurisdiction over the EPA, he became concerned about financial irregularities at Superfund and the EPA's failure to enforce the law. His concern was based on agency leaks and evidence brought in an Environmental Defense Fund suit against the EPA. Oversight of the Superfund was the responsibility of Rita Lavelle, who was reported to have had conflicts of interest. In September 1982, Dingell requested that Gorsuch provide documents about hazardous waste and Superfund data, a request that the Department of Justice and President Reagan opposed. Though she was personally willing to supply the documents, Gorsuch refused a subpoena in December of 1982 and was cited for criminal contempt of Congress, the first such citation of an executive agency head.

In February 1983, Gorsuch asked Rita Lavelle to resign. She refused. Intense media attention on EPA activities and a further subpoena to Gorsuch led to her resignation on March 9, 1983. She married Robert Burford, the Director of the Bureau of Land Management (BLM), a month before her resignation.[2] An obituary in 2004 referred to a 1986 book by Gorsuch that contained acerbic comments about the Reagan administration, and the following quip: "The nation's capital is too small to be a state but too large to be an asylum for the mentally deranged" (Sullivan, 2004). Gorsuch was replaced by the respected first EPA administrator, William Ruckelshaus, who moved quickly to restore EPA operations and enforcement to previous levels. In 1987, President Reagan signed the Montreal Protocol against chlorofluorocarbons, which is considered one of the most successful UN environmental initiatives. The treaty phased out use of chlorofluorocarbons (CFCs), a class of halogenated hydrocarbons widely used for refrigeration, air conditioning in automobiles, fire protection and electronics. They had been shown to erode the ozone layer over Antarctica, opening a hole that allowed the transmission of dangerous levels of ultraviolet radiation.

While it was supported by five environmental NGOs, the book by Lash largely avoids polemics, as Stegner indicated.[3] It described Ann Gorsuch as inexperienced in government administration and overcommitted to Reagan's ideological agenda, but also intelligent and able to learn from experience. It cites sympathetic episodes in a turbulent tenure ending with her abrupt resignation. Based on over 400 interviews, the book provides a detailed chronology of chaotic events during the first three years at the EPA and is one of the more balanced and insightful accounts of high-level federal politics known to the author.

Lash's book offers only a discursive, minimally detailed treatment of James G. Watt's controversial tenure as Secretary of the Interior, beginning with a lengthy account of a proposal for oil drilling in the Salt Creek Wilderness area near Roswell, New Mexico. It continues with a history of US land-use law and related developments, followed by a brief history and characterization of James Watt and the Reagan administration's goals of making more land (including wilderness areas) and resources available for development. It criticizes the Watt administration for proposing to limit acquisition of land for new national parks. The next section of this book draws on another detailed exposition of the turbulent first Reagan administration, and my personal experience.

### *James Gaius Watt and the Department of the Interior*

I served in the Department of the Interior during the tenure of James Watt. On Monday, January 26, 1981, an unusual event took place in the Department's auditorium in Washington, D.C. Watt had been confirmed by a Senate clerk five days earlier. That morning he confirmed the President's hiring freeze at the Department, issued a freeze on all but the most essential travel, ordered a review of all existing consulting contracts, appointed longtime confidant Steve Shipley as executive assistant, and sent letters to the governors of all 50 states. He then held introductory meetings with Interior employees. Instead of formal introductions by a senior official, the slight, balding Watt stepped out from a curtain behind the stage to a microphone and addressed the department employees, 700 at a time. After brief introductory comments, he continued in shockingly blunt fashion.

> On November 4, the people of America spoke with great clarity. They called for a dramatic new beginning and a change in our course of government. It will come as no great surprise, I am sure, that I am hereby accepting the resignations of all appointees of the Carter Administration. The fact is that you were terminated on November 4, and I am simply putting the decision of the American people into effect. I expect you be prepared to depart at the end of work today … The changes President Reagan has commanded me to bring to the management of our environment and our resources will be exciting for those of you committed to the multiple use of our lands, for those of you committed to preserving the best values of our natural and cultural heritage … To those of you who do not share this commitment, you will be happier if you seek employment opportunities elsewhere [this was followed by a gasp from the audience]. (Arnold, 1982)

The foregoing quote differs only in minor detail from a film of the speech archived by the US Geological Survey. Watt announced that he would clean house at Interior and place change makers throughout the half-dozen agencies for land use and resource management. No one had ever heard a high official speak like this—totally without circumlocution or bureaucratese. He maintained the same directness whether speaking with a group of geologists or with senators on Capitol Hill (Manheim, 2009).

Watt began expanding leasing of federal land for grazing, lumbering, and mineral extraction. He initiated an inventory of wilderness sites and announced budget cuts of $383 million in Fiscal Year 1981 and $877 million in Fiscal Year 1982 from the Carter administration budget (BIA, 1981) in a speech:

> The economy is in disarray—whether we look at it from the standpoint of inflation, unemployment, productivity, or interest rates. The budget is out of control. President Reagan and I are committed to a fundamental change of course. We have concluded that massive reductions in the budget, together with streamlining of programs and elimination of excessive regulations, are necessary actions to improve the state of the economy.

The most substantive book about James Watt's tenure[4] is a rarely cited authorized biography by Ron Arnold (1933–2022), one of the best-informed critics of the environmental movement[5] (Arnold, 1981; see also Arnold, 1997, 1999, 2010). Arnold founded the Wise Use movement in 1988 to advocate "productive harmony between people and nature." His treatment of the Watt administration resembles Lash's treatment of the EPA in terms of detail and lack of polemics. A drawback is that it was published in 1982 and therefore provides no coverage after April of that year. Besides biographical detail and quotes from hearings for Watt's nomination, Arnold offers history on US land law and related issues, such as the rise of the ecology movement.

A European perspective on political and policy developments in the first Reagan administration is provided by Lees and Turner (1988). It cites a critical book by Brownstein and Easton (1982) describing EPA administrator Ann Gorsuch Burford: "She had no administrative experience in government at any level … but had a reputation for shrewdness … [and] sought to improve administrative efficiency at EPA and implement the deregulation agenda of the administration."

Arnold added details about Watt's proposals. The BLM, the Bureau of Reclamation projects, the National Trust for Historic Preservation, and the US Geological Survey received significant cuts, and Youth Conservation Corps funding was eliminated. Land acquisition funding for the Park Service would be cut by 90 percent, but the Park Service budget for restoration

**Table 7.1:** Results of Department of the Interior achievements in 1981

| | |
|---|---|
| Oil production: 10.1 | Revenue from coal leases: 79.4 |
| Natural gas production: 0.2 | New acreage for National Parks (proposed): -90 |
| Offshore oil and gas acreage leased: 96 | New acreage for National Parks (approved by Congress): -70 |
| Lease revenues: 47.6 | Recovery plans for endangered species: 63.1 |
| Coal acreage leased: 424 | New area for wildlife refuges: 24,000 acres |
| Coal tonnage sold: 275 | |

Note: Data refer to the percentage change from the Carter administration in 1980, except for acreage of wildlife refuges.

Source: Based on Arnold (1982)

and improvement was doubled. Table 7.1 summarizes or recalculates the results of the first year of the Department of the Interior described by Arnold compared to the percentage change from spending in the Carter administration in 1980.

Arnold reported that the time for water project planning was reduced from 17 to seven or eight years, and that for the first time, a reservation Indian was placed in charge of Indian Affairs, under whom 24 Indian schools were rehabilitated. He acknowledged a negative report published by the National Wildlife Federation on April 29, 1982, titled *Marching Backward: The Department of the Interior under James G. Watt.* Subsequent events in the Watt administration are taken from my book (Manheim, 2009).[6]

Watt met his ambitious goals in 1981, and bold initiatives continued in 1982. In January 1982, Watt engineered the divestiture of the US Geological Survey's Conservation Division, which was responsible for the oversight of offshore minerals and oil and gas recovery operations. The USGS was known for its scientific integrity, but not for its promptness and efficiency. Many employees from the Conservation Division were transferred to a new federal agency, the Minerals Management Service (MMS), which became focused and effective. The trade-off was that it lost the USGS's scientific expertise and relied on contractors for external scientific and technical support. Without the USGS's reputation for objective investigation and reporting, the MMS became a policy arm of the government. Critics claimed that the MMS's planning and environmental impact statements would invariably reflect administrative policy.

Watt was aggressive in Western leasing policies for grazing and mining, especially for coal. The FLPMA of 1976 directed the BLM to conduct wilderness reviews as part of its land-use planning. Watt announced an accelerated schedule for completion of wilderness review by 1984, along with budget cuts of 42 percent (Baker, cited in Manheim, 2009). He was equally bold in offshore oil and gas leasing, announcing area-wide lease sales in the Gulf of Mexico, Alaska, and the Atlantic Coast, while reducing management budgets. Area-wide leases were upheld by courts against a multi-organizational suit *Secretary of the Interior v. California*, 1984. Critics called the large tracts "fire sales" and "giveaways" while oil companies defended them. Some independent observers felt that the large tracts allowed more efficient planning similar to systems used in Canada and Norway. A report to Congress by the comptroller of the General Accounting Office (GAO, 1981) found merit in area-wide leasing, but raised eyebrows about Watt's reduced budget.

Watt was instrumental in President Reagan's announcement on March 10, 1983 of an offshore Exclusive Economic Zone to extend 200 miles from the coast. It would include minerals, energy resources, and fisheries, and expanded US jurisdiction to an area equal to three quarters of the US continental land area. It was used to exclude Russian and Polish fishery fleets that had been operating in the Gulf of Maine.

Previous presidential appointees often reported difficulty in effecting change in their agencies. This was obviously not the case with Watt, given his administrative zeal and the tools provided by Carter's CSRA. William Bettenberg, former Director of the Mineral Management Service, stated in an interview (see the Acknowledgments section to this volume) that Watt was the most effective Secretary of the Interior in history. However, "Watt was tone deaf to opposition, concerns, or even questions about his plans and objectives to a degree that can only be explained by his belief that he had a higher calling" (Manheim, 2009). For example, "Watt sent Governor Edmund Brown of California a brusque letter informing him that compromise [oil] leases off California, which had been laboriously negotiated by [previous Interior Secretary] Cecil Andrus with local and legislative leaders and with the Governor, would be restored to their original scope."

When protests emerged at hearings preliminary to land and offshore leasing, Watt simply terminated hearings. These and other actions aroused such wide opposition that Interior employees wore T-shirts showing an upside-down buffalo (the symbol of the agency). Democratic members of Congress lashed back, beginning to insert moratoria for offshore areas into Interior funding bills. After intemperate comments to members of a panel reviewing coal leases created a media firestorm, Watt resigned on November 8, 1983. He was replaced by William Clark and then followed by Donald Hodel, who served out the remainder of the Reagan administration.

Congressional moratoria were eventually extended to virtually all the Exclusive Economic Zones (EEZ) areas around the conterminous US coast, except the central Gulf of Mexico. Perceiving an inability to avoid the moratoria, President George H. W. Bush, who was elected in 1988, incorporated them into an area-wide moratorium proclamation in 1990.[7]

### *Politics: tax cuts and changes in national political relationships*

Led by Speaker Tip O'Neill, the House of Representatives under Reagan was controlled by the Democrats, while the Senate was controlled by the Republicans, led by Majority Leader Howard Baker. Urgent measures were needed to deal with stagflation that reached peak interest rates of 18 percent in October 1981. The Reagan administration's top priority was tax reduction, and on August 14, 1981, Congress approved the *Economic Tax Reduction Act of 1981* (Kemp-Roth Act), which cut the top marginal tax rate from 70 to 50 percent, the largest cut in history. President Reagan's gallant humor after a near-fatal assassin's bullet on March 30, 1981[8] was met with a wave of national sympathy that helped pass the bill.

Sponsored in part by two Democratic leaders, Representative Richard Gephardt of Missouri and Senator Bill Bradley of New Jersey, the *Tax Reform Act of 1986* further cut the top federal income tax rates from 50 percent to 28 percent, while the bottom rate was raised from 11 percent to 15 percent. The capital gains tax was raised from 20 percent to 28 percent. The top rate was subsequently increased to 32 percent in the Bush administration and to 38 percent in the Clinton administration, which achieved the last balanced federal budget in 2000. The Reagan tax cuts resulted in a decline in federal revenue of 9 percent, while supposed compensatory cuts in federal spending never happened (Wessel, 2007). This resulted in a doubling of the federal debt from $980 billion to $2 trillion during the Reagan administration.

It was noted in Chapter 6 that the early environmental laws had overwhelming bipartisan support. Even the environmentally zealous Sierra Club accepted offshore lease sales after careful scrutiny and hard bargaining. An example was the "Position adopted by the Sierra Club Board of Directors, 1975: The Sierra Club believes that no offshore petroleum exploration should occur unless and until the following conditions are met" (website cited in Manheim [2009] and no longer available). Subsequently, however, the Sierra Club came to categorically oppose all new offshore leasing. Michael Scott of the Wilderness Society stated that up to the Watt administration, "conservation had been a bipartisan policy going back to the time of Theodore Roosevelt. Watt made it a partisan issue and the Democrats see the advantage of it being a partisan issue" (Scott, 1983).

In summary, the environmental management system enacted by bipartisan framers in the 1970s, along with the Supreme Court decisions that increased the breadth of application of the laws, led to economic decline. Efforts to revive the economy in the first Reagan administration overreacted against regulations. This in turn led to a counter-response by Congress. Contention over environmental regulatory policy and governmental operations was recognized by the subsequent Presidents Bush and Carter, and reforms movements are described Chapter 8.

# 8

# Global Climate Change: George H. W. Bush to Bill Clinton-Al Gore

## Global climate change

Carbon dioxide emissions took on special prominence with Congressional testimony by James Hansen, Director of the NASA Goddard Institute for Space Studies, on June 23, 1988. Hansen and coworkers had published a series of papers modelling global climate trends, for example (Hansen et al, 1988). He reported that he was 99 percent certain that global warming was occurring and that greenhouse gas effects were the primary cause.[1] As a more recent summary by the McKinsey Company put it: "In past cases, humanity was merely a 'taker' of change; it is now also its maker" (Trittipo et al, 2023). Hansen's status and blunt statement, without the usual qualifications expected from scientists, was a watershed event. It created awareness in the public, new concern among scientists and environmentalists, and increased research and publications on climate change. The first Intergovernmental Panel on Climate Change (IPCC), sponsored by the World Meteorological Organization and the United Nations Environment Programme, was held that same year. It now has 195 member states who recommend scientists to participate in scientific assessments. The sixth assessment by the IPCC was published in 2021–2023.

Figure 8.1 shows an updated plot of atmospheric temperatures from 1880 to 2023 provided by Dr. Hansen, revealing a systematic rise in temperature since 1970.

Let's go back to the first discovery of the significance of carbon dioxide emissions for global temperature. In 1896, Swedish physical chemist Svante Arrhenius published a paper that would have echoes 100 years later (Wikipedia—Svante Arrhenius). He observed that carbon dioxide ($CO_2$) and water vapor absorbed solar radiation reflected by the Earth. Absorption was mainly in long wavelengths, that is, infrared radiation, and it increased the temperature of the Earth. Aided by estimates of atmospheric

**Figure 8.1:** Atmospheric temperature anomalies, 1880–2023

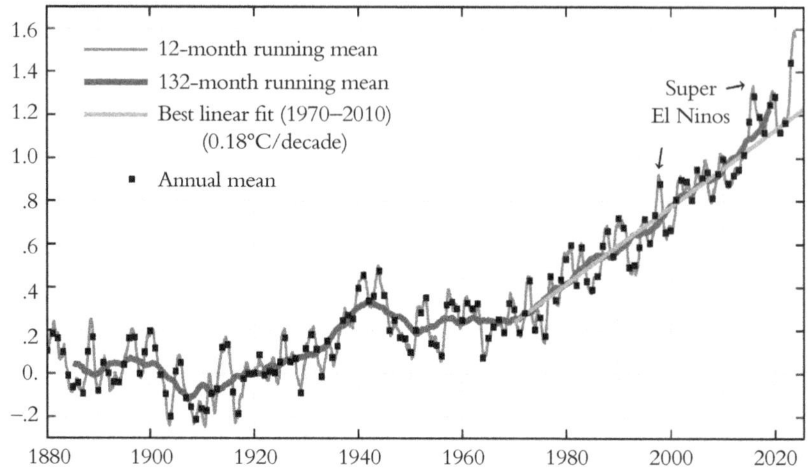


Note: The 132-month running mean differs significantly from the best linear fit in most recent years.

Source: Jim Hansen, Director, Climate Science, Awareness and Solutions Program, Columbia University Earth Institute, January 7, 2025

$CO_2$ concentrations by another Swedish scientist, A. G. Högbom (1894), Arrhenius calculated that a doubling or tripling of $CO_2$ could raise the temperature of the Earth by 5–10°C, which was in rough agreement with an estimated global temperature of 8 –9°C higher than the present in Tertiary time, when rock strata revealed that tropical plants and animals existed in the Arctic. Conversely, reduction in $CO_2$ by a factor of 0.5 to 0.6 of present levels would lead to a new glacial period. In short, atmospheric $CO_2$ was the primary factor controlling Earth's temperature. Without the blanket of greenhouse gases, subsequently shown to include methane (11–18 percent), nitrous oxide (4 percent), and fluorocarbons (2 percent) in proportion to their role in warming, the Earth's surface temperature would be about -19°C (Wright, 2005).

Climate scientist Charles Keeling began measuring atmospheric $CO_2$ levels from the top of the Mauna Loa volcano in Hawaii in 1958. His measurements provided the first accurate global averages of atmospheric composition because Mauna Loa is in the mid-Pacific Ocean, far from major industrial emissions, and sampled atmospheric levels. Högbom's early global estimate of 450 ppm $CO_2$ had been too high because sampling sites in his time were influenced by industrial emissions. Precise measurements showed that small decreases in $CO_2$ concentration occurred each year in summer when terrestrial plants absorbed $CO_2$. These were followed by increases in winter, when vegetation decayed. Continuing observations show that $CO_2$

**Figure 8.2:** Carbon dioxide emissions by source since 1880

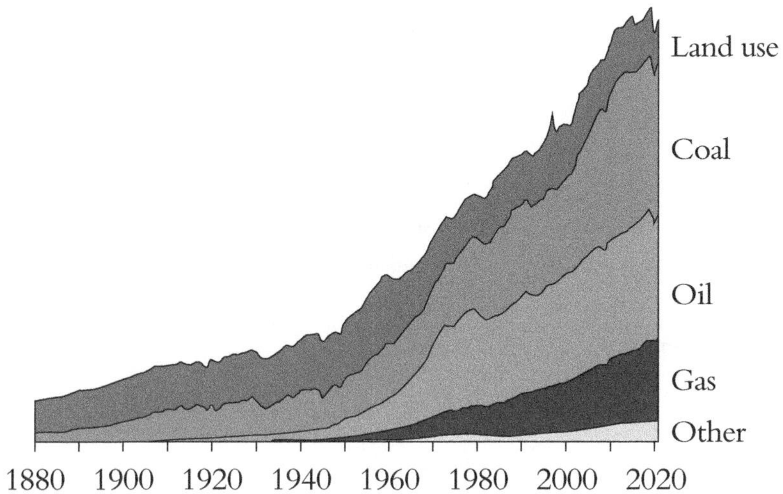


Source: Wikipedia—Climate Change

concentrations have risen from 315 parts per million (ppm) in 1958 to 424 ppm in November 2024 (NOAA, 2024), the highest in recorded history. Temperatures reached 1.48°C warmer than at the onset of the Industrial Revolution in 1800.

Figure 8.2 shows that while land sources of emissions have remained roughly constant, the overwhelming proportion of $CO_2$ emissions have come from the combustion of fossil fuels. These data are from a comprehensive summary of climate change (Wikipedia—Climate Change) illustrated by dozens of images and documented by 429 references. Additional sources of $CO_2$ emissions are from cement and aluminum production and steel smelting. Methane emissions come from livestock, manure, rice cultivation, landfills, wastewater, coal mining, oil and gas extraction, and melting of permafrost. Coal use, the most concentrated source of energy, surged in the 1970s around the time of the first Arab oil embargo. The article states that by 2019, concentrations of $CO_2$ and methane had increased 48 percent and 160 percent, respectively, since 1750: "$CO_2$ levels are higher than they have been at any time during the last 2 million years. Concentrations of methane are far higher than they were over the last 800,000 years."

Global warming is most pronounced in the polar regions, air temperature having increased an average of 0.25°C per decade in the Arctic since 1940. It is the lowest in equatorial regions. Warming tends to promote extremes in environmental conditions. It increases drought in dry areas like the Sahel and the US Southwest, while in wetter areas, higher moisture levels in air promotes increased rainfall and episodic flooding. Warming may expand

**Table 8.1:** Ranked asset risk of sea-level rise for low-lying cities

| Rank | Country | Urban area | Assets ($billion) |
|---|---|---|---|
| 1 | US | Miami | 416.29 |
| 2 | US | New York-Newark | 320.2 |
| 3 | US | New Orleans | 233.69 |
| 4 | Japan | Osaka-Kobe | 215.62 |
| 5 | Japan | Tokyo | 174.29 |
| 6 | The Netherlands | Amsterdam | 128.33 |
| 7 | The Netherlands | Rotterdam | 114.89 |
| 8 | Japan | Nagoya | 109.22 |
| 9 | US | Virginia Beach | 84.64 |
| 10 | China | Guangzhou | 84.17 |
| 11 | China | Shanghai | 72.86 |
| 12 | India | Mumbai | 46.2 |
| 13 | Thailand | Bangkok | 38.72 |
| 14 | China | Hong Kong | 35.94 |
| 15 | India | Kolkata (Calcutta) | 31.99 |

Source: Nicholls et al (2007), OECD publication

forest growth and agriculture in high-latitude areas, but dire outcomes are predicted for the ultimate consequences of warming in a book by Jeff Goodell (Goodell, 2023). Of immediate concern for human populations is the rise in sea level of 104 mm since 1993, roughly 2.8 mm per year (NASA, 2023), due to melting of glaciers and ice caps in Greenland and Antarctica, compounded by thermal expansion of sea water. A ranking of major coastal cities in terms of financial risk as a result of sea level rise is provided in Table 8.1. A number of low-lying island nations are at more existential risk (Gebhardt, 2023).

The foregoing discussion offers a brief sample of the complex issues associated with global climate change. They are of sufficient gravity that 195 nations committed themselves to limit greenhouse gas emissions in the Paris Agreement of December 12, 2015. However, beyond a small but well-published group of contrarian scientists (Chapter 11), a countermovement against reduction of $CO_2$ emissions is currently led by the $CO_2$ Coalition, now headed by Gregory Wrightstone (Wrightstone, 2023), which holds that $CO_2$ increase is beneficial, noting its stimulation of plant growth. Wrightstone's arguments can be nontrivial and persuasive with conservatively oriented American political leaders.

## Problems in arguing the climate change issue

In the US, the vast increase in publications that followed the testimony of James Hansen ranged from formal publications in scientific and policy media to trade journals and popular books and articles. However, an old adage may apply: "There are two ways to be badly informed: to not have enough information, or to have too much." A query on the key phrase "global climate change" in Google Scholar and Google returned 2.45 million and 1.24 billion titles, respectively. A book by George Marshall, a leading British expert on climate change communication, cited numerous pitfalls involved in efforts to promote support for climate-friendly policies (Marshall, 2014). The US has experienced especially intense efforts by both government since the Obama administration, and nongovernmental organizations (NGOs) to promote information and actions against greenhouse gas emissions. However, a striking example of problems in communication referred to by Marshall (2014) is provided by the career of Al Gore, which will be described in a later section.

### *The George H. W. Bush presidency*

The administrations of George H. W. Bush and Bill Clinton were described as a time for "refinement, recoil, and rejuvenation of environmental regulations" in a leading textbook of environmental law (Percival et al, 2000). In the election campaign of 1988, former Vice President Bush sought to dissociate himself from the dissension over environmental policy that had grown during the Reagan administration, claiming that he would be "the environmental president" and make reauthorization of the Clean Air Act a major priority. In his campaign for the 1980 election, he had famously criticized Reagan's tax cut proposals as "voodoo economics," but moved in conservative directions once he accepted the role of vice president in the Reagan administrations. In the 1988 campaign, he made another memorable statement, ending a pledge to not raise taxes with the quote: "Read my lips. No new taxes." However, rising inflation fueled by the huge tax cuts in the Reagan administration forced him to violate that pledge.

Foreign relations were Bush's greatest strength. He had sought an end to the Cold War in negotiations with Soviet leader Mikhael Gorbachev and supported the reunion of East and West Germany after the fall of the Soviet Union. He pursued arms reduction, better relations with China, and worked for a reduction of tensions in the Middle East. When Iraqi leader Saddam Hussein invaded Kuwait in 1990, Bush, aided by Secretary of State James Baker, mobilized an international force and quickly defeated Hussein, but refrained from deposing him or controlling Iraq. His performance gained Bush a public approval rating of 89 percent, then the highest on record.

"Bush surprised almost everyone by actively soliciting environmentalists' advice and appointing a number of environmental leaders to his administration" (Kraft, 1997). He appointed William Reilly, President of the World Wildlife Fund, as EPA administrator and Michael DeLand, formerly EPA director for New England, as chairman of the Council on Environmental Quality. However, he appointed a conservative former Congressman from New Mexico, Manuel Lujan, Jr. as Secretary of the Interior, indicating that Western land policies would not see major change.

Bush's greatest contribution was supporting market-based solutions to environmental pollution in the *Clean Air Act Amendments of 1990*, one of the last 1970s laws to be updated. The legislation was initially contested by both environmental organizations and industry. But active support by Bush, along with contributions by Senate Majority Leader George Mitchell, EPA administrator Reilly; Paul Portney, President of Resources for the Future (a leading think tank), and Fred Krupp, President of the Environmental Defense Fund, facilitated the passage of the Act. Its three most important features were a new approach to removal of sulfur dioxide discharged by coal-fired power plants, a reduction in air pollution in 80 urban areas not meeting 1977 air quality standards, and lower concentrations of some 200 toxic airborne chemicals (Vig and Kraft, 1997). Krupp's contribution was a system of marketable pollution allowances for sulfur dioxide emissions. It was wildly successful, reducing the cost of pollution reduction by 80 percent over conventional command and control systems. The system was later adopted for $CO_2$ emissions by the European Union (Manheim, 2009).

In 1990, Bush consolidated offshore drilling moratoria that had been passed by Congress in response to James Watt's aggressive offshore oil and gas leasing. His executive order covered 85 percent of the US Exclusive Economic Zone (EEZ) for the lower 48 states. The Sierra Club's rise in membership, which tripled during the first Reagan administration, stopped after Bush's actions (see Table 8.2). The Sierra Club has been a leader among some 270 US environmental and conservation organizations. Other environmental organizations with aggressive litigation policies include Friends of the Earth, the Natural Resource Defense Council, Friends of the Earth, and the Center for Biological Diversity, which currently claims 1.7 million members and online activists.

Bush's tenure ended with a mixed record on environmental issues. He was excoriated for refusing to support the international movement to reduce carbon dioxide emissions, calling for more research. His Domestic Policy Council, chaired by Allen Bromley, proposed revisions for the definitions of wetlands that would have removed half from federal jurisdiction. However, a

**Table 8.2:** Membership of major US environmental organizations (in thousands)

| Organization | 1971 | 1981 | 1992 | 1997 | 2004 |
|---|---|---|---|---|---|
| Sierra Club (1892) | 124 | 246 | 615 | 569 | 736 |
| National Audubon Society (1905) | 115 | 400 | 600 | 550 | 550 |
| National Parks Conservation Association (1919) | 49 | 27 | 230 | 375 | 375 |
| Izaak Walton League (1922) | 54 | 48 | 51 | 42 | 45 |
| Wilderness Society (1935) | 62 | 52 | 365 | 237 | 225 |
| National Wildlife Federation (1936) | 540 | 818 | 997 | 650 | 650 |
| Defenders of Wildlife (1947) | 13 | 50 | 77 | 215 | 463 |
| The Nature Conservancy (1951) | 22 | 80 | 545 | 865 | 972 |
| WWF-US (1961) | n.a. | n.a. | 970 | 1,200 | 1,200 |
| Environmental Defense Fund (1967) | 20 | 46 | 175 | 300 | 350 |
| Friends of the Earth (US) (1969) | 7 | 25 | 30 | 20 | 35 |
| Natural Resources Defense Council (1970) | 5 | 40 | 170 | 260 | 450 |
| Greenpeace USA (1975) | n.a. | n.a. | 2,225 | 400 | 250 |

Source: Wikipedia—Environmental Movement in the United States

memorial for Bush by Fred Krupp, President of the Environmental Defense Fund, praised his leadership for the Clean Air Act Amendments, which led to an 88 percent decline in sulfur dioxide emissions and stopped acid rain. A memorial from the Environmental and Energy Study Institute cited Bush's signing of the *Energy Policy Act of 1992*, which promoted energy efficiency and encouraged incentives for alternative fuels, including ethanol, hydrogen, electricity and biodiesel (LaPorte, 2018).

*The End of Nature*, an influential environmental book, was published by Bill McKibben during the George H. W. Bush administration (McKibben, 1989). It was the first in-depth book on climate change written for laypersons and became an international bestseller, translated into 24 languages. Born in 1960, McKibben attended Harvard University, where he became the editor and president of *The Harvard Crimson*. After graduation in 1982, McKibben worked as a writer for *New Yorker Magazine*. Reacting against the libertarianism of the Reagan administration, McKibben turned down a job offer from the *New York Times* and committed himself to writing on the environment and nonviolence.

In 2007, McKibben cofounded 350.org to organize international public opinion on behalf of the campaign against climate change. The name "350" evokes James Hansen's earlier statement that 350 parts per million $CO_2$ in the atmosphere would be unsafe. McKibben is the author of a dozen books and a recipient of the Gandhi Peace award in

2013. A professor at Middlebury College, McKibben's style is informed, but uniquely down to earth and compelling. He was appointed to the Democratic Party platform drafting committee by candidate Bernie Sanders in 2016. While McKibben has been unrelenting in opposition to the fossil fuel industry, characterizing it as "a rogue industry, reckless as no other force on earth" (Nisbet, 2014), he normally avoided confrontational language in his writings, a style that increased his influence beyond the environmental movement.

### *The Clinton-Gore administration*

The environmental revolution of the 1970s created a complex environmental regulatory framework. It made major progress against pollution and environmental hazards, but also had adverse impacts on the economy and business. The first Reagan administration's attempt to roll back enforcement had overreacted and failed. The EPA's enforcement was restored by the end of the second administration. However, the efficiency of the system was problematic, as indicated by a quote in a leading environmental policy textbook: "After more than thirty years, efforts by federal, state, and local governments to eliminate air and water pollution ... air and water remained seriously polluted" (Rosenbaum, 2007).

Recognizing that governmental procedures were cumbersome and inefficient, and that legal battles impeded progress (Kagan 2001), the William Jefferson (Bill) Clinton administration (1992–2000) placed Vice President Al Gore in charge of the Reinventing Government initiative. Its name was taken from the title of a book (Osborne and Gabler, 1992), and the project's goal was to make government "more effective, efficient, and user friendly" (Nakamura and Church, 2003).

Based on studies over a decade, the latter authors cited the *Comprehensive Environmental Response, Compensation and Liability Act of 1980* (CERCLA), or Superfund Act, as problematic. It was "one of the most expensive and controversial environmental programs in history ... it consumes a substantial portion of the entire staff and financial resources of EPA." A major problem with Superfund was that to clean up hazardous waste sites, it assigned liability to businesses and state and local governments with relationships to waste sites even though their relationship might have been only minor. The authors described Superfund as representing regulation "in its most unpalatable and politically vulnerable form ... roundly criticized for lengthy delays, high costs, and limited accomplishments."

In 1995, after Republicans captured both houses of Congress in the election of 1994, EPA administrator Carol Browner announced the Reinventing EPA project. This was a key element of the Clinton-Gore initiative because the EPA dominated government environmental regulations. Addressing the EPA's negative image with the business community, its goal was to "transform the fundamental legal and political character of its regulatory programs" (Rosenbaum, 2007). CERCLA and other relevant statutes had no provisions to balance risk and cost, and in the EPA's early years, zealous officials also showed scant interest in the concerns of business. Court decisions relating to NEPA and the CAA had excluded economic factors from environmental enforcement. Now, however, tradeoffs and reducing cleanup and administrative costs came to the fore. Legislative remedies failed in 1994 (Nakamura and Church, 2003), but high-level administrators took risks in introducing major changes in the EPA's operating policies. The agency began to talk with its clients and show interest in their concerns. No legislative reforms were enacted, but administrative reforms improved the agency's public image and efficiency.

Clinton's Secretary of the Interior Bruce Babbitt, a former Arizona governor and head of the League of Conservation Voters, reversed earlier land-use policies of James Watt. He supported protection of endangered species and biodiversity, created a National Landscape Conservation System managed by the Bureau of Land Management, and instituted large, "consensus-based" environmental restoration projects. He attempted to increase fees for grazing rights on public lands, but was blocked by Western states' legislative delegations.

The official White House biography of the Clinton administration cites among its positive achievements low unemployment and inflation and reduced crime rates. After signing a law raising top personal income tax rates to their present level, Clinton proposed the first balanced budget in decades and achieved a budget surplus. He called for a national initiative to end racial discrimination as a part of the celebration of the millennium in 2000. The White House biography (Anonymous, no date) acknowledges that the administration's health initiative failed and that:

> as a result of issues surrounding personal indiscretions with a young woman White House intern, Clinton was the second US president to be impeached by the House of Representatives. He was tried in the Senate and found not guilty of the charges brought against him. He apologized to the nation for his actions and continued to have unprecedented popular approval ratings for his job as president.

In 1994, Republicans gained a historic victory in the House based on their "Contract with America," a sweeping proposal of eight principles and ten bills promised to be initiated by the Republican Party if it gained control of Congress. As reviewed by veteran journalist James Fallows (1994), some of the proposals were overdue, like stopping Congress's practice of imposing unfunded mandates on the states, creating a "loser pays" rule for lawsuits, and a line-item veto for the president. However, other parts of the plan offered unrealistic measures. Nevertheless, its boldness helped Republicans win both houses of Congress, with Newt Gingrich becoming Speaker of the House of Representatives. Gingrich, who had a PhD in history and was known for his flamboyant ideas, was a leader in the initiative.

Fallows noted that the bills offered grandiose visions, but few details about implementation, and Republicans often failed to consider the views of their Democratic counterparts. Examples of Republican bills related to environmental regulatory reform are as follows:

- H.R. 46: To delay for two years [the] implementation date for enhanced vehicle inspection and maintenance under the Clean Air Act.
- H.R. 603: To authorize States to regulate certain solid waste.
- H.R. 1080: To authorize States to control movement of municipal solid wastes generated in their jurisdictions.

The problem was that bills proposing environmental regulatory reform could be so poorly drafted that they failed to get out of committee. Others were passed in the House but defeated in the Senate or vetoed by President Clinton. A single regulatory bill, Unfunded Federal Mandates 1995, became law. The Republican Contract with America had the goal of improving the performance of Congress, but it failed because the framers did not communicate with Congressional Democrats, who would have to live with the reforms.

The Clinton administration's Reinvention of Government initiative recognized that the existing regulatory system was focused on controls, but not on efficiency and the impacts of controls on business and the public at large. As noted earlier, a poster child for the problem was the Superfund law, which sought to pay for the cleanup of contaminated sites by targeting any linked entity, regardless of its degree of responsibility. It spent more on litigation and administration than on cleanup, which created animosity and ill will for the EPA (Nakamura and Church, 2003). While the reinvention project did not result in reform legislation, it brought about major changes in the way in which the EPA and other regulatory agencies interacted with business and the public.

Major regulatory reform proposals emerged as a part of the National Performance Review effort. These included bills for large-scale government reorganization in 1995 and 1996; however, they were not approved. This was the last major opportunity to reduce antagonism over the regulatory system and associated gridlock in Congress. The failure was particularly unfortunate because reforms could have avoided gridlock in Congress and reduced antagonism over regulatory policies, both of which were factors that accentuated subsequent political polarization. Though the current political climate is not conducive to consensual and lasting Congressional reforms, pathways to future reform are discussed in Chapter 13.

### *The tragic legacy of a gifted political and environmental leader: Al Gore*

Al Gore came from a prominent political family, his father serving as a Democratic senator from Tennessee. At Harvard College, Gore did not major in science, but his interest in the environment and global climate change was sparked by a class with Roger Revelle, an internationally known ocean scientist and expert on global warming (Wikipedia—Al Gore) After military service, a stint as a reporter with the *Nashville Tennessean*, and law studies at Vanderbilt University, a Tennessee Congressional seat that Gore's father once held open up. Gore left his law studies without completing his degree and won the election, becoming a Congressional representative aged 28. He won re-elections easily, maintained interest in science and technology, and supported the development of the internet. In the election of 1984, he won the Tennessee Senate seat formerly held by Republican Howard Baker.

James Hansen's testimony in 1988 fired Gore's interest in climate change. His book *Earth in the Balance* (Gore, 1992) was the first by a US politician to become a *New York Times* bestseller since John F. Kennedy's *Profiles in Courage* (Kennedy, 1956). It was written in popular style, but was full of information on climate change and its global impacts. It revealed an informed and creative intellect that would have gained prominence had Gore pursued a career in science. Gore expressed strong opinions, but leaned toward moderation in politics and also in environmental issues—for example, he described the deep ecology movement pioneered by Norwegian ecologist Arne Naess, as "dangerously wrong."

Given this background, a surprising feature in Gore's book was attacks on President George H. W. Bush and the Republicans. In the introduction, Gore quotes a speech by presidential candidate Bush saying that he would "confront the greenhouse effect with the White House effect." Gore followed with: "It was, as we now know, an empty promise." He gave qualified credit to Bush for supporting an update of the Clean Air Act, but other references to the president's or Republican policies are critical.

The problem with mixing partisan politics in a serious book on environmental issues was that it lost scientific credibility and stoked political hostility. Tensions between Democrats and Republicans had risen during the first Reagan administration, but Republican support was needed to pass bipartisan legislation. Irrespective of their potential validity, Gore's political barbs were counterproductive. A potential explanation may lie in his service in Congress from 1977 to 1985. As described in the previous chapter, the former bipartisan consensus on environmental policy was replaced by partisan polarization by the Reagan administration's campaign to roll back enforcement of environmental regulations. Gore may have been influenced by the partisan atmosphere of that time, with Congressional backlash and the resulting resignations of Gorsuch and Watt.

In the same year as the publication of Gore's book, Clinton and Gore defeated President Bush in the election of 1992. They won re-election in 1996, although the Republicans took control of both houses of Congress in 1994. Though exceptionally qualified as the Democratic candidate for the presidency in 2000—a former Representative, Senator, sitting Vice President, and with expertise in government reform and environmental policy, Gore was defeated by George W. Bush in a highly disputed election. After losing his bid, Gore devoted his full energy to the climate issue. His film *An Inconvenient Truth* (Remnick, 2006) dramatized the risk of warming to the planet. Released in 2006, it gained wide attention and was described in a *New Yorker* review as a "brilliantly lucid, often riveting attempt to warn Americans off our hellbent path to global suicide" (Remnick, 2006). Gore received two Academy Awards for his documentary as well as the Nobel Peace Prize in 2007, sharing it with the Intergovernmental Panel on Climate Change.

In his passionate commitment to the climate issue, Gore is again suggested to have made an underrecognized error by doubling down on politics in his film and book. His title, *An Inconvenient Truth*, is barbed. Given the dire consequences he described for the planet, it is not hard to identify Republicans and business leaders as those who found his truths inconvenient. His criticisms of the Exxon-Mobil Company, the American Petroleum Institute, President George W. Bush, skeptical scientists, and media that gave too much exposure to controversy over climate change disregarded long-accepted principles for effective communication, first expounded on in Aristotle's treatise *On Rhetoric* (Aristotle 332 BCE). Dale Carnegie's bestselling *How to Make Friends and Influence People* (Carnegie, 1936) offered telling examples that attacking or confronting people creates hostility. It was also arguably not useful to stoke passion among his partisans in ways that could promote radicalism.

I had experience with the negative impact Gore's film had on Republican congressmen needed for bipartisan legislation. While attending a public conference at the House of Representatives in 2007, I fell into conversation with an official from the Interior Solicitor's Office, on loan to the House Natural Resources Committee. The official described a meeting of Republican members of the Committee where the new Gore film was discussed. They agreed unanimously that they would not watch it.

In contrast, Ronald Reagan's amicable relations with political opponents gained him legislative success, despite a House of Representatives dominated by the Democratic Party. In at least one case, which is described in Chapter 12, Democratic cooperation is interpreted to have led to undesirable developments, but it illustrates the power of positive human relations.

A Wikipedia article on *An Inconvenient Truth* cited moderate Republican senator Lamar Alexander's polite assessment: "Because (Gore) was a former vice president and presidential nominee, he brings a lot of visibility to the issue. On the other hand, it may be seen as political by some, and they may be less eager it to be a part of it." Polling by the Gallup organization shows that an equal number of Democratic and Republican respondents expressed concern about climate change in 1998, but after 2000, opinion on the question diverged (Dunlap and McCright, 2008).

9

# George W. Bush and Barack Obama

## The George W. Bush Administration

*The power of election strategy*

George W. Bush defeated Vice President Al Gore for the presidency in the bitterly contested election of 2000. He lost the popular vote, but a 5-4 decision of the US Supreme Court halted the recount of the close Florida vote, letting Bush win the state, and thereby the election, by a margin of only 547 votes. The election campaign highlighted an outcome of the electronic revolution in the 1970s. Al Gore had unusually strong qualifications: experience as a Congressional Representative, Senator, and sitting vice president of the US. He was the author of a bestselling book on global climate. Bush's political experience was a single term and re-election as Governor of Texas. In his favor was the family name, personal charisma, and one of the most successful campaign managers in America, Karl Rove, who had an overwhelming record of victories in campaigns in which he had the leading role (Wikipedia—Karl Rove). In short, the Bush victory illustrated the critical importance of campaign strategy in the era of instant electronic communications reaching millions of voters.

Traditional assets for presidential candidates were political experience, name recognition, ability to articulate issues, and party support, However, a review of presidential elections from 1976 to the present found that the critical factor in nearly all successful campaigns was superior campaign strategy, usually led by campaign managers or advisors (Manheim, 2023b). Innovative campaign managers like Hamilton Jordan, James Carville, Lee Atwater, Karl Rove, and David Axelrod brought victory to their candidates against individuals with superior qualifications.

A reason behind the new trend beside changes brought by the electronic era included the decline of public interest in and knowledge of public affairs, underscored by the Annenberg Public Policy Center surveys of

American voters. One poll revealed that only one American in four could name the three branches of the federal government (Annenberg, 2017). Newspaper readership and audiences for TV news, formerly mainstays of public information declined (Lipka and Shearer, 2023). In the increased competition for audience, the media tended to focus on human-interest stories and on sensational or instant-interest news instead of in-depth journalism. Public opinion on political candidates became increasingly volatile. The new conditions made political campaigns increasingly complex and expensive. Campaign success was achieved by campaign managers with insight into public psychology and who made effective use of public polling. A corollary for success in campaigns was candidates' willingness to accept independent advisors whose strategies might not agree with candidates' preferences.

### *Bush's background, campaign, and administration*

After early education at the elite Phillips Academy and then Yale University, Bush served in the Texas Air National Guard. Though he had a mediocre scholastic record, he gained an MBA from the Harvard Business School before becoming active in the oil industry in Texas. He lost a campaign for Congress in 1978 and struggled with alcoholism. Influenced by Billy Graham, his recovery was assisted by Christian conversion. Bush moved to Washington in 1988 to work on the presidential campaign of his father George H. W. Bush's unsuccessful 1992 presidential campaign (Wikipedia—George W. Bush).[1] Bush's assets included his gregarious and friendly persona, a modest demeanor, but strong personal confidence.

Under the campaign guidance of Karl Rove and Karen Hughes, Bush won the Texas governorship against popular Democratic governor Ann Richards in 1994. Bush's environmental record as governor was mixed. Texas ranked near the bottom of states in environmental ratings, but Bush signed a law requiring electric power companies to buy energy from renewable sources. This and Texas's high-wind energy expanses helped it become the leading producer of wind energy in the US. Bush's push for Texas's largest tax cut in history and support for an increase in teacher salaries helped him gain a landslide reelection in 1998.

Guided by Karl Rove, Bush became a contender for the Republican nomination for president in 2000. His major opponent, Senator John McCain, had a heroic war record and was noted for ethics and candor. While McCain's politics were conservative, he was labeled a maverick by the media for his willingness to depart from his party's voting patterns and cooperate with Democrats. In a memorial on his death in 2018, Environmental Defense Fund President Fred Krupp lauded McCain as being the most vocal Republican on climate change: "Along with his friend, Democratic Sen. Joe

Lieberman, McCain sponsored the *Climate Stewardship Act* in 2003, which would have capped US carbon-dioxide emissions at the 2000 level" (Krupp, 2018). McCain's campaign, with its emphasis on political reform, proved to be no match for Rove's campaign wizardry. To counter the McCain record for bipartisanship, Rove coined the campaign slogan "reformer with results." He emphasized grassroots campaigning and town meetings that exploited Bush's persona.

Rove recognized the importance of a unifying theme in campaigns. For Bush's campaign against Al Gore, Rove adopted the slogan "compassionate conservatism." The Bush campaign had included a commitment to reduce greenhouse gas emissions and Bush was said to have favored William Danforth, a moderate Republican and ordained Episcopal priest, as vice president. However, Richard Cheney, former president of the Halliburton Company, a leading oilfield supplier, was ultimately given the office and, after Bush's election, assumed a leading policy role. The commitment to reducing greenhouse gases was quickly abandoned, and a subsequent task force meeting on energy policy was limited to participants chosen by Cheney. Halliburton later gained a huge sole-source federal contract for logistical support in Iraq.

A Wikipedia article focused on the Bush administration environmental record (Wikipedia—Climate Change Policy of the George W. Bush Administration) reported that he refused to implement the international Kyoto Protocol on reducing greenhouse gas emissions, but provided tax credits to businesses that used renewable energies. Government science reports about climate change were edited and pressure was exerted on scientists to modify writings relating to climate change. Climate scientist James E. Hansen, director of NASA's Goddard Institute for Space Studies, claimed in a widely cited *New York Times* article that his superiors at the agency were trying to silence him (Revkin, 2006): "To head up the council [Council on Environmental Quality (CEQ)], Cheney installed James Connaughton, a former lobbyist for industrial polluters, who once worked to help General Electric and ARCO skirt responsibility for their Superfund waste sites."

I was a scientist in the Department of the Interior during the period in question. While I do not endorse the polemics in *The Republican War on Science* (Mooney, 2006), my experience confirms critical material in it. Bush's first EPA administrator, Christine Todd Whitman, was respected, but resigned after disagreements with the administration. She was replaced by Michael Leavitt and Stephen Johnson. Bush's public approval ratings had extreme variation. Following his response to the 9/11 terrorist attack, Bush enjoyed the highest presidential ratings in recorded history, but he also had the lowest ratings as a consequence of the 2007–2008 financial crisis. The Bush administration's reputation further suffered for initiating a war against

Iraq's Saddam Hussein on the wrong assumption that he had weapons of mass destruction. Bush's positive achievements included his cooperation with Senator Ted Kennedy to pass an education reform bill, the *No Child Left Behind Act of 2002* and initiating the President's Emergency Plan for AIDS Relief in Africa in 2003.

## The Barack H. Obama administration

### *Obama's background*

Barack Obama was born in Hawaii, the son of a White mother and a Black father from Kenya. He moved with his mother's second husband to Indonesia and returned to Hawaii in 1971. After further schooling in Los Angeles, Obama transferred to Columbia University and graduated with a degree in political science. He worked as a community organizer in Chicago before entering Harvard Law School, where he became the first African-American editor of the Harvard law journal. Returning to Chicago, he taught constitutional law at the University of Chicago Law School before being elected to the Illinois Senate in 1996. With the aid of advisor David Axelrod, Obama won election as US senator from Illinois in 2004.

As Ronald Reagan had done in the Republican Convention in 1964, Obama drew national attention with a speech at the Democratic National Convention in 2004—and again when he won an Illinois Senate seat in the same year. A powerful speaker, he was asked by the Democratic Party to speak at campaign events, where he drew enthusiastic crowds, and the question of higher office was increasingly raised. He left the Senate before the end of his term to run successfully for president, and his election as the first Black President of the United States was a milestone for the nation. Obama showed unusual leadership capabilities, but his rapid rise to the presidency was also aided by the transformation in American politics referred to previously. His advisors in the 2008 campaign were David Axelrod, architect of his 2004 Senate campaign, and David Plouffe, his campaign manager. The campaign employed thousands of paid staff with major teams in most states (Wikipedia—Barack Obama 2008 Presidential Campaign), and employed innovative database technologies.

### *The Obama presidency*

The University of Virginia's Miller Center website on the American presidents suggested that in his cabinet appointments, Barack Obama adopted a "Team of Rivals" approach, a reference to the award-winning book by Doris Kearns Goodwin, *A Team of Rivals: The Political Genius of Abraham Lincoln* (Goodwin, 2006). Ten years in the writing, it chronicled the presidential campaign leading to Lincoln's election in 1860 and how Lincoln appointed his political rivals to high cabinet positions. Obama nominated his rival for the Democratic nomination, Hillary Rodham Clinton, for Secretary of State and appointed two Republicans: Robert Gates as Secretary of Defense and Ray Lahood as Secretary of Transportation. This was unusual in a polarized time; his immediate predecessors had appointed no opposite party members to cabinet positions.

This gesture to bipartisanship was not just an inspiration from the Goodwin book. Brad Berenson, Obama's classmate at Harvard Law School, observed that conservative classmates later supported Obama's election because "he was more open-minded and would listen to the conservatives, and would value and accept their contributions in a way that some of the other candidates would not" (Shapiro, 2012).

The Obama administration immediately faced the horrific financial crash that had taken place in the last years of the Bush administration. Obama used the Bush administration's $700 billion Troubled Asset and Relief (TARP) initiative to save banks, General Motors, and Chrysler from bankruptcy. Obama also proposed an $800 billion economic stimulus package for the 2008 budget: the *American Recovery and Reinvestment Act* (ARRA), one third of which would involve infrastructure projects. This sector included special emphasis on projects involving renewable energy. However, the Act did not get a single Republican vote in the House of Representatives and only three or four Republican votes in the Senate.

The second edition of Richard Lazarus's treatise *The Making of Environmental Law* (Lazarus, 2023) provided a detailed review of Barack Obama's environmental policies, which I draw on here. It noted that Obama cared more deeply about climate change than any previous president. He was keenly aware that "the US was responsible for the largest share of greenhouse gases that had accumulated in the atmosphere." He understood that only global action could constrain the increase in global warming, and that agreement would be unlikely unless the US made a serious effort to reduce its emissions. His immediate goal, therefore, was national climate legislation, including implementation of a "cap-and-trade program for market exchange of greenhouse gas emission allowances." He appointed a series of established leaders to senior positions in his administration, among whom were John Holdren, a professor of physics at Harvard University and an expert on climate science, Steven Chu, a Nobel Prize-winning biophysicist who became an aggressive and innovative Secretary of Energy, and Jane Lubchenco, head of the National Oceanic and Atmospheric Administration. Marcia McNutt, now President of the National Academy of Science, Engineering, and Medicine, was named Director of the US Geological Survey.

The Democratic Party had large margins of control in both houses of Congress. Leading Republicans like John McCain, who had held hearings to educate Senate colleagues about climate change, Lindsay Graham, and Newt

Gingrich, supported climate legislation. The prospects for new legislation appeared strong, but a new popular movement led by the Tea Party emerged. Favoring lower taxes, reduction of the national debt and federal budget deficit through decreased government spending and governmental controls, it opposed the ARRA budget bill and climate legislation. Its campaign targeted any Congressional members who favored or voted for the bill by supporting opponents in primary elections. The energy legislation passed in the House of Representatives in June 2009, but never reached a vote in the Senate. The Tea Party and associated conservative movements were so successful that in the election of 2010, the Republicans regained control of the House and left the Democrats with a thin margin in the Senate. President Obama acknowledged that the Democrats had gotten a "shellacking."

An important environmental event had earlier taken place on April 10, 2010. Deepwater Horizon, a drilling vessel leased by British Petroleum, had a catastrophic blowout. Eleven crew members were killed and four million barrels of crude oil were dispersed into the Gulf of Mexico. The Minerals Management Service, which had jurisdiction over offshore drilling, was so enmeshed in bureaucratic control that it released no information on the spill for 11 days until it received instructions from Interior Secretary Salazar. Offshore oil production in the Gulf of Mexico was a profitable undertaking for both industry and the federal government. In 2008, federal revenues "had topped $18 billion," some of which was shared with coastal states.

Industry claimed that American companies had a strong safety record for the dangerous technology of offshore drilling in the Gulf, but that British Petroleum had a particularly questionable record in its offshore operations. An important conclusion from the massive reexamination of governmental policy that took place was that governmental agencies responsible for environmental and regulatory safety had to be separated from revenue generation. That had been the case when the US Geological Survey had responsibility for monitoring offshore operations before the transfer of authority to the Minerals Management Service, an independent agency engineered by James Watt in 1982. Another conclusion from the *Macondo* (Deepwater Horizon) event was that low-income, marginalized communities in the Gulf Coast had been disproportionately affected by the spill, which impacted fishing and oyster populations. Service workers in the tourist industry lost jobs, and there were also reports about unfairness in distribution of remedial funds (Osofsky et al, 2012).

Gridlock in Congress and the conservative stance of the Bush administration under the influence of Vice President Cheney had thwarted previous efforts to promote energy legislation. Despairing of Congressional action, environmental organizations in cooperation with the State of Massachusetts succeeded in gaining a 5-4 decision by the Supreme Court in the case of *Massachusetts v. EPA* in 2007, declaring $CO_2$ to be an environmental pollutant. This was a tactic of last resort, given the fact that $CO_2$ was the chief greenhouse gas but also essential for photosynthesis by plants and life on Earth. However, it represented a huge victory for regulation of carbon emissions because it allowed the EPA to control emissions without Congressional approval. This was now a primary means for the Obama administration to control greenhouse gas emissions, with special application to automobile emissions and electrical power plants powered by fossil fuel energy.

The Obama administration's first climate change initiatives were incorporated into the *American Recovery and Reinvestment Act of 2009*: its $90 billion for strategic clean energy and tax incentives made up the largest investments in no-carbon or low-carbon energy in history. They led to major increases in wind and solar power (Obama, 2012; see also the data in Chapter 10).

Another major initiative was EPA's Clean Power Plan, primarily based on the *Clean Air Act*. The plan included more stringent emissions limits on light-duty motor vehicles, including a waiver of the ban on California's still more stringent limits, new efforts to control federal government emissions and promote more efficient energy use, and rules by the EPA and the Department of the Interior to control methane emissions, which involved oil and gas facilities and landfills. The Department of the Interior limited new coal leasing on federal lands and withdrew large areas from oil and gas leasing on the outer continental shelf. The administration denied support for the Dakota Access Pipeline, and President Obama vetoed Congressional legislation that would have authorized the completion of the Keystone XL Pipeline to transport oil from Canada to the Gulf Coast. A host of new regulations for pollution and natural resource control emerged, and new measures were introduced to encourage alternative energy sources like wind and solar energy. According to Lazarus (2023), the final EPA plan was published "a little more than a month before the international climate negotiations were scheduled to begin in Paris." The administration's plan committed to reduce power plant emissions by 30 percent over the next 15 years. President Obama joined China in signing the 2015 Paris Agreement on September 3, 2016.

A major achievement of the Obama administration with more lasting effect than the Clean Power Plan (which would be rescinded in the first Trump administration) was the *Affordable Health Care Act of 2010*, or "Obamacare." It was the first major national healthcare legislation since the Johnson administration. The achievement was credited in significant measure to Henry Waxman, an indefatigable Democratic Representative from California (1975–2015).

Recognizing the state of political polarization in the nation, and more candid in acknowledging positions different from his own than most politicians, Obama expressed the goal of bringing the country together.

However, achieving political harmony faced a formidable obstacle in the attitude of Republicans, expressed in a statement by Senate Minority Leader Mitch McConnell: "The single most important thing we want to achieve is for President Obama to be a one-term president" (Kessler, 2017). It also faced obstacles in Obama himself.

Obama had a conceptual desire for bipartisan cooperation, but his voting record had been the most liberal in the Senate in 2007. During an in-depth interview with Obama on *Fox News*, Chris Wallace posed the question of whether unity for Obama meant unconditional surrender by Republicans. Obama's ideological commitments and natural reserve limited communication with Republicans except Speaker John Boehner, who had the most liberal voting record among Republicans, and who eventually retired in disgust from the contention of Republican politics. There were minimal initiatives in either the Republican or the Democratic Parties to achieve balance or take into consideration the concerns of opponents. An example of lack of realism in policies is seen in the Obama White House archives for climate change (obamawhitehouse.gov), which lists 104 achievements but offers no indication of failures or policy problems. Chapter 11 will indicate that leading European nations take more realistic approaches to law making and governance.

Despite his many assets, the second Obama administration saw a rise in polarization. In addition to the conservative movement described previously, this was contributed to by a surge in illegal immigration and the declaration by Obama and his Attorney General that his administration would not enforce the *Declaration of Marriage Act (1996)* that had been passed by Congress and signed by President Clinton. The business community also expressed opposition to the new powers of EPA in regarding carbon dioxide as a pollutant. These factors would aid in the unexpected election of Donald J. Trump, a business mogul who had no prior experience in public service, as will be described in Chapter 10.

10

# Upheaval: Donald Trump, Joe Biden, and Trump 2.0

## Trump's background

*An underrated master of media manipulation*

In this section, I offer details about Donald Trump's history in order to reveal background, skills and strategies overlooked by the media and political experts.[1] On October 12, 2015, the C-Span broadcast of the No Labels Problem Solvers Conference for presidential candidates in New Hampshire was chaired by the late senator and vice-presidential nominee, Joseph Lieberman (Glueck, 2015), and featured speeches by Donald Trump and other candidates. The media largely dismissed Trump's speech, but I was intrigued by detail that suggested there was more to Trump than a business mogul with a flamboyant style. He spoke of a skating rink in Brooklyn that city authorities had been unable to renovate for eight years, but which his organization rebuilt in four months after gaining agreement from unions and all the relevant officials. The story would prove roughly correct, but the rarity of a Republican candidate interested in labor attracted interest.[2] Trump described Middle Eastern airports that were more advanced than anything in the US. This revealed foreign experience and lack of the America-centric focus of most American politicians. I ordered books by and about Trump to learn more about him.

The authoritative biography of Trump by journalist Gwenda Blair (Blair, 2005) chronicled Trump's education, rise in the New York real estate scene, near-bankruptcy in 1990, and his association with the "quintessential fixer," lawyer Roy Cohn, who was associated with mob figures as well as leaders from both political parties. Other biographers describe Trump's impulsivity and short attention span, but a former business associate noted Trump's careful preparation for real estate deals (Ross, 2008).

Mainstream media widely but wrongly assumed that Trump's books were ghostwritten or otherwise of little consequence. After Trump's election, claims proliferated that he was poorly informed and did not read books. A Google Scholar query on the phrase "Trump ignorance" in 2020 yielded more than 19,000 hits. David Graham, a senior writer for *The Atlantic*, cited author Michael Wolff: "He didn't read. He didn't really even skim. Some believed that for all practical purposes he was no more than semiliterate." Gary Cohn was also cited: "It's worse than you can imagine … Trump won't read anything—not one-page memos, not the brief policy papers, nothing" (Graham, 2018). An article in *The Week* magazine repeated the same theme (Mann, 2020):

> Trump's ghostwriter for *The Art of the Deal*, Tony Schwartz, speculated that Trump has never read a single book in his adult life, not even a book about him or "by" him … Trump processes data orally … the putative author of three books with "Think" in the title, doesn't like to think. Trump is a know-it-all who knows almost nothing.

These opinions pose a riddle. How did a supposedly ignorant businessman who never held public office gain the highest office in the US—an achievement denied to accomplished leaders of both parties? Careful analysis of Trump's 15 books through the 2016 election indicated that dismissive characterizations of Trump were fatally misguided. They fed into his strategies. Had material in his policy-oriented books been given full attention, American political history might be different.

Most of Trump's books after *The Art of the Deal*, a *New York Times* bestseller, are potboilers about real estate or gaining wealth, but unlike his transactional verbal statements, they offer glimpses of his operating methods and motivations. Eleven of his books have subordinate coauthors. Trump would collect material for nine months to a year and then hand it to a writer assistant (most often, Meredith McIver) to organize into book format (Manheim, 2023a) That the content of the books was his is supported by ensuing examples.

The co-author of *The Art of the Deal*, Tony Schwartz, claimed in an interview that he was the real author, asserting that he "put lipstick on a pig" (Mayer, 2018). An examination of the history of the book (Manheim, 2023a) showed that Trump hired Schwartz, a facile writer with liberal views, to follow him for 18 months and compile the results in a book. Schwartz had no history of background in New York politics, real estate, or Trump family history; the concept for and the content of the book came from Trump. Beyond serving as a paid scribe, Schwartz's claim was grossly misleading.

*Think Like a Champion* (Trump and McIver, 2009) challenges claims about Trump's illiteracy. After an introductory chapter that praises President Barack Obama's first year in office, the book's short chapters feature quotes from famous authors, including Pythagoras, Albert Schweitzer, Albert Camus,

Oscar Wilde, Pearl Buck, Abraham Lincoln, Henry Ford, Mark Twain, and many others. The selections focus on achievement and are followed by two to three pages of personal observations on each author and the theme. Trump's favorite book was *The Art of War* by the fifth-century BC Chinese general Sun Tzu, who emphasized the importance of surprise—a noted tactic for Trump. Excerpts of author quotes and Trump's comments illustrate the style of the book:

Ralph Waldo Emerson: *Whatever games are played with us, we must play no games with ourselves*

> "In the *New York Times Book Review* of September 30, 2007, is an essay by Stephen King … in reviewing the state of the short story today, he notes that they seem to 'feel show-offy', and written for editors and teachers, rather than for readers."

Washington Irving: *Great minds have purposes, others have wishes*

> "Charles De Gaulle … came from a family of historians and writers. His father taught literature and philosophy. But young Charles de Gaulle had a passionate interest in military matters and he was determined to pursue this unexpected passion. It's a good idea to take your own pulse … instead of just focusing on what masses are doing."

Aldous Huxley: *Experience teaches only the teachable*

> "Comprehensive education dissolves the line between knowing too much and knowing too little on a variety of subjects—subjects that are necessary for success."

Robert Louis Stevenson: *Everyone who got where he is has had to begin where he was*

> "A lot of people think I'm a natural at business. In some ways they might be right, but it's also an acquired skill that takes discipline and focus, just as being an athlete or a musician takes perseverance and years of training."

A search in Google for the book's co-author, Meredith McIver, found no references. Her major in college had been ballet, suggesting that she was a longtime writer assistant who compiled Trump's draft material into books, but did not contribute substantive content. Trump had an exceptionally wide range of interests, but his short attention span suggests that his reading style involved rapid skimming for topics of potential relevance. In his candidacy for the 2024 election, Trump's ability to fend off four separate indictments, doing the research needed to endorse or pan Republican candidates, while planning and pursuing a competitive election campaign, shows multitasking capabilities that were already emphasized in *The Art of the Deal* (Trump and Schwartz, 1987).

In this first bestselling book, Trump referred to his ability to attract media attention: "They are hungry for good stories, the more sensational the better." Once his political interests re-emerged after the success of *The Apprentice* TV show, Trump's books continue their didactic style, but take on a more cynical character. The heading of a chapter in *Trump: Never Give Up* (Trump and McIver, 2008) offers insights into Trump's carelessness about grammar and factual data: "It takes a lot of smarts to play dumb: Keep them off balance. Knowledge is power, so keep as much of it as you can to yourself."

Unlike politicians whose insights into societal issues are constrained by partisan ideological commitments, Trump's freedom from ideological constraints are demonstrated by his books and political history. He proposed a single-payer national health policy and a 14.25 percent wealth tax as an abortive candidate for the Reform Party in 2000 (Trump and Shiflett, 2000). He supported Democratic politicians like Harry Reid, Charlie Rangel, and Senate Majority Leader Chuck Schumer, and the campaign of John Kerry against George W. Bush in 2004. He made multiple contributions to Hillary Clinton's campaign and donated $100,000 to the Clinton Foundation. The first chapter of *Think Like a Champion* (Trump and McIver, 2009) praised the first year of Barack Obama's presidency, and Trump was a signatory among business leaders who took out a full-page ad in the *New York Times* on December 6, 2009 urging action on climate change (Anonymous, 2009).

However, by 2010, Trump saw new political opportunity in weaknesses in the Democratic administration and public discontent. In 2011, Trump's second policy book, subtitled "Making America #1 Again" (Trump, 2011), harshly criticized the Obama administration. His contributions switched to the Republican Party. In the same year, he initiated the "birther" controversy about President Obama's American citizenship, which artfully distracted attention from his previous political affiliations. Beginning in 2013, Trump called climate change a hoax (Trump, 2013).

The ultimate political coup took place on June 16, 2015, when Trump's inflammatory announcement of his candidacy for the Republican presidential nomination created headlines in the media. Prior to this, an aggregate of nationwide polls for the Republican primary showed Trump at 4 percent. One month later, he surged ahead of 16 credentialed Republican candidates. The announcement of his candidacy and rally speeches were couched in language gauged by the Flesch-Kincaid readability test to be at the fourth-grade level (Schouten, 2015). Google searches found no mention of Trump's earlier political positions and active support for Democrats and Barack Obama in any US media following his announcement, except for a passing mention in the *New York Times*: "Trump had supported both Democrats and Republicans in the past" (Burns, 2015). In short, the huge increase in readership following the sensation that Trump created apparently weighed more heavily for editors than doing due journalistic diligence and revealing Trump's schemes. He became so confident of media obliviousness that the brazenly acknowledged in his 2016 campaign book (Trump, 2015):

> I use the media the way it uses me—to attract attention. Once I have that attention it's up to me to use it to my advantage ... So sometimes I make outrageous comments and give them what they want—viewers and readers ... I learned a long time ago how to talk directly to the people who matter—to regular Americans.

In short, Trump is not the crude, poorly informed individual with mysterious demagogic skills portrayed in the media, but a knowledgeable, resourceful, and ruthless tactician. Confident of his instincts, as he noted in books, he makes bold but calculated moves that confound opponents. Another Trump principle is to not admit mistakes, but move on. This style helps account for his ability to sustain the confidence of his core supporters despite setbacks or compromising developments.

Trump's Democratic opponent in the 2016 election campaign was Hillary Clinton, who had promising qualifications for high office. She had White House experience as First Lady; had been a Senator from New York State, and Secretary of State in the Obama administration. In contrast, Trump had many negatives. However, Clinton tended to follow her instincts in the campaign and failed to take advantage of the political skills of her husband, Bill Clinton. Against predictions, Donald Trump shocked the Democrats by winning a close election.

## The first Trump presidency

### *Appointments*

A number of individuals appointed to cabinet and other positions were terminated or resigned owing to disagreements or for deterring Trump from actions regarded as illegal or unwise. Prominent among these were Chief of Staff John Kelly, Secretary of Defense James Mattis, Secretary of State Rex Tillerson, Attorney General Bill Barr, National Security Advisors John Bolton and H. R. McMaster, National Security Advisor. Scott Pruitt was among eyebrow-raising appointees. As Attorney General of Oklahoma, "Pruitt opposed abortion, same-sex marriage, the Affordable Care Act, and environmental regulations." As a self-described "leading advocate against the EPA's activist agenda," he had sued the EPA at least 14 times in his role" as attorney general of Oklahoma (Wikipedia—Scott Pruitt). Pruitt also denied the scientific consensus for climate change. In the wake of 14 separate federal investigations, Pruitt resigned and was replaced by Andrew Wheeler in July 2018 (Wikipedia—Environmental policy of the first Donald Trump administration).

Wheeler had stronger professional credentials than Pruitt. He was named by the *National Journal* as one of the Top Congressional Staff Leaders in 2005, had been a deputy assistant administrator in the EPA, and had a more nuanced position on climate change. However, he was a former chief counsel for the Senate Committee on Environment and Public Works under Chairman James Imhofe, the Senate's most adamant critic of climate change policies. He had also served as a lobbyist for coal and industrial firms. With expanded influence over federal agencies made possible by President Carter's *Civil Service Reform Act of 1978*, Trump nominated individuals for 20 policy-making positions in the Department of the Interior. His first nominee for Secretary was Montana Congressman and former Navy Seal, Ryan Zinke. Zinke was replaced by David Bernhardt after an Inspector General report that he had violated ethics rules and lied to investigators (Wikipedia—Ryan Zinke).

### *Administrative actions*

Among his first actions on inauguration on January 20, 2017, Trump issued a directive weakening the Affordable Care Act "in anticipation of its withdrawal," a ban on travel to the US by citizens of eight Muslim nations, and suspension of refugee admissions for 120 days. Subsequent environmental and regulatory actions soon followed. An in-depth Wikipedia article (Wikipedia—Donald Trump) reported that "During his first six weeks in office, he delayed, suspended, or reversed ninety federal regulations, often after requests by the regulated industries." It cited an Institute for Policy Integrity study that found that 78 percent of Trump's proposals were blocked by courts or did not prevail after litigation.

Within the first five months of his administration, Trump issued major executive orders relating to the environment, regulatory matters, and government organization examples of which are shown in Table 10.1.

The first executive order, on January 24, was on infrastructure involving the Keystone XL and Dakota Access pipelines, referred to in Trump's election campaign (The White House, 2017). It stipulated that all new pipelines in the US must be constructed using materials and equipment produced in the US.

**Table 10.1:** Executive Orders by Donald J. Trump relating to regulatory and environmental policies

| EO | Date | Text |
|---|---|---|
| 13766 | Jan. 24 | Expediting Environmental Reviews and Approvals for High Priority Infrastructure Projects |
| 13771 | Jan. 30 | Reducing Regulation and Controlling Regulatory Costs |
| 13778 | Feb. 28 | Restoring the Rule of Law, Federalism, and Economic Growth by Reviewing the "Waters of the United States" Rule |
| 13781 | Mar. 13 | Comprehensive Plan for Reorganizing the Executive Branch |
| 13783 | Mar. 28 | Promoting Energy Independence and Economic Growth |

Source: Data from the *Federal Register*, "2025 Donald J. Trump Executive Orders," Available from: https://www.federalregister.gov/presidential-documents/executive-orders/donald-trump/2025

As proposed by Russell Vought, the Director of the Office of Management and Budget (OMB), the January 30 order required agencies proposing a new regulation to identify two existing regulations to be eliminated. Vought was subsequently associated with the development of Project 2025, a series of policy proposals by the conservative Heritage Foundation to restructure the executive branch of government (Dans and Groves, 2023). Project 2025 was reviewed with alarm by Democrats, but Trump claimed he had no information on its details.

The key feature of EO 13778 required the EPA administrator and Assistant Secretary of the Army (overseeing the US Corps of Engineers) to interpret the US regulatory code for Waters of the United States (WOTUS) in a manner consistent with the minority opinion in the Supreme Court decision *Rapanos v. United States* (2006), which reduced federal regulatory jurisdiction over isolated waterways. Justice Scalia's opinion for the minority went further, recommending that courts override "evidence-based standards" in favor of Congressional intent.

Unlike other early presidential orders, proposed reform of the executive branch's numerous agencies by EO 13781 gained favorable attention in the mainstream media. An article in *The Washington Post* (Rudalevige, 2017), listing previous presidents and their reform proposals concluded that "when Trump—for real this time—complained about 'duplication and redundancy everywhere,' and urged more 'efficiency, effectiveness and accountability of the executive branch,' he was preaching to a bipartisan, historical presidential choir." The need for governmental reforms has long been expressed by administrative scholars like Paul Light (Light, 2009).

On March 28, Trump released EO 13783, a far-reaching order that reviewed or rescinded most of the Obama administration's environmental and energy policies, including the New Source rule for power plants, the

Clean Power Plan, the EPA's ambient air, automobile, and methane emission standards, and restrictive rules pertaining to oil and gas development. It also ordered review of 1970s laws: the Endangered Species Act (ESA), NEPA, and the *Marine Mammal and National Marine Sanctuaries Acts of 1972*. Finally, EO 1392 directed the Secretary of the Interior to review national monuments greater than 100,000 acres that had been created since 1996 and that had been expanded by at least 100,000 acres.

### *Digression: problems with the* **National Environmental Policy Act**

ESA and NEPA are more than 45 years old. They are fiercely defended, but have long been objects of antagonism. The latter is only seven pages long, but as described in Chapter 6, its scope of application was expanded by federal court decisions and Council on Environmental Quality regulations. It became an administrative procedure rather than a law promoting wise planning and coordination, as the framers had envisioned. NEPA was originally designed to apply to actions by federal agencies, but it now applies to activities that require passage across federal lands, are funded wholly or in part by the federal government, or that affect air or water quality. It fosters litigation by opponents of developments, who can claim that environmental statements were inadequate for any concern. In short, NEPA needs reform, but the unilateral approach of the Trump administration, without consultation with the Democrats, brought a storm of opposition. It had no chance to foster prudent modification, and nearly all of Trump's executive orders, including modified regulations for NEPA by the Council on Environmental Quality, were revoked by the succeeding Biden administration. NEPA continues to create multiyear delays of infrastructure projects through its environmental impact provision and litigation, though the first reform measure is described in the account of the Biden administration.

### *The COVID-19 pandemic*

A major crisis in the Trump administration was the COVID-19 pandemic. The first infections were announced by the Chinese government on December 31, 2019. President Trump had a mixed record on the pandemic. He admitted in interviews reported in a book by Bob Woodward (2023) that he delayed the announcement of the pandemic. Trump White House archives note that the president created a Coronavirus Task Force in early 2020 and "launched *Operation Warp Speed*, which successfully saw two safe and effective Coronavirus vaccines in distribution by the end of 2020." (Oversight 2021). Vaccines normally requiring years to produce were distributed in record time. The archives also state that Trump invoked the

*Defense Construction Act of 1950* 100 times to supply ventilators and testing kits to states and ordered the US Corps of Engineers to deliver products.

On the negative side, an article in *Public Administration* (Parker and Stern, 2022) reported on the impact of delays and lost opportunities by the administration. A Congressional committee reported a list of obstructive interferences by the president with professional officials and agencies, and his ostentatious refusal to wear masks in public, violating CDC guidelines.

### *Impeachment, the re-election campaign, and January 6*

Trump's presidency was challenged by two failed impeachments: the first on charges of abuse of power and obstruction of Congress (2019), and the second in 2021 on a charge of incitement to insurrection. After his loss in the 2020 presidential election, Trump became the first losing candidate in US history to refuse to concede the results of an election. An article in *Politico* chronicles his claim that the election was stolen and his efforts to overturn the outcome (Kumar and Orr, 2020). In addition to 62 court challenges of election results (61 of which were rejected), Trump sought to manipulate state electors. Texas Attorney General Kenneth Paxton initiated a Supreme Court suit on Trump's behalf, seeking to reject the votes of swing states on grounds of election irregularities. Louisiana Congressman Michael Johnson contacted 196 of his Republican Congressional colleagues, asking them to sign an *amicus* resolution supporting the Texas suit; 126 signed it, but the Supreme Court refused to hear the case.

Republican Minority Leader Mitch McConnell acknowledged Biden's victory, but a Trump attorney, John Eastman, advanced a novel legal argument that would allow Vice President Mike Pence to defer counting of results and return the vote to the states for recertification. This would allow Republican leaders of states that Trump lost to present alternative slates of electors, giving Trump the win. Trump vilified Pence when he refused to defer certification of Biden's election. The final act in the election drama was violent mob entry into the US Capitol on January 6, 2021 (Duignan, 2024).[3] In July 2023, the Justice Department issued an indictment against Trump for instigating the attack (Savage and Goldman, 2023).

Notwithstanding the extraordinary events associated with the Trump presidency, a trio of British experts on American politics published a book titled *The Ordinary Presidency of Donald J. Trump* (Herbert et al, 2019). Its thesis was that while Trump's personal behaviors were extraordinary, his policies did not differ significantly from those of previous Republican Party platforms. Except for the passage of tax cuts by party-line vote in 2017, the book argues, the Trump administration's achievements were meager. This assessment does not include Trump's controls on influx of illegal immigrants at the southern border, reduction of regulations, and expansion of oil and gas production, presumably because these actions were reversed by the Biden administration.

## The Joe Biden presidency

Joseph Robinette Biden Jr., Vice President in the Barack Obama administration, became a candidate for the 2020 presidential election even though he would be 78 years of age by the time of his inauguration. He took this step because he was appalled by Donald Trump's statements, and concerned that Trump would defeat the leading Democratic candidate, Bernie Sanders, in the election of 2020. Senator Sanders was a self-described democratic socialist, and the history of presidential elections did not favor candidates whose politics extended beyond mainstream values.

After mediocre performances in Democratic candidate debates, Biden's fifth place in the New Hampshire Democratic primary of February 11, 2020 appeared to be a fatal blow to his campaign. His endorsement by Jim Clyburn, an African-American Representative from South Carolina and a senior Democratic leader, helped Biden win an unexpectedly large plurality in the South Carolina primary of February 26, due to Biden winning 61 percent of African-American votes. The impact of that victory helped Biden win the Democratic nomination. Campaign manager Jen O'Malley Dillon created a moderate image for Biden, which helped give him a narrow win over Donald Trump in an election decided by the swing states of Arizona, Georgia, Michigan, Pennsylvania, and Wisconsin.

Biden's campaign and inaugural address projected moderation, but as president, his policies were guided by the boldly progressive Biden-Sanders Unity Task Force Recommendations. The 110-page document listed John Kerry, Alexandra Ocasio-Cortez, and six others as co-chairs (Kerry et al, no date). It has been called the most progressive program since the Roosevelt New Deal (Stoolmacher, 2023). The task force recommendations showed the influence of Biden's style, containing human-interest vignettes and personal expressions, as well as bulleted plans with aspirational content.

The nation had made progress from the COVID-19 epidemic, and was further aided by the huge recovery budget cited in Table 10.3. In other areas, on his first day in office, Biden signed 17 presidential orders, acting more swiftly and comprehensively to reverse his predecessor's directives than any president in modern history. An executive order rejoined the US to the World Health Organization, another rejoined the Paris Climate Accords, and a further order revoked a series of Trump executive orders (see Table 10.2). Within the first 100 days, Biden issued many other orders, memoranda, and proclamations. The largest number (15) were on the COVID-19 epidemic, followed by immigration (12), equity (10), the economy (7), and the environment (5) (Hickey et al, 2021), prepared by the Biden-Sanders Unity

**Table 10.2:** Examples of Executive Orders on public health and environment by Joe Biden

| EO | Date | Text |
|---|---|---|
| 13990 | Jan. 20 | **Protecting Public Health and the Environment and Restoring Science to Tackle the Climate Crisis**<br>"[I]mprove public health and protect our environment; to ensure access to clean air and water; to limit exposure to dangerous chemicals and pesticides; to hold polluters accountable, including those who disproportionately harm communities of color and low-income communities; to reduce greenhouse gas emissions; to bolster resilience to the impacts of climate change; to restore and expand our national treasures and monuments; and to prioritize both environmental justice and creation of the well-paying union jobs necessary to deliver on these goals … review and, as appropriate and consistent with applicable law, take action to address the promulgation of Federal regulations and other actions during the last 4 years that conflict with these important national objectives." |
| 13992 | Jan. 20 | **Revokes Trump Orders** 13771, 13777,13875,13891,13893, pertaining to regulatory reduction, advisory committees, rule of law, transparency, and fairness in Civil Administration, government accountability |
| 14008 | Jan. 27 | **National Climate Task Force.** The Task Force shall be chaired by the National Climate Advisor. [Membership]<br>(i) the Secretary of the Treasury;(ii) the Secretary of Defense;(iii) the Attorney General; (iv) the Secretary of the Interior;(v) the Secretary of Agriculture;(vi) the Secretary of Commerce;(vii) the Secretary of Labor;(viii) the Secretary of Health and Human Services; (ix) the Secretary of Housing and Urban Development;(x) the Secretary of Transportation;(xi) the Secretary of Energy;(xii) the Secretary of Homeland Security;(xiii) the Administrator of General Services;(xiv) the Chair of the Council on Environmental Quality; (xv) the Administrator of the Environmental Protection Agency;(xvi) the Director of the Office of Management and Budget;(xvii) the Director of the Office of Science and Technology Policy; (xviii) the Assistant to the President for Domestic Policy;(xix) the Assistant to the President for National Security Affairs;(xx) the Assistant to the President for Homeland Security and Counterterrorism; and(xxi) the Assistant to the President for Economic Policy |

Sources: Wikipedia—Executive Orders of the US Federal Government; https://www.federalregister.gov/presidential-documents/executive-orders/joe-biden/2025

Task Force. All executive orders are available on the Federal Register. The revocations were not only for specific measures like the permit for Keystone XL Pipeline and the cancellation of other Trump rules, but also involved less partisan programs, like an apprenticeship support project.

### *The Biden administration's environmental policies*

President Biden promoted extraordinarily far-reaching environmental and climate change policies. The Paris Agreement that he rejoined in 2021 included a US pledge to reduce greenhouse gases by 50–52 percent by 2030. As summarized in the source listed in Table 10.3, Biden targeted ending deforestation and land degradation by that date, and achieving zero emissions for electrical power by 2035. All federal vehicles were to be electric. He set a goal of protecting 30 percent of US land and expanded existing national monuments as a step in this direction. The range of actions included emission limits on vehicles, advancing green building practices, restricting offshore oil and gas leasing, pausing LNG (liquid natural gas) exports, taking measures for flood management, and restoring consideration of the social impact of carbon in the EPA's environmental regulatory decisions. Wind turbines in the Atlantic margin would deliver 30 gigawatts of energy for the eastern coastal states.

The *Infrastructure and Jobs Act 2021* and the *Inflation Reduction Act of 2022*, listed in Table 10.3 provided record financial outlays for infrastructure and renewable energy development. A Biden administration law that is not mentioned in most reports is the first reform of NEPA since its passage in 1969. As discussed earlier, NEPA's environmental impact assessment requirement is probably the single greatest source of delays for infrastructure projects. *The Fiscal Responsibility Act of 2023* avoided the shutdown of the government by extending the debt limit after weeks of negotiations. Among the administration's concessions were modification of NEPA provisions, which included recommendations for a single environmental document, encouragement for establishing a single lead agency, and page limits and deadlines for environmental impact statements and assessments.

An observer from the Columbia University Climate School concluded his assessment of the Biden administration environmental program with the following statement: "No elected official has a perfect environmental record, but *Biden has the best environmental record of any president in American history*" (Cohen, 2023).

A progress report on Biden's environmental program by the World Resources Institute, a nonpartisan environmental organization, gave the Biden administration's progress four ratings: *goals achieved*, *significant progress*, *some progress*, and *off track* (Lashof, 2024). The commitment to cut total greenhouses gases by 50 percent by 2030 got the *achieved* rating, along with "tackling super pollutants" and "scaling up carbon dioxide removal." This includes scaling up carbon dioxide removal through investments in reduction, sustainable agriculture, ecologic restoration to promote natural carbon removal, and regional hubs for direct air capture. *Significant progress*

**Table 10.3:** Major laws passed under the Biden administration

| Date | Law | Funding |
|---|---|---|
| March 11, 2021 | American Rescue Plan | $1.9 trillion |
| Nov. 5, 2021 | Infrastructure and Jobs Act (IFJ) | $488 billion |
| Aug. 8, 2022 | Inflation Reduction Act (IRA) | $780 billion over 10 years |
| Aug. 9, 2022 | Chips and Science Act | $103.6 billion |
| June 3, 2023 | Fiscal Responsibility | Increased debt limit |

Sources: Wikipedia—Environmental Policy of the Joe Biden Administration; https://www.federalregister.gov/presidential-documents/executive-orders/joe-biden/2025

included the methane emissions fee stipulated by the Inflation Reduction Act (IRA), which will increase to $1,500 per metric ton of methane in 2026, and the EPA's final rule to reduce greenhouse gas emissions from passenger vehicles sold between 2023 and 2026, as well as strong standards for model year 2027. *Some progress* was assigned to "ramping up clean electricity standards to 55% by 2025, 75% by 2030 and 100% by 2035," but there was limited authority to expedite standards involving interstate transmission. The same grade was given to setting appliance and equipment standards to replace fossil fuels, setting emission performance standards for cement, steel, and plastics, and re-establishing international leadership. Taxing pollution, interpretable as placing a tax on carbon emissions, was rated as *off track*.

Not all policy analyses were supportive. The American Society of Civil Engineers raised the 2021 rating of C- for US infrastructure only to C (Webber and Phillis, 2025). A 24-page critique of the Biden administration's emphasis on environmental justice was released by the Manhattan Institute, a conservative think tank (Meigs, 2023). It accepted the validity of environmental justice concerns, but argued that Biden's *Justice40 Initiative*, committing 40 percent of outlays to the environmental justice agenda, detracted from environmental and infrastructure projects and "also made government programs less focused and less effective across the board." The point was underscored by a *New York Times* article by economist Ezra Klein (Klein, 2023):

> You might assume that when faced with a problem of overriding public importance, government would use its awesome might to sweep away the obstacles that stand in its way. But too often, it does the opposite ... it tries to accomplish so much within a single project or policy that it ends up failing to accomplish anything at all.

### *Late events*

In spite of low unemployment and other positive factors, President Biden's approval rating in public polls had difficulty rising above 40 percent. This was associated with public concern over a record influx of migrants at the US southern border in his administration. In February 2024 alone, US Customs and Border Protection reported more than 189,000 encounters (CPB, 2024), which did not include migrants crossing the border with the aid of smugglers.

Under political pressure, on June 4, 2024, President Biden issued an Executive Proclamation under the "Immigration and Nationality Act, sections 212(f) and 215(a) suspending entry of noncitizens who cross the southern border into the US unlawfully." Soon after, following his faltering performance in the Biden-Trump debate on June 28, Biden announced his withdrawal as a candidate for the presidency. At the Democratic Convention in August, Vice-President Kamala Harris was nominated as the Democratic candidate for president, with the Democratic governor of Minnesota, Tim Walz, as vice-presidential candidate. They would face Republican nominees Donald Trump and J. D. Vance, a senator from Ohio and author of a bestselling personal biography, *Hillbilly Elegy*.

Though a party loyalist, Joe Biden had in the past claimed as many friends among Republicans as Democrats. That relationship was changed by antagonism to Donald Trump and his influence on the Republican Party. Biden was committed to progressive values, especially infrastructure development, climate change policy, and human rights. In the late campaign, staff made overtures to industry groups and his inauguration speech projected moderation and a desire to bring the nation together. However, that approach was no longer evident once he became president. Biden's strengths were in personal relations, not policy or political strategy. He was most comfortable with advisors with whom he had longtime relationships, like Mike Donilon (O'Keefe and Gomez, 2024). This preference is not usually associated with effective policies. The failure by Biden to honor his earlier comment that he would serve as an interim president and his late withdrawal was among reasons cited for the subsequent upset victory by Donald Trump.

### *Underrecognized issues in the Biden administration climate change program*

Most published analyses largely focused primarily on the Biden administration's environmental and climate change objectives and laws with unprecedentedly large financial outlays. Only a *Politico* article pointed out the potential consequences of a Trump election in 2024 for Biden's agenda (Tamborino and Dabbs, 2024). Without attempting a comprehensive search,

I was not able to find accounts that systematically reviewed infrastructure progress, renewable energy development, and carbon reduction.

Three chapters of this book reviewed the history of political polarization and its barriers to US progress against climate change. I have referred to these obstacles as "the four horsemen of green energy development" (Manheim, 2021): (1) polarization and gridlock over regulatory and energy policy that has blocked meaningful Congressional action since the *Clean Air Act Amendments of 1990*; (2) bureaucratization and politization of federal aid to state and local infrastructure projects; (3) the regulatory/permitting labyrinth that resulted in a "median time of more than eight years from the first to the last permitting milestone for utility-scale wind and solar development permits from 2007 to 2015" (Bauer et al, 2024); and (4) bureaucratic barriers that deter visionary leaders from manufacturing and infrastructure development. The latter point will be elaborated upon shortly, while permitting delays are explored further in later chapters.

The power of American visionary entrepreneurship is exemplified by Thomas Alva Edison (1847–1931), whose inventions are said to have underlain one out of every six industrial jobs in the early twentieth century. Breakthrough entrepreneurship remains strong in information technology and marketing, but is absent in areas burdened by regulatory requirements, litigation, and NIMBY. The importance of visionary entrepreneurship for the environment is illustrated by Elon Musk's development of a world-leading electric vehicle. Tesla EV's led in the US market in 2023 with 55.1 percent of sales, followed by Ford with 6.1 percent (Melissa, 2024). Musk not only pioneered the Tesla but also introduced rapid charging stations and built the first US megafactory for car batteries.

The biography of Musk by Walter Isaacson (Isaacson, 2023) notes that to achieve breakthroughs in electrical vehicles and aerospace, Musk ignored a number of federal regulatory requirements. We can assume that, because his advances were so important, regulators were ultimately reluctant to jeopardize the projects. Isaacson reported on a White House celebration of electric vehicles in August 2021, to which the heads of GM, Ford, Chrysler, and the leader of the United Auto Workers Union were invited, but not Musk. Asked about his absence, Biden's press secretary, Jen Psaki, observed that the three largest employers of United Auto Workers employees were invited (Isaacson, 2023). This illustrates how political policy as well as regulatory barriers can inhibit necessary progress.[4] Notwithstanding Musk's achievements, he has become an object of disapproval by progressives for his support for Trump and other actions.

## The election of 2024 and Donald J. Trump's second nonconsecutive term as president

The election of Donald Trump, along with Republican control of both houses of Congress, took place in the late stages of the preparation of the book. This section reviews the election of 2024 and issues raised by the unexpected success of the Republican Party. It gives special attention to Trump's proposed environmental and climate change policies and related governance issues as of his election, but prior to inauguration.

### *The 2024 election*

Donald Trump declared his candidacy for the Republican nomination for president in 2024 shortly after the midterm elections of 2022. These elections resulted in a Democratic majority in the Senate and a Republican majority in the House of Representatives. Despite overwhelming court decisions rejecting claims of election fraud, Trump had continued to claim that the 2020 election were stolen, leading to Democrats' concerns that he posed a threat to the nation's democratic processes. Despite federal and state court indictments, Trump kept the support of a majority of Republican voters.

President Biden indicated in his 2020 campaign that he would serve as an interim president and bridge to younger political generations of Democratic leaders. However, in April 2023, he reversed that position and declared his candidacy for reelection. As the sitting president, he had minimal formal opposition, although age was an issue, given that he would turn 82 in November 2024.

Turbulence in the Republican-led House of Representatives finally led to the election of Louisiana Representative Michael Johnson as Speaker. Despite his strong pro-Trump background, he worked with Democratic leaders to avoid the shutdown of government, gaining Congressional approval of funding for Ukraine, Israel, and Taiwan with a major funding bill in April 2024.

As mentioned in the previous section, Biden's approval ratings had failed to rise above the low 40s, but poll ratings for Biden and Trump remained close after Biden announced his candidacy for re-election—until the unprecedented series of events in 2024, which are summarized by Mannweiler (2024):

> May 30. A New York court convicts Trump of felony crimes for fraudulent business documents regarding hush money payments made to influence the election of 2016.
>
> June 27. President Biden has a disastrous performance in a debate with Donald Trump and declines in presidential poll ratings
>
> July 1. In a 6:3 decision, the Supreme Court rules that Trump has immunity for presidential acts; the decision affects the Justice Department's indictment of Trump for subversion against the government in the January 6, 2021 assault on the Capital [sic]

July 13. Donald Trump is nearly assassinated at a rally in Pennsylvania. Leading electric vehicle and space entrepreneur Elon Musk throws full support to Trump; Musk is named by Trump as having a role in his administration, along with former presidential candidate, Vivek Ramaswamy. Shortly afterward, Trump chooses Senator J.D. Vance (OH), as his vice president.

July 15-19. Trump is nominated in Republican convention against challenger Nikki Haley, governor of South Carolina.

July 21. Responding to pressure, President Biden withdraws from the presidential race, endorsing Vice President Kamala Harris for the Democratic nomination. She draws enthusiastic Democratic support and funding, is subsequently nominated and takes the lead in presidential polls. Harris chooses Tim Walz, governor of Minnesota, as her running mate.

Sept. 15. A second assassination attempt on Trump is averted.

The election of November 5, 2024 resulted in a Trump victory. He won seven swing states: Arizona, Georgia, Michigan, Nevada, North Carolina, Pennsylvania, and Wisconsin, where both parties had concentrated money and campaign effort, as well as his former states in the 2016 election. The margin in the Electoral College was 312 for Trump and 226 for Harris. Unlike his popular vote in 2016, Trump achieved a 76.9 to 74.4 million plurality over Harris. The Republicans took leadership in the Senate from the Democrats with a margin of 53 to 47 seats. They retained narrower control of the House of Representatives by a margin of 220 to 215 members.

Unexpected demographic results were Trump's increase in support in the 18–29 age group, compared with his results in the 2016 election, and a huge gain in support by Hispanic men—54 percent compared with 36 percent in 2016 (Molski, 2024). Republicans led among voters without college degrees, while Democrats led among college-educated voters. This difference was particularly extreme for White noncollege voters, 66 percent of whom voted for Trump, while only 32 percent voted for Harris. The startling new pattern of working-class support for Republicans alarmed Democratic leaders because this group had previously been identified with the Democratic Party.

The election of Donald Trump as President, Republican control of both houses of Congress, a conservative majority of 6:3 in the Supreme Court, and Trump's stated plans created the potential for a more dramatic shift in governance than at any time since the early administrations of Franklin D. Roosevelt. The development was the more unexpected because of the widely held assumption that the increase in Democrat-favoring Hispanic populations might favor increasing Democratic Party dominance in presidential elections.

## *Environmental policy: consequences of the Trump administration*

Trump's campaign proposals included far-reaching changes in federal agencies, in foreign policy, and in domestic politics involving health, labor relations, economics, education, and, of particular interest in this book, environmental regulations and climate change policies. President-elect Trump claimed that he would repeal the IRA, which provided huge subsidies for infrastructure and renewable energy development. Before reviewing environmental and climate change issues based on information available at the time of writing, it is useful to review potential constraints on government initiatives of the new administration.

### *Enacting major legislation*

Passing or repealing law, the latter highlighted among Trump's stated plans, is subject to a longstanding Senate rule that limiting debate on a bill requires cloture, a procedure that needs approval of two thirds of a normal Senate, or 60 votes. Changes have modified the rule for nominations and for appropriations, but in principle, the Republican majority in the Senate would fall short of being able to repeal the IRA against unanimous nay votes by Democrats. The IRA commits twice as much funding to Republican-dominated areas as to those under Democratic control, a factor which might cause affected Republican senators to be reluctant to kill the law.

However, a powerful means to avoid the filibuster was introduced in the *Congressional Budget Act of 1974*. The reconciliation procedure expedites consideration of types of tax, spending, and debt limit legislation. Reconciliation bills are not subject to filibuster in the Senate, and amendments are limited. A prominent example of the use of reconciliation was the major tax cut legislation (*Tax Cut and Jobs Act of 2017*). No Democrats voted in favor and only 13 Republican members of the House voted against it (Anonymous, 2017). In the current House of Representatives, the Republican margin of control is smaller than in 2017 so that independent-minded GOP members will be a critical factor in legislative outcomes.

### *Schedule F: conversion of civil service employees*

Schedule F for the civil service was introduced during the last weeks of the Trump administration in 2020 through Executive Order (EO) 13957 (Wikipedia—Schedule F). It was not applied and was revoked by President Biden with EO 41003 on January 22, 2021, his third day in office. President Trump affirmed in his campaign that it would be re-applied early on in his administration as a principal means to "Drain the swamp." This extraordinary measure would allow the president to reclassify virtually any civil service employee with policy-making roles as political appointees, stripping them of civil service protections and allowing their termination. The legal basis for the Schedule F appointment was a section of President Jimmie Carter's *Civil Service Reform Act of 1978* (5 USC § 7511(b)(2) (CSRA),[5] which exempts from civil service protections federal employees "whose position has been determined to be of a confidential, policy-determining, policy-making or policy-advocating character" (Wikipedia—CSRA). The CSRA's role in increasing presidential control over the federal bureaucracy was discussed in Chapter 7, though the provision used to justify Trump's action was not known to have been used to target existing employees in Carter's or subsequent administrations.

The earlier Trump order went beyond the CSRA provision. It required all federal agency heads to inventory their employees and compile lists of individuals nominated for Schedule F. The lists were to be given to the OPM (headed by a presidential appointee) for decision. Affected employees could appeal decisions to the Merit Protection Board, whose members have staggered terms of seven nonrenewable years.

Trump's 2020 EO was so sweeping that, if implemented, it could return the US government to the spoils system of Andrew Jackson. The original declaration would be vulnerable to legal challenges on multiple grounds, including statutory (based on CSRA protections of employees from arbitrary dismissal and political retaliation), constitutional (based on the separation of powers and due process), and the *Administrative Procedures Act of 1946* (Anonymous, 2024). For these reasons, the application of Schedule F would likely be modified. A subject not raised for comment, except in a bombastic statement by firebrand Steve Bannon,[6] was how a Schedule F, if applied in the second Trump administration, would be dealt with in a subsequent administration.

### *Environmental policy and climate change*

The World Resources Institute reacted to the Trump commitment to roll back climate change initiatives with the quote: "The potential negative repercussions for climate and environmental action are gargantuan" (DeConcini et al, 2024). The following summary of the potential impact of the Trump election on environmental policy is partly based on the foregoing article and Gerrard (2024):

---

Constraints on Trump's promise to halt spending under the Inflation Reduction Act were reviewed in the previous section. While the law was intended to provide funding for up to ten years, the Biden administration sought to accelerate disbursal of funds to support manufacturing and infrastructure projects in support of a green energy transition. "However, the Internal Revenue Service under Trump could make it difficult to utilize tax credits by issuing very restrictive interpretations of the credits or refusing to release the necessary funds" (Gerrard, 2024).

Trump would be expected to again withdraw the US from the Paris Agreement of 2015, his previous withdrawal having been rescinded by President Biden. Action by Trump would be straightforward; "If Trump were to withdraw the US from the Paris agreement, it would make our country an international pariah, but it would not subject us to legal enforcement" (Gerrard, 2024). A more far-reaching step would be withdrawing the US from the U.N. Framework Convention on Climate Change, but this would be more difficult because this treaty was approved by the Senate. Would Republicans who supported Trump in other areas want to see the United States isolated more completely in international public and official opinion on climate change than President Putin of Russia is now isolated for his unprovoked attack on the Ukraine?

Trump would reverse a key regulation aimed at reducing emissions from power plants, and roll back key rules aimed at curbing climate change and air and water pollution. "Trump is likely to direct the EPA and the National Highway Traffic Safety Administration to freeze or weaken the [emission] standards and to revoke the California waiver, as he did during his first term. These actions, too, will face court challenge."

Coal-fired plants are subject to a 2024 EPA rule that requires their eventual closure unless they install carbon capture and storage (CCS). This might be repealed by Trump. However, Doug Burgum, Governor of North Dakota and nominated for Secretary of the Department of Energy, has favored CCS development. A significant factor limiting CCS applications has been costs and delays due to complex regulatory requirements (Hart, 2009). If Trump's reduction of regulatory requirements lowered the cost of CCS, this could be an area where reduction in regulatory burdens could reduce fossil fuel emissions.

An area of the IRA helping offset its massive outlays was a fee to be imposed on methane leakage during oil and gas production. Methane is a significant greenhouse gas and the fee would represent the first carbon tax, which Trump would be expected to oppose. Large companies like Exxon have expressed support for carbon taxes that are imposed on consumers (Exxon, 2024), but since this would be imposed on producers it would be unlikely to gain support from the fossil fuel industry.

Wind and solar energy on private land do not require federal permits, and development here is likely to continue. However, permits are required for developments on federal lands, and Trump has expressed special antagonism to wind energy. This view dates to his objection to wind turbines that he felt spoiled the view from a golf course he built on the coast of Scotland (BBC, 2019).

---

The history of the nuclear power issue and current status is discussed in the next chapter, but recent developments favor growth in low-carbon energy from this source. There has been an increase in public support for nuclear power, greater among Republicans than Democratic voters (Leppert and Kennedy, 2024). Regulatory cost would be potentially lowered by new laws passed during the Biden administration (previous section), and new technologies, especially smaller modular reactors with lower costs, have drawn increasing interest. The enormous power requirements of electronic data centers has led the Google Company to enter into contracts for power from modular reactors (Greiner, 2024). Trump has shown cautious interest in small modular reactors (Pethokoukis, 2024).

### *Regulations and enforcement: enter Elon Musk*

Even without Schedule F, the 1978 CSRA would give President Trump substantial control of federal agencies charged with administration of laws involving regulations, though probably not to the degree he has proposed. Major regulated areas beyond the environment and natural resources include banking and finance, healthcare, and education. It is here that the Department of Government Efficiency (DOGE), projected to be led by Elon Musk and Vivek Ramaswamy at the time of writing, would propose to restructure agencies and slash regulations to "save two trillion dollars" (Shuster, 2024). DOGE would be an advisory entity rather than a government agency, but given Musk's influential relationship with the president, his recommendations would be expected to carry weight.

*TIME* magazine's lead article on Musk (Shuster, 2024) points out that while Musk is the richest man on Earth, his past record has shown little interest in wealth for its own sake, but rather as a means to realize ambitious goals like electrical vehicles and space travel. An in-depth Musk biography by the respected historian Walter Isaacson (Isaacson, 2023) noted Musk's political history as a moderate Democrat who was concerned about climate change. He resigned from business advisory councils in the earlier Trump administration after Trump withdrew from the Paris Agreement. Antagonism toward regulators experienced during his industrial initiatives is a notable factor in his support for Trump's candidacy after the assassination attempt. Trump responded to Musk's support by revising his previous position against electrical vehicles. These relationships suggest the possibility that Musk might exert influence on Trump's environmental and climate change policies. However, at the time of submission of this manuscript, reports of change in Musk's previously strong commitment against climate change render a positive role for Musk doubtful (Verma et al, 2024).

In summary, the second Trump administration, supported by Republican domination of the houses of Congress, portends transformation in the US government and domestic policy comparable in US history only to the presidencies of Andrew Jackson and Franklin D. Roosevelt. The environmental agenda of the new administration is of concern to the overwhelming number of nations that recognize the gravity of global climate change. NATO nations are also concerned about Trump's statements about the 70-year-old alliance.

Chapter 11 will turn from describing recent US administrations to compare the structure and evolution of the American governmental systems and the EU as it relates to environmental law making.

# 11

# Comparisons between US and European Law Making and Renewable Energy Progress

## The United States

### *Political evolution of environmental regulations*

In a primer on regulations, Susan Dudley and Jerry Brito (2012) pointed out that the Founding Fathers did not design constitutional law-making provisions to be efficient. Recognizing headstrong proclivities in the new nation, they designed a system that "would not allow the majority to rule with an iron fist." In the words of James Madison (Madison, 1987, republished from an edition of 1840): "Ambition must be set against ambition." In order to achieve separation of powers, the federal government was divided into three branches: executive, legislative, and judicial. The legislative branch was further subdivided. Article I, Section 1 of the US Constitution reads: "All Legislative Powers herein granted shall be vested in a Congress of the US, which shall consist of a Senate and House of Representatives." A succinct description of law-making procedures is provided by the House of Representatives website (Representatives, no date):

> Laws begin as ideas. First, a representative sponsors a bill. The bill is then assigned to a committee for study. If released by the committee, the bill is put on a calendar to be voted on, debated or amended. If the bill passes by simple majority (218 of 435), the bill moves to the Senate. In the Senate, the bill is assigned to another committee and, if released, debated and voted on. Again, a simple majority (51 of 100) passes the bill. Finally, a conference committee made up of House and Senate members works out any differences between the House and Senate versions of the bill. The resulting bill returns to the House and Senate for final approval. The Government Publishing Office prints

the revised bill in a process called enrolling. The President has 10 days to sign or veto the enrolled bill.

Note that the procedure described by the House refers to "a representative" initiating a law, reflecting the fact that the Constitution makes no mention of parties. There were already groups with different philosophies for governance, but the first President, George Washington, felt that unity rather than division was needed if the new democratic republic was to survive. His deep concern about parties, reflected in his farewell address (Washington, 1796), was remarkably prescient: "The spirit of party serves always to distract the public councils and enfeeble the public administration. It agitates the community with ill-founded jealousies and false alarms, kindles the animosity of one part against another, foments occasionally riot and insurrection."

The efficient governance system of the first six administrations, with officials and workers appointed based on competence and permanent tenure, was swept away by President Andrew Jackson's spoils system, which replaced officials and government employees after each presidential election. Regional division among the states had extreme consequences. In 1860, slaveholding Southern states seceded from the union, precipitating a Civil War that cost 698 thousand lives (Barceló et al, 2024). In proportion to population, this would be equivalent to over 6 million men in current populations. Fanatics have assassinated four presidents, a leading presidential candidate, and the most prominent modern African-American civil rights leader, Martin Luther King. On January 6, 2021, after decades of increasing party polarization, a mob supporting outgoing President Donald Trump's claims of a stolen election violently entered the Capitol building. The nation already showed less respect for tradition than other nations early in its history.[1] However, since the 1960s, respect for institutions and the federal government have shown increasing decline (Pew, 2024).

Washington's recognition of the risks posed by divisiveness in society was foresighted, but his hope that parties would not prevail was unrealistic. An anomalous feature of US governmental operations is that while the nation has prided itself on championing liberty, it developed the most labyrinthine body of federal regulations among democratic nations. As described in Chapter 5, the Johnson administration failed to take timely action on urgent environmental problems. As a consequence, a national environmental crisis aroused Congress to enact a complex system of laws and regulations in the 1970s to control pollution and environmental hazards. Similar command and control laws were in force in European nations in the 1970s, but, as we will see, were replaced by more effective policies in the 1990s. The inability of the US to achieve reform was a product of serendipitous factors and tendencies for overreaction that are reviewed in Chapter 12. Polarization has become a formidable obstacle not only to progress against climate change but also to rational governance.

### *Environmental law*

With a few exceptions, such as sections of the *Rivers and Harbors Act of 1899*, current US environmental policy is governed by federal laws passed in the 1970s. They are administered by the EPA and other federal agencies that delegate specific authorities to states while retaining final regulatory authority. The EPA and agencies with regulatory responsibilities issue detailed rules and regulations that have the force of law, but federal agencies do not have the freedom to modify policies prescribed in law. In a procedure referred to as "Notice and Response" described in an introduction to US environmental law (Elliott and Esty, 2021), a proposed rule or regulation is published by the issuing agency with time allowed for public response. After review, agencies issue final rules. Affected individuals or organizations can dispute decisions by filing suit in federal court.

Under the Supreme Court decision in *Chevron v. The Natural Resources Defense Council* (1984), courts were obliged to defer disputed issues to agency interpretations when reasonable and supported by statute, but *Chevron* was subsequently overturned by the Supreme Court in 2024. See Manheim (2024) for a brief history of the controversy. Environmental organizations and US regulatory agencies vigorously supported *Chevron*, whereas industrial and trade organizations like the US Chamber of Commerce, representing nearly three million businesses, long regarded US regulations as burdensome and excessive. Policy differences between the contending movements have grown.

Since 1993, an annual snapshot of the federal regulatory state, *The Ten Thousand Commandments*, has been published by C. Wayne Crews of the Competitive Enterprise Institute, a conservative Washington think tank. The 2023 report indicates that around 3,000 rules are issued each year, and since the Federal Register began reporting rules in 1978, 215,405 have been issued (Crews, 2023). A comprehensive database and assessment of industry-specific regulations (Al-Ubaydli and McLaughlin, 2015) claimed: "The American regulatory system has no working, systematic process for reviewing regulations for obsolescence or poor performance." Over time, it is argued to have "led to a vast stock of regulations." The regulatory system curbed pollution, but its flaws inhibit infrastructure and innovation in renewable energy development.

A few amendments of 1970s statutes were passed in the 1980s, but except for the *Safe Drinking Water Act Amendments of 1996*, the last major environmental laws passed by Congress were the *Oil Pollution Act of 1990* and the *Clean Air Act Amendments of 1990*. Gridlock in Congress over environmental regulatory policy has blocked subsequent environmental and energy legislation. The last effort to reauthorize and reform NEPA and ESA in ways that included environmental goals was led by Representative Richard Pombo, Chairman of the House Natural Resources Committee, in 2005. After a detailed review of ESA, a reform bill, the *Threatened and Endangered Species Recovery Act* (TESRA), passed the House with sparse Democratic support, but campaigns by environmental organizations helped defeat it in the Senate (Manheim, 2009).

A reform bill popular with the Republican Party has been the REINS Act, passed by the House of Representatives in 2011, but rejected in the Senate. It has been revived regularly since then (Dooling, 2019, Schnell and Beitsch, 2023). The REINS Act requires that new regulations with financial impacts over $100 million be approved by Congress. In short, it attempts to reduce excessive regulation through additional regulation. As expected, it is opposed by the Democratic Party.

### *Federal land law*

A special set of laws, the first being the *Northwest Ordinance Act of 1785,* referred to in Chapter 3, dealt with the management of federal lands. As a consequence of the Jacksonian turnover in the federal government, there was no follow-up to the Northwest Ordinance Act until the Progressive Era in the late 19th century. As noted in Chapter 4, lack of federal oversight and guidelines for management of federal land had severe environmental consequences for the areas west of the Mississippi River. The uncontrolled rush to exploit rich mineral deposits in California and western federal territories left behind contaminated waste dumps, some of which remain as Superfund sites today.

The Yosemite Valley was given as a protected area grant to California by President Lincoln in 1864, and the first National Park was established in 1872 under President Grant. The *Homestead and Railroad Acts of 1862*, the *General Mining Act of 1872*, the *Timber Culture Act of 1873*, the *Desert Lands Act of 1877*, and the *Free Timber Act of 1878* allocated land and resources, but there were no provisions for managing federal lands until the *Organic Act of 1879*, which created the US Geological Survey and authorized it to map and survey federal lands and resources. A Division of Forestry was created in the Department of Agriculture in 1881, but the first law allowing the federal government to manage land (national forest areas) was the *Forest Reserve Act of 1891*, which was vigorously employed by President Theodore Roosevelt. Less than half a page long, the *Federal Antiquities Act of 1906* allowed presidents to protect scenic and other valuable land features. The Act became controversial following President Carter's use of it to sequester tens of million acres of Alaskan land in 1977.

While a monument around the Hawaiian Islands was created by President George W. Bush, the law, originally intended protect historic and especially valuable scenic areas, was increasingly employed by Democratic presidents to sequester millions of acres of land primarily to prevent them from being exploited for economic purposes.

During the Great Depression, President Franklin D. Roosevelt's Civilian Conservation Corps planted billions of trees, eradicated invasive species, and improved wildlife habitats, and the Works Progress Administration and Public Works Administration built massive infrastructure projects. Important laws passed during Roosevelt's first term included the *Federal Power Act of 1930*, which created the Federal Energy Regulatory Commission, and the *Taylor Grazing Act 1934*. For the first time, the Act authorized the federal government to regulate grazing on federal lands. After the Second World War, two major laws preserving federal lands were the *Wilderness Act of 1964* and the *Wild and Scenic Rivers Act of 1968*. Among the laws of the 1970s, the *Forest Management Act of 1976* introduced major constraints and requirements for public input into the operations of the Forest Service.

In summary, exploitative land-use policies in the colonial period were already recognized as unwise by thoughtful leaders like Thomas Jefferson and James Madison. However, the development of enlightened management policies for managing federal land was inhibited by the patronage system initiated by President Andrew Jackson in 1829. Federal administrative policies and agencies capable of overseeing the environment and public health finally emerged in the late 19th century, but the destructive effects of uncontrolled mineral exploration in federal territories of the West in the 19th century continue to influence negative attitudes toward mining and mineral recovery in the present-day environmental movement. It is a current problem for renewable energy development, which has major mineral requirements.

The environmental laws of the 1970s form the basis for the current US environmental regulatory system, but, as noted previously, their economic impacts led to a countermovement whose excesses widened disagreement over policy to political polarization in the 1980s. The resulting Congressional gridlock has affected subsequent environmental, natural resource, and energy policy. As a consequence, presidents since the 1990s have been forced to pursue policies through executive orders and actions that can be revoked by succeeding presidents. Political antagonism reached extreme levels with the election of President Trump in 2016, and most of his initiatives were reversed in favor of strong environmental and climate change policies by President Joe Biden, but Trump's re-election portends another reversal of policy. Since the 1990s, the political center has tended to disappear (McCarty, 2008) as the Democratic and Republican Parties' primary goals have been to defeat the opposition rather than seek common ground and effective policy.

### *Environmental problems*

Besides greenhouse gases, according to an assessment by Earth.org (Igini, 2024), the US's six most important environmental problems are considered to be: 1) air pollution; 2) water pollution; 3) water supply; 4) wildfires; 5) food waste; and 6) plastic pollution. Air pollution comes primarily from transportation and power generation emissions, and wildfires that have reached record levels in recent years. Wildfires are discussed in Chapter 12.

Water pollution is attributable to runoff from America's agricultural areas. Fertilizers contribute nitrates and arsenic. Nitrates and phosphates contribute nutrients to water bodies. Decay of plankton blooms from excess nutrients discharged to the Gulf of Mexico contribute to a large oxygen-poor "dead zone" in the Gulf of Mexico. Drought conditions in the West have aggravated groundwater problems as "toxins seep deeper into the soil, tainting underground drinking water supplies" (Igini, 2024).

A serious problem is water supply, 80 percent of which is consumed by agriculture. This is aggravated by drought affecting the Colorado River, which supports water supply to Oklahoma, Colorado, Texas, New Mexico, and California. Groundwater is "mined" in western states, especially Arizona—that is, consumed in volumes exceeding replenishment, causing lowered groundwater levels. Further problems are aging delivery systems like pipelines. The costs for renewal of these systems are huge.

An estimated 40 percent of US food is wasted, the highest levels among nations, while 37 percent of Americans are estimated to be food insecure (Igini, 2024). Another kind of waste is plastics, pollution with which is twice that of China and more than all European nations combined. In this context, one may mention that EPA data (EPA, 2024b) show that the US landfills approximately 50 percent of its municipal waste (EPA, 2024b), whereas Sweden landfills only 1 percent of its waste (Manheim, 2022b). Sweden has achieved low levels by producing less waste and greater recycling, but also by incinerating waste with production of electricity and regional heat (Manheim, 2022b). US environmental NGOs are opposed to waste incineration (Sierra, 2024) because of the legitimate concern for air pollution and carbon emissions. This points a common problem in the US—aspects of climate change progress and other initiatives are inhibited by conflicting environmental concerns.

### *State activities*

With the US's only Mediterranean climate, a long and beautiful coastline, and magnificent forests, California is one of the most environmentally favored among states. However, it has active oilfields and abandoned mines, and Los Angeles is surrounded by mountains that trap pollutants close to the ground with frequent temperature inversions, against which the state was early in taking active steps. The state has long been the national leader in environmental policy and regulation.

Beginning in 2002, California initiated the nation's first restrictions on automotive emissions, gaining special federal status. In 2006, its *Global Warming Solutions Act* required reduction of greenhouse gas emissions to 1990 levels by 2020. The current goals are emissions 40 percent below 1990 levels by 2030. California has the two of the four major solar thermal power facilities in the nation. However, aggressive state programs have come at the cost of having the nation's highest living and housing costs after Hawaii.

Partly offsetting its traditional leadership in oil production, Texas has become the national leader in wind energy. The US reached a peak in coal production in 2008, but there has been rapid decline, due to retirement of coal-fired power plants spurred on by environmentalist pressure. Wyoming remains the overwhelming leader in production of high-quality, low-sulfur coal. The loss of bituminous coal mining in Appalachia has left serious economic problems for these low-income areas.

The federal Bureau of Offshore Energy Management has been aggressively leasing offshore wind areas off the states of Virginia, Delaware, New Jersey, New York, Rhode Island, and Massachusetts. As mentioned in the chapter on the Biden administration (Chapter 10), these are critical initiatives, given the lack of renewable energy supplies for populated Eastern states, but their value is partly offset by the high cost of offshore versus onshore turbines, and the effect of inflation on construction and regulatory problems. Turbines would be less expensive to install in state waters, but unlike Europe, as will be noted later, they are currently excluded because of environmental restrictions.

Florida is most exposed to risks associated with climate change, with increasingly damaging hurricanes, and cities and populated areas concentrated in low-lying coastal areas. It has huge discard piles of high-uranium-content gypsum, waste products of the Florida phosphate mining industry. These could become a source of uranium for nuclear power plants if technologies for winning uranium with gypsum as a byproduct were developed.

Significant progress was made in renewable energy development during the Obama administration, initiatives that were aggressively resumed during the Biden administration. Among the more permanent developments were wind turbine development in the high-wind mid-western swath, especially in Texas, and significant solar energy development. However, necessary progress in infrastructure development, nuclear energy, and carbon sequestration remains inhibited by regulatory obstruction, without considering anti-environmental policies of Donald Trump's administrations.

## Europe

### *Political evolution of environmental policy*

This review of European governance draws on my earlier summary, which begins: "In the ashes of World War II, seeds of hope were sown, survived, and grew among former enemies" (Manheim, 2009). Visionaries in Western Europe charted a new course that would avoid the blood feuds of the past and laid the economic and social groundwork for what evolved into the EU.

At The Hague in the Netherlands in 1948, leaders began a network of cooperation that would become one of the most stable and powerful economic and political unions in the world. A founding concept was that all voices had to be heard. European governance grew slowly with careful steps and planning. Inspired by Frenchmen Jean Monnet and Robert Schuman, the Treaty of Paris, signed by France, Germany, Italy, Belgium, the Netherlands, and Luxembourg in 1951 established the European Coal and Steel Community (ECSC). It was based on the idea that economic partners would have incentives to cooperate with rather than fight each other, and its success was aided economically and philosophically by the generosity of the US Marshall Plan. The ECSC managed the steel and coal industries through a High Authority and a Common Assembly, bodies that were the precursor to the European Parliament. A Council of Ministers represented the individual interests of the member states.

Security was an unstated goal of the ECSC, but the establishment of the US-led North Atlantic Treaty Organization (NATO) in 1949 meant that European nations showed little interest in military matters and were able to devote their energies to building civil structures. The Korean War (1950–1953) prompted the US to require Europe to support more of its own defense, but the formation of a European Defense Community failed when the French Parliament rejected it in 1954. Accession to the EU by nations is chronicled in Table 11.1. Seven other nations are now candidates or in negotiations for membership in the EU. Norway, Switzerland, and the UK are not in the EU, but they cooperate closely with it and adhere to most of its policies.

Six years after the ECSC was formed, the Treaty of Rome (1957) initiated the European Economic Community (EEC)—the heart of what would later become a common market. This culminated in 1986 with the Single European Act, which allowed capital and labor to move across national boundaries, free of duties or visas (Table 11.2). Subsidies remained in some agricultural regions as the price for successful negotiations.

The Treaty of Rome also established the European Atomic Energy Community (Euratom) for the development of nuclear energy. The leading bodies of the EEC, the Commission, the Council of Ministers, and an advisory parliamentary assembly, like the hierarchy of the ECSC, were

**Table 11.1:** Accession of nations to the European Union

| Year | Country |
|---|---|
| 1951 | France, Germany, Italy, the Netherlands, Belgium, Luxembourg |
| 1973 | UK, Ireland, Denmark |
| 1981 | Greece |
| 1986 | Portugal, Spain |
| 1995 | Sweden, Finland, Austria |
| 2004 | Czech Republic, Estonia, Cyprus, Latvia, Lithuania, Hungary, Malta, Poland, Slovakia, Slovenia |
| 2007 | Bulgaria, Romania |
| 2013 | Croatia |
| 2020 | UK left EU |

Source: Wikipedia—The European Union

forerunners to the later EU. In addition to the administrative and legislative branches, a judicial branch, the European Court of Justice, was created to settle disputes involving the Treaty of Rome and the decisions that were made by the EEC.

Nations that remained outside the EEC initially formed the European Free Trade Association (EFTA) in 1960, but it had little of the dynamism of the EEC, and some members applied for EEC membership in 1961. The accession of the UK, Ireland, and Denmark to the organization took place in 1973, after challenges posed by EEC members and failed referendums in the home nations. By then, the treaty of European communities and the treaty establishing the European community customs union had been ratified (see Table 11.2).

French President Charles de Gaulle, the presidents of the Bundesbank, and British Prime Minister Margaret Thatcher were all nationalists who put the brakes on EU progress. They objected to strengthening the federal government of the EEC and the EU. De Gaulle wanted a permanent leadership role for France, while the conservative, semi-autonomous Bundesbank resisted relinquishing Germany's position as the European central banker to the new EU central bank. Thatcher was unwilling to give up either Britain's borders or its currency. Counterbalancing the nationalists were pan-Europeanists: the pre-eminent peacemaker, German Chancellor Konrad Adenauer, author of the EU Constitution, French President Valéry Giscard-d'Estaing, and early visionaries Jean Monnet and Robert Schuman.

Eventually, all three nations joined and became staunch members of the EU, working around their differences with compromise fostered by intensive

**Table 11.2:** List of major developments in EU history

| Year | Events |
|---|---|
| 1948 | The Hague Conference: European federalists meet |
| 1949 | North Atlantic Treaty Organization (NATO) |
| 1951 | Treaty of Paris: European Coal and Steel Community (ECSC) |
| 1957 | Treaty of Rome: European Economic Community (EEC) and European Atomic Energy Commission (Euratom) |
| 1960 | European Free Trade Association (EFTA), not part of EEC |
| 1967 | EEC, ECSC, Euratom merged |
| 1971 | Bretton Woods established the US dollar as the basis of internation trade: EEC currencies were weakened |
| 1979 | Initial European currency moves towards the euro (finally realized in 1999) |
| 1986 | Single European Act (SEA); common market agreements |
| 1992 | Maastricht Treaty: European Union (EU) established: common environmental policies adopted |
| 1995 | Schengen Agreement; free border movement |
| 1999 | European Central Bank (ECB) and European monetary system begin |
| 2002 | First euros circulated; UK, Sweden, Denmark abstain |
| 2004 | Accession of ten nations |
| 2004 | EU constitution ratification failed; EU continued under treaties |
| 2009 | Lisbon Treaty; reforms of legal system; establishment of President of European Council |
| 2010 | Debt crisis for some nations |
| 2012 | Nobel Peace Prize awarded to European Union |
| 2020 | UK formally leaves EU (Brexit); common approach to COVID-19 epidemic |
| 2022 | Russian attack on Ukraine: EU imposes sanctions and supports Ukraine |

Source: Expanded from Manheim (2009)

discussion and debate. After having long agitated for withdrawal of the UK from the EU, Boris Johnson became Prime Minister in 2019 and won a referendum to do just that in a close vote in 2021. However, a 2024 poll showed that 55 percent of the British public thinks it was wrong to leave the EU (Statista, 2024).

The path to a single European currency was realized in 1999, when 11 nations replaced their national currencies with the euro. Other nations subsequently joined the club, while the UK and Sweden remained the chief holdouts. The common monetary system had the effect of allowing all member States to see each other's economic progress on a level playing field. Differences among European nations in terms of gross domestic product became a problem in the late 1980s, but this was resolved by richer nations increasing aid to the poorer nations.

Some European nations were better managed than others. An important key to progress were the twice-yearly summit meetings held in different Member States and rotation of chairs of key governing bodies. At each summit, common problems were discussed, and new steps were planned. The mixture of supranational and intergovernmental bodies ensured full knowledge and agreement before each new step was taken. The strength of the EU has been its ability to allow different practices and avoid escalation of discussion into destructive rhetoric.

In 1991, the collapse of the Soviet Union ended the Cold War. Germany was reunified, and Eastern European members of the Warsaw Pact, forced into the Soviet Communist bloc after the Second World War, asserted their independence, with most joining the EU. With ratification of the Maastricht Treaty (1992), the EC became the EU. Ratification of the treaty ran into temporary opposition when it was submitted to the citizens in referendums, but after two years, ratification was achieved, with some reservations. Treaty provisions for common monetary and social policies strengthened the EU, and its benefits attracted new applicants.

A key to the success of the EU is its benefits to all member nations. Richer nations profit by the interchange of ideas, technologies, and markets for their product, while poorer nations gain from administrative policies and fiscal discipline needed to meet membership requirements and gain financial and technical assistance from the EU. The governmental transparency required for EU membership, and frequent contacts with leaders from other nations, have been factors for rapid growth in nations like Ireland, Estonia, and Romania. Ireland and Finland went from being poor countries after the Second World War to prosperous nations as a result of their EU membership.

As summarized by Yeşilada and Wood (2009), laws and regulations decided by the European Parliament involve matters of general principles and policies, while details are left to individual nations to implement. The EU does not have police powers, but consensus behind its policies and laws allows it to exert pressure on nations that lag. The Amsterdam Treaty of 1997 anticipated the influx of new Member States from Eastern Europe that lacked long experience with democracy. It upgraded EU laws and social policies and gave the Schengen Agreement of 1995 the force of law. The Schengen Agreement had eliminated border controls within the EC and was the starting point for the Charter of Fundamental Rights, which allowed free movement across national borders.

When the euro made its formal debut in 2002, the logical next step was writing a constitution for the EU. Though this did not reach agreement, EU governance functioned well based on existing treaties and adding bodies needed to serve member States. Representation for both the people and the governments of the Member States helped gain acceptance for decisions by the EU's governing bodies.

The EU is a looser confederation than the US. It has experienced numerous crises, but resolutions are facilitated by twice-yearly meetings in different capitals and open communication and transparency. Its political mechanisms have demonstrated effectiveness, maintaining flexibility and respect for the concerns of affected groups. The EU experience shows that cooperation and diverse cultures, along with 20 different languages, are not mutually exclusive. As will be described later on, its law-making provisions offer experience and insights that could help the US resolve political gridlock once recognition of the need for fundamental reforms is accepted.

## *Law making and policy*

The organization of the EU shown in Figure 11.1 describes the multiple approaches to national participation in governance. Member States' electorates choose representatives to the European Parliament. Officials of national governments appoint the members of the European Court of Justice, the European Commission, and Council of the European Union. The Council, composed of heads of state and the president of the Commission, develops concepts for future EU initiatives. The president of the European Council represents the EU in discussions with foreign nations and international councils. The Maastricht Treaty of the European Union (1992) confirmed the principle of proportionality and subsidiarity, which allows for Member States to exercise full independence on matters within their individual competence. The EU takes the lead in areas beyond these limits.

The operational heart of the EU is the European Commission, which receives proposals for laws and independently prepares them for the European Parliament. It monitors the operations of member nations and compliance with EU law, although neither it nor other top EU bodies have enforcement power. Implementation of EU laws is left to the Member States. Most EU nations have a parliamentary system under which the governing party or coalition can initiate laws. Critical details about the law-making process in advanced EU nations tend to be omitted in academic literature, but are included in an exceptionally detailed English-language exposition of German politics (Dalton, 2017). Important aspects are the role of apolitical ministry experts and exposure of draft laws to different constituencies during the law-making process. The following steps for German law making are an example of this process:

1. *Initiative.* Legislative proposals are initiated by the ruling party or coalition. Alternatively, bills may be proposed by Parliament (the Bundestag, corresponding to the US House of Representatives) or, less often, by the

**Figure 11.1:** Governance of the European Union

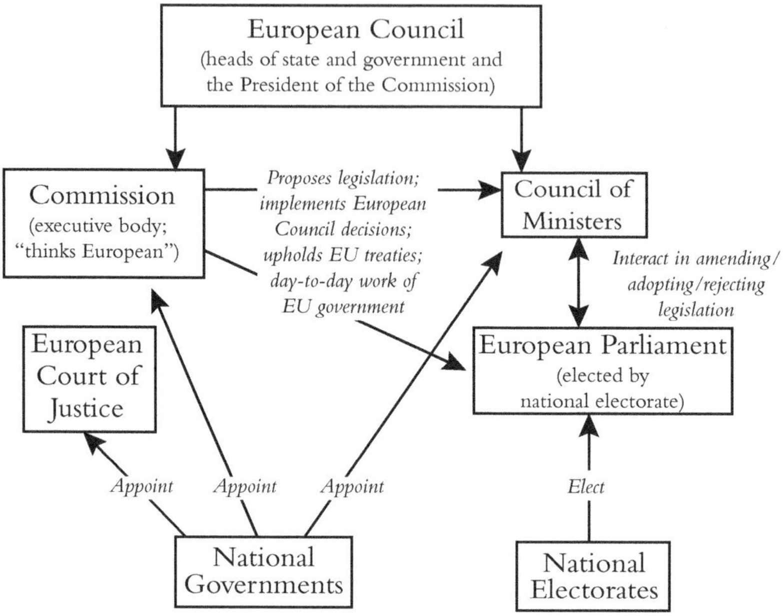


Source*:* Manheim (2009) and Yeşilada and Wood (2009)

Bundesrat, the body representing the Länder (corresponding to the US Senate); bills may also be proposed by private citizens or other bodies.

2. *Inquiry*. For major laws, the proposal is given to Bundestag committees corresponding to special fields of federal ministries. Procedural rules guide cooperation of federal ministry staff in these committees. Unlike the US, the government does not appoint heads of the committees, which operate in cooperative ways.
3. *Referral*. The revised draft is submitted to other ministries, constituencies, and stakeholders, including local political units, in order to gauge response to the bill. Consultant reports or contacts with other EU nations may be included, if appropriate. The draft bill is submitted to the Bundesrat, which may make further revisions.
4. *Government bill*. On receiving the revised draft, the government submits it to the Bundestag legislative advisory committee for refinement. This will include consideration of interactions with or potential conflict with existing laws. EU law is also considered.
5. *Parliamentary action*. The parliamentary committee submits a report on the bill, after which it is presented for debate, amendments, and voting. Once passed, the law is published and encoded in the book of law codes.

At an EPA Partnership Summit, the Environmental Counselor for the European Commission in Washington, D.C., Malachy Hargadon, described the Commission's preparation of higher-level proposals for the European Parliament as following patterns analogous to that described earlier (Hargadon, 2008). The Commission received proposed laws from a variety of sources within the EU, and its deliberations involved active interaction with all relevant constituencies. After this, draft bills were submitted to the Council of Ministers and other relevant bodies before being taken up by the European Parliament.

The critical difference between European and US law making is in the way in which laws are prepared. European policy involves the participation of apolitical experts, and drafts are shown to affected constituencies, including opposing parties. The purpose is to minimize conflict and unanticipated problems. According to Dalton (2017), between 1998 and 2002, this system led to 90 percent of laws proposed by the governing body being approved by the Bundestag, 35 percent of laws proposed by the Bundestag being approved, and 24 percent of laws proposed by the Bundesrat being approved. As in Germany, a large proportion of the debate and amendment process in England also takes place prior to the final submission of laws to the House of Commons and House of Lords (Library of Congress, 2020).

In contrast, in the US, there is no formal vetting process for bills submitted to Congress, except that bills marked up (approved) by committees for vote in Congress are scored for cost by the Congressional Budget Office. In the 117th Congress (2021–2023), 17,817 bills were submitted to Congress, but only 365 (2 percent) were signed by the president (GovTrack, 2024). It is clear that this system is enormously inefficient, engaging most of the time of members of Congress in legislation that will not gain approval. It is worth noting that the US system prior to the 1970s had greater similarities to the current European law-making system because, like the latter, apolitical professional experts from federal agencies played a significant role in Congressional law making. The nonpartisan role of US federal agencies in law making was diminished by the *Civil Service Reform Act of 1978*, which increased the president's influence on federal agencies and their policies, and reduced the role of independent civil service administrators and experts.

## *Environmental policies and principles*

In the 1970s, European nations had specialized laws with command-and-control functions. A Norwegian official stated to me that laws might, for example, specify the configuration of oarlocks on rowboats. In Germany, severe air pollution led to passage of a strict Federal Republic of Germany emission law, the *Bundes-Immissionsschutzgesetz*, following an amendment to the Federal German Constitution. This law was sparked by sulfur dioxide emissions from the industrial complex in the Ruhr valley, causing widespread damage to German forests (*Waldsterben*), which held special value for the German public. The environmental impact statement concept included in the US NEPA legislation was widely adopted in modified form in Germany as well as other European nations.

In 1987, the groundbreaking UN Commission report *Our Common Future*, chaired by Norwegian Prime Minister Gro Harlem Brundtland (Brundtland, 1987), transformed environmental policies in Europe. In her introduction to the report, Brundtland recognized that there were those who wanted proposed laws strictly limited to environmental issues. However, she stated: "The environment does not exist as a sphere separate from human actions, ambitions, and needs," adding that isolating it "would have been a grave mistake." The Brundtland Report enjoyed wide respect in Europe, and the ensuing system integrates economic and environmental issues in policy making. The report introduced the concept of sustainable development as the basis of European environmental policy.

According to the Treaty on the Functioning of the European Union (TFEU), the EU has responsibilities for all aspects of environmental policy, including air and water pollution, waste management, and climate change. Environmental policy follows the three principles of precaution, prevention, and polluter pays. Combating climate change became a specific goal with the Treaty of Lisbon in 2009.

As described previously, legislation may be initiated within the European Commission, suggested by EU Council members, or by various sources within the EU. Once proposed, laws are subjected to an impact assessment (IA) and vetted for their potential impact from all perspectives and by dialoging with potential stakeholders, including consumers, labor unions, industry, NGOs, and political bodies. A draft law is prepared for submission to committees of the European Parliament that examine potential conflicts and prepare the laws for a vote. For example, Germany proposed its *Elektrische Gesetz*, or law governing recycling of electrical appliances. After due process, the *Waste Electrical and Electronic Equipment* (WEEE) law was passed by the European Council and European Parliament on January 27, 2003. Among other provisions, the WEEE required the replacement of potentially toxic metals like cadmium, mercury, and lead in electrical and electronic equipment to the fullest extent practicable.

Four years of intensive analysis, discussion, and negotiation preceded the introduction of the *Registration, Evaluation and Authorisation of Chemicals* (REACH) Regulation, approved by the European Council and the European Parliament in December 2006. Under this law, a chemical management agency was established in Helsinki, Finland, to which producers or importers of toxic chemicals to the EU had to submit applications (The Center for Sustainable Production and Consumption).

The REACH law placed responsibility for assessing toxicities and describing safeguards for use of toxic chemicals on producers and importers, not on the agency. Applications for chemicals involving volumes exceeding 1,000 metric tons were to be submitted within three years; volumes between 100 and 1,000 tons were to be submitted within six years, and volumes between 1 and 100 tons were to be submitted within ten years—that is, by 2018 (Manheim, 2009).

Chemicals were the EU's single largest manufactured product and accounted for 31 percent of global production. Because it affects sellers to the EU, REACH has become a de facto global law, which Japan adapted (as did many nations) with variations. However, while individual US states have adapted to REACH, US laws of the 1970s and 1980s differ from REACH, which stipulates uniform standards and procedures, which are both open to the judgment of professional regulators who are empowered to evaluate and accept or reject applications for use of chemicals. REACH allows provisional use subject to future submission of supplementary data and considers requests for special waivers.

In European law making more generally, careful advance preparation of environmental proposals, assisted by the fact that they can be tested in one or more EU Member States, accounts for the fact that a large proportion of proposals are approved. Criticisms of environmental regulations that inhibited economic progress in Europe were the focus of the fifth summit of EU environmental protection agency heads in Prague in 2005, "Prague Statement" (Anonymous, 2005). The most recent (40th) meeting of the EU's EPA heads was held in Helsinki in 2023.

### *Swedish and Scandinavian environmental policy*

Widely regarded as an innovator and leader in EU environmental policy, Sweden's environmental management system has a uniquely decentralized approach (Thews et al, 2017). In 1999, Sweden consolidated 15 previous environmental laws into a single environmental code of 700+ pages. The code contained a comprehensive list of categories of activities and assigned them administrative oversight levels corresponding to their environmental hazards. For example, bulk mineral mining permits like sand and gravel pits and limestone quarries were in category C. Permitting and environmental management for this category was handled by municipal boards. Normal mining exploration except uranium was in category B, handled by län (the equivalent of US states). Nuclear power plants or full-scale mining operations were in category A, handled by one of five regional environmental courts. These courts not only made legal decisions, but also had advisory and oversight capabilities. My interview with the director of the Swedish Environmental Protection Agency in 2007 revealed the startling information that while the Swedish EPA was respected for its research and environmental guidance, it had no enforcement powers.

Decentralized approaches to environmental regulation also characterize other Scandinavian nations. The Norwegian Petroleum Directorate (NPD), for example, does not publish formal regulations for offshore petroleum exploration and leasing. Instead, it develops environmental plans and regulations as a part of contracts with each organization. The NPD no doubt has internal guidelines, but it retains the freedom to develop independent plans adapted to the circumstances of each lease. The NPD also urges companies interested in leasing in Norwegian waters to cooperate in order to share advanced environmental technology. Its policies promote efficiency and foster creative adaptation to specific environmental conditions, but they also demand high standards and trustworthiness on the part of the NPD. The stability of leadership in the NPD is indicated by the fact that Fredrik Hagemann served as founding director of the NPD in 1972 and served for 24 years until 1996 (Wikipedia—Norwegian Offshore Directorate).

Such policies attest to the efficiency gained in regulatory policies when mutual trust exists between society and governmental agencies. A Finnish book on administrative management (Harisalo and Stenvall, 2004) claimed that trust in people and organizations is more important than financial capital, and it suggested that where there is trust, government organizations can be as efficient as private organizations. The problem of regaining trust in environmental relations in the US is addressed in Chapter 13.

## Climate change policy and progress

### *Introduction*

After ratification by 198 nations, the United Nations Framework Convention on Climate Change (UNFCCC) went into effect in 1994. The urgency of controlling human influence on climate change was again affirmed by 194 nations in the Paris Agreement of 2015.[2] The only holdouts were oil producers: Iran, Libya, and Yemen (Wikipedia—Paris Agreement). Under the leadership of President Barack Obama, the US signed and actively supported the Paris Agreement, but US participation was withdrawn by his successor, President Trump, in 2017. The agreement was rejoined by President Biden in 2020. This sequence of events illustrates that political polarization in the US not only has "negative effects on the efficient functioning of the administrative state and the judiciary" (McCarty et al, 2008), but is a fundamental inhibitor for progress against climate change.

Contrasting with the Trump withdrawal, a 2023 poll by the nonpartisan Pew Research Center showed that 74 percent of Americans favored participating in international environmental agreements (Tyson et al, 2023), indicating that the US public is less polarized on this subject than political leaders. A similar conclusion had been drawn in earlier research by Fiorina et al (2010).

According to an article published by the International Renewable Energy Agency (Lyons et al, 2021), "The use of renewables coupled with reductions in energy intensity [that is, amounts of energy used for given functions] will be the principal pillars of a net-zero pathway," but this approach will need to be supplemented by $CO_2$ capture and storage and other adaptive methods. These authors estimate that adaptation has lagged in development. To reach net zero by 2050, adaptation will need to reach an amount of $CO_2$ similar to that currently removed by all global forests. Direct and indirect mitigation methods including industrial and agricultural processes are summarized in an article with 364 references (Wikipedia—Climate Mitigation), and numerous online references in Google and Google Scholar.

An in-depth economic review for lay audiences (Dorman, 2022) found that five scenarios for reaching net-zero carbon emissions by 2050 required negative emissions, such as use of energy from biomass supplemented by carbon sequestration. Another economic review of climate change policy for "puzzled citizens" (Rebonato, 2024) emphasized that while the science is reasonably settled, the economics is not. Decisions offer difficult trade-offs between concern for future citizens and the "happiness" of current citizens. The remainder of this chapter will explore greenhouse gas emission history over the past ten years, including US and European production of renewable energy.

### *The growth of carbon dioxide emissions*

Energy is a core requirement for societal development, and China and developing nations are actively increasing their energy supply. China began an enormous boom in energy production and carbon emissions after it was admitted to the World Trade Organization in 2001, with growth overwhelmingly from fossil fuels. It is now the world's leading emitter of $CO_2$, especially from coal, which currently supplies 60 percent of the nation's energy. However, China is also actively building renewable energy capacity and is estimated to provide 90 percent of the world's solar PV panels, even though its increase in renewable energy remains lower than its increase in use of fossil fuel energy. The urgency of increasing international use of renewable energy development is revealed by Figure 11.2, which plots $CO_2$ emissions from major areas of the world from 1970 to 2022. "Other countries" shown in the graph now rival emissions from China. The projections of the International Energy Agency to meet the necessary reduction requirements in terms of emissions require a dramatic increase in

**Figure 11.2:** Annual emissions of major nations and groupings, in millions of tons

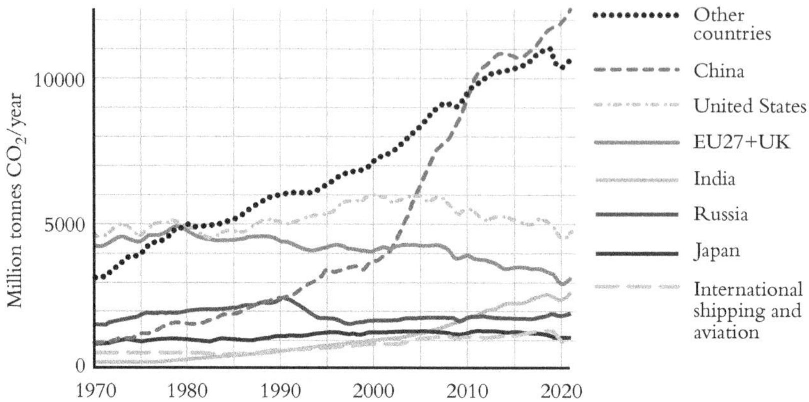


Source: Data from Crippa et al (2023) with figure created by "Tomastvivlaren"; https://sv.wikipedia.org/wiki/Användare:Tomastvivlaren

use of low-cost renewables or low-carbon energy by this group of nations (IEA, 2023).

Europe and the US began with roughly comparable carbon emissions. Europe began emissions reduction after 1990, whereas the US reductions were slower and reached a plateau after 2000. Both regions increased emissions reduction after 2008, with Europe lowering emissions to a level more than 20 percent less than the US. India increased emissions, surpassing the EU in 2023 to become the world's third-largest carbon emitter (IEA, 2024).

## *Renewable energy*

Figure 11.3 compares the supply of renewable energy for Europe and the US from diverse sources. Each row of renewable energy sources has a common scale, and the rows descend in terms of electrical power levels. For both Europe and the US, the greatest increases achieved in the last ten years are in wind and solar energy, while hydropower (created by turbines in dams of rivers and streams) has remained relatively constant. The IRENA report (Lyons et al, 2021) indicates that wind and solar overwhelmingly dominate renewable energy investments. Together, they make up 95 percent of world investments in renewable energy.

Bioenergy is in the second tier of renewable sources in Figure 11.3. However, the IRENA world renewable energy outlook report in 2021 indicated that to meet zero net carbon emissions by 2050, bioenergy should be increased fivefold from current levels, with biofuels needing to increase sixfold in order to supply air and other transportation sectors. It currently has important roles in the UK, Sweden, and Finland, where wood pellets fire powerplants and, along with the incineration of municipal waste, provide regional heat for residences. Though not part of the Europe–US comparison, Brazil's RenovaBio program has become an efficient provider of biomass energy through integrated cooperation between private producers and government regulators. Other South American nations have suitable conditions for biomass development, but have not yet adopted the necessary operational conditions. In contrast, development of bioenergy in the US has not increased because of opposition from major environmental NGOs (PFPI, 2016). In earlier years, there was significant US interest in electrical power developed from wave and tidal motion, and federal regulators received numerous permit requests. However, these opportunities have not been realized.

Figure 11.3 reveals that the US lags behind Europe in every renewable energy type except biofuels and geothermal energy, the smallest sectors. As will be reviewed in the next chapter, this condition is an anomaly in terms of earlier US history, when the nation was in the vanguard among nations in applied science and technology.

Notwithstanding record budgets for infrastructure and renewable energy development in laws passed by the Biden administration (see Chapter 10), US renewable energy development faces numerous problems. For example, a goal of 30 gigawatts of offshore power development by 2030 was set by the Biden administration for the high-wind-energy corridor along the Atlantic coast of the US. This power, roughly equivalent to 30 large nuclear power plants, was needed for the densely populated eastern coastal region, which has a shortage of alternative sources of renewable energy. A pillar of the Biden administration's renewable energy plan (Storrow, 2023), it would have provided a major part of the power needs of the New England states plus New York and New Jersey.

However, setbacks emerged for projects administered by the Bureau of Offshore Energy Management (BOEM). These included financial (for example, rising interest rates), technical, and coordination problems that caused up to half of the private operators and sponsors to withdraw from or delay projects in waters off New Jersey, Massachusetts, Connecticut, and Rhode Island. In other areas of the nation, supply problems and raw material shortages, insufficient industrial capacity, NIMBYism, and litigation combined with regulatory barriers to obstruct infrastructure electrical grids, such as those from the wind energy-rich Midwest.

### *The role of nuclear power*

With expertise in nuclear technology gained during the Manhattan Project (the atom bomb development during the Second World War), the US

**Figure 11.3:** Comparison of renewable energy production in Europe and the United States

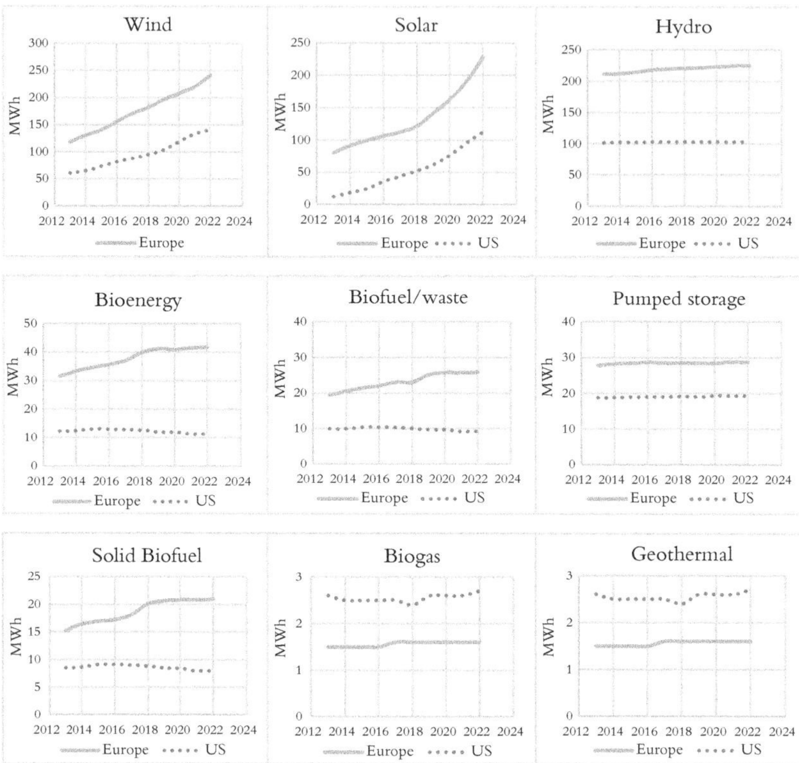


Note: European data are in solid lines, and US data are in dashed lines.

Source: International Renewable Agency (IRENA, 2023)

became the pioneer in nuclear power. Westinghouse delivered the first fully commercial pressurized water reactor in 1960. A boiling water reactor model developed by the Argonne National Laboratory and commercialized by General Electric started in the same year. The first multinational survey of levelized reactor cost (including capital and operational cost) (Lovering et al, 2016) reported that from 1954 to 1968, base costs for the earliest US reactors declined sharply from $6,800 to $1,300/Kw, with reactor size increasing from 80 MW to 620 MW. From 1964 to 1967, costs were in the $1,000–1,500/kW range, with an increase in size from 800 MW to 1,100 MW. Between 1967 and 1972, reactor costs varied between $600 and $2,500/Kw. By the late 1960s, large-scale production of nuclear power plants made the US the overwhelming world leader in installations, a position it still retains (Table 11.3). Early European experience in Germany and France was similar to that in the US. In France, for example, a domestically

**Table 11.3:** Nuclear power generation (2022), in gigawatt/h by region

| Region | GWh |
|---|---|
| US | 772.1 |
| China | 395.3 |
| Europe | 609.3 |
| France | 282.1 |
| Russia | 209.5 |
| South Korea | 167.5 |
| Canada | 81.7 |
| Ukraine | 81.1 |
| Spain | 56.2 |
| Japan | 51.9 |

Source: Wikipedia—Nuclear Power

developed gas-cooled model was changed to a modified version of the US Westinghouse pressurized water model in the later 1960s.

In the US, temporary interruption in reactor starts took place in 1971 and 1972 when increased public concern about environment pollution led to the creation of the EPA and passage of NEPA in 1970. In the same year, court decisions in a NEPA suit against the Calvert Cliffs nuclear power plant made the NEPA Act judicially enforceable and toughened rules (see Chapter 6), requiring backfitting of the plant. Anti-nuclear activism, including concern about radiation, nuclear proliferation and terrorism, and waste disposal, increased regulatory requirements and costs. Loss of confidence in the Atomic Energy Commission led to the transfer of its responsibilities to the Nuclear Regulatory Commission in 1974. Over 120 reactor proposals were cancelled (Wikipedia—Nuclear Power).

Concerns about nuclear power also arose in Germany in the 1970s, and protests led to cancellation of a proposed plant in Wyhl in 1975. However, the impact of the 1973 Arab oil embargo on France's energy provisions increased French commitment to nuclear power. In 15 years, it came to dominate France's electrical energy requirements and currently supplies nearly 70 percent of French electrical power.

In 1979, the partial meltdown of Unit 2 at the Three Mile Island plant near Harrisburg, Pennsylvania, created a sensation in the US and abroad, although the accident resulted in no deaths or health risks to workers or the public (NRC, 2024). Lovering et al (2016) compiled data on the costs of reactors in construction before and after the accident. They ranged from $1,800 to $11,000 per kW, with costs rising steeply in the latest starts. New regulatory requirements and environmentalist opposition, often initiated through NEPA, lengthened permitting and construction times. Increased costs associated with these changes made nuclear power uncompetitive, and new plant starts stopped.

The Reagan administration recommitted to nuclear energy, leading to a modest number of reactor completions, expansions, and new starts in the 1980s. However, the disastrous explosion in the Chernobyl reactor in the Soviet Union (now Ukraine) in 1986 created a worldwide shock. It disseminated radioactive iodine-131, cesium-134 and 137 into the atmosphere, affecting areas in the Ukraine, Belarus, and Russia. Atmospheric air currents spread fallout as far west as France and Italy and north to Sweden. It led to Germany's decision to phase out nuclear energy, which required Germany, despite its commitment to reduce greenhouse gases, to resume burning low-quality coal and lignite to provide energy for electrical power. A similar decision by Sweden to phase out nuclear reactors affected more than 30 percent of its electrical power. However, the decision was reversed in 2009, and current plans call for the construction of new large nuclear reactors by 2035. In the US after Chernobyl, high costs for nuclear power construction and declines in the cost of alternate fuels made nuclear power no longer competitive, effectively shutting down new nuclear power plant starts since 1990 except for two installations in Georgia.

Nuclear power represents a difficult resource problem. All major international projections recognize the need for nuclear power to meet $CO_2$ emissions goals. It offers stable power, can serve as backup to intermittent renewables, and complements them by potentially providing blue hydrogen as transportation fuel. No serious operational problems have occurred since the Chernobyl disaster, which was caused by a flawed Soviet reactor design, compounded by workers who made major mistakes. Along with other nuclear nations, Russia now supports the International Atomic Energy Agency and its recommendations. New technologies like small modular, high-temperature, fast-neutron, and molten salt reactors promise improvements in performance and economics, safety, and waste profiles (Grossi, 2024).

Along with wind and solar, nuclear energy is among the safest energy sources, based on deaths per terawatt of power (Ritchie, 2024). The US Office of Nuclear Energy points out that nuclear power plants require only 1/75th and 1/300th of the space required for equivalent power production by solar photovoltaic and wind, respectively. Waste is concentrated and requires far less space than waste from discarded solar panels. It can also be reprocessed.

However, powerful forces oppose nuclear energy. Opposition is especially strong in the US, where major environmental NGOs like the Sierra Club (Jealous, 2023) oppose it. Besides using Chernobyl as symbols of the dangers of nuclear power, valid environmentalist arguments include concerns about nuclear proliferation and threats from terrorists, unpredictable natural events such as those that happened at Fukushima, Japan in 2011, and most persuasively, excessive cost. Germany, Belgium, Switzerland, and Taiwan have all committed to phasing out nuclear power, although delays have taken place. It is mainly China that is actively building new nuclear power plants.

However, environmental pressures have been the main factor elevating costs for nuclear power installations in the US. Even the Chernobyl disaster raised costs only modestly in France, and South Korea has been building nuclear power plants at costs comparable to those in the US prior to Three Mile Island (Lovering et al, 2016). Experts have pointed out that government regulations adopted to assure the public or to minimize legal challenges require elaborate precautions that responsible operating organizations take as a matter of course. An underrated problem is that industries that lack operational flexibility will not attract dynamic and innovative leaders. High executive and worker pay in the large existing US nuclear industry may have helped maintain qualified staff.

Beyond the need of data centers for high-capacity sources of electrical power, factors and policies that can help overcome the challenges to expanded use of nuclear energy include carbon pricing, that is, placing a fee of $CO_2$ emissions, clean energy standards, and advanced reactor technology. Core issues like lack of public trust and overregulation are discussed in Chapters 12 and 13.

Data summarized in this chapter indicate that the US lags behind Europe in progress against climate change. It is hampered by outdated regulatory policies and domestic conflict. The problem is exacerbated by the fact that without an ability to create consensus-based policy and gain international credibility, the US is hindered in contributing to solution of international problems, notably the demands of developing nations for energy in ways that minimize carbon emissions and global warming. Rebonato (2024) points out that without unified support from advanced nations to help developing nations achieve lowered emissions, the best of modelled plans may be beyond reach.

Both Democratic and Republican presidents and senior observers have agreed that bloat and inefficiency have accumulated in the federal government. Before the 1970s, federal agencies under the former civil service system provided apolitical, expert guidance for the Executive Office and Congressional law makers in ways that are now effectively employed in advanced European nations (see Chapter 5). They had minimum power to regulate and did not make up a "swamp" of overweening bureaucracy that the incoming Trump administration proposes to drain. This is an example of the importance of taking account of US history as well as advanced environmental and energy policies in effect in Europe and other nations in considering policy issues and pathways for future progress (see Chapters 12 and 13).

# 12

# Policy Issues and Discussion

## The information problem

A vast increase in access to information has taken place since the electronic era began. Online accessibility of data, including Google's project to digitize all books and historical documents, dramatically facilitated historical research. However, the flood of electronic media has ironically made access to balanced information about public affairs much harder. The electronic era provided new entertainment media, appeals to discretionary interests, and personal communication through social media. These diversions of public interest and the competition of derivative electronic news sources have led to a decline in journalism. An article in *The Atlantic* magazine (Farhi, 2024) cited recent losses of hundreds of journalists at the *Washington Post*, *NBC News*, *ABC News*, *National Public Radio*, *Vice*, *Vox*, and *BuzzFeed*. Major newspapers like the *Chicago Tribune* have been hollowed out after being purchased by hedge fund owners. Farhi noted that: "Denver's two dailies ... employed more than 600 journalists before the Rocky Mountain Times went under in 2009. Today the Denver Post's newsroom directory lists 59 journalists, who have to cover a region of nearly 3 million people." The situation for rural newspapers is even more dire.

Editors of mainstream media have reduced "hard" reporting on serious issues. In fairness, their decisions take into account the lack interest by the general public in societal and political affairs (Flatow, 2024). This can be seen in the content of magazine racks in any drug store or supermarket or on TV news. It was strikingly confirmed in a survey by the Annenberg Public Policy Center in 2017, which reported that only one American in four could name the three branches of the federal government. Subsequent Annenberg reports with changes in methodology have only muddied the picture.

Political polarization has contributed to loss of a common base of credible information on current affairs that was available in the Walter Cronkite era.[1] People with differing political orientations now have separate sources of information. Democratic supporters favor National Public Radio and TV, CNN, and mainstream news media like the *New York Times* and the *Washington Post*, whereas Trump supporters favor *Fox News*, *Newsmax*, *Breitbart,* and *One America* as sources. Figure 12.1 shows a kaleidoscopic distribution of US media according to political bias and type of coverage. While a lot of media, whether they lean right or left, do not deliberately misinform or provide inaccurate information, they may promote bias by selective emphasis and omission. However, even media outlets that seek balance may fail to report controversial detail found only in more ideologically oriented sources.

The loss of in-depth journalism dealing with global climate change and environment is only partly compensated for by the publications of nonpartisan organizations like the World Resources Institute, think tanks like *McKinsey & Co.*, the political magazine *The Hill* (which offers regular coverage of environmental and energy policy), *Grist,* and *Inside Climate News*, which claims to have the largest US desk dealing with climate news, and has won awards for its coverage. Older and newer print and online media like *The Atlantic, TIME, Reuters, The New Republic, The American Prospect, Substack's Free Press* and *The Bulwark, Mother Jones, Politico,* and *APNews* tend to reach informed and politically interested audiences, but not the wider public. They offer occasional opinion pieces and research articles on environmental affairs, but not consistent coverage.

Loss of public information by the public has also taken place since the 1960s because research by leading American academic institutions has become fragmented into disciplines and largely isolated from the wider society. Researchers submitting papers to flagship journals in the social sciences now pay around $5,000 if they want open publication of peer-reviewed articles—that is, publications accessible without stiff costs per article. Only students and academic faculty can view scholarly literature free through their library connections. As will be discussed later on in this chapter, the academic publish-or-perish system also led to the decline in broad syntheses of information of the kind needed by decision makers and the interested public.

Academic publications in fields under discussion are affected by political polarization even if their authors seek to avoid ideological bias. Articles on environmental policy, including publications of the National Academies of Sciences, Engineering, and Medicine, tend to skirt sensitive issues (which are often the most important) to avoid controversy. Some authors do so to avoid being labeled or risking their jobs. On the other hand, a few widely cited academic authors have abandoned scholarly conventions of objectivity in taking polemic positions like openly attacking corporations for past or present actions in environmental and health issues. Academic authors are required by leading American and international journals associated with environmental policy to demonstrate expertise in quantitative methods or conceptual contexts in ways that ensure their

**Figure 12.1:** Distribution of US media according to political bias and type of coverage

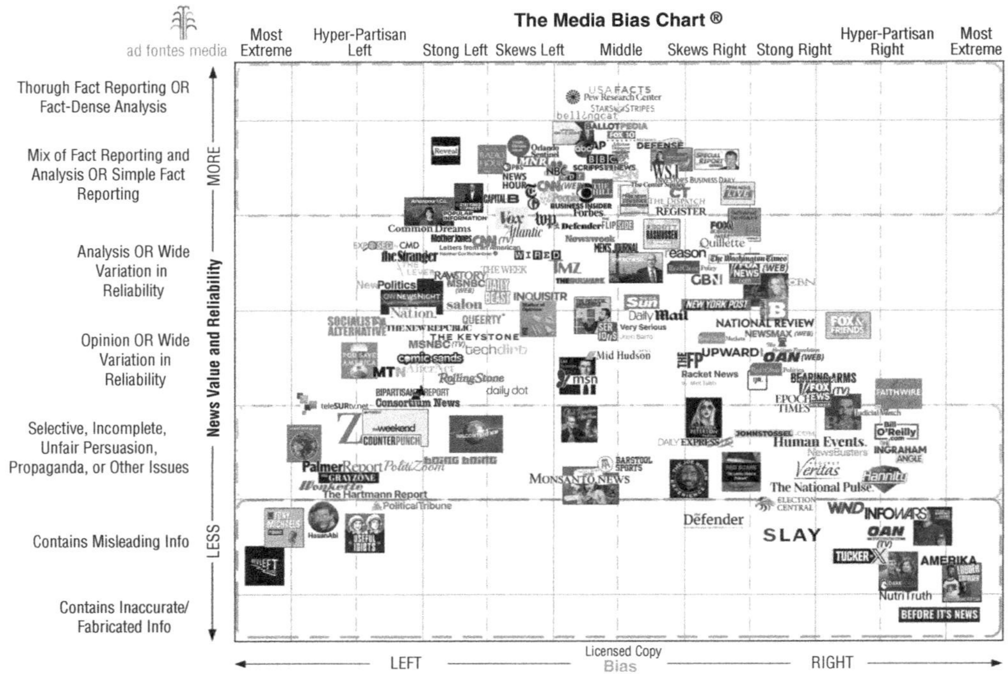


Note: Similar charts from other sources show differences in bias placement, but the overall picture is consistent. The lowest range delineates consistently misleading information and fabrications.

Source: Ad Fontes Media ratings conducted in 2024. Rating data available at https://www.adfontesmedia.com/interactive-media-bias-chart. Reproduced with permission.

work will not receive public or decision-maker attention. There is an almost complete lack of scholarly media that are designed to include wider audiences and could present objective reports informing decision makers and concerned members of the public. Another lack is historical background on critical policy issues, without which policy assessments are argued to be poorly informed.

Reliable, important information is available on the websites of the EPA, the Department of Energy's Energy Information Administration, and other government agencies like the Census Bureau and the National Weather Service, but federal agencies are no longer reliable sources of information on policy because their websites reflect the politics of the party in power, There is legitimate concern about bias that might also emerge in the EPA and the EIA, given President Trump's campaign statements.

Chapters 5, 6, and 7 offered detail on important developments that have not received previous coverage or have been underreported because of the aforementioned problems. In short, our information system is fragmented and often inadequate or unreliable. It is not conducive to providing reliable information either to citizens or political leaders. I suggest that academic leaders, by the nature of their role and resources, have the ability and responsibility to address the problem. Later sections of this chapter will provide historical summaries and discussion of additional issues.

## Historical review

In the early years of the US, federal government operations, aided by Alexander Hamilton's economic and administrative contributions, enabled rapid national developments in the administrations of the first six presidents (Light, 2009). After the War of 1812, during the "The Era of Good Feelings" (1815–1825), President James Monroe was virtually unopposed for a second term. The environmental high point during these administrations came during the presidency of Thomas Jefferson (1801–1809), whose scientific interests included fields that we now call archeology and anthropology. Following the Louisiana Purchase from France in 1803, Jefferson commissioned the Lewis and Clark Expedition to explore the little-known northwestern part of the vast new region. Expedition leaders were given special scientific training and directed to collect plant and animal specimens, skeletal remains, note major geographic features, and conduct quantitative mapping of river systems.

The introduction of the "spoils system" for appointing government employees, initiated by the Andrew Jackson administration in 1829, transformed government operations and led the nation into a long period of instability. Turnover in government agencies after presidential elections prevented the development of stable administrative structures. An absence of land use regulations for federal territories led to the contamination of western federal lands during pervasive mining operations in federal territories following the California Gold Rush in 1849.

The devastating consequences of the Civil War (1860–1865) were exacerbated by the assassination of President Abraham Lincoln, who was committed to civil rights for the former slaves while seeking to reunite rebel states into the union. Ten years of Reconstruction were followed by suppression of the African-American population in former Confederate states. Rapid economic growth, including the major expansion of the national rail network, ensued in the "Gilded Age," though the absence of stabilizing governmental agencies aggravated financial instability and hardship for large segments of the population.

A critical change in the late 19th century was administrative reform of the federal government. Public and Congressional confidence in federal agencies grew. This allowed laws to be short because detailed operational policies were delegated to career civil service leaders. Federal science agencies helped bring the US into the vanguard of nations in application of science and technology to public needs. The US led in infrastructure development, including waterway management, construction of dams, bridges, tunnels, skyscrapers, and electrical illumination. It became a world leader in agriculture and manufacturing. American engineers contributed significantly to progress. The Theodore Roosevelt administration marked a new departure in conservation of forests and valued natural areas.

In 1920, aided by the US Health Service, the US led the world in life expectancy. Efforts to ameliorate the Great Depression in the 1930s included large federal outlays for environmental remediation and the construction of major public works. The nation recovered rapidly from the Depression after the Japanese attack on Pearl Harbor in 1941, when industry and government came together in the war effort under the leadership of President Franklin D. Roosevelt, creating the greatest surge in GDP in the nation's history.

Despite the Korean War in 1952 and the demagogic attacks of Senator Joseph McCarthy, the sense of community that had developed during the Second World War continued to a considerable degree in the 1950s. The GI Bill aided millions of servicemen and service women in advancing their education, simultaneously stimulating the growth of colleges and universities. Development of a national highway system supported the economic boom, while the US manufacturing sector brought millions of workers into the middle class. The major legal victory against longstanding racial segregation achieved by African-American legal scholars and the National Association for the Advancement of Colored People (NAACP) in the Supreme Court's unanimous *Brown v. Board of Education* decision (1954) electrified African

Americans and inspired civil rights leaders in the 1960s to demand fulfillment of the court decision.

### *Sociopolitical problems and instability*

The Supreme Court decision that overturned the "Separate but Equal" *Plessy v. Ferguson* decision in 1896 marked the end to legal sanctions for segregation of African Americans—a condition that signaled inferior status in conflict with the principles of the nation. However, opposition to the restoration of Black peoples' rights continued for two more decades in former Confederate states. Longstanding marginalization of African Americans and American Indians was underrecognized in a highly regarded history textbook used in public schools for 30 years (Morison and Commager, 1930–1969).[2] Racial progress was marked by the election of Barack Obama as President in 2008. However, an activist movement centered in leading academic institutions and including a bestselling book sponsored by the *New York Times*, claimed that racism continues to pervade American society (Hannah-Jones and New York Times Magazine, 2021); see also (Kendi, 2019).

The potential danger in volatile public sentiment was of deep concern to the Founding Fathers. The first example was the Whiskey Rebellion during the presidency of George Washington. Disruptive change in federal government operations came with the patronage system introduced by Andrew Jackson, a leader popular with Irish immigrants and less educated voters in frontier states. Jackson and subsequent presidents up to Abraham Lincoln supported slavery. In the approach to the Civil War, the overwhelming majority of leaders and influential sectors in Southern society, including newspapers and the majority of Christian churches, favored slavery, underscoring the potential power of misguided public opinion.

In the immediate post-Civil War period, corruption in federal and state governments and private industry pervaded the nation. The Gilded Age was characterized by enormous wealth gained by prominent individuals sometimes labeled "Robber Barons." Many industrial magnates showed qualities of entrepreneurship and innovation, while some obtained wealth through monopolies or manipulation of financial markets. Governmental reform begun in the administration of Rutherford B. Hayes culminated in the administration of Theodore Roosevelt, who battled industrial trusts and promoted public health and environmental conservation.

Woodrow Wilson, a president with prominent intellectual credentials, advanced domestic initiatives, but also applied regressive racist policies to the federal civil service. After the First World War, he promoted international policies later seen as disruptive to European society. A national predisposition to overreaction played a role in extreme economic fluctuations in the 1920s and 1930s, referred to previously. These kinds of trends will be reviewed in more detail in the next section.

## Overreaction: a special problem in American society

Boldness and entrepreneurialism have fueled major American achievements from the early history of the nation. From the early 20th century to the 1970s, the US led the world in economic and many other areas. Special characteristics in American society not found in nations from which the immigrants came (de Tocqueville, 1835) have been associated with "American exceptionalism" (Lipset, 1996). While de Tocqueville's observations of positive qualities in the new nation were balanced by negative qualities, American exceptionalism has generally been regarded by conservatives as positive and a model for other nations. Political movements following the 2016 election of Donald Trump have highlighted patriotism and minimized flaws such as racial injustice and the highest levels of income inequality and incarceration levels among advanced nations.

The *Tragedy of the Commons* (Hardin, 1968) was a groundbreaking book that referred to the depletion of a common resource that has many users, none of whom has responsibility to maintain it. This issue has special relevance for the environment in America, where rigorous laws were enacted in the 1970s to deal with abuses of the common environment. However, a problem lies in the Americans' readiness to embrace ideas and form bandwagon movements without adequate consideration of their potential consequences. De Tocqueville noted 180 years ago that Americans tended to be headstrong—that is, have unwarranted confidence in the validity of their ideas. I interpret this as being fostered by the new world's democratic political structures and expanded opportunities compared to constraints in the old world. Limited land availability and stratification of European societies, controlled by monarchies and aristocratic elites, placed limits on both ideas and economic initiatives. The selection process for immigrants to America also favored risk takers and dissidents, which may have contributed to differences in public attitudes between the new and old worlds.

A positive product of headstrong tendencies in American society was inventors and entrepreneurial leaders who took bold risks and made spectacular leaps forward. Examples are the Erie Canal, Thomas Edison's inventions, the comprehensive rail network, skyscrapers of the early 20th century, landing a man on the moon, the invention of the Internet, Google, and, most recently, Elon Musk's breakthroughs with electric cars and in aerospace. Musk grew up in South Africa, but as with other immigrant entrepreneurs like Andrew Carnegie, it was the American environment that fostered his achievements (Isaacson, 2023).

If technical ideas and inventions are flawed or inadequately implemented, they are unlikely to work, but in the political realm, there are fewer constraints. Ideas put into effect by charismatic leaders and embraced by a wider public can have major impact. If they are unbalanced and have flaws, they may do great damage. Corrections to flawed policies may likewise go too far. The founders knew their countrymen. Concerned about the risks for the new nation, they devised the governmental system of checks and balances to limit excesses by any one branch. In a famous essay, *Federalist 51*, James Madison stated that "ambition must be made to counteract ambition" (Madison, 1788). However, a more recent disruptive factor has been the advent of instant electronic communication that began in the 1970s. This new influence intensified political instabilities inherent in American society, allowing strongly held views to gain disproportionate influence. Examples of the impact of flawed politics throughout American history are provided in the next section.

### *Overreaction and flawed politics in American history*

Most of the Constitution is remarkably foresighted, continuing to guide the nation more than 230 years after its framing. However, a fatal flaw in the document was its treatment of slavery. In order to bring all 13 colonies into the new union, the framers acquiesced to the demands of the two Carolinas and Georgia, whose economies depended on slave labor (see James Madison's notes on the Constitutional Convention, cited in Chapter 3). Beyond limiting any restriction on the importation of slaves until 1808 at the earliest, a fateful provision was the Three-Fifths Compromise, which allowed three fifths of the slave populations in Southern states to count toward representation in Congress and the Electoral College. This provision and Virginia's later movement into the pro-slavery bloc led to the election of pro-slavery presidents, beginning with Andrew Jackson in 1829. These presidents, in turn, appointed pro-slavery judges and justices of the Supreme Court. Decisions like *Dred Scott* (1846–1857)[3] intensified the split between North and South. The ultimate result was the Civil War, which can be argued to have had more severe consequences than internal conflicts in European history.

The next example is the replacement of the stable and efficient governmental appointment procedures employed in the first six administrations by Andrew Jackson's spoils system. Jackson's egalitarian arguments and populist support were earlier viewed with sympathy, for example, Schlesinger (1945). However, Jackson's flaws are now more widely recognized. The turnover in government after elections initiated by his patronage system prevented the establishment of stable administrative structures until the progressive reforms in the late 19th century. The absence of land-use laws in federal territories that would later become western states left widespread contamination after the California Gold Rush of 1849. Continuation of the patronage system after the Civil War contributed to chaotic sociopolitical conditions.

In the period leading up to the Civil War, the overwhelming proportion of leaders and influential educated sectors of Southern society embraced pro-slavery positions. Even some graduates of the US Military Academy who had sworn to uphold the Constitution and personally opposed slavery, such as Robert E. Lee, William J. "Stonewall" Jackson, and J. E. B. Stuart, chose to lead armies in defense of an inhumane institution already banned in Europe.

The century-old temperance movement led to the Eighteenth Amendment in 1919, which totally banned the making, sale, or use of alcoholic beverages. Before it was reversed by the Twenty-First Amendment in 1933, the ban brought about a reduction in alcohol-related diseases and violence (Blocker, 2005). However, as popularized in gangster films about the 1920s and 1930s, it led to illegal alcohol production and formation of gangs in urban areas like New York, Chicago, and Kansas City, as well as the flouting of law by upper-class society. Controls on alcohol sales was also put into effect in Northern European nations with high alcoholism rates, but not to the extremes as in the US, and they did not result in the rise of criminal gangs.

The stock market crash and the ensuing Great Depression of the 1930s were more extreme in the US than in other nations. The New Deal's PWA and WPA programs provided massive governmental assistance to the unemployed and were efficiently run. However, President Franklin D. Roosevelt had hostile relationships with industry in his first two administrations and the private sector remained weak. It was only when Roosevelt and industry came together after the Japanese attack on Pearl Harbor in 1941 that the nation experienced the greatest surge in productivity in its history (Anonymous, 2024). Book censorship has been periodically exercised by the US Postal Service under the *Comstock Act of 1873*. Beginning in 1930, US motion picture producers adopted codes that banned violence, sexually stimulating scenes, obscenity, vulgarity, and actions considered to degrade public morals.

Reactions against the extreme earlier societal restraints in the 1960s likewise took exaggerated form. They gave rise to an unprecedented rise in violent crime from 1960 to the 1980s, as can be seen in Figure 12.2. The rise was especially great in Massachusetts, where the relaxation of social constraints, use of illegal drugs, and radical reform of the juvenile justice system were most extreme. The increase was smaller in Virginia, which underwent less radical change. The rise in crime led to vigorous national counterprograms, including increased police and overincarceration. Despite recent reform initiatives, US incarceration rates remain greater than in all but three nations. The 1960s included the tragic assassinations of four major political leaders and new social trends, including sexual permissiveness, drug use, and anti-business attitudes. Harvard University's administration building was occupied

**Figure 12.2:** Historical graph of violent crime in Massachusetts and Virginia, 1960–2014

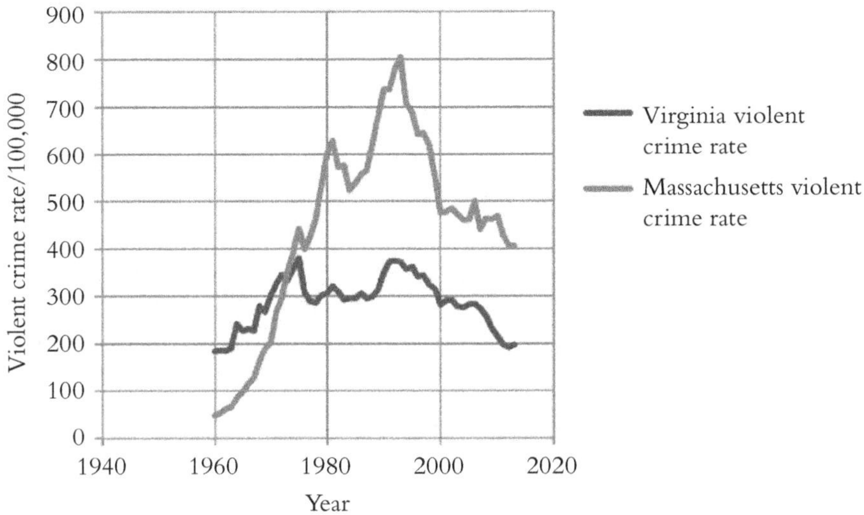


Source: FBI UCR data

by a student mob in 1969 (Eichel et al, 1970) and disorders occurred at many other college campuses.

The post-Second World War economic boom led to severe environmental pollution, including threats to the extinction of the nation's revered national symbol, the bald eagle. The latter was not a result of flawed policies, but rather a consequence of a chemical and biological developments that were not even known to the scientific establishment prior to Rachel Carson's revelations. However, they required responsive national action to deal with the problem. This book proposes that subsequent serendipitous developments, along with overreaction in environmental and regulatory policy combined to lead to the present political polarization.

Responding to Carson's book, President Kennedy announced plans to mobilize executive action to deal with the pesticide issue; he would have probably extended initiatives to other pressing issues like air pollution. However, after his tragic assassination, his successor, Vice-President Lyndon B. Johnson, failed to take effective action. Congress filled the gap in the 1960s. Triggered by an environmental crisis, Congress took transformative action in the 1970s. Fearing the influence of powerful economic forces on federal regulators, it adopted rigorous environmental laws passed by large bipartisan majorities.

As described in Chapter 6, the laws made rapid progress against pollution, but their impacts on the economy created antagonism in the business community. A radical countermovement to roll back the enforcement of the environmental laws in the first Reagan administration brought about a backlash from Congress. Conflict over environmental regulation widened to political polarization (Manheim, 2020). Another fateful development during this period was the accident at the Three Mile Island nuclear power plant in 1979. Though it caused no deaths or health hazards, it led to excessively stringent governmental controls that brought delays and costs to levels uncompetitive with energy from fossil fuel sources. New nuclear power starts were effectively shut down.

The banking crash of 2008 deserves special attention as an example of the impact of flawed politics at the highest national levels of expertise. On October 23, 2008, former Federal Reserve Board Chairman Alan Greenspan, arguably the most respected financial expert in the nation, testified grim-faced in a Congressional hearing that the banking crash had taken him by surprise: "Those of us who have looked to the self-interest of lending institutions to protect shareholder's equity (myself especially) are in a state of shocked disbelief" (cited in Manheim, 2014).[4] The US financial bubble developed with bipartisan support for credit default swaps that aggregated real estate loans into larger tradable instruments. Like the stock market boom in the late 1920s, the swaps gained popularity in anticipation of market increases, oblivious to the risks.

Federal officials' discomfiture was increased by a PBS *Frontline* report that highlighted the battle with Brooksley Born, Chairman of the Commodities Future Trading Commission (PBS, 2009). Born felt that the uncontrolled growth of credit default swaps threatened markets and the economy. However, her warning to President Clinton's Working Group on Financial Markets was rejected by powerful federal officials: Federal Reserve Board Chairman Greenspan, Treasury Secretary Robert Rubin, Deputy Secretary Larry Summers, and Arthur Levitt, head of the SEC. When she publicly proposed the regulation of derivatives trading, she was forced to resign. This episode illustrates the influence of powerful individuals and popular policies over prudent decision making. Canadian banks governed by more conservative governmental policies were minimally affected by the US financial crash (Courtney and Nivola, 2009).

Since the 1980s, the major parties have become further polarized, with the Republican Party taking an especially radical turn under influence of President Donald Trump. Despite his unprecedented conviction for criminal behaviors and indictment for others, he was supported by a majority of the nation's population for a second term in 2024. The described events and developments illustrate a progression of problems since the 1970s. In recent decades, economic downturns in the US economy, like the crash of 2008 and the COVID-19 pandemic, have been followed by relatively rapid recovery through governmental support and the country's private sector. The unexpected strength of the US economy, despite political instability, may be partly explained by traditional US resourcefulness and the fact that economic stability is one of the few areas on which Republicans and Democrats agree. This corresponds with another of de Tocqueville's observations—that materialism is a prominent trait in American society. A troubling prediction is offered by another famous writer, James Fenimore Cooper, in a now obscure book on American democracy: "Whenever the government of the US shall break up, it will probably be in consequence of a false direction having been given to public opinion ... perverted as to cause the false to seem true" (EPA, 2024).

## Environmental justice

Environmental justice is defined as fair treatment of people, regardless of race, color, or income, with respect to the implementation and enforcement of environmental laws and policies. The overview of environmental justice by the US EPA (EPA, 2024c) cites a statement by President Kennedy in 1963: "Simple justice requires that public funds, to which all taxpayers of all races [colors, and national origins] contribute, not be spent in any fashion which encourages, entrenches, subsidizes or results in racial [color or national origin] discrimination."

A notable historic environmental justice problem created by federal law was the *Housing Act of 1934*, a landmark measure that vastly expanded middle-class home ownership. However, it led the Federal Housing Administration to adopt segregation guidelines that suppressed African-American participation.

The broader environmental justice issue first gained media attention in the 1980s when populations living close to toxic waste sites in North Carolina and Alabama were shown to be dominated by African Americans (SEAS, no date). An example was the hazardous waste site in Emelle, Alabama, which received toxic waste from 48 states and three foreign countries. Professor Bunyan Bryant, a pioneering African-American environmental scientist, observed that Sumter County, Alabama, in which Emelle was located, had an approximately 70 percent Black population and was one of the poorest counties in the nation (Bryant and Mohai, 1992). Due to Bryant's work, the University of Michigan, where Bryant was a faculty member, became the first university in the nation to offer graduate and undergraduate degrees in environmental justice.

Other areas with disproportional exposure of Black populations to toxic pollutants or other hazardous conditions include Flint, Michigan, where lead pipes contaminated water supplies, leading to elevated levels of lead in the blood of the local populations. Additional examples are Cheraw, South Carolina polychlorinated biphenyls (PCBs); Warren County, North Carolina (PCBs); Baton Rouge, Louisiana ("Cancer Alley"), site of major petrochemical complexes; Centreville, Illinois (raw sewage); Newark,

New Jersey (Superfund site); and various tribal reservations (oil and gas developments). The 1987 *Clean Water Act Amendments* gave Indian tribes authority to issue and enforce water quality permits, including water bodies whose sources lay outside reservation boundaries.

In 1994, President Clinton issued Executive Order 12898, which directed federal agencies to incorporate environmental justice into their missions. Accompanying the Executive Order was a presidential memorandum that noted that Title VI of the *Civil Rights Act of 1964* prohibited recipients of federal funding from discriminating on the basis of race. Executive Order 12898, on the other hand, directs federal agencies to identify and address, as appropriate, disproportionally high adverse human health and environmental effects of their programs, policies, and activities on minority populations and low-income populations. EPA's environmental justice (EJ) mandate extends to all of the Agency's work, including setting standards, permitting facilities, awarding grants, issuing licenses, and regulations. The memorandum authorized the EPA to oversee compliance of other federal agencies.

The environmental revolution of the 1970s sought to ameliorate pollution and health problems with laws and regulations. Less affluent communities were thought to especially benefit from improved health, but a counterintuitive problem subsequently emerged. Lazarus (2004) pointed out that "sources of industrial pollution were disproportionately located where the poor and racial minorities lived. If industrial operations closed or were cut back, they could leave minority communities in worse circumstances." A notable example is West Virginia, where the coal industry was a mainstay of the economy. As concern over fossil fuel emissions increased, coal-fired power plants and coal mines became targets for elimination. The loss of the coal industry had severe impacts on the population, causing West Virginia to move from a dominantly Democratic state to a Republican one. The refinery complex around Baton Rouge, Louisiana, is known for enhanced cancer rates related to particulate matter and hydrocarbons in the atmosphere, but it is also a major employment resource and an economic hub for the Gulf region. This may have been among the reasons the EPA did not proceed with a proposed pollution crackdown in the region (Younes, 2023).

In 2024, the Biden administration announced the minor allocation of funds to remediate polluting and abandoned mine lands overseen by the Office of Surface Mining, Reclamation, and Enforcement (OSMRE) (DOI, 2024). However, even larger measures usually lack specific timeframes and do not replace a lost economic base. The problem of dealing with economic effects associated with energy transformation is exacerbated by the inability to establish cooperation between government and industry, as contrasted with government contracting, which has complex soliciting requirements that may involve political influence, and mandated requirements.

International accidents with large human impacts in the 1980s include the explosion at the Union Carbide plant at Bhopal, India, which released a toxic gas, methyl isocyanate, killing more than 2,000 local residents and injuring more than 500,000. Another was the explosion at the nuclear plant at Chernobyl in the Ukrainian Socialist Republic in 1986. Along with "forest death" in Europe, these developments underscored that domestic laws could be insufficient to control health hazards that extended beyond natural borders. However, the US has shown reluctance to join any of the international conventions with safeguards against pollution and other hazards, including the UN Law of the Sea, the Convention on Biological Diversity, and the Basel Convention on International Transboundary Movement of Hazardous Wastes (Lazarus, 2023).

Lazarus (2023) cited divisions that grew within the environmental movement over charges that some environmental proposals were driven by elite groups who wanted to preserve pristine areas for their own use or simply for preservation of natural environments, even if no humans ever saw or visited them. These movements showed little concern for Native Americans or ordinary people. For example, the early statements of the founder of the Sierra Club, John Muir, who wrote of the benefits of creating parks on land formerly occupied by Indians because "it could never have been the intention of God to allow Indians to rove and hunt over so fertile a country and hold it forever in unproductive wildness while Scotch and Irish and English farmers could put it to so much better use" (Nobel, 2016). Muir's attitudes evolved with time and acquaintance with the Tlingit Indians in Alaska. Sierra Club President Michael Brune was forced to resign after he labeled Muir a racist (Melley, 2020).

The Biden administration's commitment to environmental justice was more aggressive than that of the Obama administration. Senior Biden officials, including John Kerry and former administrator of the Environmental Protection Agency Gina McCarthy, were directed to lead the government-wide effort that involved every agency. The tools would include regulations, tax policy, and financial outlays applied to the vast array of activities led or supported by the federal government. Biden announced the Environmental Justice40 Initiative a week after taking office. This initiative committed 40 percent of federal government investments in infrastructure and renewable energy development to disadvantaged communities, stating that: "Categories of investment were clean energy and energy efficiency, clean transit, affordable and sustainable housing, training and workforce development, remediation and reduction of pollution, and the development of critical clean water and wastewater infrastructure" (The White House, 2021).

The White House statement's reference of potential applications to "hundreds of federal programs" with respect to the environmental *Justice40 Initiative* took on more significance with the passage of the major budgetary outlays referred to in Chapter 10. LaTricea Adams, founder of Black Millennials 4 Flint, sat on the White House Environmental Justice Advisory Council (WHEJAC) during the Biden administration.

Progress in environmental justice involves complex factors. It raises the problem that leaders chosen for commitment to idealistic goals like environmental justice may lack the technical, administrative, and managerial competence that can produce effective outcomes (Olasky, 1992). The reverse may also apply: leaders chosen for the effective technical leadership may give lesser attention to the human issues. As will be underscored later on, this is why an apolitical and professional civil service is likely to yield more balanced results than one influenced by partisan politics.

As discussed in Chapter 6, the regulatory system created in the 1970s offers the lesson that a focus on environmental problems without considering economic and industry perspectives reduced industrial pollution at the cost of helping drive industry abroad, a development that devastated Rust Belt regions of the country and continues to have national consequences. Black-led campaigns against segregation and for civil rights had successful outcomes because leaders like Charles Whitney Houston and Martin Luther King Jr. combined strong motivation with balanced strategy and resourcefulness. Professor Bunyan Bryant has suggested that gifted and motivated African Americans, rather than White allies, may need to take the lead in the environmental justice movement.

## Industry–environmental conflict and the origin of climate denial

The power of American industry in the earlier history of the nation is illustrated by the magnificent American rail network of 1918 (see Figure 12.3). However, after the Civil War, the absence of effective laws and corruption of government encouraged industry abuses. Early examples include battles for monopoly by railroad barons, the Crédit Mobilier scandal, and conditions in which industrial workers (and especially coal miners) worked and lived (Kiger, 2023). Contrary problems occurred when industrial sectors became impacted by social and economic changes or unwise policies. A notable example was the loss of the nation's passenger rail network after decades of erosion, due to restrictive regulations and policies favoring road and air transportation (Wikipedia—History of US Rail Transportation). The loss of urban public transit systems was compounded by a conspiracy to replace them with bus systems, for which General Motors, Standard Oil of California, and other companies were convicted in 1949 (Wikipedia—General Motors Streetcar Conspiracy).

In summary, the economic boom after the Second World War created environmental pollution. Serendipitous events and developments created

**Figure 12.3:** A Midwest segment of the US railway system in 1918

Source: Railway (1918)

conflict between American industry and the powerful environmental movement, as was described in Chapter 6. The following sections describe conflicts over forestry, fossil fuel production, and the rise of climate skepticism and denial.

### *Forestry conflicts*

Until the mid-1950s, the US Forest Service was one of the most respected federal agencies. Its employees had included Aldo Leopold, founder of the US ecological movement, Arthur Carhart, a pioneer in advancing protection of wildlife, and Robert Marshall, a founder of the wilderness movement. The June 2, 1952 issue of the popular weekly news magazine *Newsweek* highlighted the Forest Service, crediting it with "contributing to the value of recreation, wildlife management, timber stands, and pure and abundant water." Forest Service leaders were familiar with advanced practices of European nations like Austria, Germany, and Sweden that had long experience with forest management. The Forest Service initially emphasized the suppression of minor wildfire and failed to employ prescriptive burning to reduce dangerous accumulation of understory. However, in the latter half of the 20th century the agency came to embrace preventive management against disease and fire and of selective removal of mature or diseased trees (O'Toole, 1988).

The post-Second World War boom with suburbanization and predominantly wood homes expanded demand for lumber products. Congressional appropriations and laws, especially the *Multiple Use Sustained Yield Act of 1960*, built what has been described as perverse incentives into the Forest Service's budget authorizations (O'Toole, 1988). The agency expanded timber production on federal land and, by 1970, was cutting four times as much as in 1952, nearly all by clear-cutting methods. Cutting in scenic areas and old growth forests had negative effects on public opinion, leading to Congressional hearings and lawsuits by environmental organizations. It energized the preservation movement, which scored a major success with the passage of the *Wilderness Act of 1964*. The Act allowed Congress to establish wilderness areas within which all economic activity as well as public access by motorized conveyances would be excluded in perpetuity, preserve other wooded tracts, and restrict road building to limit commercial exploitation of forest resources.

### *The timber wars and the Northern Spotted Owl battle*

The most detailed account of conflict between environmentalists and the lumbering industry on the Pacific coast was published by William G. Robbins, a historian at Oregon State University (Robbins, 2004). Robbins noted that in 1938, Oregon produced the most timber of any state, much of it from old growth redwoods. Resistant to rot, redwood lumber had been used for construction and decking, and was popular for outdoor furniture throughout the nation. In the middle of the Second World War, the chief of the Forest Service had expressed concern that the trends threatened sustained yields and called for regulation "to stop destructive cutting." The Forest Service and the Bureau of Land Management sought to implement sustainable yield policies, but the postwar housing boom resulted in pressure for increased harvesting from commercial interests as well as Congress. Environmentalists opposed accommodating policies adopted by the Forest Service; conflict over cutting in the Monongahela National Forest in West Virginia helped lead to the passage of the *Federal Land Policy and Management Act of 1976* (FLPMA) and the *Forest Management Act of 1976*. These laws imposed constraints on Forest Service management of national forests, while local environmental organizations sought to protect forest resources in state areas (Mannchen, 2024).

Earlier logging pressure had grown through new technologies like gasoline-powered saws and diesel-powered cable pulling machines. The anti-regulatory policies of James Watt as Secretary of the Interior (1981–1983) added to cutting in national forests and the antagonism of environmentalists. Unable to prevail in efforts to restrain logging in old growth forests, the Sierra Club drew on a provision in the FLPMA requiring the agency to identify and protect the habitat of indicator species that could be endangered by industrial logging. In 1987, it filed suit through ESA against the Forest Service on behalf of the northern spotted owl, a bird whose habitat was old growth forests. After intense litigation battles with the lumbering industry, a federal court ruling in the *Northern Spotted Owl v. Hodel* case in 1988, and subsequent actions by the Clinton administration, cut logging on federal lands in California, Oregon, and Washington by up to three quarters (see Figure 12.4). However, a steep reduction in Western state timber production did not reduce the consumption of wood products; it mainly shifted it to imports from Canadian boreal forests.

Longstanding battles between logging interests and environmentalists radicalized the Sierra Club and other environmental organizations. The Sierra Club's earlier policies did not exclude logging or preventative maintenance in national forests. Gordon Robinson, a leading national forestry expert, served as an advisor to the Sierra Club for decades. His book (Robinson, 1988) accepted sustainable lumbering, but in the late 1990s, the Sierra Club's national board adopted a policy of opposing all cutting in national forests, even for preventative maintenance (Sierra, 1996). The presumed rationale was that the latter would provide an opportunity for logging companies to enter national forests.

The impact of drought and temperature greatly increased wildfires in the western states. However, regulatory inhibitions and lack of initiative on the part of the Forest Service prevented the necessary application of preventive measures (Brodie et al, 2024). Failure to adequately apply prescribed burns

**Figure 12.4:** Historic wood production from US national forests from their founding to 2007

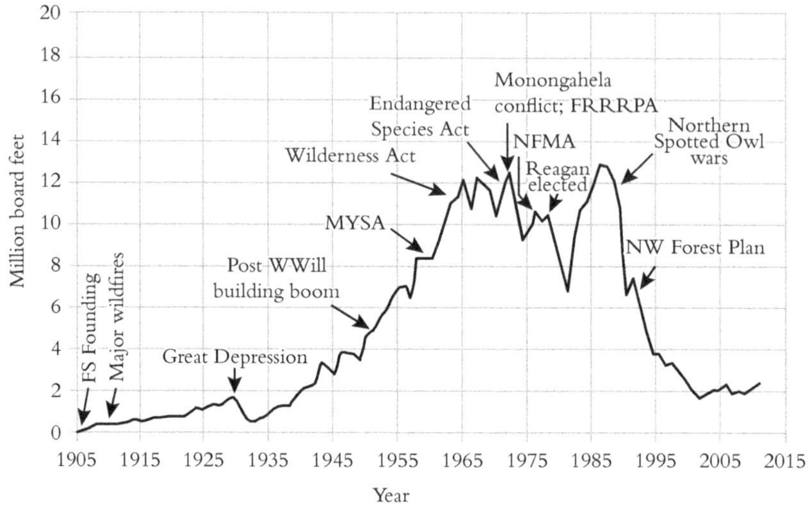


Source: US Forest Service data, annotated by Riddle (2022)

and mechanical thinning of underbrush in western forests promoted out-of-control wildfires. An estimated 22,000 acres in Oregon received prescribed burns in 2019, whereas the Northwest Region office (Washington-Oregon) reported an average of nearly a million acres a year burned by wildfires in the ten years prior to 2019. Over 50 percent of the Forest Service's budget is now consumed by combating fires, while only minor funding is allocated to preventive measures limiting the scope and intensity of fires. Roadless designations and the federal Roadless Rule in 2001 further limited the ability to gain access to forests for management and fire control.

Wildfires added an estimated $213 \times 10^{12}$ g of $CO_2$ into the atmosphere of the lower 48 states between 2002 and 2006 (Wiedinmyer and Neff, 2007). Comparing this figure with $CO_2$ emissions of approximately 6 billion tonnes in 2005 means that wildfires contributed 3.6 percent of total emissions during the cited period. Given increases in recent wildfires, the proportion must be multiplied. Compilation of annual burned acre estimates for California since 2000 (OEHHA, 2024) amounted to 20.7 million acres, or a startling 63 percent of forest cover in the state. It is not clear whether the percentage may be exaggerated by the inclusion of previously burned areas or other factors, but the foregoing data underscore that effective forest management has not been met in West Coast states (Kolb, cited in Manheim, 2010):

> Forests … represent both a potential source of atmospheric carbon dioxide if they are degraded, or the most efficient land-based sink,

> with a large capacity to absorb atmospheric carbon dioxide when trees are rapidly growing … Active forest management and the use of wood-based renewable bioenergy applied in appropriate locations will most likely result in greater forest resilience to large landscape level disturbances and increase most forest ecosystems' ability to store and sequester atmospheric carbon dioxide.

Environmental organizations like the NRDC and the Sierra Club have opposed biomass as an energy resource (Sierra, 2019). A major reason for their opposition is concern over the cutting of trees, with an ongoing bone of contention being the US wood pellet industry, which uses trees in southeastern US forests as source materials. While exceptions have been mentioned, environmentalist opposition and arguments against bioenergy have inhibited the development of an alternative energy resource that IEA regards as important in achieving net zero carbon (IEA, 2023). This includes biofuels needed to replace petroleum products for aircraft.

The effect of legislation and battles between environmentalists and the lumbering industry on historical wood production is illustrated in Figure 12.4. The previously mentioned Congressional testimony of Peter Kolb (Manheim 2010) noted that the German state of Bavaria salvaged two billion board feet of wood a year solely from killed diseased trees. This equaled the total wood production from US national forests in 2008. Kolb's report indicated that limitations on preventive measures by the Forest Service contributed to the loss of Lodgepole Pine forests in Western states due to bark beetle disease. German forests cover a third of the nation and serve both environmental and economic roles (the equivalent of $184 billion and 1.3 million jobs). Drought and warming have affected German forests through fire and insect damage, but according to the German Forest Service (Serviceburo, no date), forests are maintained by using the forest management principles given in the following list. No similar set of principles appear to apply to American national forest management since the earlier conflicts between industry and environmental groups:

- Conserving and establishing structurally diverse mixed forests.
- Planting site-adapted and stable tree species and provenances.
- Utilizing natural regeneration where soil and previous stand allow it.
- Largely avoiding clear-cutting.
- Multistoried forest structure to make maximum use of soil and air space.
- Adapting the intensity of management to individual stands.
- Stand-conserving wood harvesting.
- Maintaining soil fertility and increasing it, if possible.
- Using foreign tree species only after examining the beneficial effect of their use in ecological and economic terms.

### *Petroleum industry–environmentalist conflict: the origin of climate change denial*

Congressional testimony by James Hansen in 1988, discussed in Chapter 8, was a watershed event. It dramatically increased concern among the scientific community and the environmental movement about the emission of greenhouse gases from fossil fuel combustion. However, it also intensified division over environmental and energy policy by pitting economic benefits and plentiful energy supplies against climate change concerns.

The introduction of fracking in 2006 and increased availability of natural gas introduced further complexity. Besides reduction in the US trade imbalance and the boost to the economy, the US Energy Information Administration reported that 65 percent of the reduction in emissions from the US electricity sector from 2005 to 2019 was attributable to natural gas replacing coal-fired power plants (MIT, 2023). However, methane, the main component of natural gas, is a hydrocarbon whose combustion produces $CO_2$ as well as a potent greenhouse gas.

Antagonism to the powerful US fossil fuel industry was heightened by revelations that major oil companies had early knowledge of the role of greenhouse gas emissions in raising global temperatures, but later launched campaigns designed to minimize public concern and actively opposed governmental policies to control emissions. Internal oil industry documents revealed that beginning in the 1960s, Exxon researchers had detailed information on the impacts of $CO_2$ emissions on global warming (Mulvey and Shulman, 2015). This included climate change models comparable to those developed in advanced academic and government circles. In spite of this, in 1989 Exxon joined other American industrial organizations in forming the Global Climate Council (GCC), which used denial and deception to oppose controls on fossil fuel emissions. According to a website focused on climate disinformation (Desmog, no date), early members of the GCC included Exxon, Amoco, the American Forest and Paper Association, the American Petroleum Institute (API), Chevron, Chrysler, Ford, General Motors, Shell Oil, Texaco, the US Chamber of Commerce, and many others.

A notorious speech by Exxon CEO Lee Raymond at a World Petroleum Conference in Beijing illustrates Raymond's duplicity in minimizing concerns about climate change (Raymond, 1997):

> We ... have to keep in mind that most of the greenhouse effect comes from natural sources, especially water vapor. Less than a quarter is from carbon dioxide, and, of this, only four percent of the carbon dioxide entering the atmosphere is due to human activities... Leaping to radically cut this tiny sliver of the greenhouse pie on the premise that it will affect climate defies common sense and lacks foundation in

> our current understanding of the climate system... Forecasts of future warming come from computer models that try to replicate Earth's past climate and predict the future ... are notoriously inaccurate.

A small group of climate and other scientists lent credibility to skepticism. Their early leader was S. Fred Singer, who has been described as the "godfather of global warming denial" in a *Mother Jones* article (Jones, 2005b). Singer was an atmospheric physicist and an early leader in space research, and was appointed deputy assistant secretary with the US Department of the Interior in charge of water quality and research in 1967, but he became a skeptic regarding the adverse effects of climate change in the 1980s. He founded the Science and Environmental Policy Project (SEPP) in 1990. Its online reports continue to be published up to the present day.

Singer cooperated with others in setting up the Nongovernmental International Panel on Climate Change 2003 (NIPCC, 2019). Sponsored by the Heartland Institute, an ultra-conservative think tank, it released a number of documents, including the second volume of *Climate Change Reconsidered II*, subtitled "Biological Impacts" (Idso et al, 2014), which reportedly offered more than 1,000 pages of reviews of scientific research finding the impact of man-made global warming is benign. Gregory Wrightstone, a former gas industry earth scientist, is currently the leader of the $CO_2$ Coalition that questions climate change policy. He is the author of a book whose title, *Inconvenient Facts*, is a takeoff on Al Gore's Nobel Prize-winning film (Wrightstone, 2017). Wrightstone argues that in increase $CO_2$ is more beneficial than harmful.

The fossil fuels industry has been denounced in many books and articles—for example, Brulle (2019); Supran et al (2023); and Becker (2024). Accounts detailing the scandal of denial and deception by US industry have circulated widely in media, such as an online award-winning article by *Inside Climate News* (Banerjee et al, 2015) and a *New York Times* article on a suit by multiple attorneys general (Gillis and Krauss, 2015). A leading climate scientist, Michael Mann, has called corporations "the enemy" (Mann, 2021). The background to this controversy is provided in the following text.

## *Underexamined causes of discord*

By any measure, the conflict between industry and the environmental movement has been a political and environmental disaster for the US. The nation's earlier tradition of being at the forefront of applied science and environmental development was lost. US lag in progress against climate change (as detailed in Chapter 11) has also affected the international effort against climate change. Swedish daily newspapers have referred to the US as "an environmental gangster" (Anshelm and Hultman, 2013). There are valid judgments against the US industry's earlier actions and duplicity, but history shows that these were not simply due to self-serving behaviors. Emotionally driven attacks on industry contributed to its destabilization, the history of which will be reviewed here in greater detail.

In the 1960s, the chemical industry's attacks on Rachel Carson's revelations about chemical pesticides drew wide criticism (Lear, 1997). Concerns were raised about other hazards from industrial chemicals (Markowitz and Rosner, 2002), and general anti-business attitudes grew during the 1960s, an example being the famous "plastics" scene in *The Graduate*, a 1967 film starring Dustin Hoffman. The petroleum industry was an industrial success story and pillar of the economy, fueling the nation's cars and trucks, providing natural gas for home heating and electrical power, and petrochemicals that included feedstocks for medicines. The offshore oil industry came to rival the space program in technical sophistication.

Standard Oil Co. of New Jersey had been the largest of the companies created through the Supreme Court's 1911 breakup of the giant Standard Oil Trust. Its successor, Exxon, was the world's largest oil company[5] and a major figure in US history. A leader in all aspects of the petroleum industry—exploration and production, transportation, refining, petrochemicals, and global marketing—Exxon placed special emphasis on advanced technology and research. Its scientific achievements included basic research breakthroughs, notably the technique of ocean seismic stratigraphy that revealed global changes in sea level (Mitchum et al, 1977). Exxon had major influence in the American Petroleum Institute (API), the trade association for the oil industry.

Criticism of the oil industry was triggered by the Santa Barbara offshore oil spill in 1969 (see Chapter 6). The term "dirty oil" is traceable to public anger and media publicity about black crude oil fouling the white beaches of Santa Barbara, and by later tanker spills held to endanger marine habitats. The industry's unfavorable national image grew during the environmental revolution of the 1970s, leading to defensive policies by Exxon and other oil company leaders. The oil industry lost talented scientists and engineers and its recruiters no longer visited Ivy League schools. The oil industry withdrew from public communication and Exxon ended publication of its magazine in 1980.

Notwithstanding these developments, ethical Exxon research leaders like Roger Cohen continued to be committed to acknowledging the role of greenhouse gas emissions on global climate change and contributing to solutions. As late as 1982, a comprehensive dossier (CDD 2015) provides documentation that E. E. David, Jr, President of Exxon Research and Development Co., openly acknowledged the $CO_2$ problem in a speech to a major national scientific symposium (David, 1982), including the following excerpt:

> Few people doubt that the world has entered an energy transition away from dependence upon fossil fuels and toward some mix of renewable resources that will not pose problems of $CO_2$ accumulation … As the world continues to grapple with the profound issues posed by the $CO_2$ buildup, it could seek few better models of international cooperation than what we have already achieved.

David was a member of the US Academy of Science and Engineering and had served as science advisor to President Richard Nixon. In the foregoing speech, David referred to Exxon's research on alternative energies, which concentrated on nuclear and bioenergy applications, and suggested future directions for renewable energy development. However, nuclear energy and biomass use were opposed by major environmental organizations like the Sierra Club and other environmental organizations. Exxon was thereby placed in a difficult position. Its primary products, on which the nation was dependent, were disparaged, while its most effective potential contributions to replace fossil fuels were opposed by powerful environmental organizations.

Open hostility between the environmental movement and industry and their respective supporters further increased when the first Reagan administration sought to roll back the enforcement of environmental regulations (see Chapter 8). The Sierra Club's membership tripled. Antagonism toward the fossil fuel industry spiked after James Hansen's 1988 testimony about the role of $CO_2$ in global warming and the Exxon Valdez oil spill in Alaska in 1989.

Exxon, one of the US's most efficient and technologically advanced energy companies, moved from acknowledging the adverse effects of fossil fuels on global climate and readiness to contribute to solutions, to denial and deception. However, the circumstances leading up to its actions deserve more attention. Emotionally driven attacks that created strains on the company and losses of key staff had extended to unreasonable levels. The nation depended on petroleum for transportation fuel and other needs, and there were no immediate alternative resources. So after two decades of increasing antagonism, Exxon and its industrial allies fought back.

In the political sphere, the founding of the Intergovernmental Panel on Climate Change (IPCC) in 1989 and the United Nations Framework Convention on Climate Change (UNFCCC) in Rio de Janeiro (1992) set in motion international movements toward sustainable development. US senators and representatives, especially those from states with major fossil-fuel production, expressed concern about antagonism toward the oil industry and international movements. When the Kyoto Protocol, an international treaty committing states to reduce greenhouse gas emissions, came to the attention of the US federal government in the late 1990s, a resolution proposed by Senators Chuck Hagel (R-NE) and Robert Byrd

(D-WVA) passed with a margin of 95 to 0 in the Senate (1997). It stated that the US should not sign a climate treaty limiting greenhouse gases unless developing nations made similar commitments. The US ambassador to the UN, Peter Burleigh, signed the protocol, but the Clinton administration did not submit it for Senate approval. This prevented ratification of the Kyoto Protocol.

The first senator to openly deny climate change was James Imhofe of Oklahoma, who became chair of the Senate Committee on Environment and Public Works in 2003. Claiming in Senate speeches that global warming was a hoax, Imhofe spread his views through the conservative media and the committee website, and he also published a book entitled *The Greatest Hoax* (Imhofe, 2012).[6] Increasing numbers of Republican members of Congress came to question climate science. The Center for American Progress, a progressive think tank, published a report estimating that roughly half of the Republican members of Congress, including 30 senators, were climate change deniers (Drennan and Hardin, 2021).

An intensive research study published in 2013, traced "108 climate change denial books published through 2010" to links with conservative think tanks and self-published climate deniers (Dunlap and Jacques, 2013). The authors concluded that actions to reduce carbon emissions generated corporate fears of international action to reduce carbon emissions from fossil fuels. They "worried about restrictions on their products ... and joined forces with the US conservative movement in attacking the scientific evidence for warming, thus the necessity of reducing carbon emissions."

Only a few political leaders sought constructive and cooperative solutions to energy policy. Alone among Republicans, Senator John McCain of Arizona partnered with Democratic senator and later vice-presidential nominee Joseph Lieberman on the *Climate Stewardship Act of 2004*. Its cap-and-trade provisions, developed in consultation with both industry and environmental leaders, would have reduced carbon emissions to 2000 levels by 2010. It also would have increased the price of carbon fuels and thereby enhanced the viability of alternative energy sources (Lavelle, 2018). It gained 43 votes, but lost in the Senate. McCain received little credit in mainstream media for his initiatives, being typically described as a "maverick" for cooperative initiatives with the opposing party (Yancey-Bragg, 2018). This was typical of the sensation focus by media that reached a peak in the Trump campaign in the presidential election in 2016.

### *The alternative Danish approach*

Bjørn Lomborg, a Danish political scientist, statistician, and committed member of Greenpeace, created a firestorm with his book, *The Skeptical Environmentalist* (Wikipedia—Bjørn Lomborg). Lomborg's theses were that many tenets of mainstream environmental science were wrong or exaggerated. His claims were dismissed by the scientific community in the US, though they gained attention in popular media.

Lomborg's book was challenged by Danish scientists to the Danish Committee on Scientific Dishonesty, complaining that his work was scientifically dishonest. The committee, a body under Denmark's Ministry of Science, Technology, and Innovation, largely supported the charges against him, but they were annulled by the Ministry. Instead, Lomborg was appointed head of Denmark's new Environmental Assessment Institute. He resigned to return to University of Aarhus in 2004, where he has remained and continues to publish.

Tolerance for Lomborg's heretical views did not mean that the Ministry embraced his ideas; rather, pragmatic Danish officials appear to have recognized that academic science is subject to an "authority" syndrome whereby prominent scientists and schools of opinion can influence research and publication, avert criticism, and reject important but unconventional ideas. A Nobel Prize-winning biologist referred to this process as "a tyranny" and boycotted leading science journals (Sample, 2113).

Denmark was an early leader in renewable energy development, with special emphasis on wind energy, exploiting its high-wind-energy environment. Like other Scandinavian nations, Denmark moved to market-friendly economic policies and competition in the 1980s, but it also embraced strong environmental goals, with a critical difference from the legislative process in the US; it included industry as a partner in government policy (Wallace, 1995): "In the US, an adversarial approach to public policy has exacerbated the tensions which accompany environmental issues … Denmark has taken a similarly tough stance (on environmental policy) bolstered by general assent from Industry, which has the comfort of being closely integrated into policy-making processes."

This cooperative approach led Demark to a leadership position in environmental performance, ranking no. 1 in the Yale-Columbia Environmental Performance Index (EPI) in 2022 (Block, 2024). The former Danish Oil and Natural Gas Company (DONG) transitioned to renewable energy, from 85 percent fossil fuel-based electrical power to 15 percent, which was achieved in 2019, 21 years ahead of schedule. Renamed Ørsted, it has become the world's largest offshore wind company.

## Sustainability

*Why polarization is not compatible with climate change progress*

Regardless of how one assigns responsibility for the US lag in climate change progress, 40 years of battles over environmental and energy policy in the US offer no encouragement that continued antagonism toward the fossil fuel industry and unilateral political policies can lead to environmental progress. Evidence for this conclusion is the reversal of environmental policies after each of the last six changes in party control of the presidency, including membership in the Paris Agreement. Neither environmentalists nor industry and their political supporters have shown the ability to crush political opposition and gain more than temporary control of national policy—nor would one-party control be consistent with the US's democratic principles. In short, it seems clear that addressing climate change will be frustrated by continued conflict.

Further evidence about why radical measures to curb fossil fuel emissions are unlikely to succeed is provided by polls of public opinion by the nonpartisan Pew Research Center (Pew, 2023). A total of 59 percent of Democratic and Democratic-leaning voters regarded climate change as very important, a view held by only 12 percent of Republican voters. The only areas of common agreement between the two groups were economic development and greater cooperation by the parties. Given the importance of petroleum products for transportation, power, residential heating, and other needs for the nation, along with the insufficiency of adequate potential replacements, even the Biden administration (which was strongly committed to support for green energy policies) was hesitant to take overly aggressive action against the oil and gas industry. Price shocks or interruption in energy supplies would result in a loss of political support in an already tenuous political environment.

The US imported 57 percent of its crude oil requirements in 2006, when hydraulic fracturing first began. Fracking was the major factor in making the US become a net exporter of petroleum hydrocarbons by 2021. The benefits of fracking, whose dominant product has been natural gas, include the fact that natural gas costs in the US were a quarter of those in Europe in 2024, and that 65 percent of the US reduction in greenhouse gas emissions has been due to replacement of coal-fired power plants with natural gas (MIT, 2023). Fracking production methods have a shorter life and can therefore be reduced more quickly, without stranding resources, than production from conventional petroleum reservoirs. These factors do not reduce the urgency of reducing emissions from fossil fuels, including natural gas, but they point to the need to take the foregoing factors into account in realistic energy policy. I will discuss the problems and potential strategies in greater detail in Chapter 13.

Infrastructure development necessary for clean energy transition is subject to barriers that have been referred to as "the four horsemen of green energy development." These include Congressional gridlock and inability to pass needed legislation; bureaucratization and politization of federal aid to infrastructure projects; the regulatory/permitting labyrinth; and barriers to achieving infrastructure breakthroughs (Manheim, 2021). Polarized politics block the resolution of each of these problems.

The last major update or reauthorization of environmental law was in 1990. Federal funding for state and local infrastructure projects involves hundreds of provisions in the federal administrative code, involving complex labor, contracting, and reporting requirements, and stipulations for stakeholder representation that diffuse management decision making. The importance of the latter point is attested to by comparison with the construction of the Chrysler Building in New York City in only 20 months in 1930. Expeditious completion was facilitated by a system whereby a carefully developed engineering plan was submitted to a unitary city agency that had the experience and authority to approve of the plan and coordinate city services like sewage, electricity, water, and traffic during construction.

Major infrastructure projects have been estimated to require four and a half years for federal environmental permits (CEQ, 2020). These regulatory delays are due in part to court decisions that made NEPA's environmental impact statement provision into a complex administrative procedure. The combination of court-introduced procedures and Council on Environmental Quality regulations led to impact statement procedures requiring years to complete.

Throughout American history up to the 1970s, breakthroughs in infrastructure were created by visionary leaders. Such leadership talent today avoids projects with regulatory delays of uncertain duration. The work goes instead to firms prepared to work with the complexity of federal projects, usually under cost-reimbursement contracts that provide payment for as long as projects continue. Rapid transit development in the Washington, D.C. region offers an example.

In the greater Washington, D.C. area, a superior underground plan for extending the Silver subway line to Dulles Airport in Virginia was proposed in 2006, but it was changed to a surface option in order to gain federal support (Wikipedia—Silver Line Washington Metro 2024e). The line was finally completed in 2025. Work on the Purple Line, conceived in 1996 to extend rapid transit to the Maryland suburbs of Washington, D.C., collapsed in 2020 after litigation, delays, and deferred payments to contractors. In contrast, planning and construction of a new (2023) Kansas City International Airport that did not utilize federal support was planned and completed in five years. As discussed previously, problems associated with federal support include high-level federal politics and statutory requirements that diffuse project management and invite litigation.

## *Energy and sustainability*

The United States was the world leader in scientific recognition of and modeling of the effect of global warming. However, compared to Germany, it was slow in building renewable energy capacity (see Figure 12.5).

**Figure 12.5:** US and German renewable electrical energy production, 1990–2006

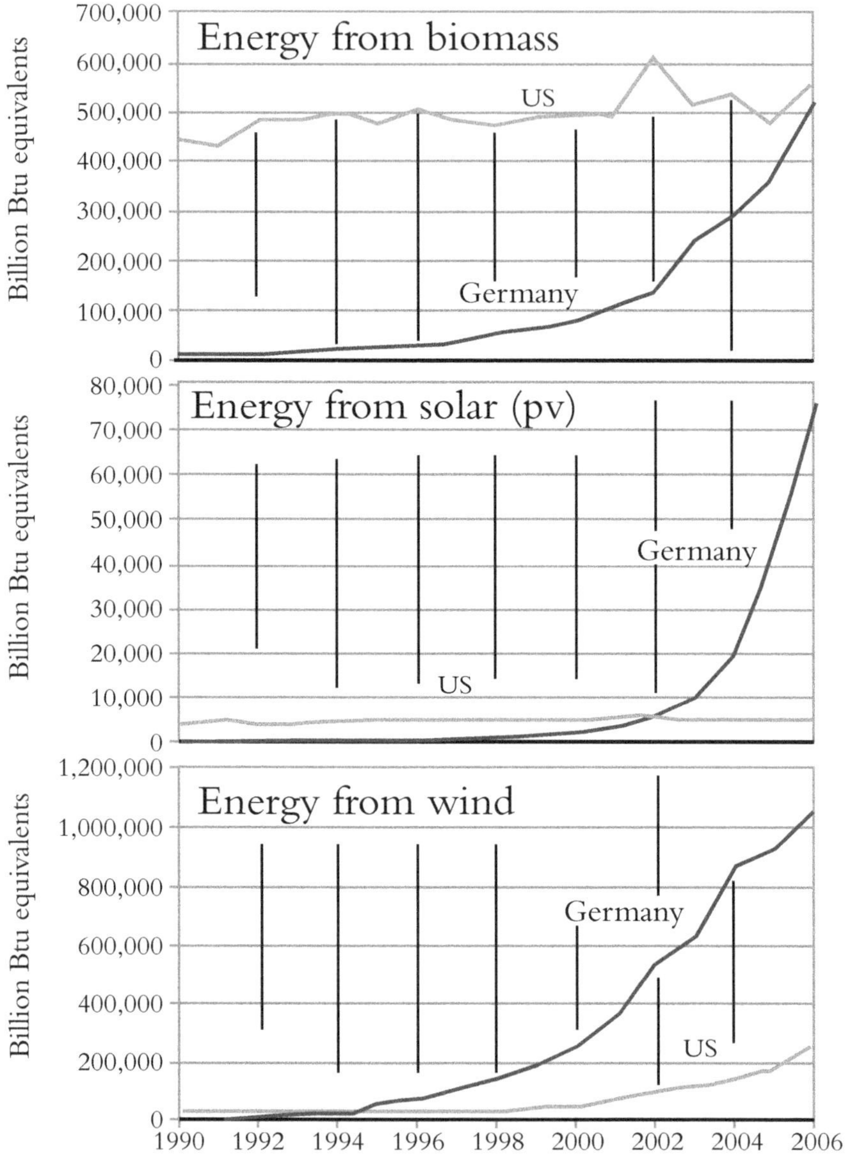


Note: Btu = British thermal unit, a measure of the heat content of fuels or energy sources

Source: Manheim (2009)

Rapid increase in wind and solar energy came first in the Obama administration (2008–2016). From 2010 to 2020, wind energy grew from 95 to 338 billion kWh, and solar energy grew from 1 to 89 billion kWh. Wind energy is currently a leading alternative energy source. It is concentrated in a large, high-wind-energy swath in the middle of the country, along with high-wind-energy belts along the coasts, in the Great Lakes, and scattered sites in mountainous areas.

Midwestern states cited in Table 12.1 lead in terms of installed wind energy capacity. However, the percentage installed versus potential capacity in megawatts shows that these states are producing only a small fraction of potentially available wind energy. The reason why these states are not producing more electrical power and transferring it to populous areas to the east was suggested to be a chicken-egg problem by a Harvard University study (Moch and Lee, 2022). The midwestern states don't produce more wind energy because of the lack of electrical grids to transport surplus power beyond local needs, but grid investors are reluctant to expand the grid if there are not guaranteed supplies to feed it. The final obstacle to expansion of the grid is getting federal permits for major infrastructure like electrical grids, involving delays involving NEPA, whose court interpretations and CEQ guidelines facilitate environmental challenges and litigation.

Renewable, low-carbon energy in the southeastern states is dominated by solar energy and nuclear power. Solar energy development is surprisingly patchily distributed, with high concentrations in California, Arizona, Nevada, North Carolina, Massachusetts, South Carolina, Georgia, and Florida. Total electrical power generation from solar is shown in Table 12.2.

Reaching energy sustainability goals will require major increases in electrification to provide heat, power for electrical cars and other transportation needs, industrial processes, and green hydrogen or synthetic fuels for transportation needs like air travel and sea transport. According to the study by Moch and Lee (2022), the US currently has 600,000 miles of electrical grids connected to 1 million MW of electrical generating capacity. However, 70 percent of this network is over 25 years old. The study projected that over one million more miles of network must be built by 2050. The challenge of achieving net carbon neutrality by 2050 is further indicated in Figure 12.6, which provides a historical graph of total energy sources in the US from the founding of the nation to 2022. The Energy Information Administration lists the total quantity of energy consumed in five main sectors in the country in quadrillion ($10^{12}$) British thermal units (BTU): electric power 37.75 quads; transportation 27.47 quads; industry 23.18 quads; and commercial 4.90 quads. The graph shows that the steep decline in coal consumption is offset by an increase in natural gas use. Nuclear power plateaued after the 1970s. Bioenergy, which has become important in European nations, is not separately listed.

**Table 12.1:** Installed and potential wind energy capacity (in MW)

| State | Installed capacity | Potential capacity | Percentage installed/ potential capacity |
|---|---|---|---|
| Texas | 37.10 | 1,300 | 2.8 |
| Oklahoma | 11.79 | 360 | 3.3 |
| Iowa | 10.01 | 280 | 3.6 |
| Kansas | 8.77 | 506 | 1.7 |
| Illinois | 7.67 | 191 | 4.0 |
| California | 6.19 | 300 | 2.1 |
| Colorado | 4.84 | 395 | 1.2 |
| Minnesota | 4.18 | 183 | 2.3 |
| New Mexico | 4.02 | 653 | 0.6 |

Note: Energy in meters/second

Source: Data from DOE (2024)

**Table 12.2:** Energy sources for electrical power

| Energy source | Billion kWh | Share of total | Percentage of total |
|---|---|---|---|
| **Fossil fuels (total)** | | 2,505 | 60.00 |
| Natural gas | | 1,802 | 43.10 |
| Coal | | 675 | 16.20 |
| Petroleum (total) | | 16 | 0.40 |
| **Renewables (total)** | | 894 | 21.40 |
| Wind | | 425 | 10.20 |
| Hydropower | | 240 | 5.70 |
| Solar (total) | | 165 | 3.90 |
| Biomass (total) | | 47 | 1.10 |
| Wood | | 31 | 0.80 |
| Landfill gas | | 8 | 0.20 |
| Municipal solid waste (biogenic) | | 6 | 0.10 |
| Other biomass waste | | 2 | 0.10 |
| Geothermal | | 16 | 0.40 |
| **Nuclear** | | 775 | 18.60 |
| **Other sources[5]** | | 10 | 0.20 |

Source: Data modified from a table published by the Energy Information Administration (EIA 2024)

**Figure 12.6:** History of energy use in the United States up to 2023

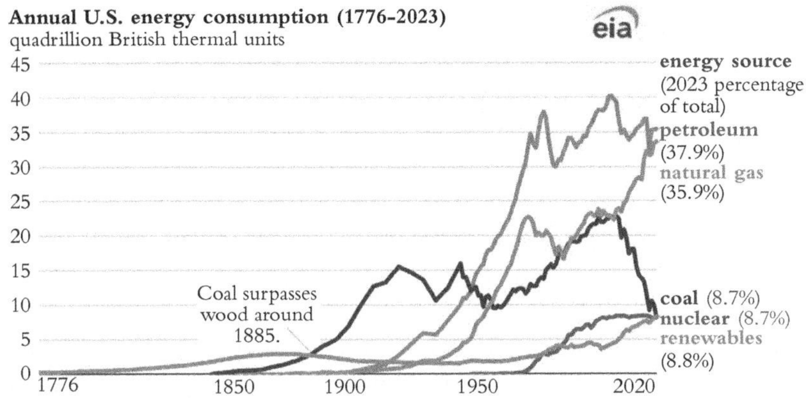


Source: EIA (2024)

Several problems can be noted here. Although nuclear energy has the lowest life-cycle $CO_2$ emissions per gigawatt hour, shares the lowest death rates (Ritchie, 2024) and has the smallest areal footprint, virtually all major US environmental organizations are on record as being in opposition to it.[7] Uncompetitive cost is among the rationales for their opposition. This fails to consider the fact that environmental pressures and opposition after the Three Mile Island accident, intensified by the Chernobyl (1986) and Fukushima Daichi (2011) accidents, led to increased regulatory requirements resulting in large cost increases and delays, effectively killing new starts after the 1970s. The accidents led Germany and Switzerland to commit to closing their nuclear power installations, but France continued to expand its nuclear network, which now supplies 69 percent of the nation's electrical power supply. South Korea also builds nuclear power plants at competitive costs (see Chapter 11). In the US, environmentalist pressures closed an operational nuclear power plant at Indian Point New York in 2021 after ten years of legal campaigns,[8] and there have been continuing efforts to close the Canyon Diablo nuclear power plant, which supplies 17 percent of California's zero carbon energy and 9 percent of its total electrical power. For a detailed review of the nuclear power debate, including 282 references, readers may refer to (Wikipedia—Nuclear Power).

Besides opposing nuclear power, a 2019 Sierra Club report disapproved of carbon capture, most bioenergies including renewable gas (biomethane), municipal waste incineration, and new, large hydrocarbon dams (Sierra, 2024). American environmental organizations' objections to carbon sequestration (geological burial) are therefore encouraging continued emissions from oil and gas. These constraints on alternative energy sources are not consistent with the policies of leading European nations. Norway, for example, began sequestering one million tonnes a year of $CO_2$ in the offshore Sleipner field in 1996. The UNFCCC and IRENA include carbon capture and storage (CCS) in sustainable energy portfolios. The Biden administration allocated a modest but significant $12 billion toward advancing the application of this technology in the IRA budget. Transportation, electrical power, steel making, and cement production will require fossil fuels well into the future, and the only currently available way to mitigate their emissions is through CCS. Major companies like Exxon have indicated their readiness to scale up this technology (Hundertmark, 2023).

The reluctance of leading US environmental organizations to accept the aforementioned alternative energy sources and strategies to reduce emissions cannot be considered in isolation. These positions are suggested to be a product of a lack of trust in industry based on historical conflicts, current industry or conservative attitudes, and fear that changes in regulatory procedures could open up the way to abuse by powerful interests. However, maintaining the status quo is not an answer to the needs.

An economic analysis of approaches to reach net zero carbon emissions by 2050 presented a critical conclusion. All five investigated scenarios required “climate intervention” involving negative carbon emissions or geoengineering to be feasible (Dorman, 2022). The most currently available approach to achieve negative carbon emissions is the generation of electrical power with biomass, combined with the geological burial of $CO_2$ emissions.

Cost is a longstanding limitation to the application of CCS. Insight on the withdrawal of the Department of Energy’s FutureGen program was provided by a Harvard Belfer Institute report (Hart, 2009). FutureGen was a public/private program designed to advance carbon sequestration that began in 2003, but was withdrawn in 2014 for costs and delays. The Hart report observed that though FutureGen was a research rather than a commercial operation, it faced regulatory constraints that included more than a dozen liability issues in aspects of its operations (Hart, 2009).

The oil industry, in this case the American Petroleum Institute, is stated to have recently maneuvered to hinder nuclear energy (Meyer, 2020). Despite criticisms about the industry’s past and present policies, oil companies are among the most efficient and technically advanced industries in the nation. Chapter 13 explores pathways and policies that might ultimately make the industry a partner in rather than an opponent of proactive climate policies.

In the past, as noted in the case of the US’s private rail network and manufacturing, policies with adverse effects on the private sector have had undesirable consequences. This has not happened with the oil and gas industry because an estimated 72 percent of US energy use remains dependent on oil and gas (USA, 2022). Renewable energy development that is subject to complex and uncertain permitting conditions rather than a rational regulatory environment has been shown to be costly and inefficient.[9] This is demonstrated by 20 years of efforts to build a federally managed offshore wind industry. In 2020, 5,341 wind turbines operated in European waters (Manheim, 2022), while only seven turbines operated in the wind-energy corridor along the US Atlantic coast (Dawes and Majkut, 2023). There are no turbines in the Great Lakes or along the Pacific coast.

## Literature highlights

The 1960s were a time of turning inward for the US. Its earlier economic and technical dominance may have added to a feeling that foreign experience was less important. Europe became the leader in environmental affairs in the 1990s, but treatment of European environmental laws and policies mainly emerged in specialized environmental law journals like the *Lewis and Clark Environmental Law Review*,[10] *Columbia Journal of Environmental Law*, *Stanford Environmental Law Journal*, *Harvard Environmental Law Review*, and *Georgetown Environmental Law Review*. These were not cited in social science publications, nor have social science publications been given significant attention in law journals to my knowledge.

Except for historical studies cited later, virtually all American books on environmental law and policy begin with the groundbreaking environmental laws of the 1970s—for example, Klyza and Sousa (2013), and multi-edition texts like Rosenbaum (2024), Salzman and Thompson (2024), and Kraft et al (2024). Their focus overlooks important historical developments in governance and environment cited in previous chapters. James Madison and Thomas Jefferson already articulated concerns about environmental conservation. George Perkins Marsh's warning about the abuse of environment to Americans in *Man and Nature* (Marsh, 1864) was regarded in the 19th century as second only to Darwin's *On the Origin of Species* in terms of importance. I propose that the 1960s "presentism" trend (Schonberger, 1974) has failed to consider history, which has contributed to environmental problems. History affects the present—longstanding polarization led to the current challenges posed by the incoming Trump administration. History offers our main guide to the future.

Environmental policy encompasses a broad range of academic approaches. Valid ideas are found in a spectrum of philosophical perspectives, from Marxism and radical ecology to free-market capitalism. If this were not so, these ideas would not attract knowledgeable adherents. Problems mainly emerge when concepts are adopted to the exclusion of others and lack pragmatic testing. Herbert Marcuse (1898–1979) was a nonconformist Marxist social philosopher of the Frankfurt school who rejected Soviet communism and had major influence on US leftist circles in the turbulent 1960s. His socioecological concepts have seen a modest resurgence in recent times (Reitz, 2022). Marcuse was a student of Martin Heidegger (1889–1976), an influential German philosopher who criticized "technological modernity's diminishment of humankind and destruction of nature" (Zimmerman, 2018). The latter author suggested that Heidegger was a forerunner of deep ecology.

A founder of deep ecology, Norwegian philosopher Arne Naess (1912–2009) distinguished deep ecology from shallow ecology (Naess and Sessions, 1984). He maintained that human and nonhuman life on Earth had value in themselves. Rejecting the utilitarian pragmatism of Western society and governments, Naess argued that a decrease in human population was needed to achieve balance. In contrast to Naess, William Devall, and George Sessions, the broader American school of ecology was influenced by Aldo Leopold's book *A Sand County Almanac* (Leopold, 1949). In addition to his rigorous training in forest science in the US, Leopold's concepts for land management were influenced by advanced German and Austrian forest and game management practices. A widely influential book by climate activist Bill McKibben extends the ecological view of nature to global climate change (McKibben, 2006). McKibben combines a warm human approach and evocative prose with solid science, avoiding polemics and exhortation while calling for a fundamental shift in humankind's relation to nature.

Robert (Bob) Marshall, a Forest Service employee who became chief of the Division of Recreation and Lands, was a leader in the movement for pristine wilderness and founder of the Wilderness Society in 1935. He was the first public official to openly oppose racial discrimination in the Forest Service and wrote *The Peoples' Forests* (Marshall, 1933), which argued for public ownership of industrial timberlands to ensure the sustainability of the forest industry and preservation of wilderness. With wealth inherited from his father, Marshall supported the Wilderness Society, civil rights, and socialist organizations (Sierra, 2019).

A book published by Kevin Hillstrom (Hillstrom, 2010) compiles original documents relating to environmental policy and politics from earliest American history (1620) to a commencement address by Nobel Prize-winning biophysicist and Secretary of Energy, Steven Chu, in the Obama administration (2009). A wide-ranging survey of environmental theory and politics was published by British political scientist Neil Carter in *The Politics of the Environment* (Carter, 2001), with a revised version released in 2018.

Five authors have published comprehensive books on US environmental history and law. The first was Roderick Nash (Nash, 1967), who chronicled America's engagement with wilderness. The others are social and political historian Samuel P. Hays (Hays and Hays, 1987; Hays, 2000); philosopher and historian Carolyn Merchant (Merchant, 2007); professor of environmental policy Richard N. L. Andrews (2020); and professor of environmental law Richard J. Lazarus (Lazarus, 2023). The books by Merchant and Andrews, who died in 2024, offer valuable details on early environmental history.

Lazarus has been regarded as the most balanced chronicler of the evolution of environmental law. His treatment offers the only summary of policy developments up to and including the Biden administration other than recent editions of policy textbooks referred to earlier.

Two authors stand out as critics of radical environmentalism. The first is Alston Chase (1935–2022), a former philosophy professor whose *In a Dark Wood* (Chase, 1995) depicts the fight over forests and the "tyranny of ecology," that is, the concept that humans are no better than snail darters. Chase claims that ecosystems ecology "infused all environmental law and policy and changed the character of US government." The other author is Ron Arnold (1937–2022), who published eight books, including an authorized biography of James Watt, Secretary of the Interior in the first Reagan administration (Arnold, 1981). This now little-known book provided documentation for Chapter 6, as did *Ecology Wars* (Arnold, 2010). These authors' controversial views are useful because they are supported by data and are largely free of ideological arm waving.

Contrasting perspectives on the future of climate change are available in the work of James Lovelock, environmental futurist and award-winning author of the Gaia Theory, and Daniel Esty, a Yale University professor and co-developer of the Yale-Columbia EPI (Block et al, 2024). The Gaia theory linked living organisms on Earth with the physical environment to form a synergistic system. A later controversial book by Lovelock (2000) claimed that it is too late to stop climate from flipping into a new equilibrium that will threaten civilization. Only expanded use of nuclear power could modify its impacts. Esty's reform proposals are discussed in the next section.

As was mentioned in Chapter 10, Donald Trump and a significant proportion of Republican members of Congress are now climate skeptics, a stance suggested have emerged from sociopolitical discord rather than claimed scientific rationales.

Finally, a British physicist and economist recently published an unusual work directed to the "perplexed but open-minded citizen" (Rebonato, 2024). It offers potent arguments that "while climate science is reasonably settled, the economics is not." The in-depth treatment looks objectively at major issues involved in arriving at integrated assessment models that seek to arrive at optimum decisions between abatement efforts based on social altruism (concern for future generations), delays to allow greater maturity of technological advances, and the real-world strivings of current society.

## Regulation, constitutional doctrine, and reform

"The growing obsolescence of our environmental statutes has become particularly troubling with the heightened urgency of climate change" (Schoenbrod et al, 2010).[11] This statement refers to conditions that have emerged since passage of the environmental of the 1970s. The optimism about environmental progress expressed in a 1,291-page summary of American environmental regulations (Percival et al, 2000) is no longer tenable and Eisner (2007) concluded that we need to look for alternative ways of governing the environment. The US Federal Register for 2023 has 90,402 pages of rules and regulations (Crews and Smith, 2023), a number that few experts justify as being conducive to effective governance. The strategy review by Esty (2017) points out that the command-and-control system built in the 1970s led to decades of Congressional deadlock, resulting in the effective paralysis of law making on environmental and natural resources issues. The Yale-Columbia EPI for 2024 ranked the US 34th among nations, just ahead of Romania (EPI, 2024).[12] The comparisons presented in Chapter 11 confirm that the US has fallen far behind Europe in terms of the development of renewable energy.

In the 1970s, major European nations had environmental laws similar to those in the US. However, the EU adopted flexible sustainability policies in the 1990s, stimulated by the UN report, *Our Common Future*, led by Norwegian Prime Minister Gro Harlem Brundtland (Brundtland, 1987). These policies fostered cooperation rather than coercion and helped lead European nations to assume world leadership in environmental policy and performance. In 2024, European nations occupied the first 21 ranks in the EPI index.

Economic development has been a priority for American society since the founding of the nation. However, after the Second World War, the industrial and economic boom created serious health and environmental impacts. Chapter 5 offered background for subsequent developments, which included the revelation of the threat of economically important pesticides to valued birds, the assassination of President J. F. Kennedy, and the failure of the Lyndon B. Johnson administration to act on Kennedy administration plans to control environmental pollution. The Santa Barbara offshore oil spill in 1969 created a sense of national environmental crisis. It fostered a sense of urgency that led to new laws by Congress. The overreactive features of these laws were introduced in part because of skepticism about the ability of existing federal and state agencies to serve as stewards of the environment. The new regulatory system included the private enforcement of public law, a provision found in no other advanced nation.

## *Unintended effects of the* National Environmental Policy Act

Responding to the sense of environmental crisis, NEPA announced that henceforth, the environment must be considered in all federal government decisions. The environment became the prime focus of a series of federal laws. Long-overdue recognition of the importance of the environment in public policy was hailed by environmentalists and the ecological movement. NEPA and environmental laws in general were vigorously embraced by these movements.

The seven-page NEPA had no provisions for enforcement or litigation and does not prohibit activities. However, court interpretations in environmentalist suits (see Chapter 6) gave NEPA powerful legal clout by allowing complaints of inadequacy in environmental impact statements called for by the Act to become grounds for suit in federal court. Impact statements came to require a multiplicity of modeling techniques and procedures to predict potential effects of proposed activities (Hyman and Stiftel, 1988). NEPA became a favored administrative tool for opponents to change. It fostered NIMBY objections to stop renewable energy initiatives and other needed projects, so that even the Sierra Club came to recognize it as a problem (Motavalli, 2021). In short, over time, NEPA became the single most important barrier to infrastructure development, because almost any environmentally linked concern, not only those that might be critical, were grounds for court challenges by local residents or other persons or groups that had "standing"—that is, would be affected by proposed developments. By the 1980s, environmental policy and law experts already recognized that reform in the US environmental regulatory system was needed (Bardach and Kagan, 1982; McGarity, 1987). However, owing to developments described in Chapter 7, opportunities for reform were overtaken by political conflict.

### *Legal and Constitutional doctrines*

This section deals with issues of legal and constitutional doctrine that arose from regulatory controversy. Environmentalists' calls for more stringent policies to control greenhouse gases were countered by conservatives' concerns about expanded federal controls on American society and their effects on the economy. These concerns go beyond environment and include laws like the *Dodd-Frank Banking Act of 2010*, which became a subject of debate that reached the Supreme Court (Iuliano and Whittington, 2017). Conservative justices held that a broad delegation of societal control to federal agencies amounted to a dereliction of Congress's responsibilities, while liberal justices argued that Congress does not surrender its legislative power by delegation; by doing so, it exercises that power (Mortenson and Bagby, 2020).

The issues contrast nondelegation, as when Congress created specific laws to protect the environment, with delegation, when because of Congressional gridlock, execution and interpretation of the laws by federal agencies took place later with no Congressional ability to exercise control. Recent debates over constitutional authority came to a head with the Supreme Court's overturn of *Chevron v. Natural Resources Defense Council* of 1984. This famous case declared that in the event of disputes about a law's intent, courts should give deference to federal agencies. In following decades, the complexity and range of federal regulations administered by federal agencies extended beyond the environment to banking and finance, health and safety, transportation and infrastructure, education, and criminal justice.

The recent case was brought by a group of fishing companies (Loper-Bright) who challenged the National Marine Fisheries Service's assessment for monitors it assigned to the ships. The D.C. district court rejected the suit, citing *Chevron*'s deference to the agency, but on appeal, the Supreme Court sided with Loper-Bright, overturning *Chevron*. The case had political dimensions because the justices in the 6–3 decision included three conservative justices appointed by President Trump. Criticism of the decision by liberal justices and environmentalists was based on the argument that the judgment of expert federal agency staff should have greater weight than that of courts. The counterargument of the conservative justices was that polarization had led to politization of agency personnel, and that this overrode the intent of Congress when it passed the law.

In summary, the legal and regulatory framework for environmental policy in the US is at the center of national political hostility and conflict, which has expanded over time, jeopardizing US programs against climate change. An assessment by the World Resources Institute, a leading nonpartisan environmental organization, finds that while "The potential negative repercussions [of the election of Donald Trump] for climate and environmental action are gargantuan," opportunities for progress remain (DeConcini et al, 2024). There is the possibility—hopefully the likelihood—that recent developments will increase recognition of the need for the reform of existing environmental law, whose effects have fostered conflict for 40 years. The discussion in Chapter 13 takes up the question of how reform might be realized. Past efforts in this direction are taken up in the following discussion.

### *Reform proposals*

Stephen Breyer, later appointed as a Supreme Court justice, was an expert on and advocate of regulatory reform, as indicated by the title of his book, *Breaking the Vicious Circle* (Breyer, 1993). In it, Breyer rejected both deregulation and "democratizing regulation," that is, changing policy by each administration. He recognized that "well-meaning, intelligent regulators, trying to carry out their jobs sensibly, can nonetheless bring about counterproductive results." He noted that "the Congressional tendency to respond directly to public perceptions worked against the development of a systematic, coordinated approach to regulating risks." He also found problems in giving courts significant roles in overseeing regulation. His solution was a new mission-oriented "independent agency commanding significant prestige and authority." Bringing about the latter concept will be explored in Chapter 13.

Given the problems with regulation and the models offered in Europe and other nations, I was surprised to find only a few authors besides Breyer who have given serious attention to constructive environmental regulatory reform. Among them is Daniel J. Fiorino, former director of the EPA's Environmental Performance program (Fiorino, 2006), and lawyer and author Philip K. Howard (Howard, 2019). Books by David Schoenbrod and co-workers offer detailed critiques on existing regulatory processes and reform proposals (Schoenbrod, 1993; Casazza et al, 2008; Schoenbrod et al, 2010). However, Daniel Esty's 78-page analysis for an Aspen Institute symposium offers what I suggest may be the most realistic available strategy to overcome "ideological, structural, and operational issues that have led to political gridlock and blocked environmental policy reform" (Esty, 2017). Because of this country's large greenhouse gas emissions and influence in global affairs, reforms are essential if Lovelock's pessimistic scenario is to be avoided.

Fiorino noted that the existing environmental regulatory system required compliance, but offered no incentive for superior performance. Howard's book states that "statutory accretion has resulted in "progressive public paralysis … and a cornucopia of unintended results," and he also criticizes liberals who "have their heads in the sand" believing that environmental review should be preserved as it is, even if it is unintelligible to any citizen and doubles the necessary infrastructure costs. Howard also scored conservatives who distrust all authority and criticize the regulatory system, but whose only reform proposal has been the REINS Act that requires Congressional approval of new regulations, which is unacceptable to the Democratic Party and environmentalists, and does nothing about statutes that generate regulations. He also noted that business leaders have opposed regulatory flexibility in favor of certainty in regulations.

European environmental policies are relevant to meaningful reform. They have proven their effectiveness over three decades, remaining stable across changes in political administrations in 28 nations. Not least, given (at the time) President-elect Trump's positions, the current American political climate is not conducive to balanced law reform. Eventually, however, it will have to be addressed. Despite any success the Trump administration may have, Chapter 13 proposes that effective governance for the US is not compatible with continued political polarization.

13

# Pathways to Progress

## Introduction

In the 1970s, the US was the world leader in environmental policy, and it remains highly influential in world affairs. However, since the 1970s, it has declined in environmental progress and performance, ranking 34th among 180 nations in the Yale-Columbia Index of Environmental Performance for 2024 (EPI, 2024). It ranked 23rd among nations in Quality-Of-Life, just behind Poland (US News, 2024). These mediocre ratings are anomalous, given US history, affluence, world-renowned universities, as well as leadership in key areas like information technology (the internet and Google), and, not least, research on climate change. The low ratings for environmental progress parallel a Pew Research Center report on Americans' trust in government, which declined from a high of 77 percent in 1964 to 19 percent in 2023 (Pew, 2024). Causes of this decline were traced in Chapters 5–7. A summary of history and factors that have contributed to flawed political policies were reviewed in Chapter 12. The failure to deal with causes of conflict that emerged in the 1980s has led to intractable polarization and public discontent, culminating in the election and nonsequential re-election of Donald Trump.

This chapter begins with relevant historical detail on operations of the federal government and changes that led to the emergence and escalation of partisan political polarization. It continues by examining alternative approaches to reduction of conflict and concludes by exploring pathways to reform environmental and regulatory law once need for fundamental change gains acceptance. As mentioned earlier, this chapter and the body of the book reflect conditions as of reelection of Donald Trump but before his inauguration. Unexpected subsequent developments are reviewed in the Afterword.

### *The Golden Age of federal agencies*

From 1900 until the 1970s, senior civil service administrators beneath presidentially appointed leaders of federal agencies remained largely independent of politics while remaining responsive to missions and tasks assigned by the president and requests from Congress and the public. Agency heads could exercise considerable independence. A notable example was Harold Ickes, who served as Secretary of the Interior in four administrations of President Franklin D. Roosevelt. Ickes was a progressive Republican and supporter of African-American causes, having been President of the Chicago NAACP (Wikipedia—Harold Ickes). As Secretary of the Interior, he served as director of the Public Works Administration, responsible for dispersal of billions of dollars in federal programs devoted to alleviating poverty and unemployment in the depths of the Depression. Ickes was known for integrity but also clashed with Roosevelt and other cabinet members.

A critical function of federal agencies was providing guidance to Congress in preparing and amending legislation. The demanding pressures on members of Congress and committees, along with shifts in party control, made it logical for Congress to draw on the professional expertise of federal agencies. As late as 1973, the Bureau of Fisheries and Wildlife prepared a final draft for ESA before it was revised by Lee Talbot, chief scientist on the Council on Environmental Quality (Talbot, 2013). In contemporary European nations, as noted earlier, apolitical ministry task groups follow guidelines of the ruling government to prepare drafts of major legislation that are further modified by party committees before a final parliamentary vote.

### *The 1970s: Congress takes the lead in environmental regulation*

The US law-making system was transformed in the 1970s, spurred on by the failure of the Lyndon B. Johnson administration to act on pollution. In the 1960s, action moved to the Senate, where Senator Muskie of Maine, Chairman of the Senate Subcommittee on Air and Water Pollution, led in legislation like the *Air and Water Quality Acts* of 1965 and 1967. Muskie was knowledgeable and committed; instead of following normal processes of legislative development in committees, he took a personal initiative in drafting legislation (Billings, 2007). However, as noted earlier, environmental laws enacted in the 1960s continued to leave authority for pollution control to the states.

As noted in Chapter 6, the Santa Barbara offshore oil spill of January 1969 triggered powerful new laws, the first being NEPA, written largely by Lynton Caldwell, special advisor to the chairman of the Senate Committee on Interior and Insular Affairs, Senator Henry (Scoop) Jackson. The next was the CAA, spearheaded by Chairman Muskie and four senators on his Subcommittee. From this time on, environmental laws were enacted almost exclusively through Congressional initiatives, bypassing the Nixon White House's agency-drafted proposals.

The environmental expertise and legislative skills of Congressional leaders in the early 1970s enabled the CAA and the *Federal Water Pollution Act*

*Amendments of 1972* (CWA) to gain unanimous approval in the Senate en route to overwhelming approval by Congress. The framers' actions were bipartisan or, as qualified by Senator Howard Baker, nonpartisan (Manheim, 2014). However, this kind of cooperation by members of Congress was exceptional and did not last. For example, only after protracted negotiations, active support by President George H. W. Bush, Senate Majority Leader George Mitchell, input from Paul Portney of Resources for the Future,[1] and special contributions by the President of the Environmental Defense Fund, Fred Krupp, was the last amendment of the CAA passed in 1990 (Manheim, 2009).[2]

Congress is the nation's prime forum for political debate, and the Senate and the House of Representatives shift party control. Congress' initiative in creating detailed regulatory procedures affecting every industrial establishment in the nation was questionable on basic principles. Congress lacks inherent scientific or professional expertise. Congressional committees can call expert witnesses, but their selection and the ultimate creation of laws are controlled by partisan leaders who are likely to be influenced by political pressures and urgent priorities. Unlike policies modifiable by civil service experts and administrators with experience and balanced perspectives, Congressional laws can be modified only by new Congressional laws. Inevitably, regulatory policy became politicised, and ultimately could no longer be amended.

The CAA of 1970 was followed by 14 other Congressional regulatory laws by the end of 1972 (Manheim and Fuhs, 2007). Bipartisan support for environmental laws continued with the *Comprehensive Environmental Response, Compensation, and Liability Act of 1980* (the *Superfund Act*). However, by this time, the nation was in an economic downturn with stagflation. Antagonism grew in the business community. Congress continued regulatory activism after the 1980s. Laws increased in length and complexity, reaching 2,300 pages in the Dodd-Frank Banking Act (McHenry, no date). They made federal agencies executors of Congressionally mandated procedures rather than able to exercise judgment and flexibility in addressing problems. The degree to which Congress assumed responsibility for regulatory detail is illustrated by P.L. 104–142, the Mercury-Containing and *Rechargeable Battery Management Act of 1996*, which required the following:

> On each rechargeable consumer product containing a regulated battery that is not easily removable, the phrase should be seen: "CONTAINS NICKEL-CADMIUM BATTERY. BATTERY MUST BE RECYCLED OR DISPOSED OF PROPERLY" or "CONTAINS SEALED LEAD BATTERY. BATTERY MUST BE RECYCLED," as applicable.

In addition to the groundbreaking new laws, major change in the federal governance was introduced by the *Civil Service Reform Act of 1978*. Promoted by President Jimmy Carter to give the president more control over agency policies, the act created a Senior Executive Service from high-level civil service staff whose members were subject to assignment by a partisan OPM. It authorized the president to appoint temporary administrators to work under presidential nominees. The new system enabled the Reagan and subsequent administrations to effectively control the policies of agencies. As referred to in Chapter 10, the CSRA provided legal justification for Trump's earlier executive order for a Schedule F that could convert civil service personnel to political appointees. It will provide the incoming Trump administrative tools to fulfill his promise to "drain the swamp."

The environmental revolution in the 1970s had positive effects in curbing pollution. It created protection for endangered species and embedded an environmental ethic in the nation's laws. However, flaws in the system eroded the nation's industrial base and created conflict with the business community. Ensuing political polarization and Congressional gridlock prevented reform of earlier laws, freezing a now 50-year-old environmental management system in place. Polarization increased with President George W. Bush's record "signing statements," which signified that the president would decline to enforce specific provisions of Congressional laws (Mann and Ornstein, 2006). Frustrated by the paralysis in environmental law making after his inauguration in 2009, President Obama appointed a White House "climate czar" with policy-making responsibilities without Senate confirmation. This practice has been criticized as unconstitutional (Crouch et al, 2020).

The inability to modify outdated legislation prevented reforms needed to deal with global climate challenges unanticipated by the framers of the earlier laws. It has affected other needs such as revitalization of the nation's infrastructure, a healthcare system that costs up to twice that of other advanced nations, and an immigration and naturalization problem at the southern border that has become a major bone of contention. Passions aroused by conflicts cloud the judgment of factions and obstruct consideration of solutions to the many problems facing the nation (Kingzette et al, 2021).

## Shots across the nation's bow

On July 13, 2024, a mild-mannered, 20-year-old high-school graduate came close to assassinating presidential candidate Donald Trump at a rally in Butler, Pennsylvania (Guzman, 2024). The event was covered by Secret Service sharpshooters, and Thomas Matthew Crooks had no escape plan. He was ready to give up his life to kill a man he apparently feared endangered American democracy. This event, and the support of half the nation for a former president who refused to acknowledge the outcome of the 2020 election, signaled that political discord in America had reached dangerous levels.

In his acceptance speech for the Republican presidential nomination on July 18, 2024, Trump "led chants of 'drill, baby, drill' and pledged to get rid of the Biden administration's 'green new scam'", the program to encourage transition to electrical vehicles (Waldman, 2024). The startling position adopted by a leading presidential candidate, given overwhelming scientific and international support for the seriousness of climate change, suggests that long hostility to the fossil fuel industry by powerful environmental organizations and leading academic activists has not been successful policy; it fostered counterhostility and radicalization of the opposition. Hundreds of lawsuits, efforts to shut down pipelines, the export of petroleum, and constant efforts to mobilize public and political pressure against an industry whose oil and gas fuels more than 70 percent of the energy needs of the nation, produced results that are opposite to those of the successful policies of European nations.

A large scholarly literature exists on American polarization, but views of political scientists illustrated by the books in Table 13.1 suggests that scholars' conclusions may tend to deal with outcomes or diverse effects of polarization rather than core origins. The concept that polarization is a right-wing phenomenon gained ground in recent years, supported by extreme positions taken by Trump and his Republican supporters, and by greater rightward movement of earlier Republican law makers than those of Democratic politicians (DeSilver, 2022). Popular support for Trump, in spite of his challenge to the US election system and other radical positions, has given rise to prejudicial characterization of his followers. However, Bennett (2024) warned that this can divert attention from general increase in distrust in the American political system and a desire for change. It also overlooks the impacts of developments in the 1970s reviewed in Chapter 6.

**Table 13.1:** A sample of books dealing with American polarization

| Author | Themes |
|---|---|
| McCarty, Poole, and Rosenthal, 2008 | Polarization has multiple causes, especially income inequality. |
| Fiorina, Abrams, and Pope, 2010 | Polarization is a myth; politicians, not the public, are polarized. |
| Mann and Ornstein, 2012 | Polarization is a right-wing phenomenon. |
| Rosenfeld, 2017 | Polarization was created by postwar polarizers of both the Democratic and Republican Parties. |
| Klein, 2020 | Americans tend toward polarization by nature. |

Given the seriousness of the polarization problem, it is surprising that more institutional studies have not engaged with this subject in detail.[3] An important exception is a 102-page report by the Conflict and Governance Program of the Carnegie Endowment for International Peace, a leading source of independent policy research focused on society and governance (Kleinfeld, 2023). Partial conclusions from the report follow:

- Americans are not as ideologically polarized as is often assumed. Misperception is greatest for the most politically engaged people. However, people are emotionally polarized ("affective polarization")—that is, they do not like members of the other party.
- American politicians are ideologically polarized and their policies have little overlap. The trend has grown for decades.
- Pluralism programs to bridge differences (for example, ranked choice voting) are not enough. Interventions to change individuals' emotions must be paired with efforts to counter politicians' incentives to instrumentalize affective polarization as a strategy.
- Advocacy that amplifies the belief that the other party is bent on destroying democracy deepens polarization and support for anti-democratic action on one's own side (for example, Thomas Matthew Crooks). Coordination of groups to act on shared goals, despite other differences of opinion, may bridge partisanship, build trust, and advance a more just democracy.
- Polarization is a highly nuanced field, and small assumptions can lead to big mistakes.
- In the 1950s, some observers felt that the parties were too similar ideologically. A series of factors caused elite groups to become polarized from the 1980s.
- The study showed violence dramatically increasing from both left and right in 2016, especially from far-right and anti-inclusivity groups.

Another Carnegie Endowment study on polarization trends in foreign countries showed that the Scandinavian nations achieved a spectacular and sustained decline in polarization after the Second World War, but "The United States stands out today as the only wealthy Western democracy with persistent levels of pernicious polarization" (McCoy et al, 2022).

Measures to reduce polarization offered by the American Bar Association included changes in Congressional election procedures such as ranked choice voting (adopted by Alaska, Maine, and Arizona), independent citizen redistricting, "survivor" votes for the presidency, or compulsory voting, as in Australia (Foley, 2024). Ranked choice voting is advocated by the Forward Party founded by Andrew Yang after the 2020 presidential election. An in-depth review of the US federal and foreign governmental systems was published by Maxwell Stearns, a professor of law at the University of

Maryland. Among his critiques was the assertion that because of redistricting, American politicians now choose voters instead of voters choosing politicians. After reviewing parliamentary systems in foreign nations, Stearns concluded that the existing Congressional system is outdated and that transformation to a parliamentary system would be the simplest reform (Stearns, 2024).

### *Approaches to change*

US media and books often feature articles and titles ending in "and here's how to fix it," but polarization does not lend itself to simple solutions. The previously cited Carnegie Endowment for International Peace report (McCoy et al, 2022) noted that the US is the only advanced nation with pernicious political polarization. If the goal of contending factions continues to be focused on overcoming or defending against opposition, this country will likely remain with what the British call a "wicked problem"—that is, a problem with no discernible solution. Progress against climate change under such polarized politics will continue to be unacceptably slow because obstacles include: (1) political gridlock blocking Congressional legislation; (2) reversal of presidential initiatives when the presidential party in power changes; (3) inhibitions on exploitation of existing and new renewable and low carbon energy sources and technologies; and (4) regulatory delays, litigiousness, and NIMBY.

US approaches to climate change during the past 35 years have been dominated by federal government policies, with subordinate actions at the state and local government levels; efforts of research organizations, business and industry; and vigorous advocacy by NGOs. Initially modest, federal policies were strengthened in the Obama and Biden administrations. However, the Republican Party has become less supportive of climate change policies over time, reaching the point of open dismissiveness in 2024. This stalemate is argued to be the product of longstanding political polarization, the continuation of which is here suggested to be untenable for climate change policy. The next topic evaluates alternative approaches to reduce polarization and restore the US to more normal functioning.

#### *Incremental change and moderation of politics*

Recent law reforms raise the possibility that change can be evolutionary and increase as reform ideas receive greater acceptance. *The Fiscal Responsibility Act of 2023* and the *ADVANCE Act* within the *Fire Grants and Safety Act of 2024* (Capito et al, 2024) initiated the first significant regulatory reforms of NEPA and reforms to facilitate US nuclear power development. Microsoft billionaire Bill Gates committed financial support to an advanced nuclear plant in Wyoming that is based on molten sodium instead of existing pressurized water designs (Plumer, 2024), which new design would allow simplified regulations. The Wyoming plant would use the electrical transmission lines of a coal-fired power plant that would be replaced by nuclear power and would retrain its workers. If successful, transformation of coal-fired plants to nuclear power could spread more widely in the US, simultaneously reducing economic and employment problems caused by closed coal-fired plants. Success might soften major environmental opposition to nuclear power.

The foregoing developments apply mainly to nuclear energy and do not resolve uranium supply, for which the US was once an exporter, but is now an importer owing in part to laws that favor opposition to mining. From 2007 to 2012, a bubble of interest in the country's largest uranium deposit in Virginia collapsed because of the absence of state governmental systems capable of overseeing mining activity or developing cooperation with relevant federal agencies (Manheim, 2014b).

On August 2, 2024, the Senate Energy and Natural Resources Committee, chaired by Joe Manchin (D-WV), approved a major energy reform bill. Its significance lay in the fact that it reduced permitting barriers to both oil and gas leasing, supported by Republicans, as well as electrical grid development, supported by Democrats. With a favorable vote of 15 to 4 in committee, it has a chance to be the first bipartisan energy reform law in decades. Despite the fossil fuel provisions opposed by environmental NGOs, it is argued to be an important step forward because it would break existing barriers against extending the electrical grid. Without progress, electrification could not provide needed alternatives to fossil fuels.

A problem with incremental changes is that they mainly involve minor changes in or re-interpretation of existing law. They do not affect the larger regulatory labyrinth. To deal efficiently with new problems and science, laws should not involve elaborate detail, but rather allow regulatory flexibility to administering officials as modern Scandinavian law does. This would require increased public trust in officials.

An incremental avenue for reform includes ranked choice voting, which would give Congressional candidates not endorsed by major political parties the opportunity to compete in elections. Ranked choice voting became popular in American cities in the early 20th century, but was virtually eliminated after the Second World War. In 2018, Maine became the first state to adopt it for primary and general elections, as well as for its legislature and governor. Maine subsequently became the first state to expand the system to presidential elections. In 2020, Alaska approved ranked choice voting for Congressional elections, and in 2022, Nevada replaced partisan primaries with a single nonpartisan primary from which the top five candidates would advance to Congressional ballot. The Forward Party and other organizations advocate for this system in other states.

The significance of ranked choice voting lies in allowing qualified candidates to challenge dominance by the major parties, who normally support candidates that embrace the party line. However, election policies are influenced by activist wings of the Democratic and Republican Parties and tend to perpetuate partisan hostility. While Democrat-controlled states like California and Massachusetts have more local ranked choice voting activity than Republican states, four of which have banned ranked choice voting (Rodriguez, 2023), both major parties oppose ranked choice voting for presidential or Congressional elections.

According to the earlier-cited Carnegie study, there are now few centrist politicians. Most moderate members of Congress have retired voluntarily or have not run for re-election because of the threat of "being primaried," that is, defeated in primary elections by party-favored candidates. However, 37 percent of the public (Saad, 2022) and a number of political groups fall into the moderate category. The best known of the latter include the Bipartisan Policy Center, No Labels, the Forward Party, New America, and Unite America. "Keep Our Republic," another nonpartisan organization formed in 2020, has a board including former leading Democratic politicians like Richard Gephardt, Gary Hart, and Tim Wirth.

The No Labels organization has been led by prominent politicians from both parties, like John Huntsman and Joe Lieberman. It has sponsored events at which political candidates were invited to speak under conditions designed to provide policy positions more informative than the sloganeering of political campaigns. The Bipartisan Policy Center features panels of well-respected speakers representing various perspectives.

While the regulatory reforms mentioned may encourage further initiatives, they have mainly been led by Congressional members with specific interests (for example, Republican Congresswoman Shelley Moore Capito from West Virginia). That state needs nuclear plants to replace coal-fired power plants that dominate its electrical power supply. In short, there is as of yet no discernible reform bloc or evidence that moderate political groups have a following sufficient to erode the power of the major parties.

### *Popular reform movements and strong leaders*

In the 19th century, the Panic of 1873 and a wave of popular revulsion against the veniality and corruption of the federal government led both the Republican and Democratic Parties to nominate reformers as candidates for the election of 1876. Republican Rutherford B. Hayes, the winner of a highly contested election, committed himself to a single term in order to concentrate on government reform without concern for popular or political favor (Hoogenboom, 1988b). Hayes appointed cabinet officials based on qualifications rather than political loyalty, and he commissioned a study of the civil service merit system that became the *Pendleton Act of 1883*. Other examples of public action were the Prohibition movement, partly led by

Christian denominations, which resulted in the Eighteenth Amendment to the Constitution, and the Civil Rights Movement of the 1950s and 1960s, which mobilized courageous support from the African-American community and its supporters. The latter efforts led to the passage of the *Civil Rights Act of 1964*.

However, in the electronic era since the 1970s, it has become easier for public opinion to be influenced by skilled media strategy. Though polls show that the public wants less polarization, popular opinion is unlikely to lead the way to political reform. One reason is the decline in the public's information and interest in political affairs, demonstrated by a survey of the Annenberg Public Policy Center in 2017. It reported that only one American in four could name the three branches of the federal government (Annenberg, 2017).

Nineteenth-century presidents with charismatic appeal, Andrew Jackson and James K. Polk, had administrations marked by vigorous partisanship. Charismatic popular leaders who transformed American politics in the 20th century include Franklin D. Roosevelt and Ronald Reagan. Some of the laws passed in the first two Roosevelt administrations—for example, the Tennessee Valley Authority, the *Social Security Act*, and the Securities and Exchange Commission—had major importance and remain today, but other initiatives of the New Deal led to antagonistic relations between the Roosevelt administration and industry that delayed the recovery from the Depression. Although President Reagan maintained a personal rapport with the Democratic speaker of the House, his early initiatives were aggressively partisan and led to conflict with Congress. Most recently, Donald Trump pushed the Republican Party into radical policies, including curbing disagreement within the Party. The pragmatism and willingness to compromise that characterize successful Scandinavian policies seem incompatible with public opinion and the kinds of leaders that have recently emerged in the US, making it questionable whether "strong" future political leaders would achieve balanced political reform.

### *Campaign strategy*

The electronic revolution and instant communications transformed politics, elevating the importance of campaign managers and pollsters skilled in discerning the mood of a volatile public. Since the 1970s, well-strategized campaigns have been the prime pathway to political success. This has been demonstrated by presidential campaigns and social movements. The first US presidential campaign characterized by superior campaign strategy was that of Abraham Lincoln, described in detail in an award-winning book by Doris Kearns Goodwin (Goodwin, 2006). It was also the first presidential election campaign in which campaign strategy assumed a new importance. Candidates could travel to various parts of the nation through the rail network, and speeches could be transmitted by telegraph. Beginning far behind three other candidates for the Republican nomination, Lincoln traveled extensively, building his name recognition in states dominated by other candidates. When no candidate won on early ballots, Lincoln gained ground in subsequent ballots and ultimately won the nomination. Democrats, concentrated in the less populous, pro-slavery South, were soundly defeated in the election of 1860.

Jimmy Carter would not have risen politically without the political genius of Hamilton Jordan, who at age 26 managed Carter's successful campaign for governor of Georgia. In 1972, at age 28, Jordan presented an unconventional, 70-page game plan, which Carter largely followed four years later in his successful run for the Democratic nomination and then for president, when he defeated Gerald Ford (Gergen, 1992).

Bill Clinton was a skilled campaigner, but was powerfully aided by James Carville in the uphill campaign against the incumbent President George H. W. Bush in 1992. Coming off a wave of popularity after the successful expulsion of the Iraqi military from Kuwait, Bush seemed unbeatable, but Clinton prevailed in a campaign marked by Carville's now-famous dictum: "It's the economy, stupid." Carville's role was featured in an Academy Award-nominated film, *The War Room* (Wikipedia—James Carville).

Karl Rove had a critical role in electing George W. Bush as Republican Governor of Texas in the 1990s. He managed Bush's 2000 presidential campaign against Democrat Vice-President Al Gore. Gore had been a representative and senator from Tennessee, a bestselling writer on the environment, and was a sitting vice-president with wide name recognition. Yet Rove achieved a controversial victory with a candidate who was later voted the worst president in US history by 61 percent of a group of historians (Wikipedia—Public Image of George W. Bush, April 11, 2025).[4] Rove's mastery of detail was demonstrated in the final phase of the 2000 election. Bush had gained a narrow lead in Florida, but Democrats claimed errors associated with punched card ballots and their notorious "hanging chads." Rove defused the furor when he observed that the City of Chicago, controlled by the Democratic Party, used the same punch-card system (Manheim, 2023c).

In 2012, polls showed that only 18 percent of the public felt that the country was on the right track after the first term of President Barack Obama. Historical precedents showed steep odds against his re-election, and he arguably would not have won the election without the innovative database technology and skills of campaign managers David Axelrod and David Plouffe. Axelrod was hooked on politics as a teenager, selling buttons for the campaign of Robert F. Kennedy at age 13 (Manheim 2023b). Donald Trump was his own campaign strategist in 2016 and again in 2024, as described in Chapter 9.

Successful campaigns for political causes have also been characterized by skillful strategy. Charles Hamilton Houston, Vice-Dean of Howard

University's law school, devised an ingenious strategy to "chip away" at the separate-but-equal doctrine of the 1896 Supreme Court decision in *Plessy v. Ferguson*. Knowing the futility of a frontal attack on discrimination, Houston and his student, Thurgood Marshall (later a Supreme Court justice), sued Southern law schools for failing to supply separate but equal education for African-American students. He chose law schools because their mostly male students avoided the sensitive issue of miscegenation. Houston and Marshall won every case because rather than create expensive separate facilities, Southern law schools were forced to accept Black candidates.

The National Organization for Reform of Marijuana Laws (NORML) was founded to legalize recreational use of cannabis. It gained an undesirable image through its association with the hippie lifestyle in the 1960s and 1970s, so NORML's leaders artfully shifted strategy to the use of marijuana to ease the pain of suffering and terminally ill patients, gaining a foothold through federal approval of medical marijuana (Wikipedia—Medical Cannabis in the United States). With California's Proposition 215, labeled the *Compassionate Use Act of 1996*, medical marijuana dispensaries soon outstripped pharmacies and coffee shops in San Francisco and Los Angeles.

The Human Rights Campaign likewise employed strategies sensitive to longstanding social mores and Christian doctrine in order to mainstream homosexuality in the US. It shifted attention from the hedonistic images of gay parades in the 1970s to media portrayal of clean, conservative couples to promote same-sex marriage in the media. The final breakthrough occurred when, after initially favoring traditional marriage in his 2008 campaign, President Obama endorsed same-sex marriage and opposed the Congressional *Defense of Marriage Act of 1996*, signed by President Clinton. The groundwork had been laid by the Human Rights Campaign's tireless political networking over several decades (Bronski, 2012).

The importance of these campaigns is that in the electronic era of instant communications, the US has a volatile public, prone to influence by skilled political tactics and operators. The public forms opinions rapidly, joins bandwagon movements, but can also be quick to abandon them. Michael Dukakis, the Democratic Governor of Massachusetts, initially led Republican presidential candidate George H. W. Bush by 17 points in the election of 1988, but ended losing in a landslide. In 2020, Joe Biden's campaign was widely written off after he came in fifth in the New Hampshire presidential primary, but after a strong endorsement by Representative Jim Clyburn of South Carolina, Black voters gave Biden an unexpected plurality in the South Carolina primary, and the win handed him the nomination. No policy issues were involved; the only change was in public opinion. The conclusion is that effective strategy capable of mobilizing public opinion will continue to be essential for success in elections and to gain in approval of policies.

### *The role of academia*

Contemporary American social science publications lead the world in publications and academic reputation, but academic fields most related to politics and environment have weak informative and advisory connections to real-life society. This was not true earlier in American history. American political scientists like Frank Goodnow (1859–1939) and Arthur Bentley (1870–1957) included practical fields in their work. Social scientists with political influence, trained before the explosion of graduate research in the 1960s, include Robert Dahl, Gabriel Almond, Kenneth Arrow, Murray Edelson, Arend Lijphart, and Elinor Ostrom (Nobel Prize 1990), although only a few academics became active in politics, These include C. Wright Mills (New Left); Jean Kirkpatrick (advisor to President Nixon and ambassador to the UN); and especially Daniel Patrick Moynihan. Moynihan was a cabinet member, advisor, and ambassador in the Kennedy, Johnson, Nixon, and Ford administrations, as well as a longtime Democratic senator from New York and committee chairman. Since the passing of Moynihan and Kirpatrick, Ben Sasse, Nebraska Senator and subsequently President of the University of Florida, is among the few academics who became active in politics.

Some 95 percent of recent American political science publications are disseminated in professional media that are neither designed for nor used by decision makers or the concerned public (Shulock, 1999; Manheim, 2019). On the other hand, some social scientists have become involved in political advocacy (Tormos-Aponte, 2021), and an estimated 90 percent of social scientists are reported to have liberal commitments (Kaurov, 2022). Academic scientists like Naomi Oreskes, Robert Bruller, and Michael Mann have openly attacked American industry. The polarization of academic scientists was explained by Kaurov (2022) by Republican attitudes toward science—for example, *The Republican War on Science* (Mooney, 2006). Activist scholars may have valid arguments, but polemics and the abandonment of balance depart from the traditions of academic science. They undermine the independent image of academia and foster antagonism in industry and trade organizations like the American Petroleum Institute and the US Chamber of Commerce. Students trained by activist faculty are unlikely to restore societal harmony nor become candidates for leadership positions and exert positive influence on industry. In contrast, in Germany, half of corporate CEOs have PhDs.

An example of the loss of communication between academia and industry occurred during the writing of this book. My first work was as a geologist in the oil industry. I had an industry contact who was now a senior Exxon-Mobil company employee. My request for an interview on nonpolitical issues like carbon sequestration was turned down and subsequent messages were not answered. This was not my only experience with industry's disaffection with academia. This example indicates that, regardless of the causes, polarization is corrosive to society. Academia has vast intellectual resources and educates new generations, but it cannot win in battle against industry that plays a critical role in the economy. It would be wise to heal the breach and contribute insights through cooperation, not conflict. I suggest that this is not only practical, but can also be considered a responsibility.

### *Alternatives to the all-or-nothing approach*

Since the 1970s, political campaigns have been won through well-executed strategies, but reducing polarization and achieving balanced political reforms are more complex problems than winning presidential campaigns or achieving goals by unified constituencies. We know from polling that the public favors a reduction in political polarization, but the problem is that the political elites who dominate politics are committed to ideological positions and have little interest in reducing polarization; they are its main exponents. Large segments of the public regret polarization, but vote to continue the impasse at election time because they have no other options.

Historical analysis reviewed earlier suggested that the origin of conflict has been obscured by political sensitivities on both the left and right. Environmentalists are reluctant to acknowledge flaws in the existing environmental laws because this could validate complaints by industry and weaken regulations regarded as important safeguards. Conservatives who revere the Reagan legacy are reluctant to acknowledge the negative effects of the first Reagan's administration's campaign to roll back the enforcement of environmental laws, actions that replaced bipartisan cooperation on environmental legislation with animosity and Congressional gridlock.

### *A first step: recognizing the futility of polarization*

The US's "pernicious polarization" is anomalous among advanced nations and has led to public distrust of government, an inability to resolve a range of issues, and unsatisfactory progress against climate change. This suggests that a first step to resolution is recognition of the realities. Recognition does not mean accepting polarization as a regrettable but unavoidable fact of life; it means realizing that this has torn the fabric of the nation and should not continue. There is an analogy in the "Three A's" of Alcoholics Anonymous: "Awareness, Acceptance, and Action." Once alcoholics accept the reality of addiction, recovery can begin. If the futility of further hostility is recognized by the public, progress can begin. One hundred and eighty years ago, Alexis de Tocqueville noted that Americans were prone to political mistakes, but once they recognized those mistakes, they could correct them more rapidly than other nations.

### *The second step: environmentalists accept that hostility to American corporations has not benefited climate change policy*

This step, which is more difficult than the first, poses the following question: can people accept the idea that efforts by each party to overpower the other have not worked for the nation, and only worked for parties temporarily? When environmental policies could not be implemented through legislation, presidents began using executive orders and taking other actions to promote their policies. Six presidents beginning with Jimmy Carter reversed the environmental and energy policies of their predecessors. Ramming through laws by party-line vote while a party controlled both houses of Congress further stoked hostility and the opposition's determination to overturn the results.

An example is the *Patient Protection and Affordable Care Act of 2010* (hereinafter the "Affordable Care Act"). This complex law, passed when the Democrats controlled the three branches of the federal government, was ironically based on a plan earlier developed by Republican governor Mitt Romney in cooperation with the Massachusetts legislature; it incorporated other earlier bipartisan initiatives. However, it became the object of 60 Republican attempts at repeal (Wikipedia—Affordable Care Act). A principal reason for that rejection was the fact that it was passed in the face of unanimous Republican opposition.

Another example is reform of NEPA regulations by the Council on Environmental Quality during the first Trump administration. NEPA is the single greatest source of delays in infrastructure development. Making NEPA regulations more effective is therefore clearly desirable. While some of the Trump administration reforms of NEPA regulations could be considered overreach, others were arguably productive. Yet, virtually all were rescinded, and some were even expanded by President Biden within days of taking office. In these examples, the opportunity for balanced and effective law making and regulatory reform was lost because of partisan polarization.

If the idea that polarization not only harms the nation, but has not benefited political parties in the long run is accepted, it would open the way to needed reform. Energy expended in battling political enemies could be turned to constructive communication, however tenuous this might be initially. Committed partisans will find it difficult to communicate with those with whom they have deep disagreement, so initial steps will likely have to come from those less affected by polarization. Cross-party restoration of balance in public policy has been cited as critical by Jaime Dimond, CEO of the prominent J. P. Morgan Chase bank: "A president should put the most talented people, including those from business and the opposite party, into their Cabinet," Dimon wrote in an opinion piece in the *Washington Post* (Dimon, 2024).

Such actions could begin the process of defusing conflict that the majority of the public favors. Breakthroughs in political communication would allow young people to see a brighter future, which many presently do not (Harvard, 2025). Attuned to new political developments and bandwagon movements, media could publicize new initiatives and increase public support for a reduction in polarization and reform of government operations. It is important to examine the origin and rationales for political positions rather than merely presenting them as soundbites and targets for opposition. The following sections assume progress on this front sufficient to allow Congressional consideration of bipartisan reforms.

## *Reform of the* Civil Service Reform Act of 1978

The law that created the original merit system governing the appointment and administration of federal government employees was only eight pages long, yet it provided a system that served the federal government well up to 1978. The *Pendleton Act of 1883* derived from an in-depth review of the best international civil service systems undertaken by Dorman Bridgman Eaton, commissioned by President Rutherford B. Hayes. His report, published in a 469-page book (Eaton, 1880), was based on the reformed British civil service system. The law laid out principles assuring fairness and efficiency, but operational details were left to three commissioners, no more than two of whom were to come from the same party. Qualification to appointment in the federal government was on the basis of examinations testing practical knowledge and capabilities, not formal educational credentials. Higher scores qualified applicants to higher-level administrative positions.

As described earlier, President Carter felt that the federal bureaucracy obstructed his policies, so he successfully pushed through a new law of 173 pages, the CSRA. The CSRA replaced the Civil Service Commission with the OPM, which was headed by a presidential appointee (eliminating the former bipartisan system). It created a mobile Senior Executive Service, whose members could be assigned by the OPM. The new law further authorized the president to designate 10 percent of executives as temporary administrators who would serve under presidentially appointed heads of agencies and top appointees. The combination of these provisions effectively transferred control of agency policies from formerly nonpolitical civil service administrators to the executive office of the president, which enabled radical shifts in agency policies after presidential elections if the party in power changed. It fatefully contained an obscure provision allowing the president to convert civil service employees to political appointees, utilized in President Trump's 2020 Schedule F Executive Order.

To promote administrative flexibility, the CSRA decentralized hiring to local managers. While Carter opposed racial discrimination, the new provisions had a discriminatory effect on the hiring of Black professionals. Federal positions were in short supply and local managers almost always found that White candidates were a "better fit" for their needs, whereas previously positions were approved centrally according to candidate qualifications. In the US Geological Survey, in which I served, most African-American geologists were hired before 1978. With the adoption of the CSRA, African-American employees became concentrated in lower-level positions, while those with professional qualifications were largely relegated to equal opportunities or human resource positions. Complaints were raised to the Department of the Interior by the Blacks in Government (BIG) organization, but had little effect. The problem was built into the new system and difficult to counter, except where top officials were highly motivated. Another change accompanying the CSRA was that examinations for higher-level positions became replaced by educational credentials, which increased the effect of social privilege, preferentially benefiting White applicants.

Reforms to help federal agencies return to more professional operation are suggested:

1. Replace the OPM head with three directors, as in the original Civil Service Commission, with no more than two from the same party. Mandate that these be long-term positions rather than subject to arbitrary change with political administrations.
2. Return Executive Service positions to agencies. Transfers should be handled by agency leaders rather than through the influence of the executive.
3. Eliminate the president's authority to appoint temporary administrators in federal agencies and to convert civil service positions to presidential appointments subject to termination.

Marcia McNutt, former Director of the US Geological Survey, pointed out that heads of federal agencies are grossly underpaid in comparison with executives in private industry with lesser responsibilities. This prevents the retention of officials with the highest qualifications (interview cited in Acknowledgments). Constructive changes could restore leadership in federal agencies to career civil servants, who would be responsive to presidential directives, but not subservient to partisan politics. Agency performance would be improved by considering employee initiatives, and restoring the ability of agencies to plan for the future. Public respect would increase as agencies would again be able to issue reliable reports instead of websites influenced by partisan policies, which are widely ignored.

A federal agency workforce characterized by integrity and professionalism rather than partisan loyalty is counter to the plans of President-elect Trump. Trump has made clear his intent to "drain the swamp" through transformative change that would include replacing bureaucrats with loyalists. This effort was frustrated in his first administration by appointees and civil service personnel who did not fully share his vision. Late in his administration, this was planned to be countered by implementing a Schedule F for high-ranking federal employees. This might permit conversion of up to 50,000 civil service positions into political appointments who could be reassigned or separated from government. The provision was promptly removed by President Biden on his election in 2020, but Trump asserted his intention to reinstate it. It should be noted that even without a new Schedule F, the existing CSRA already provides the president with extensive potential control of federal agencies. In short, the reforms suggested here—or others restoring administrative integrity to the federal civil service—have to be deferred to a time when the importance of impartial and professional federal government operation re-emerges. A similar caveat applies to the next topic. This is separate from arguments that the federal government has become bloated and inefficient, which I can confirm from my own long government service.

## *Reforming the US environmental management system*

### ***Problems with the existing law framework***

Responding to an atmosphere of environmental crisis and urgency, including protesters at Congressional offices (Billings and Jorling, 2015), the environmental revolution of the 1970s created a regulatory system that was politically effective and achieved rapid progress against environmental pollution. It remains in place and is highly regarded by the environmental movement. However, the system contains flaws that led to partisan political polarization in the 1980s and continues to create obstacles to restoring political balance.

A basic flaw in the highly complex system was that regulatory systems created in federal law could only be modified by new law. The modification and updating of the laws to resolve problems or reflect new information, or the passage of new environmental and energy legislation, was inhibited by Congressional gridlock that arose through overreaction to the laws' adverse effects. A second problematic feature was the fragmentation of environmental management into separate laws. This expanded regulatory complexity and inhibited integrated environmental management (Ruckelshaus, 2006; Esty, 2017). It resulted in the US EPA enforcing provisions of 37 separate laws and executive orders (EPA, 2024a). In an oral history of the EPA, the respected first and fifth administrator of EPA, William Ruckelshaus, stated "there probably isn't enough money in the whole federal budget to do everything they [Congress] assign to EPA" (Ruckelshaus, 2006).

A further problem was created by adjudication of disputes and authorization of civil suits by private citizens and organizations to enforce laws in federal court. This contributed to litigiousness in the US that is unique among advanced nations. In a symposium celebrating the 35th anniversary of the EPA, Paul Portney, longtime president of the environmental think tank Resources for the Future, noted that 65 percent of the EPA's directives are challenged in court (Merget, 2006; see also Schoenbrod et al, 2010).

Finally, the overwhelming domination of the federal government in regulation weakens incentives for state and local political jurisdictions to take proactive roles in environmental management. A number of states have taken independent action on climate change policy, but the decentralization of environmental management, supported by federal agencies in research, guidance, and decision making in larger largest environmental issues, as is implemented in advanced European nations, is not feasible under present conditions.

Besides contributing to the loss of major segments of US manufacturing and industry, the 1970s regulatory system continues to inhibit the competitiveness of US manufacturing. This also applies to federal government subsidies to stimulate production of renewable energy development or infrastructure. Subsidies support companies most experienced with and willing to work with complex regulatory requirements, but not necessarily the most dynamic and innovative initiatives.

Past prejudice and stigmas need to be overcome. The US mineral industry was the most impacted among economic sectors (Manheim 2009) and lack of domestic mineral production has now become a major supply issue for renewable energy development. The International Energy Agency reported that a typical electric vehicle (EV) requires six times more mineral value than a fossil fuel-powered vehicle (IEA, 2021). Each car currently requires 100 kg of graphite, 11 kg of cobalt, 32 kg of nickel, 10 kg of manganese, and 6 kg of lithium. These minerals account for 50–70 percent of the cost of electrical vehicles. Rare earth minerals are critical for wind turbines and other advanced technology, but the trade in these minerals is largely controlled by China because it dominates the processing of rare earth ores from all sources. Huge amounts of copper are needed for electrical grids.

### *Pathways to reform*

The successful decentralization of environmental management by European environmental leaders was referred to in Chapter 11. Prospects for transferring enforcement responsibilities to local authorities in the US under the then existing conditions were disparaged by former EPA administrator William Ruckelshaus. He remarked during a symposium celebrating the 35th anniversary of the EPA:

> Even if we do decide that a problem is best handled in a smaller arena, we should recall that if you're in a fight to the death with poisoned daggers, a smaller arena is not necessarily a good thing. The point is to stop fighting and start generating creative solutions. (Merget, 2006)

Reform advocate Howard Phillips wrote (Howard, 2019):

> Neither political party has any serious proposal to fix Washington. An angry public is presented with cartoon cliches of reforms that can't possibly work. Deregulation promises amputation, but that's not the right cure for mindless bureaucracy; voters want clean air and clean water … that's why deregulation goes nowhere even when Republicans are in control of Congress.

In short, America does not currently have the conditions needed for the decentralization of environmental regulation as implemented in European nations. In 1958, "about three-quarters of Americans trusted the federal government to do the right thing almost always or most of the time", but by 2010, approval of government had declined to below 20 percent (Pew, 2024). Similar disapproval of corporations was referred to earlier. The preceding chapters have shown that the regulatory system has been the prime source of dissension since the 1980s, so the nation first needs to regain public confidence in this critical function.

A wide-ranging exploration of cases involving regulation of environment, health, and safety, with 32 contributors, included reform elements (Fischbeck and Farrow, 2001). Regulatory reforms were explored by authors mentioned in the previous chapter, the most nuanced conceptual framework for which was suggested to be a 79-page document by Daniel Esty, co-developer of the Yale-Columbia Environmental Performance Index and a distinguished legal scholar (Esty, 2017). Polarization and the complexity and controversial nature of the issues put the translation of such efforts into national law beyond the capabilities of Congress in the present and near-term future.

For the eventuality that the need for structural reform gains sufficient recognition, most options for progress would probably recognize the EPA as central to the process. Even if the president's authority to appoint temporary administrators were removed, the EPA administrator would still have strong influence on agency operations. As was suggested in an earlier book (Manheim, 2009), a way to minimize partisanship would be to lengthen the term of office of the administrator, letting the president nominate a candidate from a shortlist of qualified candidates chosen by a bipartisan commission. The director of the FBI and the Chairman of Federal Reserve serve for long terms because they are so important that both parties have recognized the need for these positions to transcend partisanship.[5] Given the EPA's responsibilities for environmental regulation of all US industrial entities, as well as carbon-emitting energy production and use in the nation, removing partisanship from EPA operations is arguably as important as it is for the FBI and the Fed chair. Bipartisan commissions have been effective in the past in spite of political polarization. They work in part because parties tend to choose members with care. Committee members who lack qualifications or hold extreme views would not enjoy respect and influence when a consensus report is to be produced.

If appointment of a broadly accepted, extended-term EPA administrator were to be approved, that official, after a demonstration of leadership in the EPA's new role, could be given responsibility to convene a taskforce of qualified experts to draft proposals for environmental law reform. Bipartisan respect for the administrator, and judicious choice of task force members would be critical for the ultimate acceptance of its recommendations. The taskforce should have wide representation and expertise in all relevant subjects, including European and Canadian environmental policy. They would draft proposals to be reviewed by representatives of affected constituencies, paralleling the way in which the European Commission develops proposed laws for the European Parliament. To repeat, a prerequisite for reform would be ending party loyalty as the prime factor influencing high-level administrators working below the top presidential appointees. Without integrity and public confidence in federal agencies, no regulatory reform would work. Prior reform of the CSRA would therefore be essential. Besides increasing the president's control of agencies, the CSRA's detailed procedures are antithetical to effective performance, which was far better under the eight-page, nonpartisan *Civil Service Act of 1883*.

In leading environmental nations like Denmark, Sweden, and Germany, industry is a full partner with government in environmental and regulatory policy making.[6] This is an essential element for these nations' progress toward decarbonization because industry is both a source of greenhouse gases and essential in production of renewable energy and infrastructure, and in national affairs. In the US, the inclusion of industry in future US Democratic administrations' policy-making process might seem unlikely in the current American political climate. However, cooperation would cost Democratic administrations little beyond disapproval by its more radical party leaders and groups because the administration would make the final decisions on policy. Industry participation would help identify weaknesses and improvements in proposed policy, results that would benefit the party in power. Industry, in turn, would become informed about environmental problems and goals, gain advance information on administration plans in ways that would be helpful for its own planning, and would have incentives to include environmentally knowledgeable leaders in company and trade association management. For these reasons, engagement in policy development would likely be more effective than cabinet positions that minimally affect environmental and energy policies.

Given Trump's hostility to climate change policies (as noted in Chapter 10), one might assume that the new administration would have little openness to sustainability. However, as previously noted, industrial megastar Elon Musk's reversal of previous policies to support Trump earlier created at least a temporary change in Trump's stated disapproval of electric vehicles. He ostentatiously displayed purchase of a red Tesla in March 2025.

An expected argument against fundamental law reform in the US environmental policy is "they'll never agree to it." That perspective seems overpowering with regard to both parties in the current political climate. Environmentalists and their supporters are deeply committed to preserving health and environmental values, and are skeptical of changes that might weaken the protection of laws. On the Republican side, a criticism of the feasibility of reform is that, in the light of the decision reversing *Chevron v. NRDC*, the Supreme Court would never agree to give additional independence to federal agencies.

An answer to the first point from the environmental perspective is that the polarized system has not delivered for environmentalists or the nation. If the condition continues, climate policy is not likely to improve because energy supply is a core requirement for the economy, and the public has shown a low tolerance for progressive measures that would impact it. However, increased stability and professionalization of the EPA and other relevant agencies could increase the efficiency of American climate policy, as superior European performance shows, and thereby encourage environmentalists to adopt more flexible positions.

An answer to the Supreme Court argument is that a rationale for overturning *Chevron* was that polarized politics infected federal agencies with the partisan biases of administrations, and they were no longer trusted by large segments of the population. The reforms I have suggested would be implemented only when the EPA was no longer subject to extreme political instability. Change can take place unusually quickly in America, a trait observed by de Tocqueville 180 years ago and evidenced in past decades. A response to the "they'll never accept it" view is the question: are we prepared to accept continued hostility and its corrosive effect on society, or do we prefer to work toward a system where professionally led federal agencies give all constituencies due consideration, no matter which party is in power? Trust systems and professional competence were enabling factors for the US's earlier monumental infrastructure achievements. They currently characterize European nations that lead in progress against climate change, while they maintain robust industrial productivity and trade balance.

Chapter 12 noted that political overreaction has been a pattern in American politics since the election of Andrew Jackson in 1828. The case has been presented that America's powerful but flawed environmental laws of the 1970s and their subsequent application led to irreconcilable conflict that has blocked the effective operation of government. The incoming Trump administration proposes extreme measures to not only tame environmental regulations, but also overhaul and presumably reduce all functions of an overreaching federal bureaucracy. The radical new challenges and Trump's past actions might call for opponents to intensify their opposition, but history reviewed in this book suggests that politics limited to ideological goals and fighting opposition has fostered unbalanced policies and popular disillusion. Unpalatable or unrealistic as the process may seem, I suggest that effective governance needs to include insights from history, the experience of other advanced nations, and the perspectives of the "other" party and groups in the formation of policies. Strategies to gain popular recognition of these realities by the public at large need to be a part of effective political policy. As Abraham Lincoln recognized, without popular approval, no policy will be effective. Ultimately, the enemy of societal harmony and progress is not a given political party, notwithstanding its flaws or ideas, but polarization.

# Afterword

This concluding chapter reflects the status quo prior to the inauguration of Donald Trump as the 47th President of the United States. The Afterword reviews the dramatic developments that followed Trump's return to office. In his 2024 election campaign, Trump dismissed the science behind global climate change and the need to reduce greenhouse gases, a position contradicted by the 195 nations that affirmed the Paris Agreement of 2015. He also promised to "drain the swamp" of federal bureaucracy. However, few experts anticipated the extent to which he would defy democratic and constitutional norms.

The power of the federal government was soon used to intimidate core institutions of American society. When the Associated Press refused to adopt the term "Gulf of America" in place of the Gulf of Mexico, its representatives were barred from the White House press pool. Billions of dollars in federal grants to Harvard University were frozen. An Associated Press (AP) article compared Trump's early actions to Hungary's transformation into an "electoral autocracy" (Spike and Riccardi, 2025). Because of the unprecedented nature of Trump's early actions, I offer detailed coverage of developments up to May 2025.

The first of 26 executive orders signed on Trump's first day in office—Executive Order 14147 (2025), titled "Ending the Weaponization of the Federal Government"—began: "The American people have witnessed the previous administration engage in a systematic campaign against its perceived political opponents, weaponizing the legal force of numerous Federal law enforcement agencies and the Intelligence Community."

This order reinterpreted criminal indictments, including those related to Trump's role in instigating the January 6, 2021 attack on the Capitol building. Subsequent orders repealed 79 Joe Biden-era directives and launched sweeping policy changes, including:

- ending birthright citizenship;
- pausing refugee admissions;
- reinstating the "Remain in Mexico" policy;
- recognizing only two sexes;
- ending Diversity, Equity, and Inclusion (DEI) programs;

- withdrawing from the Paris Climate Agreement;
- reinstating the federal death penalty;
- creating a Department of Government Efficiency (DOGE). (Wikipedia—First 100 Days of the Second Donald Trump Presidency)

Other actions included "pardons and sentence commutations for roughly 1,500 defendants charged in connection to the Jan. 6 attack on the Capitol." The administration initiated rollback of existing agencies like the Consumer Financial Protection Bureau, the Department of Education, and USAID (Gangitano, 2025). As of April 2025, Trump had signed 137 executive orders and other official directives. Many were blocked or delayed by federal court rulings. Analysts noted substantial overlap between these actions and the Heritage Foundation's Project 2025 recommendations (Cruz et al, 2025). Paul Dans, chief editor of *Mandate for Leadership*, confirmed that a central goal of the project was to enable the president to "hit the ground running."

## The role of Elon Musk and the Department of Government Efficiency

Elon Musk, a groundbreaking entrepreneur in electric vehicles (Tesla), space exploration (SpaceX), and other ventures, had supported centrist political positions and expressed concern about climate change. He resigned from Trump's first administration after the United States withdrew from the Paris Agreement (Isaacson, 2023). However, anger at federal regulators, outrage over the attempted assassination of Trump, and encouragement from the incoming president led Musk to shift his position dramatically.

Musk became a Trump advisor and assumed leadership of DOGE's campaign against the federal establishment. His radical initiatives included dismantling USAID, the Department of Education, and the Consumer Financial Protection Bureau; offering buyouts to two million federal workers; firing probationary employees; demanding progress reports from all federal staff, with noncompliance interpreted as resignation; and seeking personnel records. By April 2025, buyouts, retirements, and planned layoffs had affected about 12 percent of the federal workforce. Some firings were reversed by courts; others were quietly rescinded.

A ten-year study by Paul Light (2009) revealed that although the number of federal employees had remained relatively constant at over two million for decades, the federal government employed roughly three times as many contract workers. At the time of writing, I found no estimates of the Trump administration's impact on this contractor workforce.

Many Americans initially welcomed Musk's effort to reform what they viewed as a bloated and inefficient federal government. However, his "chainsaw" approach disregarded democratic norms and legal procedures. It failed to distinguish between flawed policies and essential services—for example, between USAID's controversial programs and those critical to public health or US diplomacy.

Musk's actions triggered lawsuits, nationwide protests, and institutional resistance (Durkee, 2025). A critic in *The Nation*, a left-leaning publication, condemned Musk for his role in what it called a "megalomaniacal and criminal junta." The article charged that Musk led a cabal of billionaires committed to "smash-and-grab capitalism," aiming to extract wealth from the nation—including its poorest residents (Mystal, 2025).

Musk also intervened aggressively in foreign affairs, with notable consequences. Tesla's profits fell by 71 percent and the company's stock price dropped sharply, erasing gains made after Trump's re-election (Wile and Ingram 2025). While electric vehicle sales in Europe rose by 24 percent, Tesla sales declined by 37 percent. Musk announced in May that his major tasks were complete and he would return to focusing on his companies. However, a well-sourced article indicated that DOGE had placed personnel throughout federal agencies, suggesting that its influence would continue (Wikipedia—US Federal Agencies Targeted by DOGE).

## White House Fact Sheets

The second Trump administration began with a stream of initiatives described by online *White House Fact Sheets.* Selected sheets issued in April 2025 are listed in Table A.1. Each sheet's title is prefaced by "President Donald J. Trump advances … promotes … reforms … demands … unleashes, etc." Comments on the initiatives follow the table.

Fact Sheets portray policies as restoring legal or constitutional balance, but many have been interpreted as having opposite effects. Examples of questionable policies are cited in the following.

- The "Straw Donor" sheet calls for the Department of Justice to investigate and remove security clearances from government employees who had investigated or criticized Trump's activities (Barrón-López et al, 2025). It singles out Act Blue, the principal Democratic fundraising organization, for investigation of alleged violations of election law, omitting Republican organizations from review.
- The content of "Probationary Periods" and "Creates New Federal Employee Category to Enhance Accountability" involve details described in Chapter 10. They expand a provision in the CSRA of 1978 to convert civil service positions to political appointments that the president can terminate. The scope of this order, and those on "Equality of Opportunity and Meritocracy" and "Protects Civil Rights and Merit-based Opportunity

**Table A.1:** Selected White House Fact Sheets issued in April 2025

| |
|---|
| *Election policies*: "Investigates Unlawful 'Straw Donor' and Foreign Contributions in American Elections" (includes investigation of ActBlue) |
| *Federal workforce restructuring*: "Creates New Federal Employee Category to Enhance Accountability"; "Strengthens Probationary Periods to Improve the Federal Service" |
| *Cultural and education issues—eliminate DEI*: "Signs Landmark Order to Restore Equality of Opportunity and Meritocracy"; "Promotes Excellence and Innovation at HBCUs"; "Reforms Accreditation to Strengthen Higher Education" |
| *Environmental policy and energy dominance*: "Simplifying the environmental review and permitting process and returning nation to energy dominance"; "Pushes the Reset Button on America's Energy Regulations"; "Protects American Energy from State Overreach"; "Reinvigorates America's Beautiful Clean Coal Industry" |
| *Permitting and deregulation*: "Directs Repeal of Regulations That Are Unlawful under 10 Recent Supreme Court Decisions"; "Brings Permitting Technology into the 21st Century for Government Efficiency"; "Restores Common Sense to Federal Procurement"; "Reforms Foreign Defense Sales to Improve Speed and Accountability" |
| *Immigration policies*: "Prevents Illegal Aliens from Obtaining Social Security Act Benefits" |
| *Trade policies*: "Regulating Imports with a Reciprocal Tariff to Rectify Trade Practices That Contribute to Large and Persistent Annual United States Goods Trade Deficits" |

Source: https://www.whitehouse.gov/fact-sheets/

by Ending DEI," are reported to bypass procedural requirements of law (Super, 2025).

- The *Prevents Illegal Aliens from Obtaining Social Security Act* is among the executive orders and documents associated with plans to deport "millions of illegal aliens." The border has been secured at the time of writing, but a breakdown of the costs for mass deportation suggests why this goal is unlikely to be realized (Chu, 2024).

## Foreign policy

Trump's foreign policies departed strikingly from the US's integrated relations with Canada and Mexico, free trade policies, and 75 years of partnership in NATO. A *Reuters* article (Spetalnick et al, 2025) summarized developments: "Trump ... disparaged NATO allies and embraced Russia's narrative about its invasion of Ukraine ... [He referred to] annexing Greenland, retaking the Panama Canal and making Canada the 51st state."

The sheet in Table A.1 entitled "Regulating Imports..." justified steep increases in tariffs on all nations—even neighboring countries Canada and Mexico—by claiming that other nations' tariff policies were responsible for US high trade deficits and loss of manufacturing—an explanation that conflicts with the history described in Chapter 6. Shocking tariff increases for US trading partners on "Liberation Day" resulted in counterresponse and flight from US Treasury bonds (Hutton, 2025). Their higher interest rates threatened increase in debt service costs already close to those of defense expenditures of $820 billion (13.3 percent of the total US budget). On April 9, Trump backtracked, announcing a 90-day lowering of all tariffs to 10 percent, except for China, whose tariff was raised to 145 percent after mutual escalations.

Stirred by the breach in longstanding US relationships with Europe and other actions, a member of the French Parliament, Claude Malhuret (Diaz-Maurin, 2025), responded with a speech that went viral. It is excerpted in translation here:

> Europe is at a critical turning point in its history ... Ukraine risks being abandoned ... Washington has become the court of Nero, an incendiary emperor, submissive courtiers, and a jester ... in charge of purging the civil service ... Trump's message is that there is no point in being his ally since he will not defend you, he will impose higher tariffs on you than on his enemies and will threaten to seize your territories while supporting the dictatorships that invade you ... Never in history has a US President supported an aggressor against an ally, trampled on the US Constitution, issued so many illegal executive orders, dismissed judges who could have prevented him from doing so, dismissed the military senior staff ... weakened all checks and balances, and taken control of social media. This is not an illiberal drift, it is the beginning of the confiscation of democracy. Let us remember that it took only one month, three weeks and two days to bring down the Weimar Republic and its Constitution.

## Environmental policies

On March 12, 2025, EPA administrator Lee Zeldin published an opinion that: "By overhauling massive rules ... we are driving a dagger through the heart of climate-change religion and ushering in America's Golden Age" (Zeldin, 2025). In an address from EPA headquarters, he presented five "pillars" guiding the new EPA:

- Pillar 1: Clean Air, Land, and Water for Every American
- Pillar 2: Restore American Energy Dominance
- Pillar 3: Permitting Reform, Cooperative Federalism, and Cross-Agency Partnership
- Pillar 4: Make the United States the Artificial Intelligence Capital of the World
- Pillar 5: Protecting and Bringing Back American Auto Jobs

Only the first pillar appears to be associated with the EPA's fundamental role. The other four support presidential priorities that include increasing fossil fuel production, emissions from which increase global warming. Trump's executive orders included eliminating the electrical vehicle mandate and other "Green New Deal" policies of the Biden administration and agencies created to support them.

An omnibus initial order, "Unleashing American Energy" (January 20), rescinded the Council on Environmental Quality's NEPA regulations and required the secretaries of relevant agencies to eliminate delays in permitting processes. It prohibited the use of "Social cost of greenhouse gases" considerations in environmental evaluation. Other orders countered the "Endangerment" finding that $CO_2$, methane, nitrous oxide, and hydrofluorocarbons threatened the public health and welfare of future generations), and sought to ban laws or regulations or laws by states that would inhibit the production or use of fossil fuels by states.

An order on April 9, "Zero-Based Regulatory Budgeting," required the "Environmental Protection Agency (EPA), Energy Department, Nuclear Regulatory Commission, Bureau of Safety and Environmental Enforcement and Fish and Wildlife Service to amend regulations so that they expire by October 2026." However, Supreme Court decisions, including those of the Court under Chier Justice John Roberts, required agencies seeking to change a policy to follow relevant procedures (Frazin, 2025).

A fundamental challenge to the ESA of 1973 redefined the word "*harm*" in a proposed rule announced by the Fish and Wildlife Service and National Oceanic and Atmospheric Administration on April 17 (Anonymous, 2025). The current definition protects habitats in which endangered species live. The new, narrower definition, long sought by businesses and other opponents, would limit the interpretation of harm to intentional killing or injury by hunting or trapping. These orders illustrate Trump's tactic of making bold pronouncements that may violate existing law, but modifying them if they encounter court challenge or other meaningful resistance.

Environmental organizations are anguished about the rejection of climate change policies by the new administration. However, the World Resources Institute published an important report titled "Trump may thwart federal climate action, but opportunities for progress remain" (DeConcini et al, 2024). Cited factors favoring continued progress against climate change follow:

- *Subnational leadership*: 4,000 mayors, governors, university presidents and business leaders signed the "We Are Still In" Declaration, committing to meet emissions-reduction targets set in the Paris Agreement and continue engaging with the international community. Twenty-four states and territories are in the US Climate Alliance with similar goals.
- *Clean energy incentives have staying power.* The Inflation Reduction Act's tax incentives are popular in red states (those leaning towards Republican politics) and many may endure.

- *Bipartisan support for climate-friendly policies*: A number of bills involving $CO_2$ removal, industrial decarbonization, critical minerals, nuclear energy, and permitting reform have bipartisan support.
- *Carbon Removal and Decarbonization*: US efforts to innovate and decarbonize include the concrete and asphalt sector. Interest in decarbonizing steel and aluminum is increased by the EU border adjustment mechanism that takes into consideration the carbon cost of imports.
- *Next generation geothermal and nuclear energy*: These energies have broad bipartisan support, including the new administration.
- *Critical minerals*: Promoting mining, processing and supply are among the goals of the administration.
- *Permitting reform*: This could reduce multiyear delays in infrastructure and assist in expansion of electrical grids.
- *Trade policies*: Tariffs may stimulate American production needed for renewable energy development; however, they could also create supply-chain problems.

Climate models indicate that zero emission goals cannot be achieved without nuclear power and carbon sequestration (Rebonato, 2024). Reduced constraints on nuclear power could be especially important, not least because of the huge power requirements for AI applications.

## Discussion

Chapter 10 described how Trump employed strategies that misled opponents into underestimating his knowledge and capabilities. By making outrageous statements, he attracted extensive media coverage while provoking attacks from political adversaries, diverting their attention from issues of greater concern to the public. This tactic not only gained him visibility but also helped cultivate an image of Trump as a fearless challenger to the establishment. His approach suggests a "method in the madness": without strategic skills, he would not wield the influence he now commands. While his oversized ego contributes to erratic decisions, his refusal to admit error can paradoxically reinforce loyalty among his supporters.

Trump's political history reflects shifting affiliations and inconsistent policy priorities, except in two sustained areas: border security and tariffs. Free from the ideological commitments that constrain many American politicians, he has been able to identify overreaches and national policy problems that contributed to public disillusionment with the federal government.

A consensus among observers suggests that the Democratic Party, beleaguered by attacks on its institutions and values, has yet to coalesce around unifying themes or effective leadership. It has failed to acknowledge the substance behind some of Trump's critiques, however extreme or counterproductive his tactics. A major example is the US's environmental regulatory system, which was established in the 1970s. While achieving significant progress, as discussed in Chapter 6, this system contributed to the decline of US manufacturing, impacted lower-income communities, and fostered business antagonism. Chapter 11 noted that regulations now hinder infrastructure and renewable energy development.

The policies advanced by Trump and Project 2025 to curtail regulation are suggested to reflect reactive policy lacking perspective supplied by history. The administration's assertion of political control over federal agencies, purging regulations, and reducing agency staff represent a more aggressive echo of the Reagan administration's campaign on the 1980s to roll back environmental regulations. As outlined in Chapter 7, this earlier effort resulted in Congressional backlash and political polarization, with long-term consequences for governance.

American history demonstrates that national progress is greatest when trust and cooperation exist between government and citizens. Policies imposed unilaterally and in the face of intense opposition rarely endure and often produce lasting harm. Chapter 5 examined the emergence of federal science agencies, which operated efficiently and contributed significantly to national progress from the later 19th century up to the Second World War. These agencies also served Congress by offering apolitical, expert guidance for legislation. A central thesis of this book is that burgeoning increase in federal institutions, political polarization, and lagging environmental progress stem in part from underrecognized developments beginning in the 1960s. They include 1968, a year which the Miller Center at the University of Virginia labeled *annus horribilis*:

> It began with the capture of the USS *Pueblo* by North Korea and the Tet Offensive in Vietnam. It continued with President Johnson's decision not to seek reelection, the assassinations of Martin Luther King Jr. and Robert F. Kennedy, riots at the 1968 Democratic National Convention, and the election of Richard Nixon. (Miller Center, 2025)

The trajectory continued with the passage of powerful but flawed environmental laws in the 1970s, the countercampaign against regulations in the early 1980s, and the subsequent partisan backlash in Congress. When the American government has failed to effectively address the defining issues of the times, instability has followed. Decades of polarization, Congressional gridlock, and increasingly partisan executive policies created the conditions for the rise of a strongman whose agenda threatens democratic norms.

Yet, a different path is possible. European nations have demonstrated that it is feasible to lead in climate and environmental policy while maintaining strong industrial bases and trade surpluses. If the US can avert lasting damage to its constitutional framework, future leaders may come to see the futility of continued partisan warfare. As was discussed in Chapter 13, renewed cooperation and national vitality could once again position the US as a global leader on climate challenges.

# Notes

## Acknowledgments

1 A search on the key phrase "environmental policy" in Google Scholar returned 2.3 million titles of scholarly articles and books.

## Preface

1 Ernest Manheim (1900–2002) was the younger cousin of the noted Hungarian-British sociologist Karl Mannheim (1893–1947).

2 Now the College of Marine Sciences.

3 Mississippi, Alabama, and Florida offshore areas in the eastern Gulf of Mexico.

4 Google's Ngram Viewer is an online program that plots the frequencies of given words or phrases occurring by year in the millions of books in Google's comprehensive database. It offers a powerful means of identifying trends in society.

5 *The Conflict over Environmental Regulation in the United States: Origins, Outcomes, and Comparisons with the European Union* (Springer 2009), 321.

## Chapter 2

1 The radiocarbon dates have since been calibrated using tree ring and other data.

## Chapter 3

1 Taylor (2001) noted that a French settlement had already been established at the mouth of the St. John's River. The inhabitants were Huguenots, and they were attacked and killed by the Spanish, who were ardent Roman Catholics.

2 Jean Baptiste d'Anville (1697–1782) was precocious, becoming geographer to the French king Louis XV at the age of 22.

3 Alexis de Tocqueville's *Democracy in America* (1835/1840) initially claimed that President John Quincy Adams terminated government employees appointed by previous presidents. Adams vigorously challenged this statement in a letter of 1837 and de Tocqueville deleted it from the 6th edition (footnote in Nolla translation (deTocqueville 1951) v. I, p 214).

## Chapter 4

1 Virginia's subsequent leaders were largely pro-slavery, although Thomas Jefferson Randolph, a grandson of Thomas Jefferson, proposed a gradual emancipation plan to the Virginia House of Delegates in 1832 after the Nat Turner rebellion.

2 Jackson fought at least five duels, in one case killing his opponent.

3 Appointments based on competence in the first six presidents probably favored persons regarded as advantaged. Schlesinger's enthusiasm for Jackson's populism discounted his grievous flaws. The book by Robert Remini, based on intensive research, is better balanced.

4 Maintenance broke down after the Second World War, leading to raw sewage discharges into the harbor. Severe contamination led to a court-ordered repair and extension of the system. My agency, the US Geological Survey, and other academic institutions became involved in analysis of contaminated bottom sediments and hydrology.

5 Linus Pauling, winner of the Nobel Prize in chemistry, took his first degree in chemical engineering at Oregon State College in 1917 because chemical engineering was the only major involving chemistry of which he was aware.

6 Besides excise taxes on a wide range of goods and transactions and the nation's first income tax, the Union also printed greenbacks, whose acceptance for public and private debts was mandated by law (the *Legal Tender Act of 1862*). The Bureau of Internal Revenue was created to manage the complex system.

7 'First Transcontinental Railroad', *Wikipedia*, http://en.wikipedia.org/wiki/First_Transcontinental_Railroad.

8 In an address on the occasion of a memorial to the Pilgrims (1907).

## Chapter 5

1 The history of the corps shows that early efforts to enforce the law were opposed by political entities and opposed by the courts. For this reason, the corps largely left enforcement to local authorities (Corps, no date).

2 In contrast to the Prudential Life Insurance Company, the Metropolitan Life Insurance Company of New York believed that profit and social responsibility were not incompatible. It organized a highly effective welfare division in 1909, and its visiting nurse program created a million nursing visits a year (Duffy, 1992).

3 The "technological advances" curve in Figure 5.4 also reveals the "Khrushchev Bubble," the upswing in Soviet science and technology enabled by the reforms initiated by Soviet Party Chief Nikita Khrushchev before he was removed from the leadership in 1964.

4 As does a more recent activist organization, the Center for Biological Diversity.

5 Besides a description of the island and its fauna and flora, industries, and the culture of major Cuban cities, von Humboldt's monograph on Cuba included social indices of the human population. These included variations in race, that is, whites, mulattos, and Africans. He had a disgust for slavery and expressed strong disapproval of the institution in a visit with President Thomas Jefferson.

6 Information from Stephen Ewart, former lawyer at the Illinois EPA.

## Chapter 6

1 Professor Don Kash noted that the USGS was so minimally funded for its oversight responsibilities that its inspectors had to use oil company boats to visit drilling rigs. He suggested that the Santa Barbara spill marked a collision between the offshore oil industry and the environmental movement.

2 A founding director of the World Wildlife Fund, President of the Conservation Foundation, Undersecretary of the Interior; Chairman of the Council on Environment; and later the second administrator of the EPA.

3 A PhD geologist and environmentalist, and later Undersecretary of the Interior.

4 A geophysicist and environmentalist; member of the National Academy of Science; and Vice Chancellor of the University of California, Santa Barbara. He was an early advocate for global climate change policy.

5 William van Ness was a co-author with Caldwell on his massive annotated bibliography in 1969, and Chief Counsel for the Senate Committee on Interior and Insular Affairs, which Jackson chaired.

6 The earlier-created EQC had been floundering and was effectively superseded by the CEQ.

7 Nader's groups included Public Interest Research Group, The Center for Auto Safety, and Public Citizen.

8 Phi Beta Kappa and president of his class at Bates College.

9 An unpublished, nearly comprehensive database of environmental and land-use laws (Manheim, 2014) contained 711 laws from the founding of Congress through 2010. It was the basis for an eightfold classification of environmental laws and has been expanded for this book.

10 Supported by 132 references.

11 Talbot was a former general director for the International Union for Conservation of Nature (IUCN).

12 Congress subsequently reacted by passing a law authorizing the completion of the dam, although it was criticized for being inefficient. Other habitats were later found for the snail darter.

13 See the authors cited in Greenstone (2002).

## Chapter 7

1 I served as Chairman of the University of South Florida Department of Marine Science, which co-led a 13-university consortium of investigators with the State University System Institute of Oceanography (Florida) in the first comprehensive survey.

2 A son from her first marriage is Neil Gorsuch, a justice of the Supreme Court.

3 Lash had a distinguished subsequent career, serving as President of the World Research Institute from 1993 to 2011.

4 Watt's personal account, *Courage of a Conservative* (echoing Barry Goldwater's *Conscience of a Conservative*) (Simon & Schuster, 1985), is largely a defense of his policies, described in an online *Library Journal* review as "treating all social problems ... as manifestations of liberal moral degeneracy."

5 Arnold was erudite. Quotes from notables like Alfred North Whitehead, Juvenal, Helen Keller, and Robert Frost followed chapter headings. He freely cited the Sierra Club, environmentalists, and political critics.

6 The author was a Geological Survey scientist serving in the Office of Coastal and Marine Geology, Woods Hole, Massachusetts during this period.

7 http://www.ncseonline.org/NLE/CRSreports/Agency/agency-16a.cfm#_1_21

8 Carried out of the ambulance after being shot, Reagan famously said to his wife: "Honey, I forgot to duck." Entering surgery in the hospital, he quipped to medical staff: "Tell me you're Republicans."

## Chapter 8

1 Hansen was deeply concerned over fossil fuel contributions to climate change. On an anniversary of his testimony, Hansen was arrested in 2009 during protest of mountaintop removal to build a coal mine by the Massey Energy Company.

## Chapter 9

1 The Wikipedia article on Bush (Wikipedia—G.W. Bush) has unparalleled depth, including 527 references, 21 separate academic references, and a primary Bush source.

## Chapter 10

1 This section draws on research for an abandoned book on Trump's history and the 2016 election, and Manheim (2023a).

2 The *Politico* review belittled Trump's speech, but provided a complete online audio copy.

3 Gripping pictures of the event are available in (Reuters, 2022).

4 After an attempted assassination of Trump at a rally in Pennsylvania, Musk declared his support for Trump in July 2024.

5 The name Schedule F appears to derive from the CSRA reference to subparagraph F, paragraph 305, in Title 5 of the US Code.

6 Bannon, a radical Trump supporter who was terminated from the first Trump administration, boasted that Maga could rule for 50 years by seizing and remaking societal institutions (Callaghan, 2024).

## Chapter 11

1 This is noted from the early years of the republic. Most nations have memorials to historic leaders. George Washington was not only a military hero and first president of the nation, but a leader of uncommon stature. Yet, it took nearly 50 years after Washington's death before his national monument was erected. The residences of Washington, Thomas Jefferson, and James Madison were only preserved by private groups.

2 In addition to books by climate change skeptics cited in Chapter 12, the relatively recent *$CO_2$ Coalition*, led by Gregory Wrightstone, cites increases in crop and forest productivity due to the increased atmospheric concentration of $CO_2$.

## Chapter 12

1 Walter Cronkite was a respected and the most widely watched national news anchor on *CBS Evening News*. He served from 1962 to 1981.

2 Later editions became a two-volume set and modified their treatment of slavery and its aftermath. More recent editions continued after 1969. See Morison et al (1970).

3 The decision was made by the court of Chief Justice Roger Taney, with seven of the nine justices having been appointed by pro-slavery presidents (Anonymous, 2024b).

4 The reference cites 16 books that predicted the financial crash.

5 The largest world oil companies are now (1) The Saudi Arabian Oil Co.; (2) China Petroleum and Chemical Corp. (SNPMF); and (3) PetroChina Co. Ltd.

6 The Sierra Club responded to growing climate skepticism by appointing Michael Brune as its youngest president at age 38 in 2010. Brune excoriated the fossil fuel industry in online messages to Sierra Club members. He was forced to resign in 2021 after he condemned the club's founder, John Muir, as a racist.

7 According to an interview with Greenpeace's director for energy policy in Germany, a prime concern about nuclear power was the potential for nuclear terrorism.

8 An article by the National Resource Defense Council cited a list of safety concerns that justified the Indian Point closure (NRDC, 2021).

9 Dependency on federal government approvals and support can encourage the Enron syndrome, named for a company that embraced politically expedient policies for unethical financial gain.

10 Founded in 1969, the *Lewis and Clark Environmental Law Review* is the oldest in the nation.

11 David Schoenbrod was young lawyer with the NRDC in the1970s and assisted in the removal of toxic lead from gasoline. However, he later became a leading advocate for reform of the US's 50-year-old legal and regulatory framework.

12 The EPI index surveys 180 nations, combining "58 indicators across 11 issue categories, ranging from climate change mitigation and air pollution to waste management, sustainability of fisheries and agriculture, deforestation, and biodiversity protection." This description and data cited are available in (EPI, 2024).

## Chapter 13

1 A major think tank founded in 1952, and the first founded to focus exclusively on natural resource and environmental issues.

2 A senior attorney for the National Resources Defense Council proposed Doniger's Law, the opposite of Moore's Law. It predicted that each successive modification of the *Clean Air Act Amendments of 1970* would take twice as long as the preceding one (Doniger, 2024).

3 A major political initiative to transform federal government operations, Project 2025, was announced by the conservative Heritage Foundation, involving some 400 conservative scholars (Dans and Groves, 2023). However, even if useful reforms were implemented, they would likely be reversed in later Democratic administrations unless approved by Congress. It would therefore tend to increase rather than reduce polarization.

4 Other polls in the article offered low but less drastic rankings of the Bush presidency in history. It should be noted that rankings by historians have tended to be influenced by trends in their times.

5 This convention may be challenged by President Trump.

6 In Sweden, Denmark, and Germany, the active involvement of industry in environmental policy making is facilitated through collaborative governance models, including public-private partnerships, advisory councils, and sector-specific agreements. These countries have built institutional frameworks that ensure industry has a say in shaping regulations that impact environmental performance. Additionally, industries in these countries often participate in voluntary environmental programs, which further strengthen their role in the policy-making process.

# References


Adovasio, J. and Page, J. (2002) *The First American: In Pursuit of Archaeology's Greatest Mystery*, Random House.

Al-Ubaydli, O. and McLaughlin, P. (2015) "RegData: A numerical database on industry-specific regulations for all U.S. industries and federal regulations (1997–2012)," *Regulations and Governance,* 11: 109–123.

Ames, K. and Maschner, H. (1999) *Peoples of the Northwest Coast: Their Archaeology and Prehistory*, Thames and Hudson.

Anderson, M. and Moratto, M. (1997) "Native American land-use practices and ecological impacts," in D. Erman and the SNEP Team (eds) *Status of the Sierra Nevada: The Sierra Nevada Ecosystem Project USGS DDS-43, Native American Land-Use*, US Geological Survey, pp 187–206.

Anderson, D. and Sassaman, K. (2012) "Mississippian complexity and contact coalescence," in *Recent Advances in Southeastern Archaeology; From Colonization to Complexity*, Society for American Archaeology Press, pp 152–190.

Anderson, D. et al (2010) "PIDBA (Paleoindian Database of the Americas): Current status and findings," *Archaeology of Eastern North America*, 38: 63–90.

Andrews, R. (1999) *Managing the Environment, Managing Ourselves: A History of American Environmental Policy*, Yale University Press.

Andrews, R. (2008) *Managing the Environment, Managing Ourselves: A history of American Environmental Policy*, Yale University Press.

Andrews, R. (2020) *Managing the Environment, Managing Ourselves: A History of American Environmental Policy*, 3rd edn, Yale University Press.

Annenberg (2017) "Americans are poorly informed about basic constitutional provisions," *Annenberg Public Policy Center of the University of Pennsylvania,* [online] Available from: https://www.annenbergpublicpolicycenter.org/americans-are-poorly-informed-about-basic-constitutional-provisions/

Anonymous (2005) "The contribution of good environmental regulation to competitiveness" ("The Prague Statement"), Network of Heads of European Environment Protection Agencies (EPA Network) [online] September 29–30, 2005, 5th EPA Network plenary in Prague, Available from: https://epanet.eea.europa.eu/reports-letters/reports-and-letters/epa-network-paper-good-environmental-implementation-and-competiveness.pdf/@download/file/EPA%20Network%20paper%20Good%20Environmental%20Implementation%20and%20Competiveness.pdf

Anonymous (2009) "An ad Trump signed supporting action on climate change," *New York Times*, [online] June 3, Available from: https://www.nytimes.com/interactive/2017/06/03/us/politics/document-Nyt-Ad-Re-Climate-Change-Trump-Signer.htmlPage

Anonymous (2015) "Jefferson, science, and exploration," *American Philosophical Society*, [online] April 10–December 27, Available from: https://www.amphilsoc.org/museum/exhibitions/jefferson-science-and-exploration

Anonymous (2018) "American Indian women," *National History Education Clearinghouse,* [online] Available from: https://teachinghistory.org/history-content/ask-a-historian/23931#:~:text=They%20usually%20owned%20the%20family%27s,%2C%20social%2C%20and%20economic%20power

Anonymous (2023) "Celebrating 50 years of success in wildlife conservation," US Department of the Interior, February 2, Available from: https://www.doi.gov/blog/endangered-species-act-celebrating-50-years-success-wildlife-conservation

Anonymous (2024) "Intro.7.2 separation of powers under the Constitution," *Library of Congress*, [online] Available from: https://constitution.congress.gov/browse/essay/intro.7-2/ALDE_00000031/

Anonymous (2025) "Rescinding the definition of 'harm' under the Endangered Species Act: A proposed rule by the Fish and Wildlife Service and the National Oceanic and Atmospheric Administration," *Federal Register,* [online] 17 April, Available from: https://www.federalregister.gov/documents/2025/04/17/2025-06746/rescinding-the-definition-of-harm-under-the-endangered-species-act

Anonymous (no date) "William J. Clinton, 42nd President of the United States," Washington DC: The White House.

Anshelm, J. and Hultman, M. (2013) *Discourses of Global Climate Change: Apocalyptical Framing and Political Antagonisms*, Routledge.

APS (American Philosophical Society) (no date) "Thomas Jefferson examines Indian languages," *American Philosophical Society,* Available from: https://www.amphilsoc.org/exhibits/treasures/vocab.htm

Arnold, R. (1981) *At the Eye of the Storm: James Watt and the Environmentalists,* Regnery Publishers.

Arnold, R. (1997) *Ecoterrorism*, Merrill Press.

Arnold, R. (1999) *Undue Influence: Wealthy Foundations, Grant-Driven Environmental Groups, and Zealous Bureaucrats that Control Your Future*, Free Enterprise Press.

Arnold, R. (2010) *Ecology Wars: Environmentalism as if People Matter,* Merrill Press.

Ayres, R. (2007) "Telephone communication about the NRDC and the Clean Air Act Amendments of 1970," F.T. Manheim.

Baker, H. (2005) "Cleaning America's air: progress and challenges." *The Edmund S. Muskie Foundation*, [online] Available from: http://www.muskiefoundation.org/baker.030905.html

Baker, K. (2016) *America the Ingenious: How a Nation of Dreamers, Immigrants, and Tinkerers Changed the World*, Artisan Press.

Banerjee, N., Song, L. and Hasemyer, D. (2015) "Exxon's own research confirmed fossil fuels' role in global warming decades ago," *Inside Climate News*, [online] September 16, Available from: https://insideclimatenews.org/news/16092015/exxons-own-research-confirmed-fossil-fuels-role-in-global-warming/

Barceló, J., Jensen, J., Peisakhin, L. and Zhai, H. (2024) "New Estimates of US Civil War Mortality from Full-Census Records," *Proceedings of the National Academy of Sciences*, 121(48).

Bardach, E. and Kagan, R. (1982) *Going by the Book: The Problem of Regulatory Unreasonableness. Environmental Policy*, Temple University Press.

Barrón-López, L., Popat, S. and Bowie, T. (2025) "Trump directs DOJ to investigate former administration officials who criticized him," *PBS NewsHour,* [TV show] April 10, Available from: https://www.pbs.org/newshour/show/trump-directs-doj-to-investigate-former-administration-officials-who-criticized-him

Barry, J. (1997) *Rising Tide: The Great Mississippi Flood of 1927 and How It Changed America*, Simon & Schuster.

Bauer, L. et al (2024) "Eight facts about permitting and the clean energy transition," *Brookings Institution*, [online] May 22, Available from: https://www.brookings.edu/articles/eight-facts-about-permitting-and-the-clean-energy-transition/

Baumgaertner, E. (2024) "Civil war toll much worse in confederate states, new estimates show," *New York Times,* [online] January 25, Available from: https://www.nytimes.com/2024/11/19/health/civil-war-death-toll.html#

BBC (2019) "Scottish government wins Donald Trump wind power legal costs," [online] February 28, Available from: https://www.bbc.com/news/uk-scotland-north-east-orkney-shetland-47400641

Becker, W. (2024) "America's biggest energy scam is happening now," *The Hill Magazine,* [online] May 13, Available from: https://thehill.com/opinion/energy-environment/4659511-americas-biggest-energy-scam-is-happening-now/

Bennett, S. (2024) "It's simplistic to assume Trump's devoted voters are irrational," *Fair Observer*, [online] Available from: https://www.fairobserver.com/world-news/us-news/its-simplistic-to-assume-trumps-devoted-voters-are-irrational/

Benson, L., Pauketat, T. and Cook, E. (2009) "Boom and bust in the context of climate change," *American Antiquity,* 74: 467–483.

BIA (1981) "Interior announces budget cuts of $383 million in fiscal 1981 and $877 million in fiscal 1982 from the Carter Administration budgets for the two fiscal years," [online] March 10, Available from: https://www.bia.gov/as-ia/opa/online-press-release/interior-announces-budget-cuts-383-million-fiscal-1981-and-877-million-fiscal-1982

Billings, L. (2007/2008) "Telephone communications about the framers of the Clean Air Act Amendments of 1970," F.T. Manheim.

Billings, L. and Jorling, T. (2015) "Leon Billings and Tom Jorling" (video interview, celebrating pioneers in environmental law) at the Environmental Law Institute.

Bivens, J. (2019) "Updated employment multipliers for the U.S. economy," *Economic Policy Institute*, [online] January 23, Available from: https://www.epi.org/publication/updated-employment-multipliers-for-the-u-s-economy/

Blair, G. (2005) *Donald Trump, Master Apprentice*, Simon & Schuster.

Blakemore, E. (2021) "How an enslaved African man in Boston helped save generations from smallpox. In the early 1700s, Onesimus shared a revolutionary way to prevent smallpox," *History*, [online] April 8, Available from: https://www.history.com/news/smallpox-vaccine-onesimus-slave-cotton-mather

Block, S., Emerson, J., Esty, D., Desherbinn, A. and Wendlin, Z. (2024) *Environmental Performance Index*, Yale University Press.

Blocker, J. (2005) "Did prohibition really work? Alcohol prohibition as a public health innovation." American Journal of Public Health, 96: 233–243.

Blue, R. (1913) "Surgeon General, letter to the Secretary of the Treasury," January 10.

Bluestone, B. and Harrison, L. (1987) *The Deindustrialization of America: Plant Closings, Community Abandonment, and the Dismantling of Basic Industry*, Basic Books.

Bookchin, M. (1964) "Ecology and revolutionary thought," *Comment Newsletter,* republished in *Anarchy* (Journal) 1965, [online] Available from: https://theanarchistlibrary.org/library/lewis-herber-murray-bookchin-ecology-and-revolutionary-thought

Bradley, B. and Stanford. D. (2004) "The North Atlantic ice-edge corridor: A possible Palaeolithic route to the New World," *World Archaeology*, 36: 459–478.

Brands, H. (1998) *TR: The Last Romantic*, Basic Books.

Brands, H. (2013) *The Man Who Saved the Union: Ulysses Grant in War and Peace*, Anchor/Penguin/Random House.

Breyer, S. (1993) *Breaking the Vicious Circle: Toward Effective Risk Regulation*, Harvard University Press.

Brinkley, D. (2022) *Silent Spring Revolution: John F. Kennedy, Rachel Carson, Lyndon Johnson, Richard Nixon, and the Great Environmental Awakening*, Harper.

*Britannica* (2023) "Albany Congress: United States history (1754)," *Encyclopedia Britannica,* [online] June 12, Available from: https://www.britannica.com/event/Albany-Congress/additional-info#history

Brodie, E., Knapp, E., Brooks, W., Drury, S. and Ritchie, M. (2024) "Forest thinning and prescribed burning treatments reduce wildfire severity and buffer the impacts of severe fire weather." *Fire Ecology,* 20(17).

Bronski, M. (2012) *A Queer History of the United States*, Beacon Books.

Brownstein, R. and Easton, N. (1982) "Reagan's regulation roulette," *Student Law,* 11: 43.

Brulle, R. (2019) "Networks of opposition: A structural analysis of US climate change countermovement coalitions 1989–2015," *Sociological Inquiry,* 91: 603–624.

Brundtland, G. (1987) *Our Common Future*, Oxford University Press.

Bryant, B. and Mohai, P. (1992) *Race and the Incidence of Environmental Hazards, A Time for Discourse*, Routledge.

Bunch, W. (2010) *Tear Down This Myth: The Right-Wing Distortion of the Reagan Legacy,* Free Press.

Burns, A. (2015) "Donald Trump, pushing someone rich, offers himself," *New York Times*, [online] June 16, Available from: https://www.nytimes.com/2015/06/17/us/politics/donald-trump-runs-for-president-this-time-for-real-he-says.htmlPage

Caldwell, L. (1998) *The National Environmental Policy Act: Agenda for the Future,* Indiana University Press.

Caldwell, L., Deville, W. and Shuchman, H. (1969) *Science, Technology, and Public Policy: A Selected and Annotated Bibliography, Volume 2*, Indiana University Press.

Callaghan, L. (2024) "Steve Bannon: Maga can rule for 50 years and Farage will be PM," *The London Times.*

Cannon, L. (1991) *President Reagan: The Role of a Lifetime,* Simon & Schuster.

Cannon, L. (no date) "Ronald Reagan: Life in brief," *Miller Center*, [online] Available from: https://millercenter.org/president/reagan/life-in-brief

Capito, S., Carper, T. and Whitehouse, S. (2024) *The Advance Act*. Senate Committee on Environment and Public Works.

Carnegie, D. (1936) *How to Win Friends and Influence People,* Simon & Schuster.

Carson, R. (1962) *Silent Spring,* Houghton Mifflin.

Carter, A. (2023) "A closer look at the visionary US Endangered Species Act," *Defenders of Wildlife Magazine*, [online] March 7, Available from: https://defenders.org/blog/2023/03/closer-look-visionary-us-endangered-species-act

Carter, J. (2000) "Why we need an Arctic Refuge National Monument," *Defenders of Wildlife Magazine*, [online] Available from: http://www.defenders.org/magazinenew/Fall2000/carter.pdf

Carter, N. (2001) *The Politics of the Environment*, Cambridge University Press.

Casazza, C., Schoenbrod, D., Stewart, R. and Wyman, K. (2008) Breaking the logjam: environmental reform for the new Congress and administration, *N.Y.U. Environmental Law Journal*, 1–17.

CEQ (2020) "Environmental impact statement timelines (2010–2018)," *Council on Environmental Quality, Executive Office of the President*, [online], June 12, Available from: https://ceq.doe.gov/docs/nepa-practice/CEQ_EIS_Timeline_Report_2020-6-12.pdf

Chase, A. (1995) *In a Dark Wood: The Fight over Forests and the Rising Tyranny of Ecology*, Houghton Mifflin.

Chu, J. (2024) "The staggering cost needed for Trump's mass deportation plan," *Wall Street Journal Online,* [online] April 11, Available from: https://www.wsj.com/video/series/wsj-explains/the-staggering-cost-needed-for-trumps-mass-deportation-plan/B4B447AE-E653-4225-8E5B-4B59B1D8508D?mod=WSJvidctr__pos5

Clark, K. (1969) "Civilisation: A personal view," in M. G. Director and P. M. Director (eds) *BBC television series.*

Cohen, S. (2023) "President Biden's environmental record," *State of the Planet,* [online] Available from: https://news.climate.columbia.edu

Conant, J. and Balint, P. (2016) *The Life Cycles of the Council on Environmental Quality and the Environmental Protection Agency*, Oxford University Press.

CORPS (no date) "US Army Corps of Engineers: a brief history." US Army Corps of Engineers, Headquarters Web Site, [online] Available from: https://www.usace.army.mil/About/History/Brief-History-of-the-Corps/Environmental-Activities

Courtney, J. and Nivola, P. (2009) "Know thy neighbor: What Canada can tell us about financial regulation," *Brookings Institution*, [online] April 23, Available from: https://www.brookings.edu/articles/know-thy-neighbor-what-canada-can-tell-us-about-financial-regulation/

CBP (Customs and Border Protection) (2024) "CBP releases February 2024 monthly update," *U.S. Customs and Border Protection,* [online] November 19, Available from: https://www.cbp.gov/newsroom/national-media-release/cbp-releases-october-2024-monthly-update

Crews, W. and Smith, F. (2023) "Biden's 2023 Federal Register page count is the second highest ever," *Forbes*, [online] December 29, Available from: https://www.forbes.com/sites/waynecrews/2023/12/29/bidens-2023-federal-register-page-count-is-the-second-highest-ever/

Crippa, M. et al (2023) *GHG Emissions of All World Countries*, Publications Office of the European Union.

Cronon, W. (1983) *Changes in the Land: Indians, Colonists and the Ecology of New England*, Hill & Wang.

Crouch, J., Rozell, M. and Sollenberger, M. (2020) *The Unitary Executive Theory: A Danger to Constitutional Government,* University Press of Kansas.

Cruz, L., Bianco, A., Messerly, M., Bhattacharyya, A. and Wiederkehr, A. (2025) "37 ways Project 2025 has shown up in Trump's executive orders," *Politico,* [online] February 5, Available from: https://www.politico.com/interactives/2025/trump-executive-orders-project-2025/

Dalton, R. (2017) "Citizens' representation in the 2009 European Parliament elections," *European Union Politics*, 18(2): 188–211.

Dans, P. and Groves, S. (eds) (2023) *Mandate for Leadership: Project 2025,* Heritage Foundation.

David, E. Jr. (1982) "Inventing the future: Energy and the CO2 'greenhouse' effect," *Exxon Research and Engineering Company.*

Dawes, A. and Majkut, J. (2023) "Tailwinds and headwinds: The U.S. offshore wind market," *Center for Strategic and International Studies*, [online] January 31, Available from: https://www.csis.org/analysis/tailwinds-and-headwinds-us-offshore-wind-market#:~:text=Despite%20significant%20potential%2C%20the%20offshore,of%2042%20megawatts%20(MW)

DeSilver, D. (2022) "The polarization in today's Congress has roots that go back decades." *Pew Research Center,* [online] March 10, Available from: https://www.pewresearch.org/fact-tank/2022/03/10/the-polarization-in-todays-congress-has-roots-that-go-back-decades/

De Tocqueville, A. (1835/1840) *Democracy in America*, Liberty Fund.

DeConcini, C., Rennicks, J. and Hyman, G. (2024) "Trump may thwart federal climate action, but opportunities for progress remain," *World Resource Institute,* [online] November 13, Available from: https://www.wri.org/insights/trump-climate-action-setbacks-opportunities-us

Demkovich, L. (1978) "Clogged federal courts—who are the culprits," *National Court Journal Virtual Library,* 10: 222–226.

Denevan, W. (1992) "The pristine myth: the landscape of the Americas in 1492," *Annals of the Association of American Geographers,* 82(3): 369–385.

Dennis, Y., Hirschfelder, A. and Flynn, S. (2016) *Native American Almanac: More Than 50,000 Years of the Cultures and Histories of Indigenous Peoples*, Visible Ink Press.

Dennison, E. (1979) *Accounting for Slower Growth: The United States in the 1970s*, Brookings Institution Press.

Desmog (no date) "Global climate coalition'. *Desmog International,* [online] Available from: https://www.desmog.com/global-climate-coalition/

Diaz-Maurin, F. (2025) "For this French senator, Trump is a traitor—and Europe is now alone," *Bulletin of the Atomic Scientists,* [online] March 6, Available from: https://thebulletin.org/2025/03/for-this-french-senator-trump-is-a-traitor-and-europe-is-now-alone/

Dillehay, T. (2000) *The Settlement of the Americas: A New Prehistory*, Basic Books.

Dimon, J. (2024) "Opinion: The next president must restore our faith in America: The country needs a leader who is committed to reaffirming our special role in the world," *The Washington Post*, [online] August 2, Available from: https://www.washingtonpost.com/opinions/2024/08/02/jamie-dimon-2024-democracy/

Dippie, B. (2023) *American Indians: The Image of the Indian*, TeacherServe.

Dobyns, H. F. (1983) *Their Number Become Thinned: Native American Dynamics in Eastern North America,* University of Tennessee Press.

Dobyns, H. F. (1966) "Estimating aboriginal American population: An appraisal of techniques with a new hemispheric estimate," *Current Anthropology,* 7: 395–416.

DOE (2024) "US installed and potential wind power capacity and generation," *Wind Energy Technology Office*, US Department of the Interior, [online] Available from: https://windexchange.energy.gov/maps-data/321

DOI (Department of the Interior) (2024) "Biden-Harris administration invests $3.7 million for states to clean up abandoned hardrock mines," US Department of the Interior.

Doniger, D. (2024) "FTM interview with David Doniger on 'Doniger's law'," *Natural Resources Defense Council (NRDC)*, [online] November 18, 2014.

Dooling, B. (2019) "Wallach on lessons from the REINS Act," May 9, *Yale Journal on Regulation*, [online] Available from: https://www.yalejreg.com/nc/wallach-on-lessons-from-the-reins-act/

Dorgan, B. (2006) *Take This Job and Ship It: How Corporate Greed and Brain-Dead Politics Are Selling out America*, Thomas Dunne Books.

Dorman, P. (2022) *Alligators in the Arctic and How to Avoid Them*, Cambridge University Press.

Drennan, A. and Hardin, S. (2021) "Climate deniers in the 117th Congress: there are 139 elected officials in the 117th Congress who still deny the scientific consensus of human-caused climate change," *Center for American Progress*, [online] March 30, Available from: https://www.americanprogress.org/article/climate-deniers-117th-congress/

Dudley, S. and Brito, J. (2012) *Regulation: A Primer*, Mercatus Center, George Mason University.

Duffy, J. (1992) *The Sanitarians: A History of Public Health,* University of Illinois Press.

Duignan, B. (2024) "January 6 attack on the U.S. Capitol by Trump supporters," *Encyclopaedia Britannica,* [online] November 22, Available from: https://www.britannica.com/event/January-6-U-S-Capitol-attack

Dunlap, R. and McCright, A. (2008) "A widening gap: Republican and Democratic views on climate change," *Environment: Science and Policy for Sustainable Development*, 50(5): 26–35.

Dunlap, R. and Jacques, P. (2013) "Climate change denial books and conservative think tanks," *American Behavioral Scientist*, 57: 699–731.

Dupree, A. (1957) *Science in the Federal Government: A History of Policies and Activities to 1940,* Belknap Press.

Durkee, A. (2025) "Here are all the major lawsuits against Trump and Musk—as USAID shutdown sparks legal battle," *Forbes,* [online] February 7, Available from: https://doggett.house.gov/media/in-the-news/forbes-here-are-all-major-lawsuits-against-trump-and-musk-usaid-shutdown-sparks

Dye, D. (2009) *War Paths, Peace Paths: An Archaeology of Cooperation and Conflict in Native Eastern North America,* AltaMira Press.

Easton, R. (1972) *Black Tide: The Santa Barbara Oil Spill and Its Consequences*, Delacorte Press.

Eaton, D. (1880) *Civil Service in Great Britain: A History of Abuses and Reforms and Their Bearing on American Politics*, Harper and Brothers.

EIA (2024) "In-depth analysis: How has energy use changed throughout US history?" *Energy Information Administration*, [online] July 3, Available from: https://www.eia.gov/todayinenergy/index.php

Eichel, L., Jost, K., Luskin, R. and Neustadt, R. (1970) *The Harvard Strike,* Houghton Mifflin.

Eisner, M. (2007) *Governing the Environment: The Transformation of Environmental Regulation*, Lynne Rienner.

Elias, S. (2014) "First Americans lived on land bridge for thousands of years, genetics study suggests," *Scientific American*, [online] Available from: https://theconversation.com/first-americans-lived-on-land-bridge-for-thousands-of-years-genetics-study-suggests-23747

Elliott, E. and Esty, D. (2021) "The end environmental externalities manifesto: A rights-based foundation for environmental law," *New York University Law Journal,* 29: 505–542.

EPA (Environmental Protection Agency) (2020) "Our nation's air: EPA celebrates fifty years," *U.S. Environmental Protection Agency,* [online] Available from: https://gispub.epa.gov/air/trendsreport/2020/#welcome

EPA (2024a) "Laws and executive orders," *U.S. Environmental Protection Agency,* [online] Available from: https://www.epa.gov/laws-regulations/laws-and-executive-orders

EPA (2024b) "National overview: Facts and figures on materials, wastes and recycling," *U.S. Environmental Protection Agency*, [online] Available from: https://www.epa.gov/facts-and-figures-about-materials-waste-and-recycling/national-overview-facts-and-figures-materials#:~:text=The%20amount%20of%20MSW%20combusted,the%20amount%20generated%20in%202018

EPA (2024c) "Environmental justice timeline," *U.S. Environmental Protection Agency,* [online] Available from: https://www.epa.gov/environmentaljustice/environmental-justice-timeline

EPI (Economic Policy Institute) (2019) "The productivity–pay gap," *Economic Policy Institute,* [online] December, Available from: https://www.epi.org/productivity-pay-gap/

EPI (2024) *Environmental Performance Index*, Socioeconomic Data and Applications Center.

Esty, D. (2017) "Red lights to green lights: From 20th century environmental regulation to 21st century sustainability," *Yale Law School Legal Scholarship Repository,* [online] Available from: https://digitalcommons.law.yale.edu/cgi/viewcontent.cgi?article=6186&context=fss_papers

Ethridge, R. and Shuck-Hall, S. (eds) (2009) *Mapping the Mississippian Shatter Zone: The Colonial Indian Slave Trade and Regional Instability in the American South*, University of Nebraska Press.

EXXON (2024) "Climate policy decisions that can help drive energy investments," *EXXON*, [online] Available from: https://corporate.exxonmobil.com/what-we-do/delivering-industrial-solutions/carbon-capture-and-storage/climate-policy-energy-investments

Fallone, E. (2012) "The roots of progressivism lie in the Republican Party?" *Marquette University Law School,* [blog] January 24, Available from: The Roots of Progressivism Lie in … the Republican Party?—Marquette University Law School Faculty Blog.

Fallows, J. (1994) "Washington and the contract with America," *The Atlantic*, [online] Available from: https://www.theatlantic.com/past/docs/unbound/jfnpr/jfreview.htm

Farhi, P. (2024) "Is American Journalism Headed Toward an 'Extinction-Level Event'?" *The Atlantic*, [online] January 30, Available from: https://www.theatlantic.com/ideas/archive/2024/01/media-layoffs-la-times/677285/

Feller, D. (ed.) (2007–2009) *The Papers of Andrew Jackson,* University of Tennessee Press.

Fiedel, S., Potter, B., Morrow, J., Faughta, M., Haynes, C. and Chatters, J. (2020) "Pioneers from northern Japan in Idaho 16,000 years ago? A critical evaluation of the evidence from Cooper's Ferry," *PaleoAmerica*, 7(7): 1–15.

Fiorina, M., Abrams, S. and Pope, J. (2010) *Culture War? The Myth of Polarization*, Longmans.

Fiorino, D. (2006) *The New Environmental Regulation,* MIT Press.

Fischbeck, P. and Farrow, R. (2001) *Improving Regulation: Cases in Environment, Health and Safety,* Resources for the Future Press.

Flatow, I. (2024) "Science journalism is shrinking–along with public trust in science," *Science Friday*, [Radio show] January 5, Available from: https://www.sciencefriday.com/segments/science-journalism-trust-in-science/

Flippen, J. (2000) *Nixon and the Environment*, University of New Mexico Press.

Flippen, J. (2006) *Conservative Conservationist: Russell E. Train and the Emergence of American Environmentalism,* Louisiana State University Press.

Foley, E. (2024) "Decreasing the political polarization of the American public," *American Bar Association*, [online] Available from: https://www.americanbar.org/groups/leadership/office_of_the_president/american-democracy/resources/decreasing-political-polarization-american-public/

Folsom, B. (1991) *The Myth of the Robber Barons: A New Look at the Rise of Big Business in America*, Young America's Foundation.

Foreman, D. (1985) *Ecodefense: A Field Guide to Monkeywrenching*, Ned Ludd Books.

Franklin, J. (2005) "Spatial pattern and ecosystem function: Reflections on current knowledge and future directions," in G. Lovett, C. Jones, M. Turner and K. Weathers (eds) *Ecosystem Function in Heterogeneous Landscapes,* Springer-Verlag, pp 427–41.

Franklin, J. (2008) "Comments on recovery plan for the northern spotted owl. Testimony of Dr. Jerry F. Franklin at the oversight hearing of the Committee on Natural Resources on the danger of deception: Do endangered species have a chance," *U.S. House of Representatives,* [online] May 21, Available from: http://resourcescommittee.house.gov/images/Documents/20080521/fc/testimony_franklin.pdf

Frazin, R. (2025) "Trump orders agencies to 'sunset' environmental protections," *The Hill*, [online] April 10, Available from: https://thehill.com/policy/energy-environment/5242921-trump-executive-order-enviro nmental-protections-sunset/

Friedman, L. (2005) *A History of American Law*, Simon & Schuster.

Friedman, L. (2024) "Trump wants to kill the E.V. tax credit. Here's what to know," *New York Times*, [online] November 15, Available from: https://www.nytimes.com/2024/11/15/climate/electric-vehicles-trump-tax-cre dit.htmlPage

Galbraith, J. (1955) *The Great Crash of 1929*, 2nd edn, Houghton Mifflin.

Gangitano, A. (2025) "Trump rolls back CFPB, USAID and Department of Education: where things stand," *The Hill,* [online] February 14, Available from: https://thehill.com/homenews/5146125-trump-rolls-back-cfpb-usaid-and-doe-where-things-stand/

GAO (Government Accountability Office) (1981) "Issues in leasing offshore lands for oil and gas development," in U.S. Congress (ed.) US Government Accountability Office.

Gebhardt, C. (2023) *Sea Change: An Atlas of Islands in a Rising Ocean*, University of California Press.

Gelinas, N. (2007) "Lessons of Boston's big dig," *City Journal,* [online] Autumn, Available from: http://www.city-journal.org/html/17_4_big_dig.html

Gergen, D. (1992) "Hamilton Jordan and Jody Powell: The team who brought Carter the presidency explains how Democrats can again take the White House," *Los Angeles Times*, [online] January 26, Available from: https://www.latimes.com/archives/la-xpm-1992-01-26-op-1273-story.html

Gerrard, M. (2024) "Trump 2.0: This time the stakes for climate are even higher," *Yale's School of Environment*, [online] November 18, Available from: https://e360.yale.edu/features/trump-second-term-climate

Gillis, J. and Krauss, C. (2015) "Exxon Mobil investigated for possible climate change lies by New York Attorney General," *New York Times*, [online] November 15, Available from: https://www.nytimes.com/2015/11/06/science/exxon-mobil-under-investigation-in-new-york-over-climate-statements.html#

Glueck, K. (2015) "Donald Trump strikes sour note at No Labels: Trump's seemingly out-of-step appearance raises questions about his broader appeal," *Politico*, October 12.

Goodell, J. (2023) *The Heat Will Kill You First: Life and Death on a Scorched Planet*, Little, Brown & Co.

Goodwin, D. (2006) *A Team of Rivals: The Political Genius of Abraham Lincoln*, Simon & Schuster.

Gore, A. (1992) *Earth in the Balance: Ecology and the Human Spirit,* Houghton Mifflin.

Gottlieb, R. (1993) *Forcing the Spring: The Transformation of the American Environmental Movement,* Island Press.

Govtrack (2024) "Statistics and historical comparison," Congress, U.S. (ed.) U.S. GovTrack.

Graham, D. (2018) "The president who doesn't read: Trump's allergy to the written word and his reliance on oral communication have proven liabilities in office," *The Atlantic,* [online] January 5, Available from: https://www.theatlantic.com/politics/archive/2018/01/americas-first-post-text-president/549794/

Graham, F. (1970) *Since Silent Spring,* Houghton Mifflin.

Green, B. (2019) "The little plant that blocked the mighty dams," *NewscenterMaine.com*, [online] June 1, Available from: https://www.newscentermaine.com/article/news/the-little-plant-that-blocked-the-mighty-dams/97-607754b0-c920-4edd-a659-4e0cf47f4222

Greenstone, M. (2002) "The impacts of environmental regulations on industrial activity: Evidence from the 1970 and 1977 Clean Air Act Amendments and the census of manufacture," *Journal of Political Economy,* 110: 1175–1219.

Greiner, L. (2024) "Data centers go nuclear for power-hungry AI workloads," *Network World* [online] December 2, Available from: https://www.networkworld.com/article/3613868/data-centers-go-nuclear-for-power-hungry-ai-workloads.html#:~:text=Most%20data%20center%20operators%20are,to%20have%20online%20by%202030

Grossi, M. (2024) "Nuclear technology review 2024, report by the director," *International Atomic Energy Agency*, [online] Available from: https://www.iaea.org/sites/default/files/gc/gc68-inf-4.pdf

Guzman, C. (2024) "What we know—and don't know—so far about the Trump rally gunman," *TIME*, [online] July 19, Available from: https://time.com/6998557/thomas-matthew-crooks-trump-rally-shooter-fbi-motive/

Hakes, J. (2022) *Energy Crises: Nixon, Ford, Carter, and Hard Choices in the 1970s*, University of Oklahoma Press.

Halliday, T. (1986) "Six score years and ten: Demographic transition in the American legal profession, 1850 to 1980," *Law and Society Review,* 20: 53–78.

Hannah-Jones, N. and New York Times Magazine (2021) *The 1619 Project: A New Origin Story*, One World.

Hansen, J. et al (1988) "Global climate change as forecast by Goddard Institute for Space Studies three-dimensional model," *Journal of Geophysical Research,* 93: 9341–9364.

Harbaugh, W. (1975) *Power and Responsibility: The Life and Times of Theodore Roosevelt*, Octagon Books.

Hardin, G. (1968) "The tragedy of the commons," *Science*, 162: 1243–1248.

Hargadon, M. (2008) "Report on EU Commission," *EPA Partnership Summit.*

Harisalo, R. and Stenvall, J. (2004) "Trust as capital: The foundation of management," in M. L. Huotan, and M. Livonen (eds) *Trust in Knowledge Management and Systems in Organizations,* Idea Group Publishing.

Hart, C. (2009) "Advancing carbon sequestration research in an uncertain legal and regulatory environment: A study of phase II of the DOE regional carbon sequestration partnerships program," *Belfer Center for Science and International Affairs, Harvard University,* [online] January 7, Available from: https://www.belfercenter.org/publication/advancing-carbon-sequestration-research-uncertain-legal-and-regulatory-environment

Harvard (2025) "Youth Poll, 50th Edition," *Harvard Institute of Politics*, [online] Available from: https://iop.harvard.edu/youth-poll/50th-edition-spring-2025

Hays, S. (2000) *A History of Environmental Politics Since 1945,* University of Pittsburgh Press.

Hays, S. and Hays, B. (1987) *Beauty, Health, and Permanence: Environmental Politics in the US, 1955-1985, Trade Books and History*, Cambridge University Press.

Haynes, C. (1964) "Fluted projectile points: Their age and dispersion: stratigraphically controlled dating provides new evidence on peopling of the New World," *Science,* 145: 1408–1413.

Heatherly, C. and Foundation, H. (1981) *Mandate for Leadership: Policy Management in a Conservative Administration,* Heritage Foundation.

Heinz, G. and Hoffman, D. (1998) "Methylmercury chloride and selenomethionine interactions on health and reproduction in mallards," *Environmental Toxicology and Chemistry*. https://doi.org/10.1002/etc.5620170202

Herbert, J., McCrisken N. and Wroe, A. (2019) *The Ordinary Presidency of Donald J. Trump*, Palgrave Macmillan.

Hickey, C., Merrill, C., Chang, R. J., Sullivan, K., Boschma, J. and O'Key, S. (2021) "Here are the executive actions Biden signed in his first 100 days," *CNN News,* [online] April 30, Available from: https://www.cnn.com/interactive/2021/politics/biden-executive-orders/

Higgs, R. (1971) "American inventiveness, 1870–1920," *Journal of Political Economy*, 79(3): 661–667.

Hillstrom, K. (2010) *US Environmental Policy and Politics: A Documentary History,* CQ Press.

Högbom, A. (1894) "Om sannolikheten för sekuläraörändringar i atmosfärenskKolsyrehalt," *Svensk Kemisk Tidskrift,* 4: 169–177.

Hoogenboom, A. (1988a) *The Gilded Age and Rutherford B. Hayes*, University Press of Kansas.

Hoogenboom, A. (1988b) *The Presidency of Rutherford B. Hayes*, University Press of Kansas.

Hornig, D. and Tukey, J. (1965) "Restoring the quality of our environment," *Environmental Pollution Panel*, The White House: President's Science Advisory Committee.

Howard, P. (2019) *Try Common Sense: Replacing the Failed Ideologies of Right and Left*, W. W. Norton.

Hundertmark, T. (2023) "You need to do the math and then explain the math: A talk with ExxonMobil's Darren Woods," *McKinsey & Company*, [online] September 12, Available from: https://www.mckinsey.com/industries/oil-and-gas/our-insights/you-need-to-do-the-math-and-then-explain-the-math-a-talk-with-exxonmobils-darren-woods

Hurst, W. (1994) *Anasazi, New Georgia Encyclopedia*, University of Georgia.

Hutchinson, D. et al (2016) "The Calusa and prehistoric subsistence in central and south Gulf Coast Florida," *Journal of Anthropological Archaeology*, 41: 55–73.

Hutton, W. (2025) "Donald Trump is now badly wounded. Europe and the UK can seize an advantage," *The Guardian,* [online] April 12, Available from: https://www.theguardian.com/us-news/2025/apr/12/donald-trump-is-now-badly-wounded-europe-and-the-uk-can-seize-an-advantage

Hyman, E. and Stiftel, B. (1988) *Combining Facts and Values in Environmental Impact Assessment,* Westview Press.

Idso, C., Idso, S., Carter, R. and Singer, S. (eds) (2014) *Climate Change Reconsidered II: Biological Impacts*, Heartland Institute.

IEA (International Energy Administration) (2021) *The Role of Critical Minerals in Clean Energy Transitions; Part of World Energy Outlook, Flagship Report,* International Energy Administration.

IEA (2023) "Outlook 2023, 1.5° C Pathway," *International Energy Agency*, [online] Available from: https://www.iea.org/reports/world-energy-outlook-

IEA (2024) "CO2 emissions in 2023: The changing landscape of global emissions," *International Energy Administration*, [online] Available from: https://www.iea.org/reports/co2-emissions-in-2023/the-changing-landscape-of-global-emissions

Igini, M. (2024) "Top 6 environmental issues the US is facing in 2024," *Americas,* [online] January 12, Available from: https://earth.org/top-environmental-issues-us/

Ikenson, D. (2014) *The Myth of a U.S. Manufacturing Decline,* Cato Institute:

Imhofe, J. (2012) *The Greatest Hoax: How the Global Warming Conspiracy Threatens Your Future*, WND Books.

IRENA (2022) *Renewable Energy Capacity 2022*, International Renewable Energy Agency.

IRENA (2023) *Renewable Energy Statistics 2023*, International Renewable Energy Agency, [online] July, Available from: https://www.irena.org/Publications/2023/Jul/Renewable-energy-statistics-2023

Isaacson, W. (2023) *Musk*, Simon & Schuster.

Iuliano, J. and Whittington, K. (2017) "The nondelegation doctrine: Alive and well," *Notre Dame Law Review,* 93: 619–645.

Jackson, A. (1830) "President Andrew Jackson's message to Congress 'On Indian removal (1830),'" *National Archives*, [online] May 10, 2022, Available from: https://www.archives.gov/milestone-documents/jacksons-message-to-congress-on-indian-removal#:~:text=In%20his%20message%20on%20December,beyond%20the%20white%20settlements%20is

James, L. A. (2011) "Contrasting geomorphic impacts of pre- and post-Columbian land-use changes in Anglo America," *Physical Geography,* 32: 399–422.

Jasanoff, S. (1998) *The Fifth Branch: Science Advisers as Policymakers*, Harvard University Press.

Jealous, B. (2023) "The fiction of a nuclear silver bullet: The nuclear industry is stuck in a 'reverse learning curve,'" *Sierra,* [online] June 15, Available from: https://www.sierraclub.org/sierra/fiction-nuclear-silver-bullet

Jefferson, T. (1785) *Notes on the State of Virginia,* Library of Congress.

Jones, M. (2005a) "Endangered species act and incentives for private landowners," *Testimony of Marshall Jones, Deputy Director, U.S. Fish and Wildlife Service. Subcommittee on Fisheries, Wildlife and Water, Senate Committee on Environment and Public Works,* July 13.

Jones, M. (2005b) "Put a tiger in your think tank," *Mother Jones,"* [online] May/June, Available from: https://www.motherjones.com/politics/2005/05/put-tiger-your-think-tank/

Kagan, R. (2001) "Adversarial legalism and American government," *Journal of Policy Analysis and Management,* 10: 369–406.

Kash, D. (2006) "Oral and written communications about Kash's service as chief of the USGS Conservation Division," F.T. Manheim.

Kaurov, A., Cologna, V., Tyson, C., and Oreskes, N. (2022) "Trends in American scientists' political donations and implications for trust in science," *Humanities and Social Sciences Communications,* 9.

Kawashima, Y. and Tone, R. (1983) "Environmental policy in colonial America: A survey of colonial statutes," *Journal of Forest History,* 27: 168–223.

Kendi, I. (2019) *How to be an Antiracist,* One World.

Kennedy, J. (1956) *Profiles in Courage*, Joanna Cotler Books.

Kerry, J. et al (no date) "Biden-Sanders Unity Task Force Recommendations," JoeBiden.com.

Kessler, G. (2017) "When did Mitch McConnell say he wanted to make Obama a one-term president?' *The Washington Post,* [online] January 11, Available from: https://www.washingtonpost.com/news/fact-checker/wp/2017/01/11/when-did-mitch-mcconnell-say-he-wanted-to-make-obama-a-one-term-president/

Kiger, P. (2023) "7 negative effects of the industrial revolution: While the industrial revolution generated new opportunities and economic growth, it also introduced pollution and acute hardships for workers," [online] 9 August, Available from: https://www.history.com/news/industrial-revolution-negative-effects

King, A. (2020) "The Cahokian Diaspora, Etowah, and South Appalachian Mississippian," in C. H. McNutt and R. M. Parish (eds) *Cahokia in Context: Hegemony and Diaspora*, University of Florida Press.

Kingzette, J., Druckman, J., Klar, S., Krupnikov, Y., Levendusky, M. and Ryan, B. (2021) "How affective polarization undermines support for democratic norms," *Public Opinion Quarterly,* 85: 663–677.

Klein, M. (1997) *The Life and Legend of Jay Gould,* Johns Hopkins University Press.

Klein, E. (2020) *Why We're Polarized,* Avid Reader Press (Simon & Schuster).

Klein, E. (2023) "The problem with everything-bagel liberalism," *New York Times,* [online] April 2, Available from: https://www.nytimes.com/2023/04/02/opinion/democrats-liberalism.html

Kleinfeld, R. (2023) "Polarization, democracy, and political violence in the United States: What the research says," *Carnegie Endowmant for International Peace,* [online] September 5, Available from: https://carnegieendowment.org/research/2023/09/polarization-democracy-and-political-violence-in-the-united-states-what-the-research-says?lang=en

Klyza, C. M. and Sousa, D. J. (2013) *American Environmental Policy: Beyond Gridlock,* MIT Press.

Kraft, M. and Vig, N. (1997) *Environmental Policy from the 1970s to the 1990s: An Overview,* CQ Press.

Kraft, M., Rabe G. and Vig. N. (2024) *Environmental Policy: New Directions for the 21st Century,* 12th edn, CQ Press.

Kramer, T. (1982) "Attorney fee awards to nonprevailing parties under the Clean Air Act," *University of Cincinnati Law Review,* 51, 635.

Kroeber, A. (1939) *Cultural and Natural Areas of Native North America,* University of California Press.

Krupp, F. (2018) "McCain was a warrior for the climate," *Wall Street Journal,* [online] August 26, Available from: https://www.wsj.com/articles/mccain-was-a-warrior-for-the-climate-1535311532

Kumar, A. and Orr, G. (2020) "Inside Trump's pressure campaign to overturn the election," *Politico,* [online] December 20, Available from: https://www.politico.com/news/2020/12/21/trump-pressure-campaign-overturn-election-449486

Kurian, G. (ed.) (1998) *A Historical Guide to the U.S. Government,* Oxford University Press.

Laporte, A. (2018) "Remembering George H.W. Bush, the 'environmental president,'" *Environmental and Energy Study Institute,* [online] December 5, Available from: https://www.eesi.org/articles/view/remembering-george-h.w.-bush-the-environmental-president

Lash, J., Gillman, K. and Sheridan, D. (1984) *A Season of Spoils: The Story of the Reagan Administration's Attack on the Environment,* Pantheon.

Lashof, D. (2024) "Tracking progress: Climate action under the Biden administration," *World Resources Institute,* [online] July 30, Available from: https://www.wri.org/insights/biden-administration-tracking-climate-action-progress

Lavelle, M. (2018) "John McCain's climate change legacy: The senator from Arizona brought climate science into Capitol Hill hearings and cap-and-trade legislation to a vote, but then moderate Republican politics changed," *Inside Climate News*, [online] August 16, Available from: https://insideclimatenews.org/news/26082018/john-mccain-climate-change-leadership-senate-cap-trade-bipartisan-lieberman-republican-campaign/

Lawson, W. (1906) *American finance: Part first.--domestic,* W. Blackwood & Sons.

Lazarus, R. (2001) "The greening of America and the graying of United States environmental law: Reflections on environmental law's first three decades in the United States," *Virginia Environmental Law Journal,* 20: 75–106.

Lazarus, R. (2004) *The Making of Environmental Law,* University of Chicago Press.

Lazarus, R. (2023) *The Making of Environmental Law*, 2nd edn, University of Chicago Press.

Lear, L. (1997) *Rachel Carson: Witness to Nature,* Henry Holt & Co.

Lees, J. and Turner, M. (1988) *Reagan's First Four Years*, Manchester University Press.

Lekson, S. (2018) *A Study of Southwestern Archaeology,* University of Utah Press.

Leopold, A. (1949) *A Sand County Almanac: And Sketches Here and There,* Oxford University Press.

Leppert, R. and Kennedy, B. (2024) "Majority of Americans support more nuclear power in the country," *Pew Research Center,* [online] August 5, Available from: https://www.pewresearch.org/short-reads/2024/08/05/majority-of-americans-support-more-nuclear-power-in-the-country/

Leuchtenburg, W. (1963) *Franklin D. Roosevelt and the New Deal*, Harper & Row.

Lewis, S., Clark, W., Harrison, S. and Bradford and Inskeep (sic) (1804) *A map of Lewis and Clark's track, across the western portion of North America from the Mississippi to the Pacific Ocean: by order of the executive of the United States in, 5 & 6* (Map). Philadelphia: Bradford and Inskeep. Library of Congress, Available from: https://www.loc.gov/item/79692907/

Library of Congress (2020) "National parliaments: United Kingdom," *Library of Congress: Law*, [online] Available from: https://maint.loc.gov/law/help/national-parliaments/unitedkingdom.php#:~:text=V.-,Legislative%20Process,must%20be%20given%20Royal%20Assent

Library (1976) "Environment. President Ford '76 fact Book", Ford Library Museum, [online] Available from: https://www.fordlibrarymuseum.gov/president-ford-76-fact-book

Light, P. (2009) *A Government Ill Executed: The Decline of the Federal Service and How to Reverse It*, Harvard University Press.

Lindstrom, M. and Smith, Z. (2002) *The National Environmental Policy Act: Judicial Misconstruction, Legislative Indifference, and Executive Neglect*, Texas A&M University Press.

Link, A. (1954) *Woodrow Wilson and the Progressive Era, 1910–1917*, Harper & Row.

Lipka, M. and Shearer, E. (2023) "Audiences are declining for traditional news media in the U.S.—with some exceptions," *Pew Research Center*, [online] November 28, Available from: https://www.pewresearch.org/short-reads/2023/11/28/audiences-are-declining-for-traditional-news-media-in-the-us-with-some-exceptions/

Lipset, S. (1996) *American Exceptionalism: A Double Edged Sword*, Norton.

Lochridge, W. (2011) "Allowing for greater admission of evidence in NEPA predetermination suits," University of Chicago Legal Forum, 2011, Article 15.

Loewenthal, D. (2003) *George Perkins Marsh, Prophet of Conservation*, University of Washington Press.

Lovelock, J. (2000) *The Revenge of Gaia: Earth's Climate Crisis and the Fate of Humanity*, Basic Books.

Lovering, J., Yip, A. and Nordhaus, T. (2016) "Historical construction costs of global nuclear power reactors," *Energy Policy*, 91(4): 371–382.

Lyons, M., Durrant, P. and Kochar, K. (2021) "Reaching zero with renewables and carbon capture," *International Renewable Energy Agency*, [online] Available from: https://www.org/-/media/Irena/Files/Technical-papers/IRENA_Capturing_Carbon_2021.pdf

Macleod, C. (1963) *Use of Pesticides*, Panel Report. Office of the White House.

Madison, J. (1788) "The structure of the government must furnish the proper checks and balances between the different departments," *Federalist No. 51.*

Madison, J. (1818) "Address to the Agricultural Society of Albemarle, 12 May 1818, Founders Online," *National Archives,* [online] Available from: https://founders.archives.gov/documents/Madison/04-01-02-0244

Madison, J. (1987) *Notes of Debates in the Federal Convention of 1787*, Norton.

Magasiner, I. and Reich, R. (1982) *Ira C. Magasiner and Robert B. Reich. Minding America's Business: The Decline and Rise of the American Economy*, Harcourt Brace Jovanovich.

Manheim, F. (2007) *Archival Material Pertaining to Natural Resources and Environment NRFG145, June 1986*, Lyndon Baines Johnson Library.

Manheim, F. (2009) *The Conflict over Environmental Regulation in the United States: Origin, Outcomes, and Comparison with the EU and Foreign Regions,* Springer.

Manheim, F. (2010) "A brief history of United States forest management policy," in V. Dudok, V. Lentiakov and L. Myklash (eds) *Forestry, Forest, and Wood Technology of the Ukraine*, National University of Forestry and Wood Technology of the Ukraine.

Manheim, F. (2014a) "Howard Baker on nonpartisan vs. bipartisan legislation," *Social Science Research Network*, [online] Available from: https://papers.ssrn.com/sol3/papers.cfm?abstract_id=2467931

Manheim, F. (2014b) "Natural resource management reform: Recommendations to Governor Terry McAuliffe," *School of Public Policy, George Mason University,* [online] January 10, Available from: https://straightstory.gmu.edu

Manheim, F. (2014c) "A new classification of U.S. environmental laws," *Social Science Research Network* [online] Available from: http://ssrn.com/abstract=2420191.

Manheim, F. (2019) "Information pollution and academic leadership," *James Madison University Library,* [online] October 4, Available from: https://commons.lib.jmu.edu/leadcc/2019/1004/1/

Manheim, F. (2020) "Fateful collision: How revolutionary environmental laws of the 1970s led to a rift in American society," *C. Boyden Gray Center for the Study of the Administrative State Research,* [online] October 6, Available from: https://ssrn.com/abstract3706466.

Manheim, F. (2021) "The four horsemen of U.S. green energy development," *The Hill*, [online] February 23, Available from: https://thehill.com/opinion/energy-environment/540002-the-four-horsemen-of-us-green-energy-development/

Manheim, F. (2022) "How the United States fell behind in climate leadership," *The National Interest*, [online] May 1, Available from: https://nationalinterest.org/blog/buzz/how-united-states-fell-behind-climate-leadership-201965

Manheim, F. (2023a) "Donald Trump's books: How neglect of Trump's books and political schemes by U.S. media and academia affected political history," *Social Science Research Network,* [online] August 9, Available from: https://papers.ssrn.com/sol3/papers.cfm?abstract_id=4527123

Manheim, F. (2023b) "Trump's 'swamp-draining' ambition builds upon Jimmy Carter's reforms," *The Hill*, [online] July 26, Available from: https://thehill.com/opinion/white-house/4116862-trumps-swamp-draining-ambition-traces-back-to-jimmy-carters-reforms/Page

Manheim, F. (2023c) "What makes presidential campaigns successful?" *The Hill*, [online] October 16, Available from: https://thehill.com/opinion/campaign/4254454-what-makes-presidential-campaigns-successful/Page

Manheim, F. (2024) "The debate over 'Chevron deference' overlooks its history," *The Hill,* [online] April 17, Available from: https://thehill.com/opinion/judiciary/4597366-the-debate-over-chevron-deference-overlooks-its-history/Page

Manheim, F. and Fuhs, G. (2007) "An annotated database of US federal environmental laws," School of Public Policy, George Mason University.

Manheim, F., Buchholtz ten Brink, M. and Mecray, E. (1999) "Contaminated-sediment database development and assessment in Boston Harbor," US Geological Survey Fact Sheet FS-078-99.

Mankiw, N. and Swagel, P. (2006) "The politics and economics of offshore outsourcing," *Journal of Monetary Economics,* 53(5): 1027–1056.

Mann, C. (2006) *1491: New Revelations of the Americas before Columbus*, Vintage Press.

Mann, M. (2021) *The New Climate War: The Fight to Take Back Our Planet*, Public Affairs.

Mann, T. and Ornstein, N. (2012) *It's Even Worse Than It Looks: How the American Constitutional System Collided with the New Politics of Extremism*, Basic Books.

Mann, W. (2020) "Trump's lethal aversion to reading," *The Week*, [online] May 21, Available from: https://theweek.com/articles/915606/trumps-lethal-aversion-reading

Mannchen, B. (2024) "History of the Sierra Club and East Texas wilderness designation," *Sierra Club*, [online] February 17, Available from: https://www.sierraclub.org/texas/houston/blog/2024/02/history-sierra-club-and-east-texas-wilderness-designation

Mannweiler, L. (2024) "The biggest moments of the 2024 presidential election: Assassination attempts, running mate picks, notable debates and more," *U.S. News,* [online] October 30, Available from: https://www.usnews.com/news/national-news/articles/2024-10-30/the-moments-that-defined-the-2024-presidential-election

Marco, G., Hollingsworth, R. and Durham, W. (eds) (1987) *Silent Spring Revisited*, American Chemical Society.

Mark, J. (2021) "A history of pre-colonial North America," *Brewminate*, [online] November 2, Available from: https://brewminate.com/a-history-of-pre-colonial-north-america/

Markowitz, G. and Rosner, D. (2002) *Deceit and Denial: The Deadly Politics of Industrial Pollution,* University of California Press.

Markowitz, M. (2003) "NYC subway token, 1953–2003," *Gotham Gazette. New York City News and Policy*, [online] April 28, Available from: http://www.gothamgazette.com/transportation/1799-nyc-subway-token-1953-2003

Marsh, G. (1864) *Man and Nature, or Physical Geography as Modified by Human Action,* Charles Scribner.

Marshall, G. (2014) *Don't Even Think about It: Why Our Brains Are Wired to Ignore Climate Change,* Bloomsbury.

Marshall, R. (1933) *The People's Forests (On Forestry in America)*, H. Smith and R. Haas publishers, reissued in 2002 by University of Iowa Press.

Martinez, E. (2013) *Early Sanitation in Boston and Evolution of Modern Sewage Systems*, University Archives and Special Collections in the Healey Library, University of Massachusetts.

Mayer, J. (2018) "Trump's ghostwriter tells all," *The New Yorker*, [online] July 18, Available from: https://www.newyorker.com/magazine/2016/07/25/donald-trumps-ghostwriter-tells-all

McCarty, N., Poole, K. and Rosenthal, H. (2008) *Polarized America: The Dance of Ideology and Unequal Riches*, MIT Press.

McCoy, J., Press, B., Somer, M. and Tuncel, O. (2022) *Reducing Pernicious Polarization: A Comparative Historical Analysis of Depolarization,* Carnegie Endowment for International Peace.

McFeely, W. (2002) *Grant*, W.W. Norton.

McGarity, T. (1987) "Regulatory analysis and regulatory reform," *Texas Law Review,* 65(7).

McKibben, B. (2006) *The End of Nature* (expanded ten-year anniversary edition), Random House.

Melissa, R. (2024) "U.S. EV market passed the 1 million mark in 2023," *Statzon*, [online] March 6, Available from: https://statzon.com/insights/us-ev-market

Meigs, J. (2023) *The Big Squeeze: How Biden's Environmental Justice Agenda Hurts the Economy and the Environment*, Manhattan Institute.

Melley, B. (2020) "Sierra Club calls out founder John Muir for racist views," *PBS NewsHour*, [online] Available from: https://www.pbs.org/newshour/nation/sierra-club-calls-out-founder-john-muir-for-racist-views

Meltzer, D. (2021) *First Peoples in a New World*, 2nd edn, Cambridge University Press.

Merchant, C. (2007) *American Environmental History: An Introduction,* Columbia University Press.

Merget, A. (2006) "Smart Policy. Sound Science. Stronger Communities: Celebrating 35 Years of the EPA with William D. Ruckelshaus," Speech.

Merritt, R. A. (1969) *Engineering in American Society: 1850–1875,* University of Kentucky Press.

Meyer, R. (2020) "The oil industry is quietly winning local climate fights," *The Atlantic*, [online] February, Available from: https://www.theatlantic.com/science/archive/2020/02/oil-industry-fighting-climate-policy-states/606640/

Miller, R. (1993) "American Indian influence on the United States Constitution and its framers," *American Indian Law Review*, 18(1): 133–160.

Miller Center (2014) "American President Rutherford B. Hayes (1822–1893)," *U.S. Presidents,* [online] Available from: http://millercenter.org/president/hayes

Miller Center (2025) "Remembering 1968, A cataclysmic year," Available from: https://millercenter.org/the-presidency/educational-resources/1968

Milman, O. (2024) "Trump says he has 'no choice' but to back EVs after Musk endorsement. Ex-president, who previously denigrated electric vehicles, says they are suitable for a 'small slice' of the population," *The Guardian*, [online] August 5, Available from: https://www.theguardian.com/us-news/article/2024/aug/05/trump-endorses-electric-vehicles-elon-musk#:~:text="You're%20not%20going%20to,mandate"%2C%20Trump%20has%20said

Mintz, S. (no date) "Historical context: The Constitution and slavery," *History Resources*.

MIT (Massachusetts Institute of Technology) (2023) "How much does natural gas contribute to climate change through CO2 emissions when the fuel is burned, and how much through methane leaks?" *Climate.MIT.edu*, [online] July 17, Available from: https://climate.mit.edu/ask-mit/how-much-does-natural-gas-contribute-climate-change-through-co2-emissions-w'hen-fuel-burned

Mitchum, R., Vail, P. and Thompson III, S. (1977) "Seismic stratigraphy and global changes of sea level, part 2: The depositional sequence as a basic unit for stratigraphic analysis," in C. Payton (ed.) *Seismic Stratigraphy: Applications to Hydrocarbon Exploration,* American Association of Petroleum Geologists.

Moch, J. and Lee, H. (2022) *The Challenges of Decarbonizing the US Electrical Grid by 2035*, Harvard University.

Molski, M. (2024) "How voting demographics changed between 2020 and 2024 presidential elections," *NBC4 Washington,* [online] November 6, Available from: https://www.nbcwashington.com/decision-2024/2024-voter-turnout-election-demographics-trump-harris/3762138/

Mooney, C. (2006) *The Republican War on Science*, Basic Books.

Mooney, J. (1928) "The aboriginal population of North America," *Smithsonian Miscellaneous Collections,* 80: 1–40.

Moreno-Mayar, J. et al (2018) "Terminal Pleistocene Alaskan genome reveals first founding population of Native Americans," *Nature,* 553: 203–207.

Morison, S., Commager, H. and Leuchtehburg, W. (1970) *The Growth of the Republic* (2 vols), Oxford University Press.

Morrisey, W. (2009) *The Dilemma of Progressivism: How Roosevelt, Taft, and Wilson Reshaped the American Regime of Self-Government*, Rowman & Littlefield.

Mortenson, J. and Bagby, N. (2020) "Delegation at the founding," *Columbia Law Review,* 121: 277–368.

Mosimann, J. and Martin, P. (1975) "Simulating overkill by Paleoindians," *American Scientist*, 63: 304–313.

Moss, M. (2011) *Northwest Coast: Archaeology as Deep History*, Society for American Archaeology.

Motavalli, J. (2021) "The NIMBY threat to renewable energy: In Vermont, everyone loves clean energy—when it comes from someplace else," *Sierra*, September 20.

Mulvey, K. and Shulman, S. (2015) "The climate deception dossiers: Internal fossil fuel industry memos reveal decades of corporate disinformation," *Union of Concerned Scientists*, [online] July, Available from: https://www.ucsusa.org/sites/default/files/attach/2015/07/The-Climate-Deception-Dossiers.pdf

Munoz, S., Mladenoff, D., Schroeder, R. and Williams, J. (2014) "Defining the spatial patterns of historical land use associated with the Indigenous societies of eastern North America," *Journal of Biogeography*, 41: 2195–2210.

Mystal, E. (2025) "This Executive Order REVEALS the Trump-Musk ENDGAME," *The Nation*, [online] February 21, Available from: https://www.thenation.com/article/politics/executive-order-independent-agencies-trump/

Nader, R. and Esposito, J. (1970) *Vanishing Air*, Grossman Publishers Collection.

Naess, A. and Sessions, G. (1984) "Basic principles of deep ecology," *The Anarchist Library*, [online] January 9, Available from: www.deepecology.org

Nakamura, R. and Church, T. (2003) *Taming Regulation*, Brookings Institution.

NASA (National Aeronautics and Space Administration) (2023) Sea level, [online] Available from: https://climate.nasa.gov/vital-signs/sea-level/?intent=121

Nash, A., Mann, D. and Olsen, P. (1972) *Oil Pollution and the Public Interest: A Study of the Santa Barbara Oil Spill*, University of California Institute of Governmental Studies.

Nash, R. (1967) *Wilderness and the American Mind*, Yale University Press.

Nast, T. (1878) *The Secretary … investigating the Indian Bureau/Th. Nast.*, 1878 (Photograph), Library of Congress, Available from: https://www.loc.gov/item/2004676470/

Nesson, F. (1983) *Great Waters: A History of Boston's Water Supply*, Brandeis University Press.

Nester, W. (2024) *Franklin D. Roosevelt and the Art of Leadership: Battling the Great Depression and the Axis Powers*, Frontline Books.

Nicholls, R. et al (2007) "Ranking of the world's cities most exposed to coastal flooding today," *OECD and Other Institutions,* [online] Available from: https://climate-adapt.eea.europa.eu/en/metadata/publications/ranking-of-the-worlds-cities-to-coastal-flooding/11240357/@@download/file

NIPCC (Nongovernmental International Panel on Climate Change) (2019) *Nongovernmental International Panel on Climate Change*, Heartland Institute.

Nisbet, M. (2014) *Climate of Extremes: Part One: How Polarizing Global Warming Strategies Backfire*, Routledge.

Nixon, R. (1970) "37th President of the United States: 1969–1974. Special message to the Congress on environmental quality," *The American Presidency Project,* [online] Available from: https://www.presidency.ucsb.edu/documents/special-message-the-congress-environmental-quality

NOAA (National Oceanic and Atmospheric Administration) (2024) "Trends in atmospheric carbon dioxide (CO2)," *National Oceanic and Atmospheric Administration*, [online] Available from: https://gml.noaa.gov/ccgg/trends/

Nobel, J. (2016) "The miseducation of John Muir," *Longreads*, [online] July 26, Available from: https://longreads.com/2016/07/26/the-miseducation-of-john-muir-2/

Northey, H. (2017) "Hannah Northey on President Trump's oil pipeline executive orders," *Washington Journal*, [online] January 25, Available from: https://www.c-span.org/program/washington-journal/hannah-northey-on-president-trumps-oil-pipeline-executive-orders/467058

NPS (National Park Service) (2016) "Ocmulgee River Corridor special resource study: Cultural and historic context report," *National Park Service, US Department of the Interior*, [online], Available from: https://npshistory.com/publications/srs/ocmulgee-rc-cult-hist-context-srs.pdf

NPS (2017) *Theodore Roosevelt and Conservation*, National Park Service.

NPS (2023) "Archaic culture" *National Park Service*, [online] Available from: https://www.nps.gov/ocmu/learn/historyculture/archaic-culture.htm

NPS (2025) "Paleoindian period," *National Park Service,* [online] Available from: https://www.nps.gov/yell/learn/historyculture/archeologypaleo.htm

NRC (2024) "Backgrounder on the Three Mile Island accident," *US Nuclear Regulatory Commission*, [online] March 28, Available from: https://www.nrc.gov/reading-rm/doc-collections/fact-sheets/3mile-isle.html

NRDC (2021) "Indian Point is closing, but clean energy is here to stay," *Natural Resources Defense Council*, [online] April 28, Available from: https://www.nrdc.org/bio/kit-kennedy/indian-point-closing-clean-energy-here-stay

O'Fallon, B. and Fehren-Schmitz, L. (2011) "Native Americans experienced a strong population bottleneck coincident with European contact," *Proceedings of the National Academy of Sciences,* 108(51): 20444–20448.

O'Keefe, E. and Gomez, F. (2024) "Biden sending senior West Wing aides, Mike Donilon, Jennifer O'Malley Dillon to oversee 2024 reelection campaign," *CBS News,* [online] January 23, Available from: https://www.cbsnews.com/news/biden-sending-mike-donilon-jennifer-omalley-dillon-to-oversee-2024-reelection-campaign/

O'Toole, R. (1988) *Reforming the Forest Service*, Island Press.

Obama, B. (2012) "State of the union speech," *The White House*, [online] Available from: https://www.americanrhetoric.com/speeches/stateoftheunion2012.htm

Obama, B. (2023) "A historic commitment to protecting the environment and addressing the impacts of climate change," *The White House Archives*, [online] Available from: https://obamawhitehouse.archives.gov/the-record/climate#:~:text=Made%20the%20largest%20single%20investment,carbon%20technologies%2C%20and%20leveraging%20approximately

OEHHA (Office of Environmental Health Hazard Assessment) (2024) "Wildfires," [online] Available from: https://oehha.ca.gov/climate-change/epic-2022/impacts-vegetation-and-wildlife/wildfires

Olasky, M. (1992) *Patterns of Corporate Philanthropy: The Progressive Deception*, Capital Research Center.

Oreskes, N. and Conway, E. (2011) *Merchants of Doubt: How a Handful of Scientists Obscured the Truth on Issues from Tobacco Smoke to Climate Change*, Bloomsbury.

Osborne, D. and Gabler, T. (1992) *Reinventing Government: How the Entrepreneurial Spirit Is Transforming the Public Sector*, Addison Wesley Publishing Co.

Osborne, F. (1948) *Our Plundered Planet*, Little, Brown, and Company.

Osofsky, H. et al (2012) "Environmental justice and the BP Deepwater Horizon oil spill," *New York University Environmental Law Journal*, 20: 101–187.

Oversight (2021) "Initial Report: Covid Select Committee," US House of Representatives, [online] Available from: https://oversight.house.gov/release/final-report-covid-select-concludes-2-year-investigation-issues-500-page-final-report-on-lessons-learned-and-the-path-forward/

Parker, C. and Stern, E. (2022) "The Trump administration and the COVID-19 crisis: Exploring the warning-response problems and missed opportunities of a public health emergency," *Public Administration*, 100(3): 616–632.

Pauketat, T. (2004) *Ancient Cahokia and the Mississippians*, Cambridge University Press.

PBS (2009) "The Warning," *Public Broadcasting System*.

Parks (no date) "Brief history of national parks," *U.S. Library of Congress*.

Percival, R., Miller, A., Schroeder, C. and Leape, J. (2000) *Environmental Regulation: Law, Science, and Policy*, Gaithersburg, Aspen Publishers, Inc.

Perdue, T. and Green, M. (2008) *The Cherokee Nation and the Trail of Tears*, Penguin Library of American Indian History.

Pethokoukis, J. (2024) "Trump and nuclear energy: There are questions," *American Enterprise Institute*, [online] October 26, Available from: https://www.aei.org/economics/trump-and-nuclear-energy-there-are-questions/

Pew (2023) "Economy remains the public's top policy priority; COVID-19 concerns decline again," *Pew Research Center*, [online] February 6, Available from: https://www.pewresearch.org/politics/2023/02/06/economy-remains-the-publics-top-policy-priority-covid-19-concerns-decline-again/pp_2023-02-06_political-priorities_00-05-png/

Pew (2024) "Public trust in government:1958-2024," *Pew Research Center,* [online] June 24, Available from: https://www.pewresearch.org/politics/2024/06/24/public-trust-in-government-1958-2024/ https://www.pewresearch.org/politics/2024/06/24/public-trust-in-government-1958-2024/

PFPI (Partnership for Policy Integrity) (2016) "Letter from MA groups to congress: Don't legislate bioenergy as having zero pollution," *Partnership for Policy Integrity,* [online] June, Available from: https://www.pfpi.net/2016/06/letter-from-ma-groups-to-congress-dont-legislate-bioenergy-as-having-zero-pollution/

PIDBA (Paleoindian Database of America) (2019) "The distribution of Clovis Points in the PIDBA database," *Paleoindian Database of America (PIDBA)*, [online] Available from: https://www.researchgate.net/figure/Distribution-of-Clovis-points-in-the-PIDBA-database_fig4_295395362

Pino, M. and Dillehay, T. (2023) "Monte Verde II: An assessment of new radiocarbon dates and their sedimentological context," *Antiquity*, 97(393): 524–540.

Plumer, B. (2024) "Nuclear power is hard. A climate-minded billionaire wants to make it easier," *New York Times*, [online] June 11, Available from: https://www.nytimes.com/2024/06/11/climate/bill-gates-nuclear-wyoming.html

Powell, J. (2004) *FDR's Folly: How Roosevelt and His New Deal Prolonged the Great Depression*, Random House.

Presley, B., Wade, T., Santschi, P. and Baskaran, M. (1998) *Historical Contamination of Mississippi River Delta, Tampa Bay, and Galveston Bay Sediment*, National Oceanic and Atmospheric Administration.

Quarles, J. (1976) *Cleaning up America: An Insider's View of the Environmental Protection Agency*, University of Michigan Press.

Raab, L. and Jones, T. (eds) (2004) *Prehistoric California: Archaeology and the Myth of Paradise*, University of Utah Press.

Railway (National Railway Publishing Company) (1918) "Historic Railroad Map of the United States," in *World Maps Online.*

Rausch, J. (2006) *Encyclopedia of the United States Congress,* Library of American History.

Raymond, G. (2018) "Here's why the endangered species act was created in the first place," *TIME,* [online] July 23, Available from: https://time.com/5345913/endangered-species-act-history/

Raymond, L. (1997) "Remarks by Lee R. Raymond, Chairman and CEO of Exxon Corporation," *World Petroleum Congress*, Beijing, Exxon Corporation.

Rebonato, R. (2024) *How to Think about Climate Change*, Cambridge University Press.

Reich, R. and Donahue, J. (1985) *New Deals: The Chrysler Revival and the American System*, Times Books.

Reitz, C. (2022) *The Revolutionary Ecological Legacy of Herbert Marcuse*, Daraja Press.

Remini, R. (1999) *Andrew Jackson*, Perennial Books.

Remnick, D. (2006) "Ozone man," *The New Yorker*, 82(10).

Representatives (no date) "United States House of Representatives," in *Congress, U.S. (ed.). House of Representatives.*

Reuters (2022) "Democracy under siege: An hour-by-hour look at the assault on the U.S. Capitol," *Reuters*, [online] January 4, Available from: https://www.reuters.com/world/us/democracy-under-siege-an-hour-by-hour-look-assault-us-capitol-2022-01-04/

Revkin, A. (2006) "Climate expert says NASA tried to silence him," *New York Times*, [online] January 29, Available from: https://www.nytimes.com/2006/01/29/science/earth/climate-expert-says-nasa-tried-to-silence-him.htmlPage

Ritchie, H., Rosado, P., Roser, M. (2024) "Our world in data--nuclear energy," *ourworldindata.org*, [online] Available from: https://ourworldindata.org/nuclear-energy?trk=public_post_comment-text

Robbins, W. (2004) *Landscapes of Conflict: The Oregon Story, 1940-2000,* Weyerhaeuser Environmental Books.

Robinson, G. (1988) *The Forest and the Trees*, Island Press.

Rodriguez, B. (2023) "Ranked-choice voting is gaining momentum. So are efforts to stop it," *The 19th News*.

Rosenbaum, W. (2007) *Environmental Politics and Policy,* CQ Press.

Rosenbaum, W. (2024) *Environmental Politics and Policy*, 12th edn, CQ Press.

Rosenfeld, S. (2017) *The Polarizers: Postwar Architects of Our Partisan Era*, University of Chicago Press.

Ross, G. (2008) *Trump-Style Management: Powerful Strategies and Tactics for Mastering Every Deal*, John Wiley & Sons.

Rowthorn, R. and Ramaswamy, R. (1997) *Deindustrialization: Its Causes and Implications,* International Monetary Fund.

Ruckelshaus, W. (2006) "Sustaining environmental protection in the face of population and economic growth: Can we do it?," in A. Merget (ed.) *Celebrating 35 Years of the EPA with William D. Ruckelshaus*, School of Public and Environmental Affairs, Indiana University.

Rudalevige, A. (2017) "Trump wants to reorganize the executive branch. Good luck with that," *The Washington Post*, [online] March 16, Available from: https://www.washingtonpost.com/news/monkey-cage/wp/2017/03/16/trump-wants-to-reorganize-the-executive-branch-good-luck-to-him/Page

Saad, L. (2022) "US political ideology steady; conservatives, moderates tie," *Gallup*, [online] January 17, Available from: https://news.gallup.com/poll/388988/political-ideology-steady-conservatives-moderates-tie.aspx#:~:text=On%20average%20last%20year%2C%2037,conservative%20and%2025%25%20as%20liberal

Salzman, J. and Thompson, B. (2024) *Environmental Laws and Policy*, 6th edn, Foundation Press.

Sample, I. (2113) "Nobel winner declares boycott of top science journals," *The Guardian*, [online] December 9, Available from: http://openscience.ens.fr/ABOUT_OPEN_ACCESS/ARTICLES/2013_12_09_The_Guardian.pdfPage

Savage, C. and Goldman, A. (2023) "The Trump Jan. 6 indictment, annotated," *New York Times*, [online] August 1, Available from: https://www.nytimes.com/interactive/2023/08/01/us/politics/trump-jan-6-indictment-2020-election-annotated.htmlPage

Sax, J. (1970) *Defending the Environment: A Strategy for Citizen Action,* Borzoi Books.

Schlesinger, A. (1945) *The Age of Jackson,* Little, Brown & Co.

Schlesinger, A. (1948) *Ratings of U.S. Presidents by Scholars,* University of California.

Schnell, M. and Beitsch, R. (2023) "House GOP votes to increase congressional authority over federal rulemaking," *The Hill*, [online] June 14, Available from: https://thehill.com/homenews/house/4050493-house-gop-votes-to-increase-congressional-authority-over-federal-rulemaking/Page

Schoenbrod, D. (1993) *Power Without Responsibility,* Yale University Press.

Schoenbrod, D., Stewart, R. and Wyman, K. (2010) *Breaking the Logjam: Environmental Protection That Will Work*, Yale University Press.

Schönberger, H. (1974) "Purposes and ends in history: presentism and the new left," *The History Teacher*, 7(3): 448–458.

Schouten, F. (2015) "Analysis: Donald Trump talks to voters at a fourth-grade level," *USA Today*, [online] October 21, Available from: https://www.usatoday.com/story/news/politics/onpolitics/2015/10/21/analysis-donald-trump-talks-to-voters-at-a-fourth-grade-level/81202230/Page

Scott, M. (1983) "Conservation is now a partisan issue," *High Country News*, [online] October 31.

Seeley, B. (1999) "The other re-engineering of engineering education, 1900–1965," *Journal of Engineering Education,* 88: 285–294.

Serviceburo (no date) "Forestry in Germany," Servicebüro Forstwirtschaft-in-Deutschland.de, [online] Available from: https://www.forstwirtschaft-in-deutschland.de/german-forestry/forest-facts/?L=1#:~:text=Forest%20management%20largely%20dispenses%20with,depending%20on%20the%20tree%20species

Shao, E. and Wu, A. (2025) "The federal work force cuts so far, agency by agency," *New York Times*, [online] April 21, Available from: https://www.nytimes.com/interactive/2025/02/11/us/politics/trump-musk-doge-federal-workers.htmlPage

Shapiro, A. (2012) "Obama made a strong first impression at Harvard," *Morning Edition,* National Public Radio.

Shulock, N. (1999) "The paradox of policy analysis: If it is not used, why do we produce so much of it?" *Journal of Policy Analysis and Management,* 18: 226–244.

Shuster, S. (2024) "The kingmaker," *TIME,* December 5.

Sierra (1996) "Guidelines on implementation of the Sierra Club's policy advocating an end to commercial logging on federal public lands (ECL policy)," *Sierra Club*, [online] Available from: https://www.sierraclub.org/sites/default/files/forest.pdf

Sierra (2019) "Why does Sierra Club oppose burning biomass for energy?" *Sierra Club,* [online] September 24, Available from: https://www.sierraclub.org/redwood/sonoma/blog/2019/09/oct-7-why-does-sierra-club-oppose-burning-biomass-for-energy

Sierra (2024) *Pollution and Waste Management Policies,* Sierra Club.

Smith, M. (1983) "Peter Stephen du Ponceau and his study of languages: A historical account," *Proceedings of the American Philosophical Society,* 127: 143–179.

Sosna, M. (1970) "The south in the saddle: Racial politics during the Wilson years," *Wisconsin Magazine of History*, 54(1): 30–49, Available from: https://www.jstor.org/stable/4634581

Southwick, C. (1976) *Ecology and the Quality of Our Environment*, 2nd edn, Van Nostrand.

Spetalnick, M., Geddie, J. and Bayer, L. (2025) "Trump's first 100 days: America First president is overturning the world order," *Reuters*, [online] April 27, Available from: https://www.reuters.com/world/us/trumps-first-100-days-america-first-president-is-overturning-world-order-2025-04-27/

Spike, J. and Riccardi, N. (2025) "Hungary's transformation into an 'electoral autocracy' has parallels to Trump's second term," *Los Angeles Times*, [online] February 15, Available from: https://www.latimes.com/world-nation/story/2025-02-15/hungarys-transformation-into-an-electoral-autocracy-has-parallels-to-trumps-second-term

Spinden, H. (1928) "The population of ancient America," *Geographical Review,* 18: 641–660.

Spurr, S. (1980) *Forest Ecology*, Wiley.

Staff (2024) "Project 2025 director Paul Dans lays out how conservatives plan to staff the federal bureaucracy," *Media Matters*, [online] February 29, Available from: https://www.mediamatters.org/steve-bannon/project-2025-director-paul-dans-lays-out-how-conservatives-plan-staff-federal

Statista (2024) "In hindsight, do you think Britain was right or wrong to vote to leave the European Union?" *Statista,* [online] December 11, Available from: https://www.statista.com/statistics/987347/brexit-opinion-poll/

Stearns, M.L. (2024). *Parliamentary America: The Least Radical Means of Radically Repairing Our Broken Democracy*, Johns Hopkins University Press.

Stone, M. (2023) "Why America has a youth mental health crisis, and how schools can help," *Education Week*, [online] October 16, Available from: https://www.edweek.org/leadership/why-america-has-a-youth-mental-health-crisis-and-how-schools-can-help/2023/10

Stoolmacher, J. (2023) "A progressive perspective: Joe Biden's the most progressive president since FDR," *The Trentonian,* [online] January 30, Available from: https://www.trentonian.com/2023/01/30/a-progressive-perspective-joe-bidens-the-most-progressive-president-since-f-d-r-irwin-stoolmacher-column/

Storrow, B. (2023) "Not a shore thing: Challenges in US offshore wind development," *Resources Radio*, [online] Available from: https://www.resources.org/resources-radio/not-a-shore-thing-challenges-in-us-offshore-wind-development-with-ben-storrow/

Sullivan, P. (2004) "Anne Gorsuch Burford, 62, dies," *The Washington Post*, [online] July 21, Available from: https://www.washingtonpost.com/archive/local/2004/07/22/anne-gorsuch-burford-62-dies/78b89129-728a-404e-8550-7b5617d5f291/

Summers, M. (1993) *The Era of Good Stealings*, Oxford University Press.

Super, D. A. (2025) "Many Trump administration personnel actions are unlawful," *Center for Budget and Policy Priorities*, [online] February 14, Available from: https://www.cbpp.org/research/federal-budget/many-trump-administration-personnel-actions-are-unlawful

Supran, G., Rahmstorf, S. and Oreskes, N. (2023) "Assessing ExxonMobil's global warming projections," *Science,* 379.

Surovell, T. et al (2022) "Late date of human arrival to North America: Continental scale differences in stratigraphic integrity of pre-13,000 BP archaeological sites," *PLOS One*, 17(4): e0264092.

Talbot, L. (2013) "A personal perspective on the Endangered Species Act of 1973 (ESA) and the Convention on International Trade in Endangered Species of Wild Fauna and Flora (CITES)," *Endangered Species Coalition,* [online] July 9, Available from: https://www.endangered.org/campaigns/wild-success-endangered-species-act-at-40/lee-talbot/

Tamborino, K. and Dabbs, B. (2024) "It would just die on the vine," *Politico*, [online] April 9, Available from: https://www.politico.com/news/2024/04/09/energy-department-loans-biden-00150180

Tamm, E. et al (2007) "Beringian standstill and spread of native American founders," *PLOS One*, 2(9): e829.

Taylor, A. (2001) *American Colonies: The Settling of North America*, Penguin.

The White House (2017) "President Trump takes action to expedite priority energy and infrastructure projects," *Trump White House Archives*, [online] January 24, Available from: https://trumpwhitehouse.archives.gov/briefings-statements/president-trump-takes-action-expedite-priority-energy-infrastructure-projects/

The White House (2021) "The path to achieving Justice40," *The White House,* [online] July 20, Available from: https://www.whitehouse.gov/omb/briefing-room/2021/07/20/the-path-to-achieving-justice40/

Thews, B., Höjding, P. and Jansson, B. (2017) "Swedish environmental law: An introduction to the Swedish legal system for environmental protection," *Digitala Vetenskapliga Arkivet (Sweden)*, [online] Available from: https://www.diva-portal.org/smash/record.jsf?pid=diva2%3A1421472&dswid=5865

Tidwell, T. (2015) "Speech on 50th anniversary of the Wilderness Act," [online] Available from: https://www.fs.usda.gov/speeches/protecting-americas-wilderness-heritage

Tormos-Aponte, F. (2021) "An organizing approach to diversifying political science," *Political Science and Politics*, 54: 163–168.

Trittipo, A., Samardari, H., Hatami, H., Krishnan, M., Koch, P. and Powis, C. (2023) "Ten key requirements for a systemic approach to climate adaptation," *McKinsely & Company*, [online] Available from: https://www.mckinsey.com/capabilities/sustainability/our-insights/ten-key-requirements-for-a-systemic-approach-to-climate-adaptation?stcr=EC66F3FEF0FC4C06AAAAEBF89D07B643&cid=other-eml-alt-mip-mck&hlkid=e2599a6bb67c4d7eb8f968eb9476e83c&hctky=3203747&hdpid=816045e8-fe14-4c20-8a6c-e2e0b33b8587

Trump, D. (2011) *Time to Get Tough: Making America #1 Again*, Regnery.

Trump, D. (2013) Tweet on December 6, "Global warming is a total, and very expensive hoax", [online] Available from: https://x.com/realDonaldTrump/status/265895292191248385

Trump, D. (2015) *Crippled America: How to Make America Great Again*, Simon & Schuster.

Trump, D. and McIver, M. (2008) *Trump: Never Give up*, Wiley.

Trump, D. and McIver, M. (2009) *Think Like a Champion: An Informal Education in Business and Life*, Vanguard Press.

Trump, D. and Schwartz, T. (1987) *The Art of the Deal*, Random House.

Trump, D. and Shiflett, D. (2000) *The America We Deserve*, Renaissance Books.

Turner, C. and Scott, G. (2014) "The dentition of American Indians: Evolutionary results and demographic implications following colonization from Siberia," *Handbook of Paleoanthropology*. DOI: http://dx.doi.org/10.1007/978-3-540-33761-4_63

Twain, M. and Warner, C. (1873) *The Gilded Age: A Tale of To-day,* American Publishing Co.

Tyson, A., Funk, C. and Kennedy, B. (2023) "What the data says about Americans' views of climate change," *Pew Research Center,* [online] August 9, Available from: https://www.pewresearch.org/short-reads/2023/08/09/what-the-data-says-about-americans-views-of-climate-change/

Udall, M. (1988) "A concurrent resolution to acknowledge the contribution of the Iroquois Confederacy of Nations to the development of the United States Constitution and to reaffirm the continuing government-to-government relationship between Indian tribes and the United States established in the Constitution," *H. Con. Res. 331, 100th Congress (1987–1988), House—Interior and Insular Affairs | Senate—Indian Affairs (Permanent Select).*

Udall, S. (2006) "Unpublished telephone interview," F.T. Manheim.

Ullman, J. (1988) *The Anatomy of Industrial Decline: Productivity, Investment, and Location of U.S. Manufacturing*, Quorum Books.

USA (2022) "What types of energy does the US produce and consume? How much energy do Americans use?" *USA Facts*, [online] Available from: https://usafacts.org/state-of-the-union/energy/#:~:text=Petroleum%20and%20natural%20gas%20sources,was%2010%25%20of%20energy%20consumption

USGS (US Geological Survey) (2019) *The Four Great Surveys of the West*, US Geological Survey.

US News (2024) "Quality of life," *US News and World Report.*

Van Ness, W. (2007) "Telephone communication," F. Manheim.

Van Riper, P. (1958) *History of the Civil Service*, University of Michigan Press.

Van Riper, P. (1983) "The American administrative state: Wilson and the founders—an unorthodox view," *Public Admnistration Review*, November–December, 477–490.

Verma, P., Dwoskin, E., Siddiqui, F. and Osaka, S. (2024) "Musk's politics hadn't seeped into Tesla. Then he axed its car of Eco Car of the future," *The Washington Post*, [online] December 10, Available from: https://www.washingtonpost.com/technology/2024/12/10/elon-musk-climate-change-worldview-trump/Page

Vig, N. and Kraft, M. (1997) *Environmental Policy in the 1990s: Reform or Reaction?* Congressional Quarterly Books.

von Humboldt, A. and Bonpland, A. (1807) "Essay on the geography of plants," Edited and translated from French by Jackson, S. and Romanowski, S, University of Chicago Press.

Waldman, S. (2024) "Trump attacks EVs, 'green new scam' in RNC speech," *E&E News Politico*, [online] July 19, Available from: https://www.eenews.net/articles/trump-attacks-evs-green-new-scam-in-rnc-speech-2/

Wallace, D. (1995) *Environmental Policy and Industrial Innovation: Strategies in Europe, the United States, and Japan,* Earthscan.

Wallace, R. (1996) *Earthquakes, Minerals, and Me*, US Geological Survey.

Wang, K. (2025) "Trump's policies are making Project 2025's vision a reality," *Wall Street Journal Online,* [online] March 18, Available from: https://www.wsj.com/video/series/wsj-explains/trumps-policies-are-making-project-2025s-vision-a-reality/A6560017-5E46-42AB-BA00-3A511B92378F

Warming, J. (1895) *Plantesamfund—Grundtræk af den økologiske Plantegeografi*, Philipsens Forlag.

Warming, E. and Vahl, M. (1909) *Oecology of Plants: An Introduction to the Study of Plant-Communities*, Clarendon Press.

Washington, G. (1796) "Farewell address, 1796," [online] September 19, Available from: https://teachingamericanhistory.org/document/farewell-address-5/

Waters, M. (2019) "Late Pleistocene exploration and settlement of the Americas by modern humans," *Science*, 365: 6449.

Waters, M., Stafford, T. Jr. and Carlson, D. (2020) "The age of Clovis—13,050 to 12,750 cal yr B.P.," *Science Advances*, 6(43).

Webber, T. and Phillis, M. (2025) "US infrastructure improved with Biden-era spending but there's a long way to go," *Financial Post*, [online] March 25, Available from: https://financialpost.com/pmn/u-s-infrastructure-improved-with-biden-era-spending-but-theres-a-long-way-to-go

Wessel, D. (2007) "How Fred Krupp's singular style serves business, environment well," *Wall Street Journal*, March 1.

Whitaker, J. (1976) *Striking a Balance: Environment and Natural Resources Policy in the Nixon-Ford Years*, American Enterprise Institute.

Wiedinmyer, C. and Neff, J. (2007) "Estimates of CO2 from fires in the United States: Implications for carbon management," *Carbon Balance and Management*, 2: 1–12.

Wiencek, H. (2012) "The dark side of Thomas Jefferson: A new portrait of the founding father challenges the long-held perception of Thomas Jefferson as a benevolent slaveholder," *Smithsonian Magazine*, [online] Available from: https://www.smithsonianmag.com/history/the-dark-side-of-thomas-jefferson-35976004/

Wile, R. and Ingram, D. (2025) "Musk says time commitment to DOGE will "drop significantly" as focus returns to Tesla," *NBC News*, [online] April 22, Available from: https://www.nbcnews.com/business/business-news/tesla-earnings-q1-musk-trump-administation-what-next-rcna202409

Williams, G. (2003) "References on the American Indian use of fire in ecosystems," *Intertribal Timber Council*, [online] Available from: http://www.itcnet.org

Williford, J. (2013) "The Agitator: William Lloyd Garrison and the abolitionists," *Humanities: The National Endowment for the Humanities*, [online] January/February, Available from: https://www.neh.gov/humanities/2013/januaryfebruary/feature/the-agitator

Wilta, A., Dunker, B., Notanwing, J. and Cheney, J. (no date) Alaska National Interest Lands Conservation Act (ANILCA) Program. *Alaska Department of Fish and Game*, [online] Available from: https://www.adfg.alaska.gov/index.cfm?adfg=habitatoversight.anilca

Woodward, B. (2023) *The Trump Tapes*, Simon & Schuster.

Woodward, B. and Bernstein, C. (1974) *All the President's Men*, Simon & Schuster.

Wrangham, R. and Peterson, D. (1996) *Demonic Males: Apes and the Origin of Human Violence*, Houghton Mifflin.

Wright, R. (2005) *Environmental Science*, Prentice Hall.

Wrightstone, G. (2017) *Inconvenient Facts: The Science That Al Gore Doesn't Want You to Know*, Silver Crown Productions LLC.

Wrightstone, G. (2023) *A Very Convenient Warming: How Modest Warming and More CO2 are Benefiting Humanity*, MCP Books.

Wulf, A. (2012) "Founding gardners," *C-ville Weekly,* [online] March 11, Available from: https://www.c-ville.com/James_Madison_father_of_environmentalism

Yeşilada, B. and Wood, D. (2009) *The Emerging European Union*, 5th edn, Routledge.

Zachary, G. (1997) *Endless Frontier: Vannevar Bush, Engineer of the American Century,* Free Press.

Zeldin, L. (2025) "EPA administrator Lee Zeldin announces EPA's 'Powering the Great American Comeback' initiative," *U.S. Environmental Protection Agency*, [online] February 4, Available from: https://www.epa.gov/newsreleases/epa-administrator-lee-zeldin-announces-epas-powering-great-american-comeback

Zeldin, L. (2025) "Lee Zeldin: EPA Ends the 'Green New Deal,'" *Wall Street Journal Online*, [online] March 12, Available from: https://www.wsj.com/opinion/lee-zeldin-epa-ends-the-green-new-deal-aa81de06

Zimmerman, M. (1994) *Contesting Earth's Future: Radical Ecology and Postmodernity*, University of California Press.

Zimmerman, M. (2018) "How pertinent is Heidegger's thinking for deep ecology?" in J. Wendland, C. Hadjioannou, and C. Merwin (eds) *Heidegger on Technology,* Routledge.

# Index of Acts and Proposed Acts

# Index

References to figures appear in *italic* type; those in **bold** type refer to tables.
References to endnotes show both the page number and the note number (95n1).